Lawrence Lessig's

THE FUTURE OF IDEAS

"Valuable advice on the care and feeding of innovation, and a wise caution against taking future scientific leaps for granted."
—*The Christian Science Monitor*

"Goes far beyond head____
stake in creating a smar____

"Brims with brilliant insi____
for serious property righ____

"An important book abo____
revolution."

"Lessig's thesis . . . is tim____
be of great interest both____
by their decisions."

"Brilliant. . . . Thanks to____
herded altogether passiv____

"An extremely important____

"Highly readable and dee____
weaving of technical cha____
well told, with a fair bala____

LAWRENCE LESSIG

THE FUTURE OF IDEAS

Lawrence Lessig is a professor of law at the Stanford Law School. Previously Berkman Professor of Law at Harvard Law School, he is a graduate of the University of Pennsylvania, Trinity College, Cambridge, and Yale Law School. He clerked for Judge Richard Posner on the Seventh Circuit Court of Appeals and Justice Antonin Scalia on the United States Supreme Court. A columnist for *Red Herring* and *CIO Insight*, he is chairman of creativecommons.org, a board member of both the Electronic Frontier Foundation and Public Knowledge, and the author of *Code and Other Laws of Cyberspace*.

Lawrence Lessig can be reached on the web at:
http://www.the-future-of-ideas.com.

ALSO BY LAWRENCE LESSIG

Code and Other Laws of Cyberspace

THE FUTURE OF IDEAS

THE FUTURE OF IDEAS

THE FATE OF THE COMMONS
IN A CONNECTED WORLD

///

Lawrence Lessig

VINTAGE BOOKS
A DIVISION OF RANDOM HOUSE, INC.
NEW YORK

FIRST VINTAGE BOOKS EDITION, NOVEMBER 2002

Copyright © 2001, 2002 by Lawrence Lessig

Grateful acknowledgment is made to the following for
permission to reprint previously published material:

Professor Arti Kaur Rai: Quote from "Regulating Scientific Research: Intellectual
Property Rights and the Norms of Science," by Professor Arti Kaur Rai, *Northwestern
University Law Review* 94 (1999). Reprinted by permission of the author.

Salon.com: Quote from "Courtney Love Does the Math" by Courtney Love (June 12, 2000).
This article first appeared in Salon.com at http://www.Salon.com.
Reprinted with the permission of Salon.com.

The Library of Congress has cataloged the Random House edition as follows:
Lessig, Lawrence.
The future of ideas : the fate of the commons in a connected world / Lawrence Lessig.
p.   cm.
Includes index.
ISBN 0-375-50578-4
1. Intellectual property.   2. Copyright and electronic data processing.
3. Internet—Law and legislation.   4. Information society.   I. Title.
K1401 .L47 2001
346.04'8'0285—dc21   2001031968

Vintage ISBN: 0-375-72644-6

Book design by Jo Anne Metsch

www.vintagebooks.com

Printed in the United States of America
10   9   8   7   6   5   4   3   2   1

To Bettina,

my teacher

of the most important

lesson.

Contents

HIS IS the second book I have written. After reading the first, *Code and Other Laws of Cyberspace*, a friend told me that the argument was too dark. Too pessimistic. Things would never turn out as negatively as I had predicted. Balance would be found soon enough. A year later, the same friend wrote that he was wrong. Events had outstripped the darkest of my predictions. If anything, *Code*, he now said, was not pessimistic enough.

I'm afraid the same may be true of this book as well. As *Code* does, *The Future of Ideas* tells the story of a certain corruption of the values of the early Internet. This corruption, I argue, is happening in both a technical and a legal sense. In the technical sense, the early end-to-end architecture of the network is being modified by layers of control that give network owners a say in how the network develops. In a legal sense, the regulations within which the network lives are increasingly shifting power away from innovators and toward those who would stifle innovation. As I argued in *Code*, the pressures toward this corruption seem unstoppable. And again, as with *Code*, however dark the book was when originally penned, actual events have proven worse than the predictions.

Yet I am still surprised. I was confident of the pessimism in *Code*. I was more hopeful about the struggle I describe here. In *Code*, the battle had a predictable political valence—it sounded like a struggle between Right and Left. The story in this book is different: It is not a struggle between Right and Left, or between commercial and non-commercial interests. The interests in innovation and creativity that I defend here are as important to Intel as to the ACLU. The changes that I describe will harm the future of Apple and Microsoft as much as NPR. The threats to innovation and creativity that this book catalogs are threats to a certain kind of future that benefits almost everyone. And yet increasingly, and without effective political opposition, that future is being sold to industries of the past.

The reason is a failure of political imagination. And the cause of this failure seems increasingly impossible to correct. I hadn't understood quite why when I first wrote this book. I began to glimpse it one day when on the road trying to sell it.

I was on a radio talk show in Washington, D.C., when the host announced that there was a call from "Hilary." To my surprise (and the surprise of the interviewer) "Hilary" was Hilary Rosen, president of the Recording Industry Association of America (RIAA). After introducing herself in the smooth and professional way that is the custom of the District, Rosen delivered the zinger, "It's ironic that [he] is on promoting a book when, if he actually went to his overall philosophy, he should essentially be giving it away on the Internet instead of selling it in a bookstore."

Hilary Rosen is an extraordinarily smart woman. (A friend who worked in the White House once told me she may be the smartest person in Washington.) But here she was displaying her political talent, not her talent for conveying truth. She knows as well as anyone that nothing I've ever said would mean that my book, or any book, should have to be "giv[en] away." But she also knows that the best way to win this debate is to frame it as a choice between zero and one—between perfect and absolute protection for intellectual property and zero protection for intellectual property. She knows that if the world thinks this is its only choice, she and the industry she represents will win. It is a brilliant strategy that has so far worked wonders.

Yet our choice is *not* between zero protection and perfect protection. No one serious in this debate is promoting the abolition of copyright. Yet the Hilary Rosens and Jack Valentis of the world have convinced policy makers and ordinary people that this is a war about basic American values, and that they, the lobbyists, represent America, while we, their opponents, are essentially communists.

This *is* a war about basic American values. It is about the values of balance and measure that should limit the government's role in choosing the future of creativity. It is about the opportunity for creators to build on the past. It is about limiting the control that legal structures such as copyright give to the industries of yesterday to ensure that they can't use law to constrain the creators of tomorrow.

In this war, the choice is not between zero and one. I am a firm believer in a properly balanced system of copyright. I am certain there are industries for which patents are essential and good. I do not for a moment believe that artists' work should be stolen. When friends show me their 500 DVD collection, purchased at a dollar a disc, I am disgusted.

But you can believe in copyright without believing copyright should be perpetual. You can believe in patents without believing that everything under the sun should be patented. You can believe in these tools to inspire innovation without believing these tools should become so bloated as to destroy the opportunity for innovation.

I believe in this balance. So did the framers of our Constitution. This battle is about whose vision of creativity—the balance in our framers' vision or the extremism of modern lobbyists—should control the future of ideas.

This message of balance, however, is difficult to sell. It doesn't fit into news bites. It takes more than ten seconds to understand. Some of you reading this will spend many hours trying to understand at least one side of the story. You should recognize how extraordinarily rare you are. As the ignorance evinced in the debates in Washington makes clear, only a tiny fraction of the policy makers at the highest levels of government have even made an effort to understand what's at stake. We are therefore stuck in the past. Issues about innovation and creativity get shoehorned into the political divide of the last generation. Those of us who argue for balance and the public domain are called hippies and leftists. Those who defend the "property" in intellectual property are linked with free marketers and growth.

But these links are fabrications. Those who have thought seriously about these issues—on both the Left and the Right—have come to find common cause in restricting the power of yesterday to control the potential of tomorrow. They see that the extraordinary changes in technology around us mean there is something new to consider.

Our politicians are not among those who have thought seriously about these issues. For different reasons, the leaders of neither political party get it. Republicans are afraid to defend the future against the past because it sounds anti-property and anti-business. Democrats are afraid to defend the future against the past because it sounds anti-Hollywood. Neither party has produced leaders who understand what's at stake. So busy is our political system raising money for the next election that no one has the time to step back and think. To listen to debates in Washington about these issues is to be thrown back five years. The world outside D.C. increasingly understands; the people in D.C. have no time even to pay attention.

This is not because politicians are corrupt or evil. Some may be; the vast majority are not. The vast majority are decent and extraordinarily hard-working people who live in a system that simply doesn't give them time to reflect. They spend more time each week raising money than they spend in a year reading about what's new. This system produces leaders who can't begin to lead, because they are leaders who haven't the time to look ahead.

There are glimmers of hope. Here's just one. In a speech about the future of a kind of Internet service called "broadband" (meaning, as these pages will explain, fast and always on), FCC chairman Michael Powell told his audience the key to growth was less regulation. Giving cable operators free rein over "their property" was a crucial step in getting them to invest to build the infrastructure of broadband. If they chose to discriminate in the platform they built (like GM building the highways so that only GM trucks run on the highway), that was a necessary price to pay for the infrastructure of the information superhighway. Giving cable companies perfect control over "their property" was the key to broadband growth.

But in the same speech, Powell raised the possibility that overly protective intellectual property laws might be inhibiting broadband growth. These property owners, the chairman hinted, may be exercising "their property" rights to inhibit innovation. Congress may need to reconsider the rights the law gave intellectual property holders, Powell suggested. He pointed to the Supreme Court's decision permitting VCRs as an example of loosening the control of intellectual property in order to spur growth and innovation.

I recounted this story at a conference at Stanford. On the panel was Sony executive Yair Landau. Landau is a strikingly brilliant and attractive figure. Young and powerful within the industry, he did not hesitate to attack the chairman's position. Powell didn't understand the importance of intellectual property, Landau blasted. He was soft. Only with perfect protection of intellectual property would we get innovation in broadband.

But later in the conversation, Landau was singing an interestingly different tune. Landau's business is developing technologies to deliver movies across the Internet. Sony has developed a pay-per-view technology that will enable it to stream movies to computers. He described a conversation with unnamed "cable families" (why cable companies are referred to as "families" is not quite clear to me) in which he was told that the "cable families" would shut the Internet down on their cable lines before they would allow it to compete with their own business. Less protection, Landau was saying, for cable companies' property was essential to innovation and growth.

When he finished his lament about the power of cable companies and how they were interfering with innovation on the Internet, I thought here, possibly, there was some hope. Here were two very different and powerful men, one a Republican, and one who dressed like a Democrat. Each had identified a case in which overprotection could stifle innovation. For Powell, it was intellectual property. For Landau, it was the ordinary property that cable companies control. Both saw the danger to growth and innovation in allowing the past to veto the future. Both presumably saw a reason to rebalance the rights that threatened the future.

No doubt they saw different threats. No Democrat has the courage to question Hollywood; no Republican could question laissez-faire for cable companies. But if others, not so firmly entrenched in the political allegiances of the last century, could look at these two different critiques, they might see a lesson that is at the core of this book: The law, through "property," can be used by the kings of yesterday to protect themselves against the kings of tomorrow, and we—especially we lawyers—should be defending tomorrow against yesterday.

The only real hope is that those outside D.C. make Washington wake up. The only hope is political action. There are a few in Washington who get it—Congressmen Rick Boucher and Chris Cannon especially. There would be more if there were a greater demand by those who have the most to lose. Yet for the most part, those who have the most to lose have cowered on the sidelines and allowed this debate to be controlled by last century's industries.

There are exceptions, but not enough. Intel sent its leading executives to Capitol Hill to stand up for the right to innovate. Vice President Les Vadasz and CEO Craig Barrett found lots of scorn and little support. But at least they acted on principle.

Where is the rest of Silicon Valley? Why isn't Apple leading a charge for the right to innovate and create that its marketing department sells so well? Where are Dell, Microsoft, and IBM in getting Washington to understand the side of this debate that favors innovation?

And where, most importantly, are you? If you survive these couple hundred pages, you will understand something most don't see. If you let that understanding lie fallow, if you don't do anything about what you come to know, then our future will be controlled as it is being controlled right now: by those whose greatest hope is to use the law to stop the promise that the Internet, and creativity, could deliver.

Through balance: We live in a world with parks as well as private property, with public roads as well as private drives. We in this world understand the importance of balance between private and public. It would be silly to

sell the sidewalks; it would be crazy to nationalize GM. Yet when it comes
to cyberspace, and in particular, to the laws that regulate cyberspace, we are
increasingly forgetting this lesson of balance. Perfect control—through
technology and law—is not resisted. Extremism in this space seems normal.

If you take one idea from the pages that follow, let it be this: We can carry
the tradition of balance that has been our past into our future. We are failing that ideal just now, but we need not fail if principle—not politics—
defines the fight.

I N 1999, in a book entitled *The Control Revolution,* journalist and legal scholar Andrew Shapiro described two futures that the Internet might take.[1] The first was the familiar story of increased individual freedom, as the network gave us greater control over our lives, and over the institutions, including government, that regulate our lives. The second was a less familiar warning—of the rebirth of technologies of control, as institutions "dis-intermediated" by the Internet learned how to alter the network to reestablish their control.

Shapiro saw good and bad in both futures. Too much dis-intermediation, he warned, would interfere with collective governance; some balance was needed. But likewise, efforts to rearchitect the Net to reenable control threatened to undermine its potential for individual freedom and growth.

Shapiro did not predict which future would be ours. Indeed, his argument was that bits of each future were possible, and that we must choose a balance between them. His account was subtle, but optimistic. If there was a bias to the struggle, he, like most of us then, believed the bias would favor freedom.

This book picks up where Shapiro left off. Its message is neither subtle nor optimistic. In the chapters that follow, I argue that we are far enough along to see the future we have chosen. In that future, the counter-revolution prevails. The forces that the original Internet threatened to transform are well on their way to transforming the Internet. Through changes in the architecture that defined the original network, as well as changes in the legal environment within which that network lives, the future that promised great freedom and innovation will not be ours. The future that threatened the reemergence of almost perfect control will.

I don't mean the control of George Orwell's *1984*. The struggle that I describe here is not between free speech and censorship, or between democracy and totalitarianism. The freedom that is my focus here is the creativity and innovation that marked the early Internet. This is the freedom that fueled the greatest technological revolution that our culture has seen since the Industrial Revolution. This is the freedom that promised a world of creativity different from the past.

This freedom has been lost. With scarcely anyone even noticing, the network that gave birth to the innovation of the 1990s has been remade from under us; the legal environment surrounding that network has been importantly changed, too. And the result of these two changes together will be an environment of innovation fundamentally different from what it was, or promised to be.

Or so it will be unless we do something now. Unless we learn something important about the source of that creativity and innovation, and then protect that source, the Internet will be changed.

With dot.busts all around, it is not difficult to argue that this is the winter of the Internet's life. The question for us is whether the spring will be as silent.

A BOOK like this does not emerge from a library. It has instead been written through hundreds of conversations over many years. I am a law professor, but my argument spans computer design to economics. It is no doubt foolish for anyone to try to pull together such a range of material, but I could never have dared to be so foolish without the patient tutoring of many different people. Among these, I am most grateful to my colleagues at the Electronic Frontier Foundation, including John Gilmore and John Perry Barlow; and the Center for Public Domain, especially Laurie Racine and Bob Young. Jeff Chester of the Center for Media Education and Mark Cooper of the Consumers Union taught me a great deal about media policy and the passion of this struggle. There is a long list of technical experts who have struggled to show me how the network works. Among these I am most grateful to Hal Abelson, Scott Bradner, Ben Edelman, Dewayne Hendricks, Joseph Reagle, David P. Reed, and Jerome Saltzer. Dewayne Hendricks and David P. Reed helped me understand spectrum and, more important, the potential spectrum offered. Peter Huber helped me understand telephone companies and the very different potential they offered.

I am grateful as well to an extraordinary collection of law professors, who have built in the field of cyberlaw an amazing community. James Boyle's book *Shamans, Software, and Spleens* was my first introduction to the issues that I address here; James Boyle the person has been a steady, invaluable guide since. Jack Balkin, Yochai Benkler, Mark Lemley, Jessica Litman, David Post, and Pam Samuelson have all taught me far more than I could return to them.

My work on this book began at Harvard Law School's Berkman Center. The theme was born in the passionate rants of its extraordinary director, Charlie Nesson. Through our work as colleagues, and on the Microsoft case as well, Jonathan Zittrain helped me see how platforms matter. He has been a constant, if neglected, friend throughout the development of the argument here.

I am also especially grateful to the hundreds of readers of *The Industry Standard* who have reacted to the snippets of this book that I have woven into columns for that magazine. While the furor of many of those readers is sometimes hard to suffer, the insights and wisdom of many have been critical in re-forming the views I express here.

Finally, there is a collection of people who figure throughout the story of this book, but who were more central to its writing than the text might reveal. These are the figures who are truly fighting for a cause. Some of them are quite well known—Richard Stallman, for example. Others are well known among lawyers, at least—Dennis Karjala, Jessica Litman, Marc Rotenberg, Pam Samuelson. But others inspire more through their simple and quiet perseverance. Eric Eldred, whom you will meet in the course of these pages, is the best example of this type. These ideas would never have been put into words without the inspiration from people like him.

EARLY VERSIONS of this book were read by a number of people. I am grateful to those who offered critical (and sometimes especially critical) comments—in particular Bruce Ackerman, Yochai Benkler, David Bollier, Scott Hemphill, Dewayne Hendricks, Tom Maddox, Charles Nesson, Richard A. Posner, Barbara van Schewick, Timothy Wu, and Robert Young. My research was aided by an army of students, including Amy Ash, Scott Ashton, Aaron Bukofzer, Sky Canaves, Brian Gustafson, Drew Harris, Scott

Hemphill, Matt Kahn, Matt Rice, Hilary Stockton, and Jonathan Sanders. Pauline Reich, Hilary Stockton, and Richard Taketa contributed examples to the text. Ken Imboden and Lee Killough provided helpful technical comments as well. Chris Guzelian was especially helpful in bringing the book to closure, through both his research and a careful and talented final edit. Bettina Neuefeind, however, remains the world's greatest editor.

I am particularly grateful to Elisa Garza Kammeyer for her work throughout this last year, first as a researcher and finally as an assistant. She will prove to be the one truly famous person mentioned in this book, though that is a story that will take many years to unfold.

THE FUTURE OF IDEAS

"Free"

AVIS GUGGENHEIM is a film director. He has produced a range of movies, some commercial, some not. His passion, like his father's before, is documentaries, and his most recent, and perhaps best, film, *The First Year*, is about public school teachers in their first year of teaching—a *Hoop Dreams* for public education.

In the process of making a film, a director must "clear rights." A film based on a copyrighted novel must get the permission of the copyright holder. A song in the opening credits requires the permission of the artist performing the song. These are ordinary and reasonable limits on the creative process, made necessary by a system of copyright law. Without such a system, we would not have anything close to the creativity that directors such as Guggenheim have produced.

But what about the stuff that appears in the film incidentally? Posters on a wall in a dorm room, a can of Coke held by the "cigarette smoking man," an advertisement on a truck in the background? These too are creative works. Does a director need permission to have these in his or her film?

"Ten years ago," Guggenheim explains, "if incidental artwork . . . was recognized by a common person," then you would have to clear its copyright. Today, things are very different. Now "if any piece of artwork is recognizable by anybody . . . then you have to clear the rights of that and pay" to use the work. "[A]lmost every piece of artwork, any piece of furniture, or sculpture, has to be cleared before you can use it."[1]

Okay, so picture just what this means: As Guggenheim describes it, "[B]efore you shoot, you have this set of people on the payroll who are submitting everything you're using to the lawyers." The lawyers check the list and then say what can be used and what cannot. "If you cannot find the original of a piece of artwork . . . you cannot use it." Even if you can find it, often permission will be denied. The lawyers thus decide what's allowed in the film. They decide what can be in the story.

The lawyers insist upon this control because the legal system has taught them how costly less control can be. The film *Twelve Monkeys* was stopped by a court twenty-eight days after its release because an artist claimed a chair in the movie resembled a sketch of a piece of furniture that he had designed. The movie *Batman Forever* was threatened because the Batmobile drove through an allegedly copyrighted courtyard and the original architect demanded money before the film could be released. In 1998, a judge stopped the release of *The Devil's Advocate* for two days because a sculptor claimed his art was used in the background.[2] Such events teach the lawyers that they must control the filmmakers.[3] They convince studios that creative control is ultimately a legal matter.

This control creates burdens, and not just expense. "The cost for me," Guggenheim says, "is creativity. . . . Suddenly the world that you're trying to create is completely generic and void of the elements that you would normally create. . . . It's my job to conceptualize and to create a world, and to bring people into the world that I see. That's why they pay me as a director. And if I see this person having a certain lifestyle, having this certain art on the wall, and living a certain way, it is essential to . . . the vision I am trying to portray. Now I somehow have to justify using it. And that is wrong."

THIS IS not a book about filmmaking. Whatever problems filmmakers have, they are tiny in the order of things. But I begin with this example because it points to a much more fundamental puzzle, and one that will be with us throughout this book: What could ever lead anyone to create such a silly and extreme rule? Why would we burden the creative process—not just film, but generally, and not just the arts, but innovation more broadly—with rules that seem to have no connection to innovation and creativity?

Copyright law, law professor Jessica Litman has written, is filled with rules that ordinary people would respond to by saying, "There can't really be a law that says that. That would be silly."[4] Yet in fact there is such a law, and it does say just that, and it is, as the ordinary person rightly thinks, silly. So why? What is the mentality that gets us to this place where highly educated, extremely highly paid lawyers run around negotiating for the rights to have a poster in the background of a film about a frat party? Or scrambling to get editors to remove an unsigned billboard? What leads us to build a legal world where the advice a successful director can give to a young artist is this:

> I would say to an 18-year-old artist, you're totally free to do whatever you want. But—and then I would give him a long list of all the things that he couldn't include in his movie because they would not be cleared, legally cleared. That he would have to pay for them. [So freedom? Here's the freedom]: You're totally free to make a movie in an empty room, with your two friends.[5]

A TIME is marked not so much by ideas that are argued about as by ideas that are taken for granted. The character of an era hangs upon what needs no defense. Power runs with ideas that only the crazy would draw into doubt. The "taken for granted" is the test of sanity; "what everyone knows" is the line between us and them.

This means that sometimes a society gets stuck. Sometimes these unquestioned ideas interfere, as the cost of questioning becomes too great. In these times, the hardest task for social or political activists is to find a way to get people to wonder again about what we all believe is true. The challenge is to sow doubt.

And so it is with us. All around us are the consequences of the most significant technological, and hence cultural, revolution in generations. This revolution has produced the most powerful and diverse spur to innovation of any in modern times. Yet a set of ideas about a central aspect of this prosperity—"property"—confuses us. This confusion is leading us to change the environment in ways that will change the prosperity. Believing we know what makes prosperity work, ignoring the nature of the actual prosperity all around, we change the rules within which the Internet revolution lives. These changes will end the revolution.

That's a large claim for so thin a book, so to convince you to carry on, I should qualify it a bit. I don't mean "the Internet" will end. "The Internet" is with us forever, even if the character of "the Internet" will change. And I don't pretend that I can prove the demise that I warn of here. There is too much that is contingent, and not yet done, and too little good data to make any convincing predictions.

But I do mean to convince you of a blind spot in our culture, and of the harm that this blind spot creates. In the understanding of this revolution and of the creativity it has induced, we systematically miss the role of a crucially important part. We therefore don't even notice as this part disappears or, more important, is removed. Blind to its effect, we don't watch for its demise.

This blindness will harm the environment of innovation. Not just the innovation of Internet entrepreneurs (though that is an extremely important part of what I mean), but also the innovation of authors or artists more generally. This blindness will lead to changes in the Internet that will undermine its potential for building something new—a potential realized in the original Internet, but increasingly compromised as that original Net is changed.

The struggle against these changes is not the traditional struggle between Left and Right or between conservative and liberal. To question assumptions about the scope of "property" is not to question property. I am fanatically pro-market, in the market's proper sphere. I don't doubt the important and valuable role played by property in most, maybe just about all, contexts. This is not an argument about commerce *versus* something else. The innovation that I defend is commercial and noncommercial alike; the arguments I draw upon to defend it are as strongly tied to the Right as to the Left.

Instead, the real struggle at stake now is between *old* and *new*. The story on the following pages is about how an environment designed to enable the new is being transformed to protect the old—transformed by courts, by legislators, and by the very coders who built the original Net.

Old versus *new*. That battle is nothing new. As Machiavelli wrote in *The Prince*:

> Innovation makes enemies of all those who prospered under the old regime, and only lukewarm support is forthcoming from those who would prosper under the new. Their support is indifferent partly from fear and partly because they are generally incredulous, never really trusting new things unless they have tested them by experience.[6]

And so it is today with us: those who prospered under the old regime are threatened by the Internet; this is the story of how they react. Those who would prosper under the new regime have not risen to defend it against the old; whether they will is the question this book asks. The answer so far is clear: They will not.

* * *

THERE ARE two futures in front of us, the one we are taking and the one we could have. The one we are taking is easy to describe. Take the Net, mix it with the fanciest TV, add a simple way to buy things, and that's pretty much it. It is a future much like the present. Though I don't (yet) believe this view of America Online (AOL), it is the most cynical image of Time Warner's marriage to AOL: the forging of an estate of large-scale networks with power over users to an estate dedicated to almost perfect control over content. That content will not be "broadcast" to millions at the same time; it will be fed to users as users demand it, packaged in advertising precisely tailored to the user. But the service will still be essentially one-way, and the freedom to feed back, to feed creativity to others, will be just about as constrained as it is today. These constraints are not the constraints of economics as it exists today—not the high costs of production or the extraordinarily high costs of distribution. These constraints instead will be burdens created by law—by intellectual property as well as other government-granted exclusive rights. The promise of many-to-many communication that defined the early Internet will be replaced by a reality of many, many ways to buy things and many, many ways to select among what is offered. What gets offered will be just what fits within the current model of the concentrated systems of distribution: cable television on speed, addicting a much more manageable, malleable, and sellable public.

The future that we could have is much harder to describe. It is harder because the very premise of the Internet is that no one can predict how it will develop. The architects who crafted the first protocols of the Net had no sense of a world where grandparents would use computers to keep in touch with their grandkids. They had no idea of a technology where every song imaginable is available within thirty seconds' reach. The World Wide Web (WWW) was the fantasy of a few MIT computer scientists. The perpetual tracking of preferences that allows a computer in Washington State to suggest an artist I might like because of a book I just purchased was an idea that no one had made famous before the Internet made it real.

Yet there are elements of this future that we can fairly imagine. They are the consequences of falling costs, and hence falling barriers to creativity. The most dramatic are the changes in the costs of distribution; but just as important are the changes in the costs of production. Both are the consequences of going digital: digital technologies create and replicate reality much more efficiently than nondigital technology does. This will mean a world of change.

These changes could have an effect in every sphere of social life. Begin with the creative sphere, and let's start with creativity off-line, long before the law tried to regulate it through "copyright."

There was a time (it was the time of the framing of our Constitution) when creativity was essentially unregulated. As we'll see in chapter 11, the law of copyright effectively regulated publishers only. Its scope was just "maps, charts, and books." That meant every other aspect of creative life was free. Music could be performed in public without a license from a lawyer; a novel could be turned into a play even if the novel was copyrighted. A story could be adapted into a different story; many were, as the very act of creativity was understood to be the act of taking something and re-forming it into something (ever so slightly) new. The public domain was vast and rich—the works of Shakespeare had just fallen from the control of publishers in England; they would not have been protected in the United States even if they had not.[7]

It's not clear who got to participate in this creativity. No doubt social norms meant that the right did not reach blindly across the sexes or races. But the spirit of the times was storytelling, as a society defined itself by the stories it told, and the law had no role in deciding who got to tell what stories. An old man fortunate enough to read might learn of the struggles with pirates in the Gulf of Tripoli. He would retell this story to others in the town square. A local troupe of actors might stage the struggle for patrons of a local pub. If compelling, the troupe might move to the town next over and retell the story.

It makes no sense to say that that world was "more creative" than ours. My point is not about quantity, or even quality, and my argument does not imagine a "golden age." The point instead is about the nature of the constraints on this practice of creativity: no doubt there were technical constraints on it; no doubt these were important and real. But except for important subject matter constraints imposed by the law, the law had essentially no role in saying how one person could take and remake the work of someone else. This act of creativity was free, or at least free of the law.

Skip ahead to just a few years in front of 2001 and think about the potential for creativity then. Digital technology has radically reduced the cost of digital creations. As we will see more clearly below, the cost of filmmaking is a fraction of what it was just a decade ago. The same is true for the production of music or any digital art. Using what we might call a "music processor," students in a high school music class can compose symphonies that are played back to the composer. Imagine the cost of that just ten years ago (both to educate the composer about how to write music and to hire the equipment to play it back). Digital tools dramatically change the horizon of opportunity for those who could create something new.[8]

And not just for those who would create something "totally new," if such an idea is even possible. Think about the ads from Apple Computer urging that "consumers" do more than simply consume:

Rip, mix, burn,

Apple instructs.

After all, it's your music.

Apple, of course, wants to sell computers. Yet its ad touches an ideal that runs very deep in our history. For the technology that they (and of course others) sell could enable this generation to do with our culture what generations have done from the very beginning of human society: to take what is our culture; to "rip" it—meaning to copy it; to "mix" it—meaning to reform it however the user wants; and finally, and most important, to "burn" it—to publish it in a way that others can see and hear.[9] Digital technology could enable an extraordinary range of ordinary people to become part of a *creative* process. To move from the life of a "consumer" (just think about what that word means—passive, couch potato, *fed*) of music—and not just music, but film, and art, and commerce—to a life where one can individually and collectively participate in making something new.

Now obviously, in some form, this ability predates digital technology. Rap music is a genre that is built upon "ripping" (and, relatedly, "sampling") the music of others, mixing that music with lyrics or other music, and then burning that remixing onto records or tapes that get sold to others.[10] Jazz was no different a generation before. Music in particular, but not just music, has always been about using what went before in a way that empowers creators to do something new.[11]

But now we have the potential to expand the reach of this creativity to an extraordinary range of culture and commerce. Technology could enable a whole generation to *create*—remixed films, new forms of music, digital art, a new kind of storytelling, writing, a new technology for poetry, criticism, political activism—and then, through the infrastructure of the Internet, *share* that creativity with others.

This is the art through which free culture is built. And not just through art. The future that I am describing is as important to commerce as to any other field of creativity. Though most distinguish innovation from creativity, or creativity from commerce, I do not. The network that I am describing enables both forms of creativity. It would leave the network open to the widest range of commercial innovation; it would keep the barriers to this creativity as low as possible.

Already we can see something of this potential. The open and neutral platform of the Internet has spurred hundreds of companies to develop new ways for individuals to interact. E-mail was the start; but most of the messages that now build contact are the flashes of chat in groups or between individuals—as spouses (and others) live at separate places of work with a single window open to each other through an instant messenger. Groups form easily to discuss any issue imaginable; public debate is enabled by removing perhaps the most significant cost of human interaction—synchronicity. I can add to your conversation tonight; you can follow it up tomorrow; someone else, the day after.

And this is just the beginning, as the technology will only get better. Thousands could experiment on this common platform for a better way; millions of dot.com dollars will flow down the tube; but then a handful of truly extraordinary innovations comes from these experiments. A wristwatch for kids that squeezes knowingly as a mother touches hers, thirty miles away. A Walkman where lovers can whisper to each other between songs, though separated by an ocean. A technology to signal two people that both are available to talk on the phone—*now*. A technology to enable a community to decide local issues through deliberation in virtual juries. The potential can only be glimpsed. And contrary to the technology doomsayers, this is a potential for making human life more, not less, human.

But just at the cusp of this future, at the same time that we are being pushed to the world where anyone can "rip, mix, [and] burn," a countermovement is raging all around. To ordinary people, this slogan from Apple seems benign enough; to lawyers in the content industry, it is high treason. To the lawyers who prosecute the laws of copyright, the very idea that the music on "your" CD is "your music" is absurd. "Read the license," they're likely to demand. "Read the law," they'll say, piling on. This culture that you sing to yourself, or that swims all around you, this music that you pay for many times over—when you hear it on commercial radio, when you buy a CD, when you pay a surplus at a large restaurant so that it can play the same music on its speakers, when you purchase a movie ticket where the song is the theme—this music *is not yours*. You have no "right" to rip it, or to mix it, or especially to burn it. You may have, the lawyers will insist, *permission* to do these things. But don't confuse Hollywood's grace with your rights. These parts of our culture, these lawyers will tell you, are the property of the few. The law of copyright makes them so, even though (as I will show in the chapters that follow) the law of copyright was never meant to create any such power.

Indeed, the best evidence of this conflict is again Apple itself. For the very same machines that Apple sells to "rip, mix, [and] burn" music are programmed to make it impossible for ordinary users to "rip, mix, [and] burn" Hollywood's movies. Try to "rip, mix, [and] burn" Disney's *102 Dalmatians* and it's your computer that will get ripped, not the content. Software, or *code*, protects this content, and Apple's machine protects this code. It may be your music, but it's not your film. Film you can rip, mix, and burn only as Hollywood allows. *It* controls that creativity—it, and the law that backs it up.

This struggle is just a token of a much broader battle, for the model that governs film is slowly being pushed to every kind of content. The changes we see affect every front of human creativity. They affect commercial as well as noncommercial activities, the arts as well as the sciences. They are as much about growth and jobs as they are about music and film. And how we decide these questions will determine much about the kind of society we will become. It will determine what the "free" means in our self-congratulatory claim that we are now, and will always be, a "free society."

This is a struggle about an ideal—about what rules should govern the freedom to innovate. I would call it a "moral question," but that sounds too personal, or private. One might call it a political question, but most of us work hard to ignore the absurdities of ordinary politics. It is instead best described as a *constitutional* question: it is about the fundamental values that define this society and whether we will allow those values to change. Are we, in the digital age, to be a free society? And what precisely would that idea mean?

TO ANSWER these questions, we must put them into context. That's what I will do in the balance of this chapter. Step back from the conflict about music or innovation, and think about *resources* in a society more generally. How are resources, in this vague, general sense, ordered? Who decides who gets access to what?

Every society has resources that are *free* and resources that are *controlled*. Free resources are those available for the taking. Controlled resources are those for which the permission of someone is needed before the resource can be used. Einstein's theory of relativity is a free resource. You can take it and use it without the permission of anyone. Einstein's last residence in Princeton, New Jersey, is a controlled resource. To sleep at 112 Mercer Street requires the permission of the Institute for Advanced Study.

Over the past hundred years, much of the heat in political argument has been about which system for controlling resources—the state or the market—works best. The Cold War was a battle of just this sort. The social- ist East placed its faith in the government to allocate and regulate resources; the free-market West placed its faith in the market for allocating or regu- lating resources. The struggle was between the *state* and the *market*. The question was which system works best.

That war is over. For most resources, most of the time, the market trumps the state. There are exceptions, of course, and dissenters still. But if the twentieth century taught us one lesson, it is the dominance of private over state ordering. Markets work better than Tammany Hall in deciding who should get what, when. Or as Nobel Prize–winning economist Ronald Coase put it, whatever problems there are with the market, the problems with government are far more profound.

This, however, is a new century; our questions will be different. The issue for us will not be which system of exclusive control—the government or the market—should govern a given resource. The question for us comes before: not whether the market or the state but, for any given resource, whether that resource should be *controlled* or *free*.

"Free."

So deep is the rhetoric of control within our culture that whenever one says a resource is "free," most believe that a price is being quoted—free, that is, as in zero cost. But "free" has a much more fundamental meaning—in French, *libre* rather than *gratis*, or for us non–French speakers, and as the philosopher of our age and founder of the Free Software Foundation Richard Stallman puts it, "free, not in the sense of free beer, but free in the sense of free speech."[12] A resource is "free" if (1) one can use it without the permission of anyone else; or (2) the permission one needs is granted neu- trally. So understood, the question for our generation will be not whether the market or the state should control a resource, but whether that resource should remain free.[13]

This is not a new question, though we've been well trained to ignore it. Free resources have always been central to innovation, creativity, and democracy. The roads are free in the sense I mean; they give value to the businesses around them. Central Park is free in the sense I mean; it gives value to the city that it centers. A jazz musician draws freely upon the chord sequence of a popular song to create a new improvisation, which, if popular, will itself be used by others. Scientists plotting an orbit of a spacecraft draw freely upon the equations developed by Kepler and Newton and modified by Einstein. Inventor Mitch Kapor drew freely upon the idea of a spreadsheet—VisiCalc—to build the first killer application for the IBM PC—Lotus 1-2-3. In all of these cases, the availability of a resource that remains outside the exclusive control of someone else—whether a government or a private individual—has been central to progress in science and the arts. It will also remain central to progress in the future.

Yet lurking in the background of our collective thought is a hunch that free resources are somehow inferior. That nothing is valuable that isn't restricted. That we shouldn't want, as Groucho Marx might put it, any resource that would willingly have us. As Yale professor Carol Rose writes, our view is that "the whole world is best managed when divided among private owners,"[14] so we proceed as quickly as we can to divide all resources among private owners so as to better manage the world.

This is the taken-for-granted idea that I spoke of at the start: that control is good, and hence more control is better; that progress always comes from dividing resources among private owners; that the more dividing we do, the better off we will be; that the free is an exception, or an imperfection, which depends upon altruism, or carelessness, or a commitment to communism.

Free resources, however, have nothing to do with communism. (The Soviet Union was not a place with either free speech or free beer.) Neither are the resources that I am talking about the product of altruism. I am not arguing that there is such a thing as a "free lunch." There is no manna from heaven. Resources cost money to produce. They must be paid for if they are to be produced.

But how a resource is *produced* says nothing about how *access* to that resource is granted. Production is different from consumption. And while the ordinary and sensible rule for most goods is the "pay me this for that" model of the local convenience store, a second's reflection reveals that there is a wide range of resources that we make available in a completely different way.

Think of music on the radio, which you consume without paying anything. Or the roads that you drive upon, which are paid for independently of their use. Or the history that we hear about without ever paying the researcher. These too are resources. They too cost money to produce. But we organize access to these resources differently from the way we organize access to chewing gum. To get access to these, you don't have to pay up front. Sometimes you don't have to pay at all. And when you do have to pay, the price is set neutrally or without regard to the user, inside or outside the company. And for good reason, too. Access to chewing gum may rightly be controlled all the way down; but access to roads, and history, and control of our government must always, and sensibly, remain "free."

THE ARGUMENT of this book is that always and everywhere, free resources have been crucial to innovation and creativity; that without them, creativity is crippled. Thus, and especially in the digital age, the central question becomes not whether government or the market should control a resource, but whether a resource should be controlled at all. Just because control is possible, it doesn't follow that it is justified. Instead, in a free society, the burden of justification should fall on him who would defend systems of control.

No simple answer will satisfy this demand. The choice is not between all or none. Obviously many resources must be controlled if they are to be produced or sustained. I should have the right to control access to my house and my car. You shouldn't be allowed to rifle through my desk. Microsoft should have the right to control access to its source code. Hollywood should have the right to charge admission to its movies. If one couldn't control access to these resources, or resources called "mine," one would have little incentive to work to produce these resources, including those called mine.

But likewise, and obviously, many resources should be free. The right to criticize a government official is a resource that is not, and should not be, controlled. I shouldn't need the permission of the Einstein estate before I test his theory against newly discovered data. These resources and others gain value by being kept free rather than controlled. A mature society realizes that value by protecting such resources from both private and public control.

We need to learn this lesson again. The opportunity for this learning is the Internet. No modern phenomenon better demonstrates the importance of free resources to innovation and creativity than the Internet. To those who argue that control is necessary if innovation is to occur, and that more control will yield more innovation, the Internet is the simplest and most direct reply. For as I will show in the chapters that follow, the defining feature of the Internet is that it leaves resources free. The Internet has provided for much of the world the greatest demonstration of the power of freedom—and its lesson is one we must learn if its benefits are to be preserved.

Yet at just the time that the Internet is reminding us about the extraordinary value of freedom, the Internet is being changed to take that freedom away. Just as we are beginning to see the power that free resources produce, changes in the architecture of the Internet—both legal and technical—are sapping the Internet of this power. Fueled by a bias in favor of control, pushed by those whose financial interests favor control, our social and political institutions are ratifying changes in the Internet that will reestablish control and, in turn, reduce innovation on the Internet and in society generally.

I am dead against the changes we are seeing, but it is too much to believe I could convince you that the full range is wrong. My aim is much more limited. My hope is to show you the other side of what has become a taken-for-granted idea—the view that control of some sort is always better. If you stay with me to the end, then I want you to leave this book simply with a question about whether control is best. I don't have the data to prove anything more than this limited hope. But we do have a history to show that there is something important here to understand.

THIS SHOWING moves in three steps. In the part that follows, I introduce more formally what I mean by "free." I relate that concept to the notion of "the commons" and then introduce three contexts where resources in the Internet are held in common. These commons are related to the innovation the Internet has produced. My aim in this first part is to show just how.

I then consider in part II a parallel environment for innovation and creativity in "real space"—the space not tied directly to the Internet, though increasingly affected by it. This is the space where records are now made, books are still written, and film is primarily shot. This space does not present the commons the Internet is—and for good reason, too. The character of production in real space does not permit the freedom that the Internet does. The constraint on creativity it yields there is a necessary, if unfortunate, feature of that space.

This context of creativity has been changed by the Internet. In the balance of part II, I offer examples of how. These examples will show how many of the constraints that affected real-space creativity have been removed by the architecture, and original legal context, of the Internet. These limitations, perhaps justified before, are justified no more.

Or at least, were justified no more. For the argument of the third and final part of this book is that the environment of the Internet is now changing. Features of the architecture—both legal and technical—that originally created this environment of free creativity are now being changed. They are being changed in ways that will reintroduce the very barriers that the Internet originally removed.

These barriers, however, don't have the neutral justification that the constraints of real-space economics do.[15] If there are constraints here, it is simply because we are building them in. And as I will argue, there are strong reasons why many are trying to rebuild these constraints: they will enable these existing and powerful interests to protect themselves from the competitive threat the Internet represents. The old, in other words, is bending the Net to protect itself against the new.

PART

I

///

DOT.COMMONS

Building Blocks:
"Commons" and "Layers"

THIS BOOK is fundamentally about the Internet and its effect on innovation, both commercial and non-. "Internet" and "society" are familiar enough notions. But at the core of my argument are two fairly obscure ideas that we must begin by making a bit more clear. The first of these is the idea of a "commons"; the second is the notion of "layers." The commons is an old idea; layers, in the sense made familiar by network theorists, are relatively new. But the two together organize the argument that follows. They are building blocks to an end that will help reveal the Internet's effect on society.

THE COMMONS

IF YOU'VE used the word *commons* before, you're likely to think of a park, as in the Boston Common. If you've studied economics or political science, your mind will race to tragedy (as in "the tragedy of the commons"). Both senses are related to what I mean, but neither alone is enough.[1]

The Oxford English Dictionary (mankind's first large-scale collaborative open source text project)[2] equates the "commons" to a resource held "in common." That it defines as "in joint use or possession; to be held or enjoyed equally by a number of persons."[3] In this sense, a resource held "in common" is "free" (as I've defined that term) to those "persons." In most cases, the commons is a resource to which anyone within the relevant community has a right without obtaining the permission of anyone else. In some cases, permission is needed but is granted in a neutral way.

Think about some examples:

- The public streets are commons. Anyone is free to access the streets without first getting the permission of someone else. We don't auction rights of access, selling the right to use a particular bit of highway during a particular bit of time. (Of course there are exceptions.) Nor do we insist on particular licenses before we allow people to use the streets or highways. Instead the highways are open and free—in the sense I mean a commons to be free.

- Parks and beaches are increasingly commons. Anyone is free to access these spaces without getting the permission of someone else. Access is not auctioned off to the highest bidder, and the right to control access is not handed off to some private or governmental entity. The resource—as Carol Rose calls it, "the recreational resource"—is made available to anyone.

- Einstein's theory of relativity is a commons. It is a resource—a way of understanding the nature of the universe—that is open and free for anyone to take. Access to this resource is not auctioned off to the highest bidder; the right to use the theory is not allocated to a single organization.

- Writings in the public domain are a commons. They are a resource that is open and free for anyone to take without the permission of anyone else. An 1890 edition of Shakespeare is free for anyone to take and copy. Your right to use and redistribute that 1890 text is without restraint.

Each of these resources is held in common. Each is "free" for others to take. Some are free in the sense that no price is paid (you can use most roads without paying a toll; as we will see, it would be unconstitutional in the United States to require anyone to pay to use Einstein's theory of relativity). Some are free even though a price must be paid (a park is "free" in the sense that I mean even if an access fee is required—as long as the fee is neutrally and consistently applied).[4] In both cases, the essential feature is reasonable, and that access to the resource is not conditioned upon the permission of someone else. The essence, in other words, is that no one exercises the core of a property right with respect to these resources—the exclusive right to choose whether the resource is made available to others.[5]

Economists will object, however, that my list conflates two very different cases. Einstein's theory of relativity is different from the streets or public beaches. Einstein's theory is fully "nonrivalrous"; the streets and beaches are not. If you use the theory of relativity, there is as much left over afterward as there was before. Your consumption, in other words, does not *rival* my own. But roads and beaches are very different. If everyone tries to use the roads at the very same time (something that apparently happens out here in California often), then their use certainly rivals my own. Traffic jams; public beaches crowd. Your SUV, or your loud radio, reduces my ability to enjoy the roads or beach.

The economists are right. This list of resources held in "the commons" does conflate rivalrous with nonrivalrous resources. But our tradition is not as tidy as the economists' analytics. We have always described as "commons" both rivalrous and nonrivalrous resources. The Boston Common is a commons, though its resource is rivalrous (my use of it competes with your use of it). Language is a commons, though its resource is nonrivalrous (my use of it does not inhibit yours).[6] What has determined "the commons," then, is not the simple test of rivalrousness. What has determined the commons is the *character of the resource* and how it *relates to a community*. In theory, any resource might be held in common (whether it would survive is another question). But in practice, the question a society must ask is which resources *should be,* and for those resources, *how*.

Here the distinction that the economists draw begins to help. Economists distinguish rivalrous and nonrivalrous resources because the issues or problems raised by each kind are different.

If a resource is nonrivalrous, then the problem is whether there is enough incentive to produce it, not whether there is too much demand to consume it. A nonrivalrous resource can't be exhausted. Once it is produced, it can't be undone. Thus the issue for nonrivalrous resources is whether the Edith Whartons of the world have enough incentive to create. The problem with nonrivalrous resources is to assure that I reap enough benefit to induce me to sow.

A rivalrous resource presents more problems. If a resource is rivalrous, then we must worry both about whether there is sufficient incentive to create it (if it is the sort of resource that humans produce) and about whether consumption by some will leave enough to others. With a rivalrous resource, I must still worry that I will reap enough benefit to make it worth it to sow. But I must worry as well that others not deplete the resource that I've produced. If a rivalrous resource is open to all, there is a risk that it will be depleted by the consumption of all.

This depletion of a rivalrous resource is the dynamic that biologist Garrett Hardin famously termed "the tragedy of the commons."[7] "Picture a pasture open to all," Hardin writes, and consider the expected behavior of "herdsmen" who roam that pasture. Each herdsman must decide whether to add one more animal to his herd. In making a decision to do so, Hardin writes, the herdsman reaps a benefit, while everyone else suffers. The herdsman gets the benefit of one more animal, yet everyone suffers the cost, because the pasture has one more consuming cow. And this defines the problem: Whatever costs there are in adding another animal are costs that others bear. The benefits, however, are enjoyed by a single herdsman. Therefore each herdsman has an incentive to add more cattle than the pasture as a whole can bear. As Hardin describes the consequence:

> Therein is the tragedy. Each man is locked into a system that compels him to increase his herd without limit—in a world that is limited. *Ruin is the destination toward which all men rush, each pursuing his own best interest in a society that believes in the freedom of the commons. Freedom in a commons brings ruin to all.*[8]

This "tragedy" consumes talk about "the commons." "Ruin" is taken for granted as the destiny of those who believe in the "freedom of the commons." Hardheaded sorts thus scorn the rhetoric of undivided resources. Only the romantic wastes time wondering about anything different from the perfect control of property.

But obviously Hardin was not describing a law of nature that must apply to every good left in the commons. There is, for example, no tragedy for nonrivalrous goods left in the commons—no matter how many times you read a poem, there's as much left over as there was when you started. Nor is there always a tragedy even for rivalrous goods. As researchers have shown, in many different contexts, norms adequately limit the problem of overconsumption.[9] Communities work out how to regulate overconsumption. *How* and *why* are certainly complex questions. But *that some do* is undeniable.[10]

We therefore can't just jump from the observation that a resource is held "in common" to the conclusion that "freedom in a commons brings ruin to all." Instead, we must think empirically and look at what works. Where there is a benefit from leaving a resource free, we should see whether there is a way to avoid overconsumption, or inadequate incentives, without its falling under either state or private (market) control.

My central claim throughout is that there is a benefit to resources held in common and that the Internet is the best evidence of that benefit. As we will see, the Internet forms an *innovation commons*. It forms this commons not just through norms, but also through a specific technical architecture. The Net of these norms and this architecture is a space where creativity can flourish. Yet so blind are we to the possible value of a commons that we don't even notice the commons that the Internet is. And, in turn, this blindness leads us to ignore changes to the norms and architecture of the Net that weaken this commons. There is a tragedy of the commons that we will identify here; it is the tragedy of losing the innovation commons that the Internet is, through the changes that are being rendered on top.[11]

LAYERS

THE IDEA of the commons may be obscure, but the notion of "layers" is more easily recognized. The layers that I mean here are the different layers within a communications system that together make communications possible. The idea is taken from perhaps the best communications theorist of our generation, NYU law professor Yochai Benkler.[12] As he uses the idea, it helps organize our thought about how any communications system functions. But in organizing our thought, his work helps show something we might otherwise miss.

Following the technique of network architects, Benkler suggests that we understand a communications system by dividing it into three distinct "layers."[13] At the bottom is a "physical" layer, across which communication travels. This is the computer, or wires, that link computers on the Internet. In the middle is a "logical" or "code" layer—the code that makes the hardware run. Here we might include the protocols that define the Internet and the software upon which those protocols run. At the top is a "content" layer— the actual stuff that gets said or transmitted across these wires. Here we include digital images, texts, on-line movies, and the like. These three layers function together to define any particular communications system.

Each of these layers in principle could be controlled or could be free. Each, that is, could be owned or each could be organized in a commons. We could imagine a world where the physical layer was free but the logical and content layers were not. Or we could imagine a world where the physical and code layers were controlled but the content layer was not. And so on.

Consider some examples to make the possibilities real.

Speakers' Corner: Speakers' Corner is a place in London's Hyde Park where people who want to speak publicly gather on Sundays to deliver their speeches. It is a wonderfully English spectacle, ordinarily filled with both orators and loons. But the system of communication is distinctive: the physical layer (the park) is a commons; the code layer (the language used) is a commons, too; and the content layer is ordinarily unowned—what these nuts say is their own creation. All three layers in this context are free; no one can exercise control over the kinds of communications that might happen here.

Madison Square Garden: Madison Square Garden is another place where people give speeches or, more likely, play games. It is a huge stadium/auditorium near the center of Manhattan, owned by Madison Square Garden, L.P. Only those who pay get to use the auditorium; and the Garden is not obligated to take all comers. The physical layer is therefore controlled. But as with Speakers' Corner, both the code layer (the language) and the content layer (what gets uttered) are at least sometimes not controlled. They too can remain free.

The telephone system: The telephone system before its breakup was a single unitary system. The physical infrastructure of this system was owned by AT&T and its affiliates; so too was its logical infrastructure—determining how and who you could connect—controlled by AT&T. But what you said on an AT&T phone (within limits, at least)[14] was free: the content of the telephone conversations was not controlled, even if the physical and code layers underneath were.

Cable TV: Finally, think of cable TV. Here the physical layer is owned—the wires that run the content into your house. The code layer is owned—only the cable companies get to decide what runs into your house. And the content layer is owned—the shows that get broadcast are copyrighted shows. All three layers are within the control of the cable TV company; no communications layer, in Benkler's sense, remains free.

These examples suggest the range of ways of organizing systems of communications. No single mix is best, though the differences among the four are important. To the extent that we want a decentralized system of communications, unowned layers will help. To the extent that we want controlled systems of communications, owned layers will help. But the point of the scheme so far is not to make predictions. The point is simply to make clear the range, and that trade-offs within this range exist.

	Speakers' Corner	Madison Square Garden	Telephone System	Cable TV
Content	Free	Free	Free	Controlled
Code	Free	Free	Controlled	Controlled
Physical	Free	Controlled	Controlled	Controlled

Now, from the language I've used so far, you might think that the Internet is a communications system free all the way down—free, that is, at every one of Benkler's layers. It is not. What is special about the Internet is the way it mixes freedom with control at different layers. The physical layer of the Internet is fundamentally controlled. The wires and the computers across which the network runs are the property of either government or individuals. Similarly, at the content layer, much in the existing Internet is controlled. Not everything served across the Net is free for the taking. Much is properly and importantly protected by property law.

At the code layer, however, in ways that will become clearer below, the Internet was free. So too was much of the content served across the network free. The Internet thus mixed both free and controlled layers, not just layers that were free.

Our aim is to understand how this mix produced the innovation that we have seen so far and why the changes to this mix will kill what we have seen so far.

3

Commons on the Wires

HE INTERNET is a network of networks. In the main, these networks connect over wires. All of these wires, and the machines linked by them, are controlled by someone. The vast majority are owned by private parties—owned, that is, by individuals and corporations that have chosen to link to the Net. Some are owned by the government.

Yet this vast network of privately owned technology has built one of the most important *innovation commons* that we have ever known. Built on a platform that is controlled, the protocols of the Internet have erected a free space of innovation. These private networks have created an open resource that any can draw upon and that many have. Understanding how, and in what sense, is the aim of this chapter.

PAUL BARAN was a researcher at the Rand Corporation from 1959 to 1968. His project in the early 1960s was communications reliability. The fear slowly dawning upon the leaders of the world's largest nuclear arsenal was that the communications system controlling that arsenal was vulnerable to the smallest of attacks. An accident, or a single nuclear explosion, could disable the ability of the commander in chief to command. Chaos—or worse—would be unavoidable.

Baran's task was to explore a more secure telecommunications system. His first step was to understand the system then in place. So he asked the then provider of telecommunications in America, American Telephone &

Telegraph, to see the plans for the AT&T network to determine whether the communications system was secure.

AT&T balked. Though Baran had the proper security clearance, and though the Defense Department supported his request, AT&T refused Baran's inquiry. They had studied the matter, AT&T reported. The system was secure.

This was "the Bell system." It is hard for us today to appreciate the power of such a company. This was not just a large company, or even a large company with a very large market share. This was a partner with the government, ruling telecommunications in America. It was therefore, in its own view of itself, the governor of communications. States and the Federal Communications Commission (FCC) might regulate it, but the information and cooperation to make that regulation possible came from AT&T. It had been, since interconnection began in earnest in 1912, America's telecommunications master.[1]

Things with telephones were not always this way. Indeed, the early history of telecommunications is essentially unrecognizable to us. Though the Bell companies held the first patents on telephone technology, once those patents expired, a vigorous competition emerged to bring telephone service to Americans. AT&T concentrated on businesses. "Independents" focused on residences. The competition produced a rapid expansion of coverage. "From 1900 to 1915, at least 45% of the U.S. cities with populations over 5,000 had competing, non-interconnected telephone exchanges. During the peak of the independent movement's strength, between 1902 and 1910, that percentage was more than 55%."[2]

Today we would not recognize the phone system that this early competition produced. Though the reach of the telephone network was great—in 1920, 38.7 percent of farms and 30 percent of residences had a telephone[3]—the networks did not interconnect. There was no guarantee that if your grandmother across town had a telephone, you, using yours, could call her. Thus when you purchased telephone service, your decision in part depended upon whom you wanted to call and what service they were likely to have.

The world was then with telephones as the world was with personal computers ten years ago,[4] or as the world with instant messaging is today. Though there was a dominant system (AT&T for phones; Microsoft/Intel for computers; AOL's AIM for instant messaging), there was vigorous competition among other systems (the "independents" for phones; Apple's Macintosh or IBM's OS/2 for computers; Yahoo! or MSN for messaging). This competition effectively pushed the dominant system to become better and different. Just as the windows of Macintosh pushed Microsoft to Windows, so too the rural service of the "independents" pushed AT&T to extend its reach to farmers.

After a while, however, AT&T grew weary of this competition. The view grew within the company that security would come only by merging with the competitors. From 1908 to 1913, the Bell system adopted a number of strategies to destroy the independents, including selective interconnection and acquisition of competitors. If it could not gain customers through direct competition, it would gain customers by purchasing competitors.[5]

Initially, this consolidation inspired skepticism among regulators and the public. AT&T was attacked as a monster seeking monopoly. But by the early 1920s, antitrust enforcement in the United States was waning. The spirit of the time favored consolidation and rationalization; competition was viewed as "ruinous." Thus AT&T was slowly able to secure agreements with the government that essentially permitted it to extend its reach while protecting it against antitrust review.

Paradoxically, AT&T's most effective weapon in this expansion was to offer competitors the ability to interconnect. Though our intuition is likely to tell us that it was the failure to interconnect that hampered competition, in fact, as economist Milton Mueller has effectively argued, it was a lack of interconnection that spurred competition.[6] As each independent interconnected to the AT&T system, any distinctive advantage it could offer as an independent disappeared. Consumers had no further interest in subscribing to it over AT&T; hence the drive to AT&T as universal provider was only increased. The network advantage of AT&T would grow relative to other independents; hence the power of AT&T's increasing monopoly was enhanced.

Independents at the time understood this dynamic. Associations of independents vigorously attacked the "traitors" among them that chose to interconnect with AT&T.[7] But these competitors were increasingly seen as inconveniences, by both regulators and the public. The idea of a world of "universal service"—meaning not a telephone in every house, but a system where every phone could reach every other phone—was too seductive.[8] So in 1913 the government entered into an agreement with AT&T that would secure its monopoly in telecommunications in America, even though it was sold as a solution to telecommunications monopoly.

Named after Bell vice president Nicholas C. Kingsbury, the "Kingsbury

Commitment" required that Bell "stop acquiring independent phone companies and [. . .] connect the remaining independents to Bell's long-distance network."[9] Bell also had to divest its telegraph arm, Western Union. This stopped the company from its increasingly ravenous practice of acquisition, but it "did nothing to promote competition in either telephony or telegraphy."[10] The commitment did not force local exchanges to be more competitive. It did not require interconnection with other long-distance carriers. The solution, "in short, was not the steamy unsettling cohabitation that marks competition, but rather a sort of competitive apartheid, characterized by segregation and quarantine."[11] As a major treatise on telecommunications describes it:

> The Kingsbury Commitment could be viewed as a solution only by a government bookkeeper who counted several separate monopolies as an advance over a single monopoly, even absent any trace of competition among them.[12]

Monopolies are not all bad, and no doubt this monopoly did lots of good. AT&T produced an extraordinary telephone system, linking 85 percent of American homes at the peak of its monopoly power in 1965.[13] It spent billions of dollars to support telecommunications research. Bell Labs invented fiber optic technology, the transistor, and scads of other major technological advances. Its scientists earned at least half a dozen Nobel Prizes in physics.

And it attracted a certain kind of person. As Paul Baran described it:

> They were not motivated by making a lot of money. They were in the business to provide a service: Loyalty to the organization and help to the country providing the world's best communication. And that was their motivation and their belief. It was a religion, a pure religion. . . . In their mind, they were doing the right thing.[14]

These were not fat monopolists seeking to rob the nation of a quick buck. These were "soldiers of communications," for whom control and hierarchy were key. As one publication in 1941 put it:

> Because each of them has a part in this speeding of the spoken word, the thousands of men and women who are engaged in the telephone service in America are ever conscious of the fact that theirs is a high calling.[15]

AT&T in turn succeeded during its monopoly reign in attracting the very best telecommunications researchers. Baran attributes its success to "an absolutely brilliant compensation system,"[16] but the reason may well be that AT&T was the only show in town. As Baran describes, "[F]or years and years, that was the only place in the country that was doing work in telecommunications."[17] One could research different telecommunications systems, and one could in principle even develop other telecommunications systems. But there was nothing one could do with one's innovation unless AT&T bought it.

For much of the twentieth century, it was essentially illegal even to experiment with the telephone system. It was a crime to attach a device to the telephone system that AT&T didn't build or expressly authorize. In 1956, for example, a company built a device called a "Hush-a-Phone." The Hush-a-Phone was a simple piece of plastic that attached to the mouthpiece of a telephone. Its design was to block noise in a room so that someone on the other end of the line could better hear what was being said. The device had no connection to the technology of the phone, save the technology of the plastic receiver. All it did was block noise, the way a user might block noise by cupping his hand over the phone.[18]

When the Hush-a-Phone was released on the market, AT&T objected. This was a "foreign attachment." Regulations forbade any foreign attachments without AT&T's permission. AT&T had not given Hush-a-Phone any such permission. The FCC agreed with AT&T. Hush-a-Phone was history.

Hush-a-Phone is an extreme case.[19] The real purpose of the foreign attachments rule was, at least as AT&T saw it, to protect the system from dirty technology. A bad telephone or a misbehaving computer attached to the telephone system could, AT&T warned, bring down the system for the whole region. Telephones were lifelines, and they had to be protected from the experiments of an inquisitive nation. Rules such as the foreign attachments rules were intended to achieve this protection.

Whatever their intent, however, these rules had an effect on innovation in telecommunications. Their effect was to channel innovation through Bell Labs. Progress would be as Bell Labs determined it. Experiments would be pursued as Bell Labs thought best. Thus telecommunications would evolve as Bell Labs thought best.

BARAN UNDERSTOOD this. As a researcher at a Defense Department–supported lab, he knew how the "military" thought, and AT&T was military. Thus he had reason to be skeptical about the claims that the existing system would withstand a nuclear attack. He didn't believe AT&T really understood the threat. And if it did, he believed it simply didn't want anyone else understanding its weakness.

So he pushed AT&T to let him examine the system. It pushed back. And so, from sources unnamed, Baran secured a copy of AT&T's plans—the blueprints for the telecommunications system of the United States.

When he saw the plans, Baran knew AT&T was wrong. He was certain that the system it had built would not withstand a nuclear attack. The network was too concentrated; it had no effective redundancy. So he continued to press his idea for a different telecommunications system. He had a different design for telecommunications, and he wanted AT&T to help him build it.

This different model was not the Internet, but it was close to the Internet. Baran proposed a kind of packet-switching technology to replace the persistent circuits around which the telephone system was built. Under AT&T's design, when you called someone in Paris, a circuit was opened between you and Paris. In principle, you could trace the line of copper that linked you to Paris; along that line of copper, all your conversation would travel.

Baran's idea was fundamentally different. If you digitized a conversation— translating it from waves to bits—and then chopped the resulting stream into packets, these packets could flow independently across a network and create the impression of a real-time connection on the other end. As long as they flowed fast enough, and the computers at both ends were quick, the conversation encoded in this packet form would seem just like a conversation along a single virtual wire across the ocean.

Baran was probably not the first person to come up with this idea—MIT loyalists insist that that was Leonard Kleinrock.[20] And he was also not the only person working on the idea in the early 1960s. Independently, in England, Donald Davies was developing something very similar.[21] But whether the first, or the only, doesn't really matter for our purposes here. What is important is that Baran outlined a telecommunications system fundamentally different from the dominant design, and that different telecommunications system would have effected a radically different evolution of telecommunications.

BARAN PUSHED to get AT&T to help build this alternative design. AT&T said he didn't understand telephones. Over the course of many months, he

attended classes sponsored by AT&T so that he would get with its program. But the more Baran saw, the more convinced he was. And in a final
push, the Defense Department offered simply to pay AT&T to build the system. The government promised no risk; it wanted only cooperation. But
even here, AT&T balked. As recounted in John Naughton's A *Brief History
of the Future*:[22]

> [AT&T's] views were once memorably summarised in an exasperated out-
> burst from AT&T's Jack Osterman after a long discussion with Baran.
> 'First,' he said, 'it can't possibly work, and if it did, damned if we are going
> to allow the creation of a competitor to ourselves.'[23]

"Allow." Here is the essence of the AT&T design, supported by the state-
sanctioned monopoly. In "defend[ing] the monopoly,"[24] it reserved to itself
the right to decide what telecommunications would be "allowed." As Baran
put it, AT&T "didn't want anybody in their vicarage."[25] It controlled the
wires; nothing but its technology could be attached, and no other system of
telecommunications would be permitted. One company, through one research lab, with its vision of how communications should occur, decided.
Innovation here, for this crucial aspect of modern economic life, was as this
single organization would decide.

Now again, the point is not that AT&T was evil. Indeed, quite the contrary. We get nowhere in understanding how systems of innovation work
when we personify organizations and imagine them responsible for social
goals. AT&T had an obligation to its stockholders; it had an obligation to
the government to assure consistent quality service. It was simply acting to
assure that it met both of these obligations—maximizing its profits for its
shareholders while meeting its obligations to the government.

But what's good for AT&T is not necessarily good for America. What
AT&T was doing may well have made sense for it; its vision of telecommunications may well have made sense for the interests it understood
itself to be serving. But AT&T's vision of what a telecommunications service
should be is not necessarily what a telecommunications service should be.
There is a possible—and in this case actual—conflict between the interests
of a centralized controller of innovation and the interest in innovation
generally.

Here the conflict was plain. If the Defense Department built a telecommunications system based on packets rather than circuits, then the efficiency of that system could in theory be much greater. When you're on a

circuit-switched system, listening to your lover in Paris tell you about someone new, there's lots of downtime on the line—silence—that is just wasted bandwidth. If instead the system were packets, then the data from the downtime would be silence; it's easier to send the information necessary to reproduce silence than it is to hold open a line while silence happens. The system could better utilize the wires if the architecture enabled the sharing of the wires.

The owner of a legacy system built on a different model could well decide that this challenge was too dangerous. If a more efficient system came on-line, there would be strong pressure from the government to allow the exception; that exception would not be easy to limit; the corrosion of the existing model could be great. Monopoly control would be lost.

Thus it is completely understandable that a company like AT&T would not want to give birth to this new competitor, even if this new competitor would be better for communications as a whole. The natural desire of any company is to find ways to protect its market. And the chosen desire of a competitive market is to limit the ways in which a company can protect its market—but for most of the century, this chosen desire was not telecommunications policy. For most of the century, in this context and others that we will consider later on, the chosen desire of policy makers was to back up the desire of companies to architect and support systems that protected them against competition in the market. Competition was a bother; the vision of a telecommunications system was limited; and our telecommunications architecture—including, as we will see, broadcasting and radio—was architected to maximize the power and control of the few.[26]

AT A certain point, Baran understood. When the project was pushed into the Defense Communications Agency (DCA), Baran realized the project would be bungled. As he told author John Naughton:

> I felt that [DCA] could be almost guaranteed to botch the job since they had no understanding of digital technology, nor for leading edge high technology development. Further, they lacked enthusiasm. Sometimes, if a manager doesn't have the staff but has the drive and smarts to assemble the right team, one could justify taking a chance. But lacking skills, competence and motivation meant backing a sure loser.[27]

So Baran had the project pulled. There were not "the people at the time who could successfully undertake this project, [and they] would likely screw up the program. An expensive failure would make it difficult for a more competent agency to later undertake the project."[28] Thus, this architecture of control—centralizing innovation and protecting an existing model of doing business—would not be questioned by Baran's work. At least not then.

THE INTERNET is not the telephone network. It is a network of networks that sometimes run on the telephone lines. These networks and the wires that link them are privately owned, like the wires of the old AT&T. Yet at the core of this network is a different principle from the principle that guided AT&T. Like the principle Baran confronted, this principle affects what is allowed and what is not. And like the principle that Baran confronted, this principle has an effect on innovation.

First described by network architects Jerome Saltzer, David Clark, and David P. Reed in 1981, this principle—called the "end-to-end argument" (e2e)—guides network designers in developing protocols and applications for the network.[29] End-to-end says to keep intelligence in a network at the ends, or in the applications, leaving the network itself to be relatively simple.

There are many principles in the Internet's design. This one is key. But it will take some explaining to show why.

Network designers commonly distinguish computers at the "end" or "edge" of a network from computers within that network. The computers at the end of a network are the machines you use to access the network. (The machine you use to dial into the Internet, or your cell phone connecting to a wireless Web, is a computer at the edge of the network.) The computers "within" the network are the machines that establish the links to other computers—and thereby form the network itself. (The machines run by your Internet service provider, for example, could be computers within the network.)

The end-to-end argument says that rather than locating intelligence within the network, intelligence should be placed at the ends: computers within the network should perform only very simple functions that are needed by lots of different applications, while functions that are needed by only some applications should be performed at the edge. Thus, complexity and intelligence in the network are pushed away from the network itself. Simple networks, smart applications. As a recent National Research Council (NRC) report describes it:

Aimed at simplicity and flexibility, [the end-to-end] argument says that the network should provide a very basic level of service—data transport—and that the intelligence—the information processing needed to provide applications—should be located in or close to the devices attached to the edge [or ends] of the network.[30]

The reason for this design was flexibility, inspired by a certain humility. As Reed describes it, "we wanted to make sure that we didn't somehow build in a feature of the underlying network technology . . . that would restrict our using some new underlying transport technology that turned out to be good in the future. . . . That was really the key to why we picked this very, very simple thing called the Internet protocol."[31]

It might be a bit hard to see how a principle of network design could matter much to issues of public policy. Lawyers and policy types don't spend much time understanding such principles; network architects don't waste their time thinking about the confusions of public policy.

But architecture matters.[32] And arguably no principle of network architecture has been more important to the success of the Internet than this single principle of network design—e2e. How a system is designed will affect the freedoms and control the system enables. And how the Internet was designed intimately affected the freedoms and controls that it has enabled. The *code* of cyberspace—its architecture and the software and hardware that implement that architecture—regulates life in cyberspace generally. Its code is its law. Or, in the words of Electronic Frontier Foundation (EFF) cofounder Mitch Kapor, "Architecture is politics."[33]

To the extent that people have thought about Kapor's slogan, they've done so in the context of individual rights and network architecture. Most think about how "architecture" or "software" or, more simply, "code" enables or restricts the things we think of as human rights—speech, or privacy, or the rights of access.

That was my purpose in *Code and Other Laws of Cyberspace*. There I argued that it was the architecture of cyberspace that constituted its freedom, and that, as this architecture was changed, that freedom was erased. *Code*, in other words, is a *law* of cyberspace and, as the title suggests, in my view, its most significant law.

But in this book, my focus is different. The question I want to press here is the relationship between architecture and innovation—both commercial innovation and cultural innovation. My claim is that here, too, code matters. That to understand the source of the flourishing of innovation on the

Internet, one must understand something about its original design. And then, even more important, to understand as well that changes to this original architecture are likely to affect the reach of innovation here.

SO WHICH code matters? Which parts of the architecture?[34]

The Internet is not a novel or a symphony. No one authored a beginning, middle, and end. At any particular point in its history, it certainly has a structure, or architecture, that is implemented through a set of protocols and conventions. But this architecture was never fully planned; no one designed it from the bottom up. It is more like the architecture of an old European city, with a central section that is clear and well worn, but with additions that are many and sometimes confused.

At various points in the history of the Net's development, there have been efforts at restating its principles. Something called "RFC 1958," published in 1996, is perhaps the best formal effort. The Internet was built upon "requests for comments," or RFCs. Researchers—essentially grad students— charged with the task of developing the protocols that would eventually build the Internet developed these protocols through these humble requests for comments. RFC 1 was written by Steve Crocker and outlined an understanding about the protocols for host ("IMP") software. Some RFCs specify particular Internet protocols; some wax philosophical. RFC 1958 is clearly in the latter camp—an "informational" document about the "Architectural Principles of the Internet."[35]

According to RFC 1958, though "[m]any members of the Internet community would argue that there is no architecture," this document reports that "the community" generally "believes" this about the Internet: "that the goal is connectivity, the tool is the Internet protocol and the intelligence is end-to-end rather than hidden in the network."[36] "The network's job is to transmit datagrams as efficiently and flexibly as possible. Everything else should be done at the fringes."[37]

This design has important consequences for innovation—indeed, we can count three:

- First, because applications run on computers at the edge of the network, innovators with new applications need only connect their computers to the network to let their applications run. No change to the computers within the network is required. If you are a developer, for example, who wants to use the Internet to make telephone calls, you need only develop that application and get users to adopt it for the Internet to be capable of making "telephone" calls. You can write the application and send it to the person on the other end of the network. Both of you install it and start talking. That's it.

- Second, because the design is not optimized for any particular existing application, the network is open to innovation not originally imagined. All the Internet protocol (IP) does is figure a way to package and route data; it doesn't route or process certain kinds of data better than others. That creates a problem for some applications (as we'll see below), but it creates an opportunity for a wide range of other applications too. It means that the network is open to adopting applications not originally foreseen by the designers.

- Third, because the design effects a neutral platform—neutral in the sense that the network owner can't discriminate against some packets while favoring others—the network *can't* discriminate against a new innovator's design. If a new application threatens a dominant application, there's nothing the network can do about that. The network will remain neutral regardless of the application.

The significance of each of these consequences to innovation generally will become apparent as we work through the particulars that follow. For now, all that's important is that you see this design as a *choice*. Whether or not the framers of the network understood what would grow from what they built, they built it with a certain philosophy in mind. The network itself would not control how it would grow. Applications would. That was the key to end-to-end design. As the inventor of the World Wide Web, Tim Berners-Lee, describes it:

Philosophically, if the Web was to be a universal resource, it had to be able to grow in an unlimited way. Technically, if there was any centralized point of control, it would rapidly become a bottleneck that restricted the Web's growth, and the Web would never scale up. Its being "out of control" was very important.[38]

NETWORK ARCHITECTS Saltzer, Clark, and Reed were not the only people to notice the value of an end-to-end design. Quite independently, if later, the idea became apparent within AT&T itself. In the early 1990s, while trying to implement an improvement in the voice quality of the AT&T network (competition was beginning to have an effect: the effort was in response to the claim by Sprint that on its network you could hear a pin drop), Bell Labs researcher David Isenberg became increasingly frustrated with the "smart" network that AT&T was: at every layer in the distributional chain, the AT&T network had been optimized for voice telephony. But this optimization meant that any effort to change a layer in the AT&T distributional chain would disable other layers. Tweaking one part threw other parts into disarray. The system was in no sense "modularized," so change became impossibly difficult.

This led Isenberg to a treasonous thought: what if the problem was in the fundamental design of the network itself? What if the whole idea of a smart network was a mistake? What if a better design would be a "stupid network," with intelligence built into the devices, and the network itself kept as simple as possible?[39]

Isenberg had arrived through frustration at Saltzer, Clark, and Reed's fundamental insight: A simple, or, as Isenberg described it, stupid network would facilitate the greatest degree of innovation. A smart, or intelligent, network would perhaps be optimized for certain users, but its own sophistication would inhibit different or new uses not initially understood. By "build[ing] in assumptions about what the business proposition of the network is, you constrain what's possible."[40] The AT&T network was burdened by the intelligence built into it. A simpler design could beat the sophisticated design, at least along the dimension of innovation and change.

When Isenberg started to discuss his seditious thoughts, his employer, AT&T, was not happy. In the early summer of 1997, he was permitted to post a reply to an article that sang the virtues of smart networks. But soon after his article was posted, it was republished in many different places on the Net. Finally, in August 1997, Harry Newton published the article in his *Computer Telephony* magazine—without AT&T's permission. Isenberg became the enemy from within the AT&T network. He was told not to accept invitations from others to discuss his ideas. This control, understandably, became intolerable. As he told me, "[T]he AT&T pension became portable on January 1, 1998. I quit on January 2, 1998."

However disliked high up within the fortress, Isenberg's ideas began to catch on both outside and inside. The virtues of "stupid networks" became increasingly obvious, as the power of this simple network, the Internet, became undeniable. Isenberg's idea echoed the end-to-end principle: the two were the same, and both showed why the Internet would flourish.

*   *   *

THE INTERNET isn't the only network to follow an end-to-end design, though it is the first large-scale computer network to choose that principle at its birth. The electricity grid is an end-to-end grid; as long as my equipment complies with the rules for the grid, I get to plug it in.[41] Conceivably, things could be different. In principle, we might imagine that every device you plug into a grid would register itself with the network before it would run. Before you connected, you would have to get permission for that device. The owner of the network could then choose which devices to prohibit.

Likewise, the roads are end-to-end systems. Any car gets to enter the highway grid (put tolls to one side). As long as the car is properly inspected, and the driver properly licensed, whether and when to use the highway is no business of the highway. Again, we could imagine a different architecture: each car might first register with the grid before it got on the highway (the way airlines file flight plans before they fly).

But these systems don't require this sort of registration, likely because, when they were built, such registration was simply impracticable. The electronics of a power grid couldn't handle the registration of different devices; roads were built stupid because smart roads were impossible. Things are different now; smart grids, and smart roads, are certainly possible. Control is now feasible. So we should ask, would control be better?

In at least some cases, it certainly would be better. But from the perspective of innovation, in some cases it would not. In particular, when the future is uncertain—or more precisely, when future uses of a technology cannot be predicted—then leaving the technology uncontrolled is a better way of helping it find the right sort of innovation. Plasticity—the ability of a system to evolve easily in a number of ways—is optimal in a world of uncertainty.

This strategy is an attitude. It says to the world, I don't know what functions this system, or network, will perform. It is based in the idea of uncertainty. When we don't know which way a system will develop, we build the system to allow the broadest range of development.

This was a key motivation of the original Internet architects. They were extremely talented; no one was more expert. But with talent comes humility. And the original network architects knew more than anything that they didn't know what this network would be used for.

As David Reed describes, "[T]here were a lot of experiments in those days," and "we . . . realized that [there] was very little in common [other] than the way they used the network. There were sort of interesting ways that they used the network differently from application to application. So we felt that we couldn't presume anything about how networks would be used by applications. Or we wanted to presume as little as possible. . . . We basically said, 'Stop. You're all right' as opposed to running a bake-off."[42] These designers knew only that they wanted to assure that it could develop however users wanted.

Thus, end-to-end disables central control over how the network develops. As Berners-Lee puts it, "There's a freedom about the Internet: as long as we accept the rules of sending packets around, we can send packets containing anything to anywhere."[43] New applications "can be brought to the Internet without the need for any changes to the underlying network."[44] The "architecture" of the network is designed to be "neutral with respect to applications and content."[45] By placing intelligence in the ends, the network has no intelligence to tell which functions or content are permitted or not. As RFC 1958 puts it, the job of the network is simply to "transmit datagrams." As the NRC has recently concluded:

> Underlying the end-to-end argument is the idea that it is the system or application, not the network itself, that is in the best position to implement appropriate protection.[46]

In chapter 2, I introduced the idea of a commons. We can now see how the end-to-end principle renders the Internet an *innovation commons*, where innovators can develop and deploy new applications or content *without the permission of anyone else*. Because of e2e, no one need register an application with "the Internet" before it will run; no permission to use the bandwidth is required. Instead, e2e means the network is designed to assure that the network cannot decide which innovations will run. The system is built—constituted—to remain open to whatever innovation comes along.

This design has a critical effect on innovation. It has been, in the words of the NRC, a "key to the explosion of new services and software applications" on the Net.[47] Because of e2e, innovators know that they need not get the permission of anyone—neither AT&T nor the Internet itself—before they build a new application for the Internet. If an innovator has what he or she believes is a great idea for an application, he or she can build it without authorization from the network itself and with the assurance that the network can't discriminate against it.

At this point, you may be wondering, So what? It may be interesting (at least I hope you think this) to learn that the Internet has this feature; it is at least plausible that this feature induces a certain kind of innovation. But why do we need to worry about this feature of the Internet? If this is what makes the Internet run, then as long as we have the Internet, won't we have this feature? If e2e is in the Internet's nature, why do we need to worry about e2e?

But this raises the fundamental point: The design the Internet has *now* need not be its design *tomorrow*. Or more precisely, any design it has just now can be supplemented with other controls or other technology. And if that is true, then this feature of e2e that I am suggesting is central to the network now can be removed from the network as the network is changed. The code that defines the network at one time need not be the code that defines it later on. And as that code changes, the values the network protects will change as well.

THE CONSEQUENCES of this commitment to e2e are many. The birth of the World Wide Web is just one. If you're free from geekhood, you are likely not to distinguish the WWW from the Internet. But in fact, they are quite distinct. The World Wide Web is a set of protocols for displaying hyperlinked documents linked across the Internet. These protocols were developed in the late 1980s by researchers at the European particle physics lab CERN—in particular by Tim Berners-Lee. These protocols specify how a "Web server" serves content on the WWW. They also specify how "browsers"—such as Netscape Navigator or Microsoft's Internet Explorer—retrieve content on the World Wide Web. But these protocols themselves simply run on top of the protocols that define the Internet. These Internet protocols, referred to as TCP/IP, are the foundation upon which the protocols that make the World Wide Web function—HTTP (hypertext transfer protocol) and HTML (hypertext markup language)—run.[48]

The emergence of the World Wide Web is a perfect illustration of how innovation works on the Internet and of how important a neutral network is to that innovation. Tim Berners-Lee came up with the idea of the World Wide Web after increasing frustration over the fact that computers at CERN couldn't easily talk to each other. Documents built on one system were not easily shared with other systems; content stored on individual computers was not easily published to the networks generally. As Berners-Lee writes:

> Incompatibility between computers had always been a huge pain in everyone's side, at CERN and anywhere else. . . . The real world of high-energy physics was one of incompatible networks, disk formats, and character-

encoding schemes, which made any attempt to transfer information between computers generally impossible. The computers simply could not
communicate with each other.[49]

Berners-Lee thus began to think about a system to enable linking among
documents—through a process called "hypertext"—and to build this linking on top of the protocols of the Internet. His ideal was a space where any
document in principle could be linked to any other and where any document published was available to anyone.

The components of this vision were nothing new. Hypertext—links from
one document to another—had been born with Vannevar Bush,[50] and
made famous by Bill Atkinson's HyperCard on the Apple Macintosh. The
world where documents could all link to each other was the vision of Robert
Fano in an early article in the *Proceedings of the IEEE*.[51] But Berners-Lee
put these ideas together using the underlying protocol of the Internet.
Hyperlinked documents would thus be available to anyone with access to
the Internet, and any document published according to the protocols of the
World Wide Web would be available to all.

The idea strikes us today as genius. Its success makes us believe the idea
must have been obvious. But what is amazing about the story of the birth of
the World Wide Web is how hard it was for Tim Berners-Lee to convince
anyone of the merit in the plan. When Berners-Lee tried to sell the plan at
CERN, management was unimpressed. As Berners-Lee writes:

What we hoped for was that someone would say, "Wow! This is going to be
the cornerstone of high-energy physics communications! It will bind the
entire community together in the next ten years. Here are four programmers to work on the project and here's your liaison with Management Information Systems. Anything else you need, you just tell us." But it didn't
happen.[52]

When he went to a meeting of hypertext fans, he could get few to understand the "ah-ha" of hypertext on the Net. For years he wandered from expert to expert, finding none who understood the potential here. And it was
only after he started building the Web out, and started informing ordinary
people on a hypertext mailing list about the protocols he was developing,
that the Net started to grow.

The experts didn't get it. Someone should put that on a bumper sticker
and spread it around. Those controlling the resources of the CERN com-

puter lab wouldn't support the technology that would give the world the Web. Only those innovators outside of the control of these managers saw something of the potential for the Web's growth.

Berners-Lee feared that competing protocols for using the Internet would wipe away interest in the WWW. One protocol built about the same time was called Gopher. Gopher enabled the easy display of a menu of options from a site. When you went to a Gopher-enabled site, you would see a list of links that you could then click on to perform some function. Gopher was extremely popular as an Internet application—running on the Internet protocols—and use of Gopher took off in the early 1990s.[53]

But for the purposes that Berners-Lee imagined, Gopher was extremely limited. It would not enable the easy construction of interlinked documents. It was closer to a universal menuing system than a system for linking ideas. Berners-Lee was afraid that this inferior standard would nonetheless stick before the new and better WWW became well known.

His fear, however, was not realized, both because of something Berners-Lee did and because of something the creators of Gopher did—and both are lessons for us.

Berners-Lee was no bully. He was not building a protocol that everyone had to follow. He had a protocol for displaying content on the World Wide Web—the HTML language that Web pages are built in. But he decided not to limit the content that one could get through a WWW browser to just Web pages. Instead he designed the transfer protocol—HTTP—so that a wide range of protocols could be accessed through the WWW—including the Gopher protocol, a protocol for transferring files (FTP), and a protocol for accessing newsgroups on the Internet (NNTP). The Web would be neutral among these different protocols—it would in this sense interconnect.[54]

That made it easy to use the Web, even if one wanted to get access to Gopher content. But the second doing was much more important to the death of Gopher as a standard.

As Berners-Lee describes it, high off its success in populating the world with Gopher, the University of Minnesota—owner of the right to Gopher—suggested it might exercise its rights to charge for the use of the Gopher protocol.[55] Even the suggestion of this terrified developers across the world. (It was, Berners-Lee writes, "an act of treason."[56]) Would developers be hijacked by the university once they depended upon their system? How much would they lose if the platform eventually turned against the developers?

Berners-Lee responded to this by convincing CERN to release the right to the Web to the public. At first he wanted to release the protocol under the GPL, or General Public License (the "GNU General Public License," which we will see much more of in chapter 4). But when negotiations over that bogged down, he convinced CERN simply to release the rights into the public domain. Anyone had the right to take and use the protocols of the WWW and build anything upon them that they wanted.[57]

The birth of the Web is an example of the innovation that the end-to-end architecture of the original Internet enabled. Though no one quite got it— this the most dramatic aspect of the Internet's power—a few people were able to develop and deploy the protocols of the World Wide Web. They could deploy it because they didn't need to convince the owners of the network that this was a good idea or the owners of computer operating systems that this was a good idea. As Berners-Lee put it, "I had designed the Web so there should be no centralized place where someone would have to 'register' a new server, or get approval of its contents."[58] It would be a "good idea" if people used it, and people were free to use it because the Internet's design made it free.

THUS TWO networks—the network built by AT&T and the network we call the Internet—create two different environments for innovation. One network centralizes creativity; the other decentralizes it. One network is built to keep control of innovation; the other constitutionally renounces the right to control. One network closes itself except where permission is granted; the other dedicates itself to a commons.

How did we get from the one to the other? What moved the world governing our telecommunications system from the centralized to the decentralized?

This is one of the great forgotten stories of the Internet's birth. Everyone knows that the government funded the research that led to the protocols that govern the Internet.[59] It is part of the Internet's lore that it was the government that pushed network designers to design machines that could talk to each other.[60] The government in general, and the Defense Department in particular, had grown tired of spending millions for "autistic computing machines."[61] It therefore wanted some system for linking the systems.

Yet we are practically trained to ignore another form of governmental intervention that also made the Internet possible. This is the regulation that assured that the platform upon which the Internet was built would not turn against it.

The physical platform on which the Internet took off came prewired. It was the telephone wires that linked homes to homes. But the legal right to use the telephone wires to link to the Internet did not come preordained. That right had to be earned, and it was regulation that earned it. Nothing guaranteed that modems would be permitted on telephone lines. Even today, countries in Asia regulate the use of modems on telephone lines.[62] What was needed before the revolution could begin was permission to connect the Net to this net.

And what made that permission possible? What made it possible for a different use to be made of the telephone wires from that which AT&T had originally imagined?

Here a second kind of regulation enters the story. Beginning in force in 1968, when it permitted foreign attachments to telephone wires, continuing through the 1970s, when it increasingly forced the Bells to lease lines to competitors, regardless of their purpose, and ending in the early 1980s with the breakup of AT&T, the government increasingly intervened to assure that this most powerful telecommunications company would not interfere with the emergence of competing data-communications companies.

This intervention took many forms. In part it was a set of restrictions on AT&T's permissible businesses.[63] In part it was a requirement that it keep its lines open to competitors.[64] In part it was the general fear that any effort to bias communications more in its favor would result in a strong reaction from the government.[65]

But whatever the mix, and whichever factor was most significant, the consequence of this strategy was to leave open the field for innovation in telecommunications. AT&T did not control how its wires would be used, because the government restricted that control. By restricting that control, the government in effect created a commons on AT&T's wires.

In a way analogous to the technical requirements of end-to-end, then, these regulations had the effect of leaving the network open and hence of keeping the use of the network neutral. Once the telephone system was used to establish a circuit, the system was kept free for that circuit to send whatever data across it the user wished. The network thus functioned as a resource left open for others to use.

This is end-to-end operating at a different layer in the network design. It is end-to-end not at the layer determining the connection between two phones on the telephone system. That connection may well be formed by a system that does not comply with the end-to-end rule.

But once the circuit is connected, then the environment created by the mix of technical principles and legal rules operating upon the telecommunications system paralleled an end-to-end design at the network layer. This mix of design and control kept the telephone system open for innovation; that innovation enabled the Internet.

ARE THERE costs to the e2e design? Do we lose something by failing to control access to the resources—the bandwidth—of the network?

Certainly the Internet is not without its weaknesses. The capacity of the Net at any one moment is not infinite, and though it grows more quickly than the demand, it does at times get congested. It deals with this congestion equally—packets get transported on a first-come, first-served basis. Once packets leave one end, the network relays them on a best-efforts basis. If nodes on the network become overwhelmed, then packets passing across those nodes slow down.[66]

For certain applications, "best efforts" is not enough. Internet telephony, for example, doesn't do well when packets carrying voice get delayed. Any delay greater than 250 milliseconds essentially makes the system unusable.[67] And as content on the Net moves to real-time, bandwidth-demanding technology, this inability to guarantee quality of service becomes increasingly costly.

To deal with this problem, technologists have begun to propose changes to the architecture of the Net that might better enable some form of guaranteed service. These solutions generally pass under the title "Quality of Service" (QoS) solutions. These modifications would enable the network to treat different "classes" of data differently—video, for example, would get different treatment from e-mail; voice would get different treatment from the Web.

To enable this capacity to discriminate, the network would require more functionality than the original design allowed. At a minimum, the network would need to be able to decide what class of service a particular application should get and then treat the service accordingly. This in turn would make developing a new application more complex, as the programmer would need to consider the behavior of the network and enable the application to deal with that behavior.

The real danger, however, comes from the unintended consequences of these additional features—the ability of the network to then sell the feature that it will discriminate in favor of (and hence also against) certain kinds of content. As the marketing documents from major router manufacturers evince, a critical feature of QoS solutions will be their ability to enable the network owner to slow down a competitor's offerings while speeding up its own—like a television set with built-in static for ABC but a clear channel for CBS.

These dangers could be minimized depending upon the particular QoS technology chosen. Some QoS technologies, in other words, are more consistent with the principle of end-to-end than are others.[68] But proponents of these changes often overlook another relatively obvious solution—increasing capacity.[69] That is, while these technologies will certainly add QoS to the Internet, if QoS technologies like the "RSVP" technology do so only at a significant cost, then perhaps increased capacity would be a cheaper social cost solution.[70]

Put differently, a pricing system for allocating bandwidth solves certain problems, but if it is implemented contrary to end-to-end, it may well do more harm than good.

That is not to argue that it *will* do more harm than good. We don't know enough yet to know that. But it raises a fundamental issue that the scarcity mentality is likely to overlook: The best response to scarcity may not be a system of control. The best response may simply be to remove the scarcity.

This is the promise that conservative commentator George Gilder reports. The future, Gilder argues, is a world with "infinite" bandwidth.[71] Our picture of the Net now—of slow connections and fast machines—will soon flip. As copper is replaced with glass (as in fiber optics) and, more important, as electronic switches are replaced by optical switches, the speed of the network will approach the speed of light. The constraints that we know from the wires we now use will end, Gilder argues. And the end of scarcity, he argues, will transform all that we do.[72]

There is skepticism about Gilder's claims about technology.[73] So, too, about his economics. The economist in all of us can't quite believe that any resource would fail to be constrained; the realist in all of us refuses to believe in Eden. But I'm willing to believe in the potential of essentially infinite bandwidth. And I am happy to imagine the scarcity-centric economist proven wrong.

The part I'm skeptical about is the happy progress toward a world where network owners simply provide neutral fat (or glass) pipe. This is not the trend now, and there is little to suggest it will be the trend later. As law professor Tim Wu wrote to me about Gilder's book:

I think it is a "delta dollar sign" problem as we used to say in chemistry (to describe reactions that were possible, but not profitable). Private actors seem to only make money from infrastructure projects if built with the ability to exclude. . . . [H]ere in the industry, all the projects that are "hot" are networks with built-in techniques of exclusion and prioritization.[74]

Here *is* a tragedy of the commons. If the commons is the *innovation* commons that the protocols of the Net embrace, e2e most important among them, then the tragedy of that commons is the tendency of industry to add technologies to the network that undermine it. But this is an issue for the dark part of this book. For now, my aim is only brightness: to get you to see the commons that has been built through a set of protocols that defined the Internet that was.

THE INTERNET was born on a controlled physical layer; the code layer, constituted by the TCP/IP, was nonetheless free. These protocols expressed an end-to-end principle, and that principle effectively opened the space created by the computers linked to the Net for innovation and change. This open space was an important freedom, built upon a platform that was controlled. The freedom built an innovation commons. That commons, as do other commons, makes the controlled space more valuable.[75]

Freedom thus enhanced the social value of the controlled: this is a lesson that will recur.

4

Commons Among the Wired

IRED IS a magazine that was first published in early 1993. Its title is un-defined, but it aspires to signal those who are connected or, as one on-line dictionary puts it, "with it" with respect to all things digital. To those outside the world of "things digital," the "wired" are those caffeine-chugging techheads staring at C code as the clock chimes 0100 (military time). But to those inside digital culture, "the wired" are those who understand the poten-tial of this place called cyberspace and who are making that potential real.

The character of this group has changed. In the early 1990s, they were more intrigued by fast code than fast cash. Today, it is more the opposite. Yet if there is a group that can still be called "connected"—those who have built and are building the Internet that we have come to know—then this chap-ter is about them, about the commons among them, and about the innovation this commons built.

This commons had three aspects. One is a commons of code—a com-mons of software that built the Net and many of the applications that run on the Net. A second is a commons of knowledge—a free exchange of ideas and information about how the Net, and code that runs on the Net, runs. And a third is the resulting commons of innovation built by the first two together—the opportunity, kept open to anyone, to innovate and build upon the platform of the network.

A certain culture made each of these commons possible, as did a certain feature about the stuff these coders built—code. Something, that is, about the norms that first defined this world, as well as something about the na-ture of the code. My aim in this chapter is to explore both the character of this culture and the nature of this code, and how the two interact to produce a layer of freedom at the content layer.

For the content layer is the layer at which the commons in this chapter lives. The commons of the last chapter, built by end-to-end, is a commons at the code layer of the network. The commons here lies on top, even though built, like the code layer below it, in software. Code here is content, and at the birth of the Net, much of this content was free.

As will become clearer in chapter 11, however, the content of code is not fundamentally different from the content we are more familiar with— music, or film, or (at least digital) texts. As I will argue, in the digital world, all the stuff protected by copyright law is in one sense the same: It all depends fundamentally upon a rich and diverse public domain. Free content, in other words, is crucial to building and supporting new content. The free content among the "wired" is just a particular example of a more general point.

TO INTRODUCE these commons, however, we need to think a bit more about code. Our world is increasingly constituted by environments built in code—in the instructions inscribed in either software or hardware. Yet our intuitions about "code" are likely to be incomplete.

"Code" is written (primarily) by humans, though the code that humans write is quite unlike the code that computers run. Humans write "source code"; computers run "object code." Source code is a fairly understandable collection of logical languages designed to instruct the computer what it should do. Object code is a string of ones and zeros impenetrable to the ordinary human. Source code, however, is too cumbersome for a computer to run; it is therefore "compiled" before it is run, meaning translated from human-readable to machine-understandable code.

Object code is therefore the lifeblood of the computer, but it is the source code that links computers and humans. To understand how a program runs; to be able to tinker with it and change it; to extend a program or link it to another—to do any of these things with a program requires some access to the source.[1]

Things were not always this way. When computers were first built, they didn't have "software." Their functions were literally wired into the machines. This way of coding was obviously cumbersome. By the early 1960s, it was essentially replaced.[2] While some computer functions are still performed by "hard-wired" code (for example, the code in the ROM chip that is executed when you boot up your computer), the meat of computers today is software.

At first, no one much cared about controlling this code. In the beginning of commercial computing, computer companies wrote software, but that software was peculiar to each company's machine. Each company had its own operating system (OS, the underlying program upon which all other programs are run). These operating systems were not compatible. A program written for an IBM machine would not run on a Data General machine. Thus, the companies had very little reason to worry about a program being "stolen." Computer companies were in the business of selling computers. If someone "stole" a program meant for a particular computer, they could run it only if they had that computer.

This was a world of incompatible machines, and that troubled those who depended upon many different kinds of machines to do their work. The government, for example, spent millions on computers but grew frustrated that these machines could not talk with one another. The same was true of the company that would build perhaps the most important operating system in the history of computing: AT&T.

For in this chapter, for at least this part of this chapter, AT&T is the hero. AT&T purchased many computers to run its national network of phones. Because of a consent decree with the government in 1956, however, it was not permitted to build and sell these computers itself. It was therefore dependent upon the computers that others built and frustrated, like the government, by the fact that these other computers couldn't talk to each other.[3]

Researchers at Bell Labs, however, decided to do something about this. In 1969, Ken Thompson and Dennis Ritchie began an operating system that could be "ported" (read: translated) to every machine.[4] This operating system would therefore be a common platform upon which programs could run. And because this platform would be common among many different machines, a program written once could—with tiny changes—be run on many different machines.

In the history of computing, this urge for a cross-platform-compatible language was long-standing. ALGOL was an early example.[5] So too was COBOL, when the government announced that it would not purchase or lease any computer equipment that could not run COBOL.[6] But the birth of Unix—the name given to AT&T's ur–operating system—was the most important. For not only did AT&T develop this foundational operating system, it also gave it away. Because of the restrictions imposed by the 1956 consent decree, AT&T was not allowed to sell a computer operating system. Thus, Thompson and Ritchie succeeded in convincing the company to simply give the OS to anyone who wanted it.

The first takers of this free OS were universities.[7] Computer science departments could use the source code (within limits) to teach their students about how operating systems were written. The system could be critiqued, just as English grad students can critique Shakespeare because they have the text of the Shakespeare plays to read. And as this system became understood, fixes to bugs in this system were contributed back to AT&T. The process produced a vast and powerful network of people coming to speak the language of Unix and of a generation growing up tutored by Unix.

In this way, for this period, Unix was a commons. The code of Unix was a commons; the knowledge that this code generated was a commons; and the opportunity to innovate with and on top of this code was a commons. No one needed permission from AT&T to learn how its file system worked or how the OS handled printing. Unix was a trove of knowledge that was made available to many. Upon this treasure, many built.

OVER TIME, however, the openness of commercial code began to change. As products became more numerous and users became more diverse, and as the cross-platform compatibility of programs grew, the companies producing these products exercised more and more control over how the products might be used. The code thus "forked"—developing in different and incompatible ways, increasingly proprietary. Users became less partners in the process of developing and using computer systems and more consumers. And suppliers of code were less eager to permit their code to be copied by others.

One instance of this increase in control turned out to be quite important in the history of computing. Richard Stallman was a researcher at MIT. He was an early disciple of the norms of openness (as in "the open society") or, more generally, freedom. The whole world, of course, was not open. But throughout much of the 1970s, the norm in computing was. Exceptions were scorned.

The lab where Stallman worked had a printer connected to the network. The clever coders in this lab had written a program to notify them when the printer malfunctioned. A jam, for example, would generate a message to users on the network, and someone close to the printer could then go correct the problem.

In 1984, the lab updated the software (a driver) that ran the printer. Stallman then asked the company supplying the printer for a copy of the source code so that he could replicate the notification function in this new version of the printer driver. The company refused. The code to the printer driver was now closed, Stallman was informed. No one was allowed to tinker with it.[8]

To Stallman, this was a moral offense. The knowledge built into that driver had been produced by many people, not all of whom had been employed by the company. There was something wrong, then, with the company locking up that knowledge. And this wrong sowed the seed in Stallman's mind of a movement to resist this closing.[9]

In 1985, that movement was born. Stallman founded the Free Software Foundation. Its aim was to encourage the development of software that carried its source with it. The aim was to assure that the knowledge built into software was not captured and kept from others. The objective was to support a *commons for code*.[10]

AT&T gave the movement an important boost, quite unintentionally. In 1984, after AT&T was broken up, the company was freed of the restrictions on computing that it had been living under since 1956. Once freed of these restrictions, AT&T decided to enter the computing business. One of its most important assets in this business was Unix. Hence, AT&T decided to exercise control over Unix. After 1984, Unix would no longer be free. Companies, universities, and individuals wishing to use Unix would have to license the right from AT&T.

To many, this too was betrayal. A generation had devoted its professional career to learning and building upon the Unix system. Now AT&T claimed the exclusive right to the product of this learning. Although AT&T had taken the suggestions that had been made, although Unix had been improved in response, the company now wanted to trade on these improvements by making the code exclusive and unfree.

The reactions against AT&T's take-back were sharp. Berkeley had a version of Unix that it had been distributing; after AT&T's change, the Berkeley release had to undergo a massive retooling to extract the AT&T code so that it could release a version of Unix (BSD Unix) that was free of AT&T's restrictions.

But Stallman responded in a more productive and ambitious way. He wanted to build a free version of Unix that would, by design, always be free. So the Free Software Foundation launched project GNU—a recursive acronym meaning "GNU's not Unix." The GNU project was first to develop the suite of tools necessary to build an operating system and then to use those tools to build the GNU OS.

Throughout the 1980s, Stallman worked to do just that. Slowly he added tools to the project. Beginning with an extraordinary editor, Emacs, and then, even more important, with a compiler, the GNU C Compiler (GCC),[11] the project slowly pulled together the tools an operating system would need.

But as the 1980s came to an end, Stallman's project began to slow down. Stallman had developed a problem with his hands. For a while he lost the ability to type. As he turned to the final step in the project—building a kernel (the heart of an OS) for the GNU operating system—his pace had been cut dramatically. He had mixed all of the ingredients needed for an operating system to function, but he was missing the core.[12]

IN FINLAND, a young student studying computer science wanted the chance to experiment with an operating system. Unix was the gold standard; Linus Torvalds had little gold.[13]

Instead, Torvalds started playing with Minix, an educational version of an OS released by computer science professor Andrew Tannenbaum. Minix ran on a PC but was designed as a teaching tool. It was therefore incomplete. So in 1990, Torvalds began building an alternative to Minix, which he released to the Internet in 1991. That code was released subject to a license called the General Public License (GPL). (We'll see more of this later.) It was therefore free for anyone to take and use, as long as they didn't bottle up what they took.

People rapidly realized, however, that with a little bit of work linking the parts of an OS that Stallman had built to the core of the OS that Torvalds had released, Stallman's objective of an open and free Unix-flavored OS could be realized. Quite quickly, then, Linux—or GNU/Linux for those who want to keep the contributions in view—was born.[14] GNU/Linux was a platform that came with its source; anyone could take and build upon this platform. Because it came with its source, anyone could tinker with it to make it better. Many did, and in a very short period of time, GNU/Linux became quite good.[15]

SO GOOD, in fact, that GNU/Linux is now the fastest-growing operating system in the world. It is supplied by a host of companies, commercial and non-. It has been ported to every major chip—the "most widely ported operating system available for PCs," Torvalds reports.[16] There is a version of Linux on the PPC chip (used by Macintosh computers). There is a version on the chip used by Sun. It is quickly becoming the Unix that Thompson and Ritchie imagined—a platform to which the world can "write once, run anywhere."[17] Like Mother Nature herself, GNU/Linux is quickly becoming universal and free.

IN THE terms that I have described, GNU/Linux is an "open code" project. It is software that carries its source code with it, and it requires that its source be kept available for others. The source code can be viewed and modified by a user; parts can be taken and used by other coders. It therefore builds a commons of (1) code, (2) knowledge, and (3) innovation upon that code.

But Linux is just one example of a large number of open code projects that populated the network at its birth. It is neither the first, nor the only, nor even perhaps the most important open code project. To keep the importance of the open code movement in view, we should remember these other projects as well.

For example, more successful (in market share, at least) and just as important is the project that built the Apache server. A server is that part of the Net infrastructure that "serves" content. When you go to a Web page and view the contents of that page, the computer delivering the content is a "server." In the first days of the Web, the expectation was that companies like Netscape Corporation would build and sell servers. Netscape did, as did others, including Microsoft. But in addition to these commercial ventures, there was a version of a Web server that was made available for free. This was the HTTP'd server produced by the National Center for Supercomputing Applications (NCSA).

The NCSA server was adequate but buggy. Because it was government funded, however, its source code was free. The only requirement the NCSA imposed on users, or modifiers, of the NCSA code was that they give NCSA credit.

A group of early adopters of the HTTP'd protocol began to share "patches" to the server—improvements as well as bug fixes that would make the code run more efficiently. At a certain point, the group decided to form a collective that would build a new server on top of the NCSA server. This server—called the Apache server both because of the pride associated with the Apache name and because, as a series of patches, it was "a patchy" server—was then released to the world as a free, open source server.

Apache quickly took off. As its market share grew, users fed more patches back. Developers worked hard to integrate these patches. The quality of the server quickly improved. Apache soon became the number one server in the world. To this day, two-thirds of the servers on the World Wide Web are Apache servers. As writer Glyn Moody describes it, "[A]lthough the debate still rages fiercely about whether open source software such as GNU/Linux can ever hope to best Microsoft, Apache has already done it."[18]

The coders who built the Apache servers were not paid by any company called "Apache." Many of the developers worked part-time, paid by the companies they worked for. One of the leaders of the project, Net wizard Brian Behlendorf, says this "essential volunteerism" was crucial for the project. The work done for the project had to come from people who were motivated to help the project, not from people just paid to code from nine to five.

Linux and Apache are the two most prominent open code projects. But there are others still. Perl, developed by Larry Wall, is a programming language that enables high-power manipulation of text. It is the glue that makes most Web sites run. It too was developed as an open source project, and it is by far the dominant language of its class, ported to every important operating system. And deeper in the guts of the Internet's code are other systems that are even more crucial to the Net. The Berkeley Internet Name Daemon (BIND) system (which connects names, such as lessig.org, to IP addresses, such as 123.45.67.89) was developed originally as an open code project at the University of California at Berkeley; at version 4.9.2, Paul Vixie became its principal architect.[19] Some believe that BIND is "the single most mission-critical Internet application."[20] Whether it is or not, it was built through open code. Likewise was "sendmail," which processes mail routing, an open code project developed by Eric Allman.[21] It now runs on 75 percent of servers in the world.[22]

These projects together constitute the soul of the Internet. Together with the public domain protocols that define the Internet (governed by no license at all but free for all to take, referred to collectively as TCP/IP, including the core protocols for the World Wide Web), this free code built the Internet. This is not a single program or a single operating system. The core of the Internet was this collection of code built outside the proprietary model.

For the property obsessed, or those who believe that progress comes only from strong and powerful property rights, pause on this point and read it again: The most important space for innovation in our time was built upon a platform that was free. As Alan Cox, second only to Linus Torvalds in the Linux chain, puts it in an essay in response to Microsoft's attack on open code values:

> [M]ost of the great leaps of the computer age have happened despite, rather than because of, [intellectual property rights (IPR)]. [B]efore the Internet the proprietary network protocols divided customers, locked them into providers and forced them to exchange much of their data by tape. The power of the network was not unlocked by IPR. It was unlocked by free and open innovation shared amongst all.[23]

Not strong, perfect control by proprietary vendors, but open and free protocols, as well as open and free software that ran on top of those protocols: these produced the Net.

THIS FREE code builds a commons. This commons in turn lowers the cost of innovation. New projects get to draw upon this common code; every project need not reinvent the wheel. The resource thus fuels a wide range of innovation that otherwise could not exist.

Free code also builds a commons in knowledge. This commons is made possible by the nature of information. My learning how a Web page is built does not reduce the knowledge of how a Web page is built. Knowledge, as we've seen, is nonrivalrous; your knowing something does not lessen the amount that I can know.

There is something particular about how free code builds this knowledge commons. Code is performative; what it says, it does. Hence one learns about code not just by reading the code, but also by implementing it.

Think about the code that builds the World Wide Web. Web pages are written (primarily) in a markup language called HTML. That language is a set of tags that mark text or graphics to be displayed on a Web page. Every major Web browser has a function that reveals the source of the Web page being viewed. If you see a page and want to see how it was built, you simply "reveal source" on the page, and the Web page turns into the set of codes that generated the page.

This feature of the World Wide Web meant that it was extremely easy for coders to learn how to build Web pages. Most of the early learning was simply copying a page and modifying it as the coder wished. Even if the code building a Web page was copyrighted, others could learn from it. Again, because the code here performs as well as expresses, the feedback for teaching was strong.

This feature of the World Wide Web was chosen. There was no necessity that the source code for a Web page be viewable. Other languages—such as Apple's AppleScript language—enable authors to easily hide the code that makes the script run. Hiding could well have been the default on the World Wide Web.

But had it been the default, then the knowledge commons of the World Wide Web would have been vastly smaller. And had it been smaller, the growth and innovation of the World Wide Web would have been much less. Designing the Web to be open meant that the Web would grow more quickly.

Finally, and most important to the argument of this book, free code at the content layer builds a commons in innovation, just as end-to-end at the code layer does. By keeping its teachings open, and hence by assuring that others can build upon these teachings differently, free code assures that innovation cannot be chilled. Like the simple, neutral network of e2e, free code hasn't the power to discriminate against new innovation.

This innovation commons, however, unlike end-to-end, is protected by law. The principles of end-to-end are protected (if at all) through norms. Software engineers decide whether to implement software that complies with end-to-end. But law protects the innovation commons that open code built.

My aim in the balance of this chapter is to show just how.

THE LAW that protects the innovation commons built by open code is a combination of contract law and copyright. We will consider copyright law in greater depth in chapter 11, but for now suffice it to say that a copyright attaches to essentially any creative work at the time that creativity is fixed in a tangible form. Your e-mails are copyrighted at the time you write them, your love letters when you pen them.

The law creates this "exclusive right"—aka monopoly right—to help solve a problem that exists with creative information.[24] As we saw in chapter 2, information is naturally nonrivalrous. If you use it, I still have as much left as before. It is also naturally nonexcludable. In Jefferson's poetry, "[H]e who receives an idea from me, receives instruction himself without lessening mine; as he who lites his taper at mine, receives light without darkening me."[25] But these two features create an incentive problem for authors. If there were no way for an author to control the copies of his or her created work, then there would be no easy way for the author to profit from that work. For some authors, that would mean less time spent producing. And that in turn would mean less creative work.

Copyright tries to remedy this problem by giving authors a limited right—an exclusive right to control some uses of their work for a limited time. This right is designed to remedy the problem of incentives.

But obviously it does the author no good if the author must exercise his or her exclusive right alone. Writers aren't publishers. Thus, through contracts (written against the background of copyright law), the right to use copyrighted work is granted. That granting is a contract called a "license."

So far I've been speaking of "open code," or "free code," but these terms describe two very different kinds of licenses. The original open code license was developed by the Free Software Foundation. This is the "General Public License," or GPL.

The GPL sets the terms under which one has the right to use free software.[26] Among software licenses generally, the GPL is unique. While most licenses serve to limit the copies a licensee may make, the GPL serves to limit the *restrictions* on copying that a licensee can make. Anyone can use or modify a GPL work, as long as, in the words of the license preamble, "you . . . give the recipients all the rights that you have. You must make sure that they, too, receive or can get the source code."[27] As Richard Stallman describes it:

> A program is free software, for you, a particular user, if: You have the freedom to run the program, for any purpose. You have the freedom to modify the program to suit your needs (To make this freedom effective in practice, you must have access to the source code, since making changes in a program without the source code is exceedingly difficult.). You have the freedom to redistribute copies, either gratis or for a fee. You have the freedom to distribute modified versions of the program, so that the community can benefit from your improvements.[28]

The consequence of this license is that copyrighted work licensed under the GPL is *always* available to others to use or modify as they wish, *as is the code that derives from GPL-protected code*. This combination of copyright law and contract law essentially renders GPL code, as well as code derivative of GPL code, "free."

The GPL is not the only license used within the open code movement. A second class of licenses is ordinarily called "open source." Open source licenses are less restrictive (or less freedom enhancing, depending upon your perspective) than free software licenses. While free software licenses require that derivative work be free, open source licenses have no such requirement (where, again, "free" means that the source code must be made available to other users, not necessarily free of charge).[29] Microsoft is free to use the Apache server (licensed under an open source license) and incorporate it into a proprietary product; Microsoft is not free to take Linux and incorporate it into Windows.

This is an important difference, no doubt, but not so much for our purposes here. The GPL is enough of a model to understand the argument that follows, so the argument that follows presumes the GPL as the license. Where there is a reason to distinguish, I will be careful to make sure you see the differences in these two kinds of (legal) code.[30] But for now, let's assume the legal code governing this free code is the code of the GPL.

AS I said, the Linux operating system is licensed under the GPL. That means that the source code of Linux travels with the code itself. Anyone can tinker with the code; anyone can see how it works.

Any code that derives from this open code must itself be licensed under GPL. This code, and the knowledge it teaches, is therefore open and free.

Proponents of open code sell it on the promise that users are not hostage to open code projects. That claim is true, but in two very different senses—one small, one big. The smaller claim is just that users, or coders adopting open code, can tinker with that code. They can control the code, changing it as they wish. As Peter Wayner puts it, the "free source world . . . [is] a return to the good old days when you could take apart what was yours."[31] You can add functionality or fix functionality that is imperfect as supplied.

Other operating systems are not open or free. Apple, for example, licenses and sells Macintosh computers. Macintosh computers come with the Mac OS. Bundled in the package of programs shipped with the Mac OS 9 is a program called File Synchronization. The aim of File Synchronization is to allow a user to keep two sets of files synchronized. If you have laptop and desktop computers, then the objective of File Synchronization is to allow you to make sure that the files on both systems are kept up to date.

But File Synchronization has a problem. If you try to synchronize files whose icons have been customized (icons are the pictures on the desktop that you double-click on to open a file), then the program gets an "out of memory" error. The program thus has a bug; that bug makes it impossible to use the program on systems where the icons have been modified. But, of course, modifying the icons is one of the freedoms the Mac OS builds into its system. So those who take advantage of this freedom in the Mac OS system can't take advantage of the free synchronization program that Apple bundles with the computer.

All code has bugs; there's nothing special about the Mac OS in this respect. But what is significant about this story is how long this simple bug survived. Though this program, File Synchronization, was released in 1998, the bug remained, even in 2000. Fixing this memory allocation error in this small part of the Mac OS was not important to Apple Computer. So the bug remained unsquashed.

Had at least this part of the Mac OS been open, however—had the source code been available—then no doubt someone out there would have found it worthwhile to correct the mistake that the code had created. This coder could have taken the code that the Mac OS supplied and fixed the problem that the Mac OS created. And whether the coder sold the fix to others or not, the fix would have been made long before two years had passed.[32] Users of the File Synchronization program would not have been held hostage to the flaws in that program.

THE FREEDOM to tinker is thus an important freedom. But there is a much more fundamental sense in which open code assures that users are not held hostage, and it is this feature of open code that links it to the principle of end-to-end discussed in the previous chapter. Just as end-to-end's openness assures a neutral network that runs your code and doesn't turn against your innovation, open code's openness assures that the foundation of the computing environment is neutral and can't turn against the innovator. An open code platform keeps a platform honest. And honest, neutral platforms build trust in developers.

We can see something of the importance of this by passing quickly over the most important lawsuit affecting cyberspace so far—*United States v. Microsoft*.[33]

The government's claim in *United States v. Microsoft* was essentially this: While Microsoft had built an important platform upon which developers across the world had constructed code, Microsoft had adopted a practice that chilled certain kinds of innovation. When an innovator had a technology that threatened Microsoft's platform, Microsoft, the government claimed, adopted a strategy to kill that innovation. The platform, in other words, turned against some kinds of innovation, while no doubt protecting others. And that pattern, the government alleged, stifled innovation in just the way that AT&T's control over the telephone network had stifled innovation inconsistent with AT&T's business model.[34] Unlike a network that remained committed to end-to-end, Microsoft, the government argued, built discrimination into its platform, and this discrimination harmed innovation.

To understand the government's claim requires a bit of context. About the time that Torvalds released to the world the kernel of the Linux OS, Microsoft was releasing to the world its latest version of a program called Windows. This latest version was receiving an extraordinary response in the user community. Windows 3.0 was finally a stable and powerful tool simulating a "graphical user interface" (GUI) operating system. It was not itself an operating system; it was simply a program that ran on the underlying operating system DOS. But it was efficient enough that a huge portion of the DOS market wanted to buy or upgrade to this version of Windows.

Before Windows, users of PCs with the Intel chip architecture—"IBM-compatible" PCs, as they were called—were stuck with command line interface.[35] When you booted up the system, it presented to you a simple command line—for example, "C:>"—and it expected you, the user, to then enter a command to launch a program. It was a Unix-inspired system, initially intended for the talented who played with Unix.

Microsoft was the originator of the "disk operating system" (DOS).[36] When IBM decided to release a personal computer, it licensed the operating system for that computer from Microsoft. Microsoft, however, guided by perhaps the smartest businessman of our generation, Bill Gates, kept the rights to DOS. IBM would develop after a bit its own version of DOS—called PC-DOS. But Microsoft was always free to build and sell MS-DOS.

MS-DOS quickly became the market leader because Microsoft was better at responding to consumer demand. Its coders were better at solving coding problems. And by the late 1980s, MS-DOS was by far the dominant operating system in a world dominated by PC-compatible computers.

But there was significant pressure on Microsoft. First, Microsoft was not the only DOS producer. A company called Digital Research developed a different DOS—DR-DOS—that was increasingly viewed as superior to Microsoft's DOS. In 1990, BYTE magazine said of DR-DOS 5.0 that it "cures many (but not all) of MS-DOS's shortcomings" and was a vastly superior DOS.[37] Other reviews said much the same.[38]

Second, graphical user interfaces were threatening Microsoft. As consumers adopted the PC, they were increasingly frustrated with the command line interface and started to look at other PC products. The most attractive of these other PC products was the Apple Macintosh, introduced by Apple in 1984. The Macintosh offered a simple GUI interface that made it easy to use a PC.

Gates admired the Mac. His company first wrote Word and Excel for the Mac. And in 1985, Gates tried to license the Macintosh OS to port it to the Intel chip architecture.[39] In what may have been the worst decision in corporate computer history, Apple declined the offer. Gates therefore turned his crew to the task of building Windows.

It is hard for us today to recall the significance of the threat that Gates felt then. Microsoft was a tiny company compared with Apple. In 1984, Apple's annual sales were $1.5 billion; Microsoft's were $98 million.[40] In hindsight, the inevitable success of Windows seems assured, but at the time, many at Microsoft certainly felt the threat of a world of competitors, some building better OSs (DR-DOS) and some building better user interfaces or, more precisely, GUIs, pronounced "gooeys" (Apple). Gates therefore pushed the firm to develop something better of each.

By 1991, Gates realized that the future would be a world with one integrated GUI-OS. Windows 95 would be that OS, but it would take some time to get to Windows 95. Windows 95 would integrate the GUI of Windows 3.0 with DOS, giving users a powerful and integrated system comparable to that of the Apple Macintosh.

The key, however, was to make sure that while making the switch, Microsoft didn't lose its customer base. Most were using MS-DOS; everyone wanted Windows. So the key in the next four years, the company believed, was to hold the field.

This is where things got legal, and the account that follows is nothing more than the allegations made by the antitrust enforcers (and others) about how Microsoft responded to the threat it faced. But the allegations are substantial, the parallel to later allegations is clear, and they will help make the story of the *commons* clear if we map this (alleged) story of control.

To hold the field, Microsoft had to assure that no competitor would succeed in stealing its operating system customer base. The threat of defection was strong, given the increasingly strong competition of other DOSs. But the tool to assure no great defection was the powerful and popular program Windows 3.0. Everyone wanted Windows 3.0, and it was more important for a computer manufacturer to be selling Windows 3.0 than it was to be selling any particular DOS.

Microsoft thus used, the government alleged, its power over Windows to avoid competition with DOS. Both through pricing strategies that made it economically infeasible for an equipment manufacturer to sell any version of DOS other than MS-DOS and, according to the European Union's antitrust enforcement wing, by directly tying the sale of Windows 3.0 to the sale of MS-DOS, Microsoft made it impossible for competitors to gain any foothold in the Microsoft base. Thus, Microsoft could hold the field of its own users until it could enable the migration of its users over to Windows 95.

Microsoft was behaving, the government alleged, *strategically*.[41] It was limiting the options of its customers so as to protect its own market position. And this form of competition, the government alleged, was anticompetitive. Rather than allowing competition in operating systems to flourish, Microsoft was threatening competitors who were building products threatening it.

In 1994, the government notified Microsoft that it was about to file suit against it. The claim was illegal pricing and tying behavior in securing the field for Microsoft products. After extensive negotiations, Microsoft signed a consent decree, promising the government that it would not engage in a string of listed behaviors. The government accepted Microsoft's promises, and the case with Microsoft was settled.

A consent decree is just a contract. The government promises not to sue if Microsoft promises not to engage in certain behaviors. Nothing in the contract concedes that the behavior challenged was illegal; nothing in the contract binds the government never to sue Microsoft for other anticompetitive behavior. The decree is just a simple way for the government to stop the harm it believes a company is doing, without a long and expensive trial proving that the behavior is, in fact, illegal. If the company that signed a consent decree breaches the agreement, then the government is able to get a court to enjoin the breaching behavior.

After the government settled the case, it announced to the world that it had made the world free for operating system competition. Assistant Attorney General Anne Bingaman promised there would now be a great deal of competition among operating systems.[42] The field had been opened up, Bingaman said; competitors would flock to the field. Microsoft would face important competitive pressures; its monopoly position would be erased.

Microsoft had a different view of the decree. It believed it would have no real effect. Said Bill Gates to the press, "None of the people who run those divisions are going to change what they do or think or forecast. Nothing. There's one guy in charge of [hardware company] licenses. He'll read the agreement.' "[43]

It turned out that Microsoft was the better predictor. Soon after the announcement of the decree, DR-DOS folded. IBM announced it was pulling its development of its competing operating system, OS/2. All the competitors for the desktop PC-compatible operating system essentially disappeared. The consent decree was law, but reality was unaffected. The decree was too late in coming, and by the time it came, the reality it regulated had changed.

In 1997, however, the government was back at it. Once again, the government claimed, Microsoft was mucking about with the market. Once again, the government argued, it was behaving strategically to disable competition. This time, however, the strategy was not to protect DOS. This time the aim was to protect Windows 95 against a nascent form of competition, the Internet.

Before 1995, Microsoft had not yet come to understand what the Internet would become. Bill Gates didn't take it seriously. But in 1995, Gates got religion. In a series of meetings, he increasingly made it clear that he believed the Internet was the next great revolution and the revolution that was Microsoft's greatest threat.

When Microsoft woke up to the revolution, there was an image that kept Gates awake at night. The story went something like this: Microsoft's power came from the fact that applications developers wrote their applications to the Microsoft platform. To the extent they continued to write to the Microsoft platform, Microsoft's power would remain strong. But the Internet presented a different opportunity for developers. Through a browser technology like Netscape, tied to an application programming language like Java, developers would increasingly find it valuable to write programs to the network directly. This would reduce dependence on Windows, which would in turn reduce the power of the Microsoft monopoly. A partial substitute for Windows then threatened to undermine the power of Windows.[44]

Whether you believe this threat or not, there is fairly clear evidence that *Bill Gates* believed this threat.[45] Hence Microsoft once again shifted into defensive mode. As with DOS in the early 1990s, it needed to hold the field with users of Windows 95 until it could develop a network-based application suite that would compete with the threat posed by Java/Netscape.

It held the field with a familiar strategy. As with the MS-DOS/ Windows 3.0 strategy, the aim here was to assure that a significant portion of the base did not move away from Windows 95 before Windows 95 could be migrated into a network-based world. This time the strategy would be implemented not through a fancy application that everyone would want. This time the tie would be effected by linking a Microsoft browser to the underlying operating system, Windows 95. Every computer manufacturer that wanted to sell a PC (with an Intel architecture) had to sell it with Windows 95. Microsoft took advantage of that fact by making sure the buyers also got Internet Explorer.[46]

How it made sure the two went together changed over time. At first, the program was a simple addition bundled within the operating system—just as File Synchronization on the Macintosh is bundled with the OS. But eventually the program was "integrated" into the operating system, making it easy for programs to move to the Internet and hard for another browser to be located within the Windows 95 system.

The government charged that this bundling behavior was in effect the same sort of tie as the one attacked between Windows 3.0 and DOS. It also claimed the objective was the same: Microsoft was using its power over the operating system to behave strategically against an innovation that threatened it.

THE STORY of this battle between the government and Microsoft is not yet (at this writing) over. But the significance of the case to the argument that follows has little to do with what the appellate courts eventually say. For whether the claim is proven or not, its essence has a parallel to the lessons from chapter 3: Microsoft was accused of strategic behavior designed to protect its monopoly position. It was accused, that is, of using its power over the operating system to kill innovation that threatened this power. As *Wall Street Journal* writer David Bank puts it:

> Any product that was popular represented a potential threat to the Windows platform because it could become a platform itself. Integration was Microsoft's weapon for disabling the threats to Windows. . . . Anyone who competed against Microsoft's platform lost.[47]

Again, that's not to say that Microsoft chilled innovation generally. Obviously, and again, the Windows platform has been an extraordinary boon for innovation. Thousands of programs have been written for it; hundreds of thousands of coders have used its structure to their own advantage. But sometimes an innovation challenges Microsoft, either by challenging the monopoly Microsoft has been said to hold or by making its business model less attractive in the future. And here, the government charged, Microsoft has been quick to respond. If your business model threatens it, then Microsoft will respond by killing your business. Gates was not, the government alleged, willing to play on a level playing field. (Indeed, as David Bank quotes Gates "yelling" at executive Paul Maritz, "You're putting us on a level playing field! You're going to kill the company.")[48]

Whether or not you believe that Microsoft engaged in the behavior that the government charged (and whether or not the Court of Appeals and the Supreme Court ultimately rule that such conduct violates the antitrust laws), the important point is this: Microsoft could engage in the behavior alleged by the government only *because Microsoft controlled its own code*. The source code for the Microsoft operating system is closed; Microsoft does not reveal the source to the public generally. Thus, Microsoft can change and direct its source code in ways that advance its own strategic vision. It is capable, that is, of behaving strategically, by changing its code to challenge competitors, because its code is closed. It can "control the pace of innovation" because only it can muck about with its code.[49]

Yet this is just the power that open code doesn't have. An open code project can't bundle a product the users don't want; users, because source code is there, are always free to unbundle. An open source project can't undermine a competing system; the competing system is always free to take the open source system and fight back. The source code for open source projects is therefore a check on the power of the project; it is a limit on the power of the project to behave strategically against anything written to the platform.

This "check" is realized in the perpetual possibility of an open code project to "fork." Forking occurs when a project led in one direction splits and develops in two or more directions. This right to split is guaranteed both by the code (because the source code is available) and by the law (because the license for open code projects guarantees that people are free simply to take the code and develop it in different directions). From the same code base, developers are free to develop different versions. These different versions can take on a life of their own. And conceivably, a fork could divide the user community into different sects. A project thriving because it had x thousand users could then collapse if not enough users support the project.

This threat of forking is not idle. Important open source projects, such as the BSD Unix clone, have forked in the past.[50] There is nothing in the current licenses of open code projects that would undermine this threat in the future.[51] Instead, the possibility of forking keeps pressure on the guardians of an open code project to develop the project in a way that the broadest range of users wants. As author Peter Wayner puts it, "[I]t prevents one person or clique from thwarting another group."[52]

This is democracy brought to code. An open code system can't get too far from the will of the users without creating an important incentive among some users to push the project a different way. And this in turn means the platform cannot act strategically against its own. The threat that created a federal case in *United States* v. *Microsoft* is not a threat if an operating system is built on open code. And the absence of strategic behavior in turn inspires others to build for this code.

Now my claim is not that this neutrality is the only factor that affects whether coders build to one platform rather than another. If 99 percent of the world is on a closed platform, and 1 percent is on an open platform, then regardless of the benefits of the 1 percent platform, there are naturally strong pressures to code for the 99 percent.

Yet this factor is not well enough understood, and its effect on innovation is systematically ignored. The effect here is similar to the effect we've seen in other contexts, and our aim, here and in other contexts, should be to better appreciate its role in building the Internet we have seen.

THE USERS of an open code project are not therefore hostages. That's the lesson argued so far. They are not hostages to bad code—the right to tinker is assured. And they are not hostages to strategic code—open code can't behave strategically. These two features together constitute the innovation commons that the Internet creates. They capture the public value that open code supports.

But there is a challenge with open code projects that many believe is insurmountable. This is the challenge to assure that there are sufficient incentives to build open code. Open code creates a commons; but the problem with this sort of commons is not the problem of overgrazing. (Indeed, as "accidental revolutionary" Eric Raymond puts it, open code creates an "inverse commons." "Grazing" does not reduce the code that is available. Instead, "in this inverse commons, the grass grows taller when it's grazed on.")[53]

The problem instead is to assure a sufficient incentive to supply new or improved code—a provisioning problem, in other words. In a world where software is sold like chewing gum, and where great value is believed to reside in the power to control who can copy this code, it is hard for many to see how there would be enough incentive to build code that is given away to anyone who wants it.

Here, however, we must work as empiricists, not ideologues. For we just have to look around to see the extraordinary amount of open code being written, despite the inability to control its copying. As Richard Stallman has said, "We do develop a lot of free software. If a theory says we can't, you have to look for the flaws in the theory."[54] The fact of this coding means that coders must have very different reasons for participating in open code projects. This reality means that the ability to control the code is not necessary for individuals to have an incentive to code.

Instead, there are plenty of examples of businesses that find it worthwhile to support open code projects without an assurance of perfect control. IBM is the most famous example. In 1998, IBM decided to dump its own server product and embrace the open source Apache server. It was free to do this because the open source Apache server was free for the taking. And IBM was inspired to do this because of the quality of that server.

This began an important relationship between IBM and open code. After it adopted the Apache server, IBM then embraced the Linux operating system. Rather than support ten different operating systems for its ten different systems, IBM found a great benefit in standardizing on a single system. In 2000, the market value of Linux-related IBM servers was $30 million. By 2004, IBM expects this value to increase to $3.4 billion.[55] And because the operating system across IBM's different computer systems will be the same, the ease with which code from one project can be carried to another will increase.

But IBM has not simply leeched off the wealth of open code projects. It has committed its own resources—in excess of $1 billion, it reports—to supporting the development of Linux and Apache. The company is therefore committing its own money for something it might otherwise get for free.

Why? What incentive could a company have to pay for what it could get for free?[56]

IBM's behavior is at first hard to understand, but not if you focus a bit on the nature of the project it supports.

IBM makes money by selling equipment. It sells more equipment if the software that runs that equipment is better. Thus, the free software it supports simply adds to the value of the equipment it sells.

More important, IBM adds services on top of the free software it supports.

The Apache server software has been folded into a suite of software that IBM sells—WebSphere. WebSphere does a range of Internet-related functions that Apache doesn't. The value of WebSphere therefore increases as the power of Apache improves.

Thus, IBM's willingness to improve Apache and Linux is not in itself hard to understand. The puzzle is why it gives its improvements back to the public. Why doesn't it simply take the Apache server and fold it into WebSphere but then keep its improvements to itself? Why, in other words, doesn't IBM simply take the resources of Apache and then defect from the open source movement?

The incentive not to defect comes from something special about the character of software development. Software is not static; it needs to evolve. If IBM were to fork Apache, taking a version of the Apache server private, it would face an even greater cost in keeping that forked version up to date as the functionality of the server was improved. The contributions of others to the Apache design would have to be folded into IBM's proprietary design. Tracking and implementing those changes would be extremely costly.

It therefore makes more sense—from a purely commercial perspective— for IBM (at least) to support the open coding that builds Linux and Apache, even though it can't capture the full value of the code it contributes.

Or from a different perspective, IBM loses more from hiding its improvements than it gains.[57]

If this behavior still seems bizarre, then you need to put it into a broader context. The reigning view about software speaks as if a rational company would never write code unless it has perfect control over what it produces. But perfect control is rarely assured in any free market, not with code or anything else.

This is a hard fact for lawyers to understand (protected as they are by exclusionary rules such as the bar exam), but most of production in our society occurs without any guarantee of government protection. Starbucks didn't get a government monopoly before it risked a great deal of capital to open coffee shops around the world. All it was assured was that people would have to pay for the coffee they sold; the idea of a high-quality coffee shop was free for others to take. Similarly, chip fabricators around the world invest billions in chip production plants, with no assurance from the government that another competitor won't open a competing plant right next door.

In each of these cases, and in the vast majority of cases in a free economy, one person's great idea is open for others to take. Burger King and McDonald's; Peet's Coffee and Starbucks; Peapod and Webvan. No doubt the first movers would like it if others couldn't use their idea or if others wouldn't notice their idea until long after a market is set. But it is in the nature of the limits on patent rights, and in the nature of transparency in the market, that innovators in the ordinary market can't keep their good ideas to themselves. Some protection for ideas, and a bit more for expression, is provided by the legal system. But this protection is incomplete or leaky. Perfect control is never its character.

Innovators nonetheless innovate. And they innovate because the return to them from deploying their new idea is high, even if others get the benefit of the new idea as well. Innovators don't simply sit on their hands until a guaranteed return is offered; real capitalists invest and innovate with the understanding that competitors will be free to take their ideas and use them against the innovators.

Thus, rather than puzzling about why anyone would code for free systems, we might as well puzzle about why anyone would innovate without a government-granted monopoly to protect them. Indeed, history will teach that, at an earlier time, this was very much the view. Mercantilists believed that exclusive rights were needed before any investment made sense; the English monarchy at an earlier time protected many ordinary investments through a state-backed monopoly.

Free markets, however, function on a very different basis. We don't grant every merchant a guaranteed market; we don't reward every new marketing plan with a twenty-year monopoly; we don't grant exclusive rights to each new way of doing business. In all these cases, because the market produces enough incentive on its own, the fact that others can free-ride doesn't kill innovation.

The same lesson is being relearned in the context of code. No doubt IBM would be happier if it could control improvements to Apache; but the return from better server sales is enough to induce IBM to invest without getting the benefit of perfect control.[58] Likewise if IBM offers services that run on its servers: fast-running, more reliable servers will make it easier to sell the services that would run on top.

What's true for Big Blue is being learned elsewhere as well. Mercantilism among coders is dying. And as it dies, coders learn what free markets have taught since Smith called them free: that innovation is best when ideas flow freely.[59]

This is not to argue that software should be totally free, or that innovation should be completely unprotected. I am not an opponent of protection, where protection is properly justified. My aim is not to argue against systems of control generally. It is simply to resist a mistaken inference: that if some control is good, then more control must be better.

MY AIM in this chapter has been twofold. The first part has been to introduce the idea of open code and to demonstrate how it operates at the content layer to inspire a wide range of innovation. It does this both for the reasons that technologists give—it is fast, cheap, and powerful—and for reasons that are too often missed. By offering to the world a wide range of code and hence coding resources, open code lowers the barriers to entry for innovators.[60] By building a neutral platform, open code invites a different kind of innovation. By protecting that neutral platform, both through licenses and through distributed source code, the system assures developers that the platform will remain neutral in the future.

This feature of open code, however, is not limited to code. The lesson of open code extends to other content as well. As we will see when we consider the law of copyright, this balance between free and controlled resources is precisely the balance that the law must strike in intellectual property contexts generally. And while our intuition is that more control produces more innovation, this commons among the wired suggests at least that the story is more complex. Less control over code at the content layer has arguably produced more innovation and development of this code. Keeping this resource in a commons increases the value of the resource—both because others can draw upon this resource and because it mitigates the number of strategic games played by others. We will see something more of these strategic games in chapter 11.

5

Commons, Wire-less

"THE RADIO SPECTRUM" refers to that swath of electromagnetic radio frequencies that are used today for everything from the transmitting of AM radio to the broadcasting of television and cellular phones. Technically it refers to the use of radio waves, for any purpose, between 3 kilohertz and 300 gigahertz.

This spectrum is regulated. The *Titanic* gave us that regulation. In the aftermath of her sinking, navy analysts argued that had the radio spectrum been better regulated, a ship less than twenty miles from the wreck could have saved hundreds of passengers.[1] The chaos in the spectrum confused the ship, however, so it missed the calls of help from the sinking luxury liner. The government used this confusion as a reason to begin to regulate access and use of the spectrum.

By the fall of 1912, the push to extend this regulation was great. Congress enacted the Radio Act of 1912, vesting in the Secretary of Commerce the right to license the operation of a radio apparatus.[2] In 1926, after a series of court decisions limiting the power of the Department of Commerce, then Secretary of Commerce Herbert C. Hoover said the authority was insufficient. Congress responded with the Radio Act of 1927, vesting in the Federal Radio Commission (FRC) control over the radio spectrum.[3] The FRC thus established a process by which the right to use a certain spectrum was licensed. Any use without a license was a criminal offense.

Thus spectrum, after 1927, at least, was not a commons. To use the spectrum required the permission of someone else—the government. That permission was granted according to the government's view of what uses were best. There was no neutrality in the government's decisions about who got to use this "public" resource. This was a resource that was fundamentally controlled, with the government as the controller.

This control had an increasingly profound effect upon radio programming. Early radio programming was different from today's. The spectrum was not filled with commercial broadcasters and Rush Limbaugh. Indeed, there was no such thing as a radio commercial. Radio at its start looked a lot like the Internet at its start. Broadcasters on early radio included a wide range of noncommercial, religious, and educational services. Commercial radio was just a tiny fraction of the total.[4]

But once the government got involved, all this quickly changed. It is an iron law of modern democracy that when you create a regulator, you create a target for influence, and when you create a target for influence, those in the best position to influence will train their efforts upon that target. Thus, commercial broadcasters—NBC and CBS in particular—were effective in getting the government to allocate spectrum according to their view of how spectrum should be used.[5] (This was helped by the broadcasters' practice of offering free airtime to members of Congress.)[6] The period from 1927 to 1934 saw an extraordinary shift in the nature of radio use—from a diverse collection of uses, some commercial, most not, to a single dominant use of the radio spectrum—namely, commercial radio. As Thomas Hazlett writes, "[B]y the mid-1930s, [NBC and CBS] would be responsible for an astounding 97% of night-time broadcasting."[7]

This transition was not without opposition. When radio stations started advertising, they incited a massive and continuous campaign of opposition. Herbert Hoover said of the trend, "It is inconceivable that we should allow so great a possibility for service to be drowned in advertising chatter."[8] Poll after poll indicated that the people hated the emerging commercial system.[9]

Over time, however, people got used to the commercials, and the opposition died. By the mid-1930s, Congress was ready for a new statute, the Communications Act of 1934. The act charged a renamed agency (the Federal Communications Commission) with the duty to regulate "as public interest, convenience or necessity" requires within certain spectrum-defining areas.[10] And it empowered the FCC to make decisions about how best to use the spectrum in the public interest.

This extensive regulation of what before 1912 had been a purely unregulated practice of wireless communication was upheld by the Supreme Court in 1946. Regulation of the radio spectrum was necessary, Justice Felix Frankfurter argued, because "[t]here is a fixed natural limitation upon the

number of stations that can operate without interfering with one another."[11]
Justice Frank Murphy, though dissenting from the Court's opinion, agreed
with the Court at least this far:

> Owing to its physical characteristics[,] radio, unlike the other methods of
> conveying information, must be regulated and rationed by the govern-
> ment. Otherwise there would be chaos, and radio's usefulness would be
> largely destroyed.[12]

It was in the *nature of things*, the government argued and the Court
agreed, that only if spectrum were controlled by the government would
spectrum be usable. Spectrum could not be free.

ABOUT THE time the Supreme Court came to this conclusion, an English
economist was concluding just the opposite. In a review of the FCC's regulation of spectrum, economist Ronald Coase concluded that there was no
justification for political regulation of access to spectrum.[13] Spectrum was
no more "scarce" than land or trees were scarce. Scarcity is the nature of all
valuable resources; but not all valuable resources are allocated by the
government — at least, not in a free society.[14]

Rather than a regime of licensing, Coase argued, spectrum should be allocated into property rights and sold to the highest bidder.[15] A market for
spectrum would better and more efficiently allocate spectrum than a system
of government-granted licenses.

History has been kinder to Coase than to the regulators of the early FCC.
In 1991, he won a Nobel Prize for his work on transaction cost economics.
And long before the Nobel committee recognized his genius, many policy
makers in the United States came to believe that Coase's system was better
than the FCC's. A market in spectrum would more efficiently allocate spectrum than any system controlled by the government.

This is the debate I described at the start of the book. It is a debate
between two regimes for controlling access to a resource — in this case, spectrum. One regime (the FCC's) relies upon the government; the other
(Coase's) relies upon the market. Both presume that spectrum must be controlled. They differ only in the controller. Both thus reject a model of spectrum as a commons.

Among these proponents of a market for spectrum, none is more vocal
and persuasive than American Enterprise Institute Fellow Thomas Haz-

lett.[16] A system of government licenses, Hazlett argues, chills innovation. A world where holders of rights in spectrum cannot sell those rights chills the process by which new uses of spectrum develop. Far better, Hazlett argues, if the holders of spectrum rights had the freedom to sell those rights to the highest bidder. Then, Hazlett argues, more creative and innovative uses of spectrum would be enabled.[17]

Hazlett has done an extraordinary service demonstrating the harm of government-managed spectrum. He is certainly right that the current regime stifles innovation in spectrum use. If the innovator must first get permission from the government, then the innovator is much less likely to try. Permission from the government is an expensive commodity. New ideas rarely have this kind of support. Old ideas often have deep legislative connections to defend them against the new.

But to demonstrate the harm in government control of a resource is not yet to demonstrate the need for private control. Hazlett is right if control is necessary. But is control necessary? Even if the market is a better system for allocating control than the state, is the market in spectrum better than free spectrum, if no ex ante allocation is required?

THE ANSWER is: Maybe not.[18] Increasingly, there are strong technical arguments for a different way of allocating spectrum—or, better, arguments for a different way of *not* allocating spectrum. These "different ways" we can abbreviate as "wideband technologies." These technologies include "spread spectrum" technologies as well as technologies that allow some spectrum uses to be "overlayed" on top of others.[19] Wideband technologies would allow many different users to "share" spectrum without the government or the market handing out rights to use the spectrum up front. Just as users of the Internet "share" the resources of the Internet through protocols that coordinate multiple, unplanned use, so too users of spectrum could "share" the resources of spectrum through protocols that coordinate multiple, unplanned use. Rather than controlled, spectrum would be, in this model, "free." Rather than permission to use it, the right to use it would be granted to anyone who wanted it. Rather than property, spectrum would be a commons.

This would not mean, as I will explain more fully below, that use of the spectrum would not be regulated. The regulation would simply be different. We speak of the "freeway" system to refer to highways. Highways are "free" in the sense that I mean: they are a commons open to anyone to use.

But the devices that use the highway system are highly regulated. You can't take a go-cart onto Route 66; you can't drive a tank down your local street. Regulations control the devices that can be used on a highway. But regulation does not control who gets to go where. Use remains, in our terms, free.

The same could exist for spectrum. But to see how, we need to think a bit differently about what spectrum is and how it is used. As David Reed says of policy makers, so is it for most of us: We are "grounded in theory or common sense [about spectrum] that does not match the phenomena we are seeing every day."[20]

TO UNDERSTAND the possibility of free spectrum, consider for a moment the way old versions of Ethernet worked. Ethernet is the protocol you most likely use to connect your computer to your company's local area network. If you have a cable modem at home, it is the protocol used to connect your computer to the cable modem. It is essentially a way for many devices on a single network to "share" the resources of that network. But the critical feature of this sharing is that it occurs without any central authority deciding who does what when.

How?

When a machine on an Ethernet network wants to talk with another machine—when it wants, for example, to send content to a printer, or to send an e-mail across the Internet through an e-mail server—the machine requests from the network the right to transmit. It asks, in other words, to reserve a period of time on the network when it can transmit. It makes this reservation only if it hears that the network at that moment is quiet. It behaves like a (good) neighbor sharing a telephone party line: first the neighbor listens to make sure no one is on the line, and only then does she proceed to call. Likewise with the old versions of Ethernet: the machine would first determine that the network was not being used; if it wasn't, it would send a request to reserve the network.[21]

What if two machines sent that request at the very same time? If that happened, the network would record a "collision" on the network, and each machine would register that its request had failed. Each machine would need to request access to the network again. But rather than each machine requesting access at the same time, each waits for a random amount of time until it sends its request again. Ethernet technologies demonstrate that this protocol for dealing with collisions is quite good at facilitating coordinated use of a common network.

In this story, the Ethernet network is functioning as a commons. It is a resource that is made available generally to everyone connected to the network. Of course, everyone on the network must request permission to use the resource. But this permission can be content neutral. The network does not have to ask what your application is before it reserves space on the network.

More important, these protocols are a way for many different machines to share this common resource, without the coordination of any top-down controller. No one licenses the use of one machine over another; no system for selling rights to use the Ethernet network is needed. Instead, many different machines share access to this common resource and coordinate its use without top-down control.

Ethernet is not radio spectrum, though it is "spectrum in a tube."[22] And wideband technologies work differently from Ethernet protocols, though the Ethernet protocols do at least show how bottom-up coordination is possible. This bottom-up coordination of spectrum in a tube should in turn suggest the possibility of a different way of controlling spectrum in the air. It should suggest, that is, the possibility that radio spectrum might be allocated in this shared bottom-up way, rather than in the traditional top-down model of coordination advocated by the licensors-of-property types.

HOW WOULD such a system work?

The existing paradigm of radio spectrum broadcasting embraces the opposite of end-to-end principles. The ends in the broadcast medium—receivers—are stupid, not smart. All the intelligence is in the broadcaster itself. A receiver just listens for the strong signal separated by silence. When another strong signal comes close to the signal it's listening to, existing receivers get confused. They can't decide which signal to focus upon, so they wander in and out among them all.

A different paradigm for broadcasting imagines smart radios (smart receivers and transmitters) replacing the dumb. These receivers can distinguish the transmissions they are to focus on from background noise. They distinguish the good from the bad either because each transmission, coming as a packet of data, tells the system where to listen next or because there is a fixed pattern of listening that the receivers are programmed to follow. In either case, smart receivers make it possible for many receivers to effectively share the same spectrum range. And through technologies that facilitate coordination—again, analogous to the technologies of Ethernet—this system would permit many receivers, and hence many broadcasters, to coordinate use of the same radio spectrum.[23]

The idea for this way of allocating spectrum reaches back to World War II, and to the work of actress Hedy Lamarr.[24] Lamarr and her partner, George Antheil, were exploring ways for submarines to communicate without detection. They invented a system where a transmitter would hop along the radio spectrum—transmitting for a moment at one frequency, and then jumping at the next moment to another—while the receiver, knowing the pattern the transmitter would take, would tune to the different frequencies at precisely the right moment in time.

Lamarr's technology was taken up by the Defense Department, though her invention was never deployed. Instead, work on the technology was classified. In the mid-1980s, however, information about this research was declassified, and interest in this mode of using spectrum increased.[25] The deployment of the idea, of course, was now different. Digital processors made it possible to jump across the spectrum much more quickly and efficiently. And researchers increasingly saw that not only would this be a more efficient way to use the radio spectrum, but communications using this technology would be more secure. Rather than simply tuning in to a conversation on a cell phone (as many "scanners" do now), the conversation on the cell phone would be spewed across many different channels. The receiver would be unable to keep up unless it was clued in to the pattern of the transmission.

This is the Internet sans wires. The data being transmitted—for instance, a song or a TV show—are carved up into packets of data; those packets are sent across the radio spectrum along a broad swath of spectrum. They are then collected at the other end and reassembled by the smart receiver. Collisions or mistransmissions are retransmitted, as on the Internet. A vast array of spectrum is in turn effectively shared, in just the way "spectrum in a tube" (the wires of the Internet) is shared. No central controller is needed, just as no controller on the Internet is needed. Anyone with an idea, and a device that obeyed simple spectrum rules, could deploy that idea, just as anyone with an idea for the Internet, and a computer that obeyed TCP/IP, could deploy that idea to the whole of the Net.[26]

AROUND THE early 1980s, the rules governing spectrum became an obsession with a retired West Point officer, David Hughes. Hughes had begun online community life in Colorado by setting up one of the first on-line

bulletin boards in the nation. His aim was to find a cheap way for communities to connect, and he was located in rural America, where the thought
of wires being used to connect was neither obvious nor useful.

So Hughes began exploring radios and soon came across the explod-
ing technologies of spread spectrum radio. Using cheap (and increasingly cheaper) radio devices, Hughes began setting up spread spectrum
experiments—demonstrating the power of a technology that did not depend
upon spectrum being owned.

Though this work was technical, Hughes's motivation was "community—
not politics, not business, not technology, not government—community in
all of its parts."[27] As he explained:

> My work with radio has been based upon how you reach the smallest com-
> munities, and across community. Not just to it, but within it. . . . It's always
> been to the end of the highest level of connectivity at the lowest cost for
> every community on the face of the globe.[28]

Hughes began to push free access to spectrum. His work was designed to
demonstrate how open spectrum could connect communities much more
cheaply. At the core of his plan was a technology for sharing spectrum rather
than allocating it—in other words, a plan for making the physical layer of
spectrum *free* by treating the physical layer as if it were in a commons.

Hughes worked for a time with FCC technical adviser Dewayne Hendricks. Hendricks too was eager to exploit this new technology. In the early
1980s, the FCC announced its plan to explore using spectrum as a commons. Hendricks was eager to develop technologies to do just this. While
Hendricks was at the FCC, he pushed Chairman William Kennard's program to experiment with these alternative uses of spectrum. But when the
FCC slowed its progress, Hendricks decided to follow the path of Hughes,
leaving the government to build what many in Washington said could not
be built.

The problem was again the FCC. While the FCC had allocated a range
of spectrum to be "unlicensed"—meaning people could use this spectrum
without receiving a license—it was not encouraging this alternative use. So
Hendricks had the idea to go elsewhere to explore new ways to use the spectrum. The Kingdom of Tonga was receptive to this alternative model for
regulating spectrum use. Hendricks packed his bags.

In Tonga, Hendricks built a system to deliver high-speed Internet access
to all citizens in Tonga. This access would use the radio spectrum; the speed

was two to five times faster than the fastest cable modem in the United States.[29] Once built, the system would deliver this content at just about zero marginal cost.

Hendricks could build this system in Tonga because he was free of FCC regulations. Tonga has its own rules for allocating spectrum; it chose to make a sufficient amount free to enable this free Internet use. Rather than fight with the skeptics over whether the system would work in theory, Hendricks decided to prove it would work simply by building it.

Hendricks has not stopped with Tonga. Encouraged by the FCC's push to develop Internet infrastructure in Native American tribal lands, he has now begun a program to give Native American tribes access to free spectrum.[30] Within eight tribal lands, he is building a similar system to that in Tonga. Native Americans on those reservations will have access to superfast, supercheap wireless Internet technologies—long before the rest of America does.

How can Hendricks do this, given the rules of the FCC? Hendricks's plan starts within the rules the FCC has set; when he runs against the rules, he will shift to plan B: The Native American tribes argue that they are sovereign nations. The Supreme Court has agreed. Their claim is that they are free to regulate spectrum on their lands as long as they don't interfere with spectrum off their lands. Hendricks's system won't interfere. And by the time the lawyers resolve the battle, these Native American tribes will be connected at a higher speed than the fastest cable modems in AT&T's labs. This is regulatory activism in its finest form.

HUGHES AND HENDRICKS are just two of a gaggle of innovators experimenting with these alternatives to allocated spectrum. Some of the most famous innovations are the "Bluetooth" protocols, which enable low-power connections between mobile devices and PCs. Millions of devices now embed the protocol, which uses one of the few "unlicensed" bands that the FCC has allowed.[31] Another example is Apple Computer's AirPort technology, enabling wireless links to computer networks using a protocol called 802.11b.[32] (Real Madison Avenue whizzes, these protocol namers!) This technology enables extremely fast wireless connections between computers and a network.

But these are just the beginning.[33] Consider the work of Charmed Technologies. Founded by MIT Media Lab alumnus Alex Lightman, Charmed Technologies aims to develop wearable computing systems. These wearable devices will link to the Internet and feed information in real time back to the user or wearer. Think of *Robocop*, with the wearer as the robot—able to see a person and have the computer identify him or look up an address merely by pointing the viewer at a building.

Who knows whether such a system would catch on? Who at this point can tell whether being perpetually connected is what people really want? But the fact that we can't tell means the opportunity to experiment is important. And the opportunity to experiment here depends upon access to the resources needed to experiment—spectrum, in other words. Ideas like Lightman's require space to develop, without first having to prove to existing AT&Ts why each new idea is a good idea.

If Lightman's idea depended solely on the Internet—if the last leap were not across the air but simply a link to a wired computer—then he would have this right to experiment. The right to connect is guaranteed by a broadly competitive market for Internet service providers (ISPs). He could make his service available on the Net, and anyone on the Net could get access to it. But because his service depends upon a leap from a person to a server across the air, he must depend on the right to access wireless spectrum. And that right is threatened.

For if there were a broad swath of unlicensed spectrum—spectrum that anyone could use and many could link to—then many Alex Lightmans could experiment with ways to link the Net to people and the Net to things.[34] These experiments would generally fail, but a few no doubt would succeed. And it is these successes that could transform the Internet as it is. If the same opportunity for innovation and creativity existed around wireless technologies as existed initially around the Net, then the changes we should expect are the same as the extraordinary changes the Net has built. Free access to this free resource should produce the same sort of innovation that free access to the controlled resource of telephone lines produced.

This free resource would thus enable wireless access for a wide range of new services—some still unimagined, others the dream of Internet innovators. And this free resource would compete with other providers of access to the Internet, keeping competition strong in this critical part of our information infrastructure.

BY NOW you will have noticed something different about the argument of this chapter. Unlike the commons I've described so far, a broad commons in radio spectrum does not yet (generally) exist. And unlike the commons I've described so far, with wireless there is not yet a wide range of innovation to point to and ponder. Instead, in this chapter my argument is about a commons that could be, not one that already exists. My claim is that there is enough evidence of a different way to order spectrum that we should be exploring whether spectrum could be ordered as a commons.

How exactly would such a regime work? Well, again, to say that spectrum should be in a commons is not to say that the government would leave spectrum "unregulated." There would be a role for regulation even if spectrum were "free." But this regulation would look very different from the regulation that now controls spectrum. The government (or the market) would not be deciding who gets to use the spectrum. The government would simply be assuring that the technologies that use the spectrum are properly certified technologies.[35] The FCC would need to certify that the devices were properly configured. Just as the FCC does now with computers (to make sure they don't interfere with radio transmissions), it would do with radios (to make sure of the same).

Thus, the spectrum-as-commons model does not assume no role for the government. The role of the government, however, would be much less invasive than under the current regulatory regime. The government does decide who gets to drive on the highways; it doesn't sell off a right to drive on the highways; it simply makes sure that the devices that are used on the highway are certified as safe.

AS THE technological potential to share spectrum becomes increasingly clear, a wide range of scholars and technicians is now pushing the FCC to adopt a very different mode for allocating spectrum.[36] These advocates cover a broad political spectrum. As I've suggested over and over in this book, this diversity makes perfect sense. The advocates for free or open spectrum want to enable an extensive range of new technologies. They resist the efforts by entrenched interests to use government-granted rights over spectrum as a way to protect their own interests. They resist, that is, both government-granted and market-regulated licenses. Thus, when the government proposed auctioning off more of the radio spectrum, conservative economist George Gilder responded not by praising markets, but by attacking the political corruption implicit in these deals. Says Gilder:

> Still more subversive of good policy, the very auction process entrenches obsolescent technology and promotes the false idea that spectrum is the basis of a natural monopoly.[37]

Gilder favors innovation and change over state-supported monopolies. His aim is to push policies that would open up the resources of spectrum to the widest range of innovators. A spectrum commons would do just this. Just as the Internet did, it would open up a resource for the common use of a wide range of innovators. These many innovators would experiment with ways of using the network that none of us could now imagine. They would fuel a second and possibly far more important wave of innovation than the initial wave of the Internet that we have seen so far.

LIBERATING SPECTRUM from the control of government is an important first step to innovation in spectrum use. On this point there is broad agreement, from those who push for a spectrum commons to those, like Hazlett, who push for a fully propertized spectrum market. All agree that the only thing that government-controlled spectrum has produced is an easy opportunity for the old to protect themselves against the new. Innovation moves too slowly when it must constantly ask permission from politically controlled agencies. The solution is to eliminate the need to ask permission, by removing these controllers at least.

Liberating spectrum from the control of the market is a second and much more controversial step. Hazlett and others insist that the rationing of a market is necessary, both to avoid overuse and to provide a sufficient incentive to improve spectrum efficiency. A spectrum commons will invite tragedy too quickly.

For the moment, we can defer resolving the differences between these two positions, to emphasize their common view: Both want a world where the power of controllers to stifle innovation has been eliminated. Both agree that government control over spectrum is simply a way for the old to protect themselves against the new. Both therefore push for a radical change in spectrum management policies, to free innovators from the need to please politicians before they have the right to innovate.

Commons Lessons

OMMONS MAY be rare. They may evoke tragedies. They may be hard to sustain. And at times, they certainly may interfere with the efficient use of important resources.

But commons also produce something of value. They are a resource for decentralized innovation. They create the opportunity for individuals to draw upon resources without connections, permission, or access granted by others. They are environments that commit themselves to being open. Individuals and corporations draw upon the value created by this openness. They transform that value into other value, which they then consume privately.

The Internet has been built on two kinds of commons; it has the potential to move to a third. The protocols of the Net embedded principles in the Net that constructed an innovation commons at the code layer. Though running on other people's property, this commons invited anyone to innovate and provide content for this space. It was a common market of innovation, protected by an architecture that forbade discrimination.

Free or open source software provided a second commons at the content layer. The open code components of the Net were perpetual options for innovation. The ideas and implementation of code that would build the Internet were made freely available both technically and legally. Legally, to the extent that licenses that protected open code required that it remain in the commons. Technically, in the sense that the code that built core and peripheral functions—including, importantly, the World Wide Web—was made available to all.

Finally, free spectrum was the promise to produce a new commons at the physical layer. Here again, access would be uncontrolled and the use of this access would be determined by a wide range of innovators. Not solely by the handful of innovators owning these essential facilities, but by a wide range of innovators who might have a different view of how the facilities might be used.

These three commons work together. They increase the value of controlled resources by connecting them with free resources. The strands of fiber being laid across the world are all controlled by individuals and corporations. They are, for the most part, private. But the value they have is a function of the use to which they will be put. And that use is this commons called the Internet. The commons contributes to its value, and it makes the control that contributes to it possible.

NO DOUBT my account is incomplete. I have spoken of how these commons induce innovation; I have not pretended to measure how much or how significantly. I have not surveyed the full range of factors that might be said to affect innovation. My focus has been narrow and selective.

My excuse, however, is that the debate right now is not about the degree to which free or common resources help. The attitude of the most influential in public policy is that the free, or common, resources provide little or no benefit. There is for us a cultural blindness—an unwillingness to even account for the role of the commons. As Yale law professor Carol Rose argues, and as I indicated at the start, though "our legal doctrine has strongly suggested that some kinds of property should not be held exclusively in private hands, but should be open to the public,"[1] we live in a time when the dominant view is that "the whole world is best managed when divided among private owners."[2] The very idea that nonexclusive rights might be more efficient than exclusive rights rarely enters the debate. The assumption is control, and public policy is dedicated to maximizing control.

But there is another view: not that property is evil, or that markets are corrupt, or that the government is the best regime for allocating resources, but that free resources, or resources held in common, *sometimes* create more wealth and opportunity for society than those same resources held privately. Against the background of the commons we've seen in the context of the Internet, my aim in this chapter is to explore some reasons why. What do we gain by keeping resources free? What is lost when we allow certain resources to be controlled?

In this chapter, I draw together a few clues to answer this question. Drawing upon a wide range of writing, I want to pull together different accounts that suggest the value in keeping resources free. My aim is not proof; it is instead simply to connect ideas that are often left apart.

We can begin with our own legal tradition and with the resources that our tradition has left in the commons and the reasons why. Professor Rose has identified two reasons why our tradition has kept a particular resource— such as a public road, a right-of-way, a navigable waterway, or a town square—in common. First, these resources are "physically capable of monopolization by private persons."[3] Monopoly means power, and the monopolist would be capable of exerting power over the community. Second, the public has a superior claim to these resources because "the properties themselves [are] most valuable when used by indefinite and unlimited numbers of persons."

The easiest example here is the case of a road. A road is kept in the commons because the opportunity for "holdouts" would be too great if the road were private. If a road became the common path along which all commerce passed, if along that path other businesses were built and other services were provided, then there would be a great value secured by this common road. And selling that road might then risk a hijacking by the owner of the road. The public gets great value out of the road, and the road has value because of the "publicness" of the road. The risk this value creates is that a private actor might take advantage. The property is thus "affected with a public interest" in the sense that the road's value comes from the public's dependence on it.[4]

Likewise with a town square. No doubt in any town there are many different places that might be a town square. But over time, one place is the town square, and it may well become valuable just because it is associated with custom and history within a given community. Keeping this resource in the hands of a community is a way to assure that no single actor takes advantage of the value the community has created. The value of this particular square comes not from the actions of its owner, but from a tradition that invests it with significance above others.[5]

In both these cases, the resource is kept in the commons because of the risk of an unfair capture if the resource were private. But why "unfair"? Why isn't it completely fair that the "owner" of the property be able to extract all of its value?

Here is the great insight in Carol Rose's analysis. Where the resource has a value *because of its openness*—where its value increases just because more use it; where "the more the merrier"—then it makes sense to attribute much of the value of this resource to the "publicness" of the resource. Indeed, as Rose argues, "the usual rationing function of pricing could be counter-productive [in these cases]: participants need encouragement to join these activities, where their participation produces beneficial 'externalities' for other participants."[6]

These are cases where "increasing participation *enhances* the value of the activity rather than diminishing it." Or, we might say more precisely, these are cases where the value from increased participation outweighs any cost from increased utilization. The value, in these cases, comes from the convergence of many upon a common use, or standard, or practice. And in these cases, keeping the resource in the commons is a way to assure that that value is preserved for all.[7]

These arguments from tradition are thus grounded in both fairness and efficiency, and economists have extended the arguments from efficiency.[8] One extension in particular links back directly to the end-to-end argument.

The linking goes like this: Some resources have an understood purpose. We know what we will do with a certain resource, or at least the range of possible uses for that resource is small. But other resources don't come with their purpose preset.

Take telephone wires in the 1910s. Communications wires had been strung in America since the early 1800s. When they were first strung, their use was simple: telegraph. Given the technology at the time, there was little more that the wire could be used for; it was single-purpose. When telephones came along, there was a second possible use for the wire. That led to a new shake-up in business models. But here again, given the technology, the range of possible uses for these wires was not great.

Contrast this with computer networks. The most striking feature of the early history of the Internet is the repeated assertion by those at its founding that they simply didn't know what the network would be used for. Here they were building this large-scale computer network, with a large number of resources devoted to it, but none of them had a clear idea of the uses to which this network would be put. Many in the 1980s believed the Internet would be a fair substitute for telephones (they of course were wrong); none had any idea of the potential for many-to-many publishing that the World Wide Web would produce.[9]

Where we have little understanding about how a resource will be used, we have more reason to keep that resource in the commons.[10] And where we have a clear vision of how a resource will be used, we have more reason to shift that resource to a system of control.

The reason is straightforward. Where a resource has a clear use, then, from a social perspective, our objective is simply to assure that that resource is available for this highest and best use. We can use property systems to achieve this end. By assigning a strong property right to the owners of such resources, we can then rely upon them to maximize their own return from this resource by seeking out those who can best use the resource at issue. But if there is no clear option for using the resource—if we can't tell up front how best to use it—then there is more reason to leave it in common, so that many can experiment with different uses.[11] Not knowing how a resource will be used is a good reason for making it widely available.[12]

Scott Bradner and Mark Gaynor have captured this insight in a paper that uses "real options theory" to value different network designs. Their conclusion is that where uncertainty is highest, network designs that embrace end-to-end maximize the value of the network; and where uncertainty is low, then end-to-end is not a particular value.[13]

In this case, end-to-end is a stand-in for a commons. Here too is a resource that can be used in any number of unpredictable ways. As David Reed describes the founding of the network design, "[T]he idea was we didn't want to decide. . . . We felt that we couldn't presume anything about how networks would be used by applications."[14] And given the unpredictable character of the ways it might be used, there is something gained by keeping the resource open.

There is a second line of work that suggests another efficiency-based reason why open resources may have more value than closed resources. This work derives from the theory of management, and it helps explain why control can sometimes systematically fail.

The idea here has been made familiar by Professor Clay Christensen of the Harvard Business School in his book *The Innovator's Dilemma*.[15] The dilemma describes a perfectly understandable series of decisions that leads well-managed companies to miss the opportunities of disruptive technological change. Leading companies within a particular market will outperform others in perfecting the technology that defines their existing market. They will consistently develop superior products for continuing the development of their product line.

What these companies can't do is identify and develop disruptive technologies. (As David Isenberg puts it, "[T]he milk of disruptive innovation doesn't flow from cash-cows.")[16] And this is not because a company is irrational or because it doesn't understand the nature of the market. The blindness that keeps the company fixed in a dying path is actually its clear understanding of probable returns. It sees real revenue from existing customers who need marginally better technology. It doesn't see the revenue from radically new technologies that depend upon unidentified or undeveloped markets. From its perspective, given its customers and reasonable expectations, these successful companies rationally fail.

Christensen offers the disk drive industry as an example. Disk drives have increased in capacity while falling in physical size at a dramatic rate.[17] Overall, we can see that this shrinking created an extraordinary new market for computing power. In hindsight, it is clear that victory would go to the company that developed the smallest, most powerful drive.

But at each stage of that development, this obvious truth was missed by the very best disk drive manufacturers. The progress that led to the market we see now was not continuous; it was punctuated by disruptive changes in disk drive size. At each of these moments of disruption, the change occurred not because some genius had discovered a new technology that permitted the drive to shrink in size. The technology of each smaller drive was familiar and available to all. Instead, the disruptive changes occurred when an outside firm saw a new market and was willing to bet the firm on the success of this market. This new market was always more competitive than the old. The size of this market was uncertain. So from the perspective of the dominant player, moving into this new market seemed like a bad move. Its customers wanted nothing like the technology of the new drives; and it didn't have a vision that showed it the potential of a radically different market.

This blindness of successful companies comes not from management's failing. This pattern of failure can be seen in the very best firms. This is not the market's acting irrationally; it is the product of a rational strategy, given the market as it appears at any one time.

As David Reed says about AT&T: It was not willing to bet on data given that "the known applications couldn't justify it and they weren't willing to bet on the unknown applications."[18]

Others have described a similar blindness. Jim Carlton tells the story of Apple Computer's failing to see the potential of a market where its OS was licensed to Microsoft. Apple looked at the margins it was getting from its relatively small but rich market for PCs, and it compared those margins to those of other computer manufacturers. Apple's position looked far superior, so, rather than licensing the OS, Apple kept it closed.

Carlton describes this as pathology.[19] It was the product, he suggests, of committee decision making. And trading upon what happened since 1985, the reader is left with the view that mismanagement has accounted for Apple's failure.

But the Christensen story suggests how it was Apple's success that caused Apple's failure. Its inability to see was not a function of its blindness. Its inability to recognize the value in a radically different model of doing business may well have been a rational decision, given the information available. What Christensen teaches is why, systematically, the view of what is rational from the perspective of a single actor may well prove irrational from the perspective of the market as a whole.

The Innovator's Dilemma offers its own strategy for dealing with this blindness. But we can see in the Internet a strategy for dealing with the very same blindness. If firms will be focused on continuing progress, if they will ignore new markets that fail to promise the same level of supracompetitive returns, if they will miss disruptive technologies that in fact produce radical new industries, then we have another reason, in theory, to keep at least some critical resources for innovation within a commons. If the platform remains neutral, then the rational company may continue to eke out profit from the path it has chosen, but the competitor will always have the opportunity to use the platform to bet on a radically different business model.

This again is the core insight about the importance of end-to-end. It is a reason why concentrating control will not produce disruptive technology. Not necessarily because of evil monopolies, or bad management, but rather because good business is focused on improving its lot, and disruptive technologists haven't a lot to improve. The disrupters are hungry to build a different market; the incumbent is happy to keep the markets as they are.

This last point suggests a third line of work suggesting an efficiency-based reason for preferring open rather than controlled resources. If the Christensen story is of the blundering giant, then this is the story of the malevolent giant. Here the actor—a company or an individual holding some monopoly privilege—fully understands how a new technology might increase social value. But the giant also realizes that there is no way it can capture this increase in social value. Unable to capture the gain, and certain to lose its own rents, the malevolent giant acts to resist the technological change, as a way of preserving its own power.

Such cases are easy to describe in the abstract; proving they exist in reality is much harder. Whatever its intent, the malevolent giant rarely has the power to control a technology completely; and even where it does have the power, other market forces may be adequate in checking the exercise of the power.

We as a society should favor the disrupters. They will produce movement toward a more efficient, prosperous economy. Christensen argues for management structures that would facilitate that; the Internet is an architectural structure that does the same.

This link between innovation and architecture is the focus of the work of two other Harvard Business School professors as well. Professors Carliss Baldwin and Kim Clark have demonstrated the importance of modular design in facilitating design evolution and hence industry innovation. In the first volume of an intended two-volume work, they demonstrate the fundamental shift in the design of the computer industry, as IBM increasingly modularized the design of its systems, and as regulators increasingly forced IBM to permit the modules to be provided by others. This change reduced the market value of IBM, but that reduction was overwhelmed by the increase in value in the rest of the industry. As they describe it, a "multiplication and decentralization of design options led to the emergence of a new industry structure for the computer industry," and this in turn radically increased the value of the industry.[20]

Modularity liberates control resources, as the multiplication of interfaces frees innovators to develop new and competing designs. It is another example of how free resources enable innovation.

Efficiency is not the end of the reasons why free resources might prove valuable. Instead, one final set of values also indicates the value in keeping a resource in common. These are democratic values.

The democratic tradition is our strongest ground for resisting the system of control. Why don't we simply sell the right to govern to the highest bidder? (The cynical will say we already have in effect. Maybe, but I'm talking formally.) Why don't we have a system where we auction off the rights to control the government as a permanent property right?

This is clearly not how we arrange governance today. The right to participate in a democracy is kept in common. We don't permit people to sell their right to vote. We permit neither the government to control how that resource is used nor the market to control how that resource is used. Instead, we keep that resource in common hands, whether perpetually (in democracies that can be recalled at any moment) or periodically (in democracies like that in the United States, where elections are held every few years).

Democracies thus forbid propertizing the right to control government. Why? This is not a hard question to answer, though raising it as a question will help us think through this problem elsewhere. We don't sell the right to vote because the currency—cash—is not the only or most important dimension of value in our society. There are people who devote themselves to careers that don't make them wealthy—schoolteachers and civil servants. We don't think they, by virtue of that choice, should have less power to control how their government is run. They've made choices that result in their having less power in the marketplace; but the marketplace is not a proxy for every domain of social power. As the philosopher Michael Walzer properly observes, there are many spheres of social influence in our lives.[21] And we permit power in one sphere to dominate power in another in very few contexts. We don't in the United States permit sex to be purchased; we don't sell wives for dowries; we don't sell babies; and we don't sell votes.[22] These transactions are blocked because allowing the market to control them would be to allow one sphere total power over all others. This we have chosen not to do.

A similar insight gives more reason for certain resources to remain in common. Access to locations where protest happens—town halls, or town squares, or, in the language of First Amendment law, public fora—remains open to all if open to any, or remains open on equal terms. Here the market is not permitted control.

And likewise, one might well argue, when the resource becomes foundational to participation in a society, then we assure that it remains in the commons. The right to vote is a foundational resource in our society; we don't allow it to be bought or sold. Access to the roads or highways is central to social freedom; we don't auction off such access and thereby restrict the right to travel. And some have argued that basic infrastructure—like phones or emergency services—should be considered common resources that must be made available to all. The specifics we can argue about, but the general point should be clear: There are values that a commons could serve that are lost if the resource is privatized.

IN ADVOCATING the commons, I have not argued for a world with only a commons. Not all resources can or should be organized in a commons. Not all resources must be organized as a commons just because some are. There are public streets as well as private drives, freeways as well as toll roads. The Internet links seamlessly with networks that are completely private. A world with open wires radio spectrum is perfectly consistent with a world where exclusive cable lines are reserved to those who pay. The open and the closed always coexist and depend upon each other in this coexistence.

But there are *reasons* why some resources need to be controlled and others do not. We've seen these reasons before, but we are in a better position now to understand them. While some resources must be controlled, others can be provided much more freely. The difference is in the nature of the resource, and therefore in the nature of how the resource is supplied.

This was the insight of many in the Enlightenment and, within our tradition, Thomas Jefferson most forcefully. Listen to Jefferson writing to Isaac McPherson in 1813 about the character of the patent power:

> [1] If nature has made any one thing less susceptible than all others of exclusive property, it is the action of the thinking power called an idea, which an individual may exclusively possess as long as he keeps it to himself; but the moment it is divulged, it forces itself into the possession of everyone, and the receiver cannot dispossess himself of it. [2] Its peculiar character, too, is that no one possesses the less, because every other possesses the whole of it. He who receives an idea from me, receives instruction himself without lessening mine; as he who lites his taper at mine, receives light without darkening me. [3] That ideas should freely spread from one to another over the globe, for the moral and mutual instruction of man, and improvement of his condition, seems to have been peculiarly and benevolently designed by nature, when she made them, like fire, expansible over all space, without lessening their density at any point, and like the air in which we breathe, move, and have our physical being, incapable of confinement, or exclusive appropriation. [4] Inventions then cannot, in nature, be a subject of property.[23]

I've added numbers in brackets to Jefferson's text to make clear the distinct points he is making:

First, Jefferson is describing the nature of an "idea." An idea is, in the terms of the economist, *imperfectly excludable*. I can keep a secret from you (and therefore exclude you from the secret), but once I tell you the secret, I can't take it back. We can't (yet) erase what has entered our heads.

Second, he is describing the *nonrivalrous* character of resources like ideas. Your consumption does not lessen mine, as your lighting a candle at mine does not darken me.

These two points then suggest a third: that "nature" has made this world to guarantee that "ideas should freely spread from one to another over the globe." Enlightenment was in her plan.

Thus it follows that without government, in the state of nature, there would be no such thing as a "patent" since patents are granted for "inventions" and inventions, "in nature," cannot be "a subject of property."

What is striking about this passage is the glee with which Jefferson reports this fact of nature. Here is the first patent commissioner showing just why nature is against the work of the U.S. Patent Office. But the motive of his glee is the betterment of man. This fact about nature means that of all the resources, information can be the freest.

Yet obviously, Jefferson's story is not true of all resources, or even all resources in the commons. His is an account of a nonrivalrous resource. A rivalrous resource would not permit your consumption without lessening mine. And his argument cannot be taken to mean that there should be no control that governs nonrivalrous resources. Nature may not protect them, but neither does nature erect governments. Jefferson was not arguing against patent protection; he was instead arguing against the idea that patent protection was in some sense a *natural right.*

This distinction between resources helps us isolate the different reasons why a resource might need to be controlled.

1. If the resource is rivalrous, then a system of control is needed to assure that the resource is not depleted—which means the system must assure the resource is both *produced* and not *overused.*

2. If the resource is nonrivalrous, then a system of control is needed simply to *assure the resource is created*—a provisioning problem, as Professor Elinor Ostrom describes it. Once it is created, there is no danger that the resource will be depleted. By definition, a nonrivalrous resource cannot be used up.

What follows then is critical: The system of control that we erect for rivalrous resources (land, cars, computers) *is not necessarily appropriate* for nonrivalrous resources (ideas, music, expression). Indeed, the *same system for both kinds of resources may do real harm.* Thus a legal system, or a society generally, must be careful to tailor the kind of control to the kind of resource. One size won't fit all.

A second point also follows and is equally important: Even for resources that are nonrivalrous, some form of control will often be required. For these resources, there is still the need to assure an adequate incentive to supply or to provision the resource. Thus, even here, some control will often be needed.

In both cases, the necessary control could be provided through a number of techniques—through law, norms, the market, or, importantly, technology. Laws against theft can protect the property interest of rivalrous resources; norms against overuse can protect some shared resources; prices imposed by the market can induce provisioning and reduce consumption; and technology can make it easier to control.

This range of techniques means that there are many different ways to provide the degree of control that any particular resource might need. The commons that Carol Rose describes are governed not by the market or by law imposed by state actors. They are instead governed by "custom" or norms within the relevant community.

> Custom thus suggests a means by which a "commons" may be managed— a means different from exclusive ownership by either individuals or governments. The intriguing aspect of customary rights is that they vest property rights in groups that are indefinite and informal, yet nevertheless capable of self-management. Custom might be the medium through which such an informal group acts generally; thus, the community claiming customary rights was really not an "unorganized" public at all.[24]

Commons in the Internet are regulated differently. "Custom" is not the typical controller anymore. It was at a certain time—USENET, for example, which facilitated a worldwide messaging board organized into separate topics, was governed by a custom that forbade commercial advertising; when that custom died, much of the value of USENET died. But in the contexts we have considered, custom is not the ruler. Controls imposed through technology instead govern many of these resources.

The cases we've seen so far are a mix of rivalrous and nonrivalrous resources, and the techniques of control within each are mixed as well. The wires that supported the network that was the original Internet are clearly rivalrous; so too may be the radio spectrum that Hendricks and Hughes want to share (though maybe not).[25] But digital copies of operating systems are not rivalrous. One copy is as good as the next, and once we have a single copy, there is no limit to the copies we might make. Likewise with music, or video that is made available in digital form.

With the rivalrous resources we've seen, technology guards against depletion. Protocols for sharing the resource assure that many can use it without anyone depleting the rest for others.

With the nonrivalrous resources, technology can't itself solve the problem of incentives. Here one kind of law (contract law, through self-imposed licenses) serves to solve some of the provisioning problems, at least with open source or free software. This is the function of the GPL and other open source licenses: relying upon the particular character of code, they create a strong incentive for coders to contribute back to the commons.

But where these incentives are not enough, the law (through the odd device of what we have come to call "intellectual property")[26] adds more. Intellectual property does this by giving the producers a limited exclusive right over their intellectual property, so they can recover the costs of producing that property and receive a sufficient return to give them the incentives to produce that property. A "sufficient return," however, is not perfect control, and intellectual property law does not, therefore, give authors or inventors perfect control. The basic premise, found in our Constitution, is that "neither the creator of a new work of authorship nor the general public ought to be able to appropriate all the benefits that flow from the creation of a new, original work."[27] Instead, some of that benefit ought to be reserved to the public, in common.

SOCIETY BENEFITS from resources that are free; but unless some system of control is implemented for resources that must be created, or for resources, once created, whose use is rivalrous, then no benefit will be received. The key is to balance the free against control, so that the benefits of each can be achieved.

Yet this balance is not automatic. There is no guarantee that the control will be enough and no promise that it won't be too much or too little. The aim of society must always be to draw the optimal balance, and our obligation over time is to assure that that drawing not become skewed. The level of control at one time might be insufficient at a different time. And the level of freedom assured at one time might become threatened as the technologies of control change.

THIS POINT should be obvious, but let's make sure.

Let's imagine a fishing village that for generations has managed to fish in equilibrium with the stocks. The fish, in this example, are held in a commons; the community doesn't allocate right of control. Fishermen have an understanding about when a catch is too much; they have boats designed with this understanding in mind.

Along comes a new technology for fishing, which if used by each fisherman would radically deplete the existing stocks. Now the community faces a decision—how best to regulate the use of this technology to assure the resource is not depleted. If the community does nothing, the norms of the community might still be sufficient to keep the catch in line. But if the norms are not enough, then the community must deploy a new technology of control.

This "new technology," however, is not determined. The solutions could be many. The community might issue a regulation that says how much each fisherman can catch; it might create a property right in the resource and allow individual fishermen to trade it. Or it might deploy some technology that would limit the catch of each fisherman over a given period of time. All of these are possible responses to the threat posed to the common resource by the new technology. Each responds to a change that undermines the old equilibrium.

The same story can happen the other way around. Consider the problem of copyright on the Internet. As I've already explained, the aim of copyright is to give an author an exclusive right sufficient to create an incentive to produce, but not so great a right as to undermine the public domain. The Constitution limits this exclusive right—Congress may not, for example, give copyright to ideas, nor may it deny a right to fair use. These limits are in addition to the express constitutional limits imposed by the clause granting Congress the power to create these "exclusive rights"—namely, that the rights be for a "limited term" and that they "promote the progress of Science."

When the Internet first became popular, there was great fear that the technology for digital copying would render useless the rights granted by law. If I could make perfect copies for free and distribute them for free, then the legal restriction would become much less useful.

This led Congress to expand the rights protected by the Copyright Act, to balance the change in technology that the Internet produced. But as many have argued, this change may have been premature. For there are technologies that can be deployed to protect copyrighted work. And if deployed successfully, these technologies may actually give copyright holders more control than they would have had absent the Internet, thereby lessening the need for law.[28]

Here the technology is expanding control beyond the balance originally set, where, as in the previous example, technology was expanding free use beyond the balance originally set. In both cases, the point is the same: the balance must reflect the technologies as they exist. And changes in technologies can significantly change this balance.

The point is more than theoretical. In essence, the changes in the environment of the Internet that we are observing now alter the balance between control and freedom on the Net. The tilt of these changes is pronounced: control is increasing. And while one cannot say in the abstract that increased control is a mistake, it is clear that we are expanding this control with no sense of what is lost. The shift is not occurring with the idea of a balance in mind. Instead, the shift proceeds as if control were the only value.

The aim in the balance of this book is to make this transformation plain. We are remaking cyberspace, and these remakings will undermine the innovation we have seen so far.

PART

II

/ / /

DOT.CONTRAST

Creativity in Real Space

THERE WAS a time before the Internet. Innovation and creativity were different then. I don't mean that creators were different then or that the process of creativity has changed. But the constraints on creativity and innovation were different. This difference can be expressed at each layer of Yochai Benkler's system. Because the physical, and code, and content layers were controlled differently, the opportunities for innovation were different.

We all know about these differences in the constraints among these layers. They are all obvious, if a bit in the background. They flow directly from the nature of real constraints within a scarcity-based economy. They are not the product of conspiracy or the will of evil minds. They are importantly unavoidable, at least in real space.

My aim in this chapter is to remind you of these things that we all know. I will rehearse the constraints on innovation that flow from the character of these different layers of communication in real space, so that we can better see how they have changed.

In real space. It is this qualification about which we must become self-conscious. Our intuitions about property, and about how best to order society, are intuitions built in a particular physical world. We have learned a great deal about how best to order that world, given the physics, as it were, of that particular world.

But the physics of cyberspace is different. The character of the constraints is different. So while there may be good reason to carry structures that define real space into cyberspace, we should not assume that those structures will automatically map. The different physics of cyberspace means that the rules that govern that space may be different as well.[1]

A *different physics*. I'm not talking about science fiction or about ideas that you've never considered before. Indeed, we've already seen a careful translation of real-space constraints into the physics of a very different world—the world of ideas. Jefferson made that translation in his writing about the nature of patent. My argument is nothing more (and certainly much less) than Jefferson's. The world we must consider is partway between the world of ideas that he describes and the world of things that colo' intuitions. Cyberspace is between these two worlds. It offers not qui freedom of the world of ideas, though it offers much more of that freedom than the world of things.

In the balance of this chapter, I want to make explicit constraints in the world of things, so that we can better see how these constraints have affected our thought about the world of ideas, and hence also about cyberspace.

One final note. My argument is not that all constraints are corrupting of something called "creativity." Certain constraints obviously enable creativity. The constraints of the classical form gave us Mozart and Beethoven. The aim is therefore not to find a world without constraint; it is to remove the constraints that might otherwise inhibit innovation. Just because it is good that sonnets forbid rambling paragraphs, it doesn't follow that a tax on books would inspire better writing.

CREATIVITY IN THE DARK AGES

PUT YOURSELF back in the dark ages, the time before the Internet took off—say, the 1970s—and ask: What was the environment for creativity then? What was required of a creator or innovator to bring his or her creativity to market? What limits were imposed? I want to consider this question in two contexts—first the arts and then commerce.

The Arts

WE CAN understand the environment for creativity in the arts with the same three layers that Benkler describes when talking of a communications system. Like a communications system, creativity in the arts is affected by constraints at the physical, code, and content layers. To author, or to create, requires some amount of *content* to begin with, to which the author adds a *creative component*, which, for a few, is then *published* and *distributed*.

CONTENT

THE CONTENT an author must draw upon varies with the "writing." Some part is new—this is the part we think of as "creative." But as many have argued, we've come to exaggerate the new and forget that a great deal in the "creative" is actually old.[2] The new builds on the old, and hence depends, to a degree, on access to the old. Academics writing textbooks about poetry need to be able to criticize and hence, to some degree, use the poetry they write about. Playwrights often base their plays upon novels by others. Novelists use familiar plots to tell their story. Historians use facts about the history they retell. Filmmakers retell stories from our culture. Musicians write within a genre that itself determines how much of the past content it needs to be within that genre. (There is no such thing as jazz that does not take from the past.) All of this creativity depends in part on access to, and use of, the already created.

In our present legal regime, some of this content is free; some is controlled. A poet has a copyright on his or her poetry. Others cannot simply take and reproduce it without the copyright holder's permission. The same with plays and novels: A play that is close enough to the plot of a novel is a derivative work. Copyright law gives the copyright holder control over these derivative works. Musical chords cannot be controlled; the design of public buildings cannot be copyrighted. These bits of content in these traditions are free, even if the control created by copyright is strong.

But this control is still limited—indeed, it is *constitutionally* limited. While a poet or author has the right to control copies of his or her work, that right is limited by the rights of "fair use." Regardless of the will of the owners of a copyright, others have a defense against copyright infringement if their use of the copyrighted work is within the bounds of "fair use." Quoting a bit of a poem to demonstrate how it scans, or making a copy of a chapter of a novel for one's own critical use—these are paradigmatic examples of use that is "fair" even if the copyright owner forbids it.

A similar limitation protects the historian. For content to be controlled, it must be "creative." Facts on their own are not "creative." As the Supreme Court has said, "[T]he sine qua non of copyright is originality. To qualify for copyright protection, a work must be original to the author. . . . [But] facts

do not owe their origin to an act of authorship. The distinction is one between creation and discovery."[3] Thus, facts remain in the commons for anyone to draw upon—even if these facts were discovered only because of the
hard work of some investigator. Hard work does not entitle someone to a
copyright. Only "creativity" does. Thus facts remain a resource that—
constitutionally—cannot be subject to a system of legal control.

So too with all creative works—eventually. Disney, for example, did not
license the right to make *The Hunchback of Notre Dame* or *Pocahontas*.
These works, though originally copyrighted, are no longer subject to copyright's control. Copyright is, in the United States, at least, constitutionally
required to be for a "limited time." After that limited time, the work falls
into the public domain—free of restraint, so that "second comers," as Judge
Learned Hand described them, "might do a much better job than the originator" with the original idea.[4]

Or at least that's the theory, though Congress has done its best in recent
years to ignore this theory. The distinctive feature of modern American
copyright law is its almost limitless bloating—its expansion both in scope
and in duration. The framers of the original Copyright Act would not begin
to recognize what the act has become.

Scope: The first Copyright Act gave authors of "maps, charts, and books"
an exclusive right to control the publishing and vending of these works, but
only if their works had been "published," only after the works were registered with a copyright registry, and only if the authors were Americans. (Our
outrage at China notwithstanding, we should remember that before 1891,
the copyrights of foreigners were not protected in the United States. We
were born a pirate nation.)[5]

This initial protection did not restrict "derivative" works: one was free to
translate an original work into a foreign language,[6] and one was free to make
a play out of a novel without the original author's permission. And because
of the burdens of registering, most works were not copyrighted. Between
1790 and 1799, 13,000 titles were published in America, but only 556 copyright registrations were filed.[7] The vast majority of creative work was free for
others to use; and the work that was protected was protected only for limited
purposes.

Time, with a little help from lobbyists, works changes. After two centuries
of copyright statutes, the scope of copyright has exploded, and the reach of
copyright is now universal. There is no registration requirement—every creative act reduced to a tangible medium is now subject to copyright protec-

tion. Your e-mail to your child or your child's finger painting: both are automatically protected.

This protection is not just against competing publications. The target is not simply piracy. Any act of "copying" is presumptively regulated by the statute; any derivative use is within the reach of this regulation. We have gone from a regime where a tiny part of creative content was controlled to a regime where most of the most useful and valuable creative content is controlled for every significant use.

Duration. The first Congress to grant copyright gave authors an initial term of 14 years, which could be renewed for 14 years if the author was living. The current term is the life of the author plus 70 years—which, for an author like Irving Berlin, would mean a protection of 140 years. More disturbingly, we have come to this expanded term through an increasingly familiar practice in Congress of extending the term of copyright both prospectively (to works not yet created) and retrospectively (to works created and still under copyright).

These extensions are relatively new. In the first hundred years, Congress retrospectively extended the term of copyright once. In the next fifty years, it extended the term once again. But in the last forty years, Congress has extended the term of copyright retrospectively eleven times. Each time, it is said, with only a bit of exaggeration, that Mickey Mouse is about to fall into the public domain, the term of copyright for Mickey Mouse is extended.[8]

You might think that there is something a bit unfair about a regime where Disney can make millions off stories that have fallen into the public domain, but no one else but Disney can make money off Disney's work—apparently forever. You'd be right about that, but we'll consider the fairness (and more important, the constitutionality) in greater detail later on. It is enough for now simply to recognize that even if the scope of controlled content has grown, in principle there is to be a constitutional limitation on this expansion. Some content is to remain in the commons, even if most useful content remains subject to control.

CONTROL, AS I have argued, is not necessarily bad. Copyright is a critical part of the process of creativity; a great deal of creativity would not exist without the protections of the law. Without the law, the incentives to produce creative work would be vastly reduced. Large-budget films could not be produced; many books would not get written.[9] Copyright is therefore an integral and crucial part of the creative process. And as it has expanded, it has expanded the opportunities for creativity.

But just because some control is good, it doesn't follow that more is better.[10] As Judge Richard A. Posner has written, "[T]he absence of copyright protection is, paradoxical as this may seem, a benefit to authors as well as a cost to them."[11] It is a benefit because, as we've seen already, creative works are both an input and an output in the creative process; if you raise the cost of the input, you get less of the output.

More important, limited protection has always been the rule. Never has Congress embraced or the Supreme Court permitted a regime that guaranteed perfect control by copyright owners over the *use* of their copyrighted material. As the Supreme Court has said, "[T]he Copyright Act does not give a copyright holder control over all uses of his copyrighted work."[12]

Instead, Congress has historically struck a balance between assuring that copyright owners are compensated and assuring that an adequate range of material remains in the public domain for others to draw upon and use. And this is especially true when Congress has confronted new technologies.

Consider the example of piano rolls. In the early 1870s, Henri Fourneaux invented the player piano, which recorded music on a punch tape as a pianist played the music.[13] The result was a high-quality copy (relative to the poor quality of phonograph recordings at the time) of music, which could then be copied and played any number of times on other machines. By 1902, there were "about seventy-five thousand player pianos in the United States, and over one million piano rolls were sold."[14]

Authors of sheet music complained, saying that their content had been stolen. In terms that echo the cries of the recording industry today, copyright holders charged that these commercial entities were making money off their content, in violation of the copyright law.

The Supreme Court disagreed. Though the content the piano player played was taken from sheet music, it was not, the Court held, a "copy" of the music that it, well, copied.[15] Piano roll manufacturers (and record companies, too) were therefore free to "steal" the content of the sheet music to make money with their new inventions.

Congress responded quickly to the Court's decision by changing the law. But the change was an interesting compromise. The new law did not give copyright holders perfect control over their copyrighted material. In granting authors a "mechanical reproduction right," Congress gave authors the exclusive right to decide whether and on what terms a recording of their music could be made. But once a recording had been made, others had the right (upon paying two cents per copy) to make subsequent recordings of the same music—*whether or not the original author granted permission.* This was a "compulsory licensing right," which Congress granted copiers of copyrighted music to assure that the original owners of the copyrighted works would not acquire too much control over subsequent innovation with that work.[16]

The effect of this compromise, though limiting the rights of original authors, was to expand the creative opportunity of others. New performers had the right to break into the market, by taking music made famous by others and rerecording it, after the payment of a small compulsory fee. Again, the amount of this fee was set by the statute, not by the market power of the author. It therefore was a far less powerful "exclusive right" than the exclusive right granted to other authors.[17]

This balance is the rule, not the exception, when Congress has confronted a new technology affecting creative rights. It did the same thing with the first real "Napster" in our history—cable television. Cable TV was born by stealing the content of others and reselling that content to consumers. Suppliers of cable services would set up an antenna, capture the commercial broadcasts made by television stations, and then resell those broadcasts to their customers.

The copyright holders did not like this "theft." Twice they asked the Supreme Court to shut cable TV down. Twice the Court said no.[18] So it fell to Congress to strike a balance between cable TV and copyright holders. Congress in turn followed the model set by player pianos: cable TV had to pay for the content it broadcast, but the content holders did not have an absolute right to grant or deny the right to broadcast its content. Instead, cable TV got a compulsory licensing system to guarantee that cable operators would be able to get permission to broadcast content at a relatively modest level. Thus content holders, or broadcasters, couldn't leverage their power in the television broadcasting market into power in the cable services market. Innovation in the latter field was protected from power in the former.[19]

These are not the only examples of Congress striking a balance between compensation and control. For a time there was a compulsory license for jukeboxes; there is a compulsory license for music and certain pictorial works in noncommercial television and radio broadcasts; there is a compulsory licensing scheme governing satellite television systems, digital audio home recorders, and digital audio transmissions.[20]

These "compromises" give the copyright holder a guarantee of compensation without giving the copyright holder perfect control over the use of its copyrighted material. In the language of modern law and economics, these rules protect authors through a "liability rule" rather than a "property rule."[21] They are perfect instances of the special character of copyright's protection, as they represent the aim to give authors not perfect control of their copyrighted work, but a balanced right that does what the Constitution requires—"promote progress."

Thus, while Congress has expanded the scope of rights protected by the Copyright Clause, as technologies have changed, it has balanced the rights of access against these increases in protection. These balances, however, are not, on balance, even: though limits have been drawn, the net effect is increased control. The unavoidable conclusion about changes in the scope of copyright's protections is that the extent of "free content"—meaning content that is not controlled by an exclusive right—has never been as limited as it is today. More content is controlled by law today than ever in our past. In addition to limited compulsory rights, an author is free to take from work published before 1923; is free to take noncreative work (facts) whenever published; and is free to use, consistent with fair use, a limited degree of others' work. Beyond that, however, the content of our culture is controlled by an ever-expanding scope of copyright.

PHYSICAL

AT THE content layer, I've argued, the law aims to strike a balance between access and control. Copyrights grant control, but copyrights are constitutionally and statutorily limited to ensure some uncontrolled access. Some parts are controlled; some parts remain free.

No such balance exists at the physical layer, and for the most part, that's a good thing, too. Writing is produced and published on paper; paper is a physical good; in our economy, physical goods are fully controlled by the market. Films require film stock; nondigital film stock is extremely expensive; no right to steal this physical stock exists in our society. Market control is the rule at the physical layer; access is at the pleasure of the property owner.

This control is largely benign, at least where markets are competitive.

If the market is not competitive, then power at the physical layer can become harmful. Control at the physical layer can, in at least some contexts, be leveraged into another layer.[22] But for this danger, antitrust law is an adequate remedy. As long as the other layers remain relatively free, the control here is not inherently troubling.

The problem, of course, is that these other layers are not relatively free — or at least they weren't free in the dark ages. They were increasingly not free for content; they were especially not free at the layer of code.

CODE

THE CORE constraint on artistic creativity in real space is at the code layer — the constraint on whose work gets produced and distributed where.

The writer becomes an author when his or her work is published. Publication is a process controlled by editors. Editors at *The New York Times* decide what goes on their pages. Editors at Basic Books decide which books they will print. No one has a right to enter Basic Books and steal access to its printing presses. Nor does anyone have a right to demand that Basic Books transport his texts. The production and distribution of printed material are a wholly privatized activity.

The same is true for music. Rock bands are plenty; many write their own content; most of that content (fortunately, perhaps) never gets heard beyond a neighborhood garage. Whether the work of a musician gets distributed broadly depends upon the decisions of publishers. Record companies choose what gets floated in the market; radio stations (in effect) get paid to play what record companies choose.[23]

So too with television. You are free to buy commercial time on television, and in some markets you are free to buy program time. But unless you're Ross Perot, these freedoms don't matter much. What gets played on TV is the decision of network owners; what gets broadcast on cable is the choice of cable companies.[24]

These constraints at the code layer plainly affect the choice of creators to create or not. If the editors of a newspaper are conservative, a liberal columnist is less likely to submit a column to that paper. If newspapers generally are unwilling to be critical of U.S. policy, then authors who would criticize U.S. policy are less likely to waste their time penning the criticism. Communists don't waste much time writing Marxist screenplays. Only the deeply ill informed waste their time translating Adam Smith's work to the silver screen. The author is constrained by the expectation of how the code layer will respond. And the code layer, in those dark ages, at least, was importantly controlled. Though the range of outlets expanded dramatically,[25] the concentration in ownership among those outlets increased as well. And the Net is an important constraint on what is made.

Obviously, the code layer interacts with the physical and the content layers. NBC gets to decide what it will broadcast. Because of trespass laws, I can't break into NBC and interrupt the evening news. If I do, I will be arrested for trespass. There is no First Amendment right that I can assert to trespass on NBC's property.

Likewise, NBC's right at the code layer is largely protected against state control by the First Amendment. Congress probably does not have the power to pass a law requiring that NBC give me access to its station. Editorial judgments of television executives are a constitutionally protected right at the code layer.

Commerce

ISSUES OF control matter not just to artists, and the dark ages did more than constrain budding Frank Sinatras. Indeed, among the most significant aspects of the Internet revolution has been the liberation it has given to commerce — not just to commerce in the mode of IBM or GM, but to commerce of the different. The commons of the Net exploded opportunities for commerce that would not otherwise have existed. And this explosion was not, given the architecture of telecommunications before the Net, predicted.

We can see this point quite quickly in two contexts that have been dramatically affected by the Internet — one in the context of coding, the other in the expansion of the market. Both of these contexts were quite different before the Internet, again because of the constraints imposed upon them by the architectures of real space. The opportunities of both have been changed as the technology of the Internet has changed.

CODING

IN 1972, Robert Fano, then a researcher at MIT, published a dark and pressing essay titled "On the Social Role of Computer Communications."[26] Fano's fear was that access to computing resources would be increasingly centralized, and that this centralization would do a great damage to democracy. As the power to understand and manipulate data about the world was held by a smaller and smaller number of people, the skew to democracy caused by this concentration would only increase: what was needed, Fano argued, was a different *architecture* for computer communications, one not centralized within a small number of organizations, but instead made available generally to many.[27]

Fano had an idea of how to build this different architecture and what this different architecture would look like. To build it would require state intervention to break up the concentrations in computer communications that had emerged. The network thus built would look much like the Internet.

Fano was wrong (though understandably so) about the future. But he wasn't wrong about the past. For computers at the time were expensive devices. Except for universities, programming for them required that you work within an institution that could afford to own one of these devices. If you wanted to work on a large-scale coding project, you needed to be within a company that was producing large-scale code.

For many people, of course, that wasn't a terrible thing. IBM and AT&T were powerful and well-paying companies. Most would consider it a great privilege to work for either.

But if you were not the sort likely to be able to work in these places—if you lived in South Dakota, where there weren't many IBM coding plants, or in China, where not many coding companies were allowed—then this reality was an important constraint. To author code in this world required working within large, typically American, corporations. And for many, this meant they could not author code at all. Just as with research in nuclear science today, the ability to do this research was limited to those who worked for specific organizations.

Again, this barrier is easy to understand. No conspiracy is needed to explain it. Computers were valuable resources; not every Joe could or should have access to play around with them. The economic and processing constraints mean that the system couldn't well leave itself open for others to take. The restrictions here were unfortunate and unintended consequences of economic constraints imposed elsewhere.

Here again we can understand these constraints in terms of Benkler's model. The physical layer of the "computer-communications" architecture was controlled; the very nature of its expense forced users to locate to the machines. Locating the machines in particular places made it easy to control access. The logic of the machine may have been open, but only those with permission were allowed in the "machine room." And finally, while the source code for these machines may not have been controlled (content layer, open), the small number of these machines meant that the value of the open code was limited. Coding, and the creativity realized in coding, was dictated by this architecture that mandated control.

This feature of the dark ages, then, limited the supply of resources to a market of production. Only those in a particular place, only those willing to work within a given structure, could work within coding projects. A wide range of talent was thereby excluded from the practice of coding. The ease with which those resources might be shared with many outside a single organization was limited by the technologies of computer communications that Fano described.

MARKETS

SO TOO are markets constrained. Technology most dramatically affects the extent of the market. The more interconnected markets are, the easier it is for goods from one area to affect the price of goods in another area. Geography is a physical constraint on that interconnection—in real space, greater distance means greater cost. But information supported by broad distributional channels can balance the constraint of geography.

Competition laws and constitutional norms keep this transportation system competitive. Competition laws make it hard for distributors to restrict or control distribution. The Dormant Commerce Clause of the U.S. Constitution makes it hard for states to bias distribution to favor themselves. These legal constraints balance natural tendencies among commercial and political actors. They produce a relatively competitive interstate market for goods and services.

Still, real space constrains. Even if the market were perfectly competitive, the cost of transportation and the high cost of information restrict the market's scope. If you want to sell very weird widgets, and only a hundred thousand people are within range, then you're not likely to be able to sell enough widgets to make it worthwhile. But if you had the world as your market— if the code layer facilitated broad distribution of selective information about widgets, thus lowering the cost of information—then you might have a market large enough to make your weird widget factory work. As Ronald Coase puts it:

> People talk about increases in improvements in technology, but just as important are improvements in the way in which people make contracts and deals. If you can lower the costs there, you can have more specialization and greater production. . . . By improving the way the market works, you can produce immense benefits, not because it invents new technologies, but because it enables new technologies to be used.[28]

The net of these layers of control in real space is relatively simple to map. Creativity may well be inspired by the protection these systems of control establish. But it is also constrained by the limits that these systems of control impose. I can write what I will, but what gets published is a function of what publishers like. I can sing in the shower, but before we sing "Happy Birthday" in a large crowd, we had better call a lawyer.[29] My home movies can be shown in my living room, but art students should not expect their films to be shown in theaters. And freedom of speech notwithstanding, no one has the right to fifteen minutes of NBC's airtime. Creativity in the dark ages lives in a world largely without a commons. Permission of others is the necessary condition of one's work being seen elsewhere.

NOW AGAIN, unlike in Lenin's Russia, these systems of control are not the product of conspiracy. The constraints that require control in these different markets for resources are real. Economics is the science of choice in the context of scarcity; it is a positive (if dismal) science that takes the world as it finds it. We can no more will a world where real-space printing presses were free than we can will a spacecraft that could fly as fast as the starship *Enterprise*.

So by contrasting this economy governed by layers of control with an economy governed by large swaths of the commons, I don't mean to criticize every system of control. Whether control is necessary for a particular good in a particular context depends upon the context—upon the technologies of that context and the character of the resource. Resources held in common in one context (among friends or in a small community) may need to be controlled in another (in a city or between tribes).

In particular, to the extent a resource is physical—to the extent it is rivalrous—then organizing that resource within a system of control makes good sense. This is the nature of real-space economics; it explains our deep intuition that shifting more to the market always makes sense. And following this practice for real-space resources has produced the extraordinary progress that modern economic society has realized.

A part, however, cannot speak for the whole, especially when changes in technology render the assumptions of the old obsolete. Even if the control model makes perfect sense in the world of things, the world of things is not the digital world. We may need fences and perfect control to assure that the world of things runs efficiently. That's what the prosperity of the market, property, and contract teach us.

But perfect control is not necessary in the world of ideas. Nor is it wise. That's the lesson our Framers taught us—in both the limits they placed on the Exclusive Rights Clause and the expanse of protection for free speech they established in the First Amendment. The aim of an economy of ideas is to create incentives to produce and then to move what has been produced to an intellectual commons as soon as can be. The lack of rivalrousness undercuts the justification for governmental regulation. The extreme protections of property are neither needed for ideas nor beneficial.

For here is the key: *The digital world is closer to the world of ideas than to the world of things.* We, in cyberspace, that is, have built a world that is close to the world of ideas that nature (in Jefferson's words) created: stuff in cyberspace can "freely spread from one to another over the globe, for the moral and mutual instruction of man, and improvement of his condition," because we have (at least originally) built cyberspace such that content is, "like fire, expansible over all space, without lessening [its] density at any point, and like the air in which we breathe, move, and have our physical being, incapable of confinement, or exclusive appropriation."

The digital world is closer to ideas than things, but still it is not quite there. It is not quite true that the stuff in cyberspace is perfectly nonrivalrous in the sense that ideas are. Capacity is a constraint; bandwidth is not unlimited.[30] But these are tiny flaws that cannot justify jumping from the largely free to the perfectly controlled. There are problems of coordination and constraints of scarcity. But the solution to these problems is not necessarily systems of control or better techniques of excludability. That cyberspace has flourished as it has largely because of the commons it has built should lead us to ask whether we should tilt more to the free in organizing this space than to the controlled that organizes real space.

Put differently: These imperfections in the capacity of cyberspace—that together may make it more rivalrous than ideas are—should not by themselves force us to treat the resources that cyberspace produces as we would treat real-space resources. If by resisting the model of perfect control we gain something important, then we should do so.

IN THE context of the media, we can be a bit stronger than this. Over the past twenty years, we have seen two changes in the media that seem to pull in different directions. On the one hand, technology has exploded the number of media outlets—increasing the number of television and radio stations as well as newspapers and magazines. On the other hand, concentration in the ownership of these media outlets has also increased. This increase in concentration especially should lead us to ask whether the control enabled in real space should carry over to cyberspace.

The statistics about increased concentration in ownership are undeniable and extraordinary. In 1947, 80 percent of daily newspapers were independently owned; in 1989, only 20 percent were independently owned. Most of the business of the nation's eleven thousand magazines was controlled by twenty companies in 1981; in 1988, that number had fallen to three.[31] Books are much the same. The independent publishing market was strong just thirty years ago; with Bertelsmann's purchase of Random House in 1998, the industry is now much more concentrated, dominated by just seven firms.[32] The significance of this concentration in books is no doubt less than that in film or other important media. There are still many independent publishers, and the range and diversity of book publishing are quite large. But the inertia is in the direction of concentration. And this inertia may be a source of concern.

Music is even more concentrated.[33] The five largest music groups in the United States account for over 84 percent of the U.S. market.[34] The same is true of radio. The top three broadcasters control at least 60 percent of the stations in the top one hundred U.S. markets.[35] The same is true in film. In 1985, the twelve largest U.S. theater companies controlled 25 percent of the screens; "by 1998, that figure was 61 percent and climbing rapidly."[36] Six firms accounted for over 90 percent of theater revenues in 1997; 132 out of 148 of the "widely distributed" films in 1997 were produced by "companies that had distribution deals with one of the six majors."[37] With this concentration, there has been a dramatic drop in foreign films. In the mid-1970s, foreign films accounted for 10 percent of box office receipts. By the late 1990s, the number had fallen to 0.5 percent. [38] Cable and television are no better. In 1999, Robert McChesney could write that "six firms now possess effective monopolistic control over more than 80 percent of the nation, and seven firms control nearly 75 percent of cable channels and programming."[39] Those numbers are now much more extreme.[40] Professor Ben Bagdikian summarizes the result as follows: "[D]espite more than 25,000 outlets in the United States, 23 corporations control most of the business in daily newspapers, magazines, television, books, and motion pictures."[41] The top firms in this set vastly outbalance the remainder. The top six have more annual media revenue than the next twenty combined.[42]

The reasons for this increase in concentration are many. I don't mean to argue, as many others have, that we should necessarily consider this in-

creasing concentration inefficient or illegal. There are important efficiencies to be gained by the mergers of large media interests; important gains in
coverage have also been realized. And while the conspiracy theories are
many and practically unending in scope, we need not believe media conspirators are behind this radical change. The government has loosened its
restrictions on concentration, sometimes for good economic reasons; technologies of transmission have changed to the great benefit of all; and the
consequence has been an extraordinary concentration in media production.[43]

But whatever the reason, the results are staggering. And they extend beyond the mere structure of the market. They affect its character as well. The
resulting mix of media is strikingly homogenous. The companies that make
up the handful of international conglomerates are cookie-cutter variations
of one another. Some are slightly larger in music than in film; others are
slightly more American in ownership and content. But if you had to char-
acterize the differences in philosophy or attitude among these different
media conglomerates, it would be extremely hard (unlike, for example, the
situation with newspapers in Britain): there are no clear philosophical or
ideological differences among them.[44]

Many have quite rightly worried that this control by a few who are not
very different from each other will have a significant effect on the kind of
news that is reported. Andrew Kreig tells a compelling story of the effect of
chain management on an American newspaper, driving the respected *Hart-
ford Courant* to more excessive, sensationalistic reporting.[45] The paper he
describes is not dissimilar from many others. There are many stories about
corporate owners influencing the news within their organizations—steering
the news away from stories that reflect negatively upon those corporate owners.[46] Congressman Newt Gingrich expressly recommended as much in
1997, when he told the Georgia Chamber of Commerce that business leaders and advertisers "ought to take more direct command of the news-
room."[47]

Even if we ignore this most blatant form of bias, if the media are owned
by a handful of companies, each basically holding the very same ideals, how
much diversity can we expect in the production of media content? How
critical can we believe these media will be? How committed to testing the
status quo is this form of organization—itself so dependent upon the status
quo—likely to be?[48]

You don't need to be a radical to be worried about this trend. Even the
most committed pro-market ideologues could at least hope for a broader

range of competition in ideas and perspective. There is good evidence that competition improves the quality of newspapers.[49] And there is a general and broad view that the only justification for the power that the media has is that there is a broad range of views with the same power.[50] No more. Never in our history has the concentration of media outlets been greater. Even a believer in the invisible hand might hope that this hand might muck things up a bit.

SOMETHING *has* mucked things up a bit. Something has entered the field in a way that could make these concentrations change—not the government or a regulation imposed by the government, but the architecture of the Internet we have been describing so far.

For the essence of this power in the handful of media companies that now dominate media internationally is control over distribution and the power it can promise artists.[51] Movies run in certain places only; getting films into those places is quite hard. CDs are distributed through predictable channels of distribution—including radio stations, whose choice of what to play or not to play determines which content is popular or not. Breaking into this distribution channel is likewise extremely hard.

The same is true with cable. While many thought that increasing the number of cable channels would mean more valuable competition, in fact, the fragmentation of channels simply induced more commercialization. Fragmentation makes it easier to "slice and dice people demographically" and "maximize . . . advertising revenues."[52] Cable has thus not been a source of new innovation (unsurprisingly, as we saw, because the physical, logical, and content layers are all controlled). Instead, as "one cable executive put it in 1998, 'Most entrepreneurs have already gotten the word that the cable field is closed.' "[53]

But the essence of the Internet that I've described so far is an architecture for distribution that admits of no controllers, architecture that neither needs nor permits the centralization of control that real-space structures demand. And while this lack of control won't on its own mean Hollywood will fail, it will mean that the success of any particular kind of content is more convincingly a function of the desire for that content. Or at least, as we'll see, this is what the traditional media fear.[54]

8

Innovation from

the Internet

IN BOTH artistic and commercial contexts in real space, there are barriers that keep innovators out. These barriers, for the most part, have been economic and real: the real cost of resources is a real constraint for most who would create. These barriers are obviously not absolute; ours is an extraordinarily creative culture; plainly some overcome the limits I've described. Indeed, if markets were perfectly competitive, one might imagine the optimal number that overcomes the barriers I have described. But markets are not perfect, and costs can be regretted. Hence these barriers are enough to keep innovators away whom we would not otherwise want to exclude. The hassle, the uncertainty, the absolute cost: no doubt these together chill many.

These barriers in real space are a function of its nature or, we could say, its architecture. Not "architecture" in its ordinary sense—buildings and streets—but architecture in a much broader sense: architecture in the sense of the set of physical constraints that one finds, even if these are constraints that man has made. The constraints that are reflected through economics are constraints of architecture in this sense. You can't perfectly and costlessly copy a nutritious meal; that takes real resources. You can't costlessly and instantly move your car from one coast to another: that takes time and energy. The constraints of real space are built into the nature of real space, and though technology presses against this nature, it is only so effective. Real constraints remain.

Cyberspace has a different architecture. Its nature is therefore different as well. Digital content can be copied perfectly and practically freely. You can move a great deal of content almost freely and instantly. And you can replicate whatever good there is in one place in many places—almost instantaneously. The barriers of cyberspace in its natural state are radically different from the barriers in real space.

"In its natural state." I spent many pages in *Code* arguing against just this way of speaking. Cyberspace has no nature. How it is—what barriers there are—is a function of its design, its code. Thus, in this abstract sense, it makes no sense to speak about the nature of this system that is wholly designed by man. Its nature is as man designs it.

But cyberspace at its birth did have a certain character. I've described some of it here and more of it elsewhere.[1] The feature of its character at its birth that is most significant for our purposes here is an architecture that disabled the power of any in the middle to control how those at the ends interacted: this is the principle of end-to-end. This design choice of end-to-end assures that those with a new idea get to sell that new idea, the views of the network owner notwithstanding.

This principle can operate at very different levels. I described it initially in the context of a network design. I have argued that the same principle applies to open code. Spectrum organized in a commons would implement the principle in the physical layer. The same idea can operate within any social system. Within law, this is the principle of subsidiarity—decisions are made at the lowest level appropriate for the decision. Within politics, it is a principle embraced by libertarians, who urge not no control, but control by the individual.

We can argue about how far this principle should extend in politics. Tomes have been written about how far it should extend in law. But my aim is to push its embrace in the context of creativity. In this domain, at least, our presumption should be libertarian. And we should build that presumption into the architecture of the space.

AS THE dot.coms crash and the pundits ask whether there was anything really new in the new economy of the Internet, it is useful to frame just what this new space has given us so far. That is my aim in the balance of this chapter. I want to show how we already have something new, or at least originally did. My hope is to link instances of innovation to changes in the layers of control that the Internet effected. This is not a survey; my examples are illustrative, not representative. But by the end we should have a clearer sense of the link between these different commons and the innovation these commons produced.

NEW PRODUCTS FROM THE NET

AT THE code layer, the Internet is a set of protocols. These protocols make new digital products possible. These are products that could not, or would not, have been built before the Net. Among these we could include the dynamically generated maps with driving directions;[2] massive translation engines, covering scores of languages, translating texts and Web sites on the fly;[3] and on-line dictionaries covering hundreds of languages that otherwise would not be available except in the largest libraries.[4]

But let's focus on a few of these products and their relationship to the architecture of the Net.

HTML Books

PHYSICAL BOOKS are extremely durable information sources. They are stable and preserve relatively well. They read well in many contexts; they will be a central part of culture for the next century, at least.

But there are things paper books can't do, and constraints on paper books that limit how far the knowledge they carry is carried. These limits thus suggest the place of a different kind of book—the "HTML book," or a book produced for the World Wide Web.

HTML books are the passion of Eric Eldred. Eldred was a computer programmer in the navy. In the mid-1980s, he became aware of the Internet. The Internet then, of course, was not the World Wide Web—the Web would not appear for another five years. Nonetheless, the Net facilitated an exchange of information long before the Web made that exchange hypertextual.

When the Web came on-line, Eldred wanted to experiment to see what the Web might do for books. Eldred's daughter had an assignment to read Hawthorne's *The Scarlet Letter.* He tried to locate the text on-line. What he found was essentially unusable. So Eldred decided to make a version that was usable. He cleaned up the text, added a few links, and created his first HTML book—a book designed to be read on the World Wide Web.

An HTML book can do things that a paper book cannot. The author of an HTML book can add links to aid the reader or to guide the reader to other related texts. It can be easily searched and copied into other texts. And because it lives on the Web, it is available to anyone anywhere—including to people who can't afford to purchase that particular work and to machines that index the work to be included within search engines.

An HTML book is a derivative work under copyright law. If the original text is protected by copyright, then to publish a derivative work, you would need the permission of the original copyright holder. *The Scarlet Letter*, however, is a work in the public domain. So Eldred was free to take that work and do with it as he wanted.

This started Eldred on a hobby that soon became a cause. With the publication of Hawthorne, Eldred began Eldritch Press—a free site devoted to publishing HTML versions of public domain works (http://eldred.ne. mediaone.net/). With a relatively cheap computer and an inexpensive scanner, Eldred took books that had fallen into the public domain and made them available for others on the Net. Soon his site had pulled together an extraordinary collection of work, including a large collection of the works of Oliver Wendell Holmes (Sr., not the Supreme Court justice).

Eldred, of course, is not the only on-line publisher of public domain works. Michael Hart's Project Gutenberg has been publishing public domain texts on the Internet since 1970. But the point is not the uniqueness of Eldred's efforts. Indeed, the point is exactly the opposite: The physical and code layers of the Net enabled this kind of innovation—for Eldred and for anyone else. The physical layer was cheap; the code layer was open. His only constraint would come at the content layer—but more on that later.[5]

MP3

INTERNET TEXTS are not the only innovation enabled by the Net. Much more dramatic is the innovation in audio and video technologies. MP3 technologies are at the core of the audio changes. They too can be considered a new product that the Internet has made available.

As I have described, MP3 is the name of a compression technology. It is a tool for compacting the size of a digital music recording. It works in part by removing parts of the file that are inaudible to humans. Dogs would notice the difference an MP3 file makes; most of the rest of us are blissfully ignorant.

Blissfully—because this deafness of ours means that music can be made available on the Internet in an efficient and simple way with relatively little loss in fidelity. A five-minute song can be compressed to a file just 6 megabytes in size. And as connection speeds increase, that 6 MB file can be shipped to someone else in less than a minute.

This means that the Net becomes a possible distributor for music, and therefore it inspires a new kind of production: music written and performed for sampling on the Internet. This is not just a substitute for CDs or audio-tapes. The cheap distribution—at different levels of quality—makes it possible to sample music in a different way. This in turn expands the market for music, as more can be tried without the commitment to purchase.

Film

A SIMILAR change has happened with film. As I suggested at the start of this book, the costs of production of film have dropped dramatically as digital equipment has become more powerful and less expensive. We are soon to enter a time when filmmakers will be able to produce high-quality film for digital devices at 1 percent of the cost of the same production with traditional tools. Apple Computer is fueling this demand, with cheap, high-quality digital film technologies bundled into its popular iMac computer. This same technology, costing a few thousand dollars today, would have cost $150,000 just five years ago.

This drop in the cost of production is due to changes in the physical layer that enables film production. It is also supported at the code layer by a wide range of tools for manipulating and editing digital images. These together create an important blurring of the line between amateur and professional. As a recent Apple ad put it, "And now you're the purveyor of, you're the generator of, you're the author of *great stuff.*"

How great, of course, is a matter of taste. In 2001, Apple proudly advertised the first iMac movie purchased by HBO—a short dealing with teenage pregnancy, produced by a fourteen-year-old kid.[6] This is not quite Hollywood in the den, but it points to a future that just ten years ago could not have been imagined—a broad range of film content produced by a wider range of creators and, in turn, potentially available to others.[7]

Lyric Servers and Culture Databases

POPULAR CULTURE is diverse and expansive. Finding information about this culture, however, is often quite difficult. Fans may be many, but the systematic cataloging of data about such creativity has, so far, been quite lacking.

Think in particular about music lyrics. Music is an important part of our life. We grow up listening to songs on the radio; we buy records and listen to those songs over and over. Our ability to recall music is extraordinary; a few bars from a song we heard thirty years before will bring back memories of a certain party or an evening at a concert.

Our memory is of both songs and lyrics. But it is often extremely hard to locate either. You might remember a particular song, but recall only a few words. Or you might remember the name of the song, but be unable to find its author.

The Internet provided an obvious solution to this problem, and by the mid-1990s, there was an explosion of lyric sites across the Web. These sites had grown from earlier sites located on the Net. But they quickly became extremely popular locations where fans might find the words that were echoing around in their heads.

These sites did not make money. They were produced by fans and hobbyists. But though there was no money to be earned, thousands participated in the building of these sites. And these thousands produced a far better, more complete, and richer database of culture than commercial sites had produced. For a time, one could find an extraordinary range of songs archived throughout the Web.

Slowly these services have migrated to commercial sites. This migration means the commercial sites can support the costs of developing and maintaining this information. And in some cases, with some databases, the Internet provided a simple way to collect and link data about music in particular.[8]

Here the CDDB—or "CD database"—is the most famous example. As MP3 equipment became common, people needed a simple way to get information about CD titles and tracks onto the MP3 device. Of course, one could type in that information, but why should everyone have to type in that information? Many MP3 services thus enabled a cooperative process. When a user installed a CD, the system queried the central database to see whether that CD had been cataloged thus far. If it had, then the track and title information was automatically transferred to the user. If it had not, then the users were given a chance to contribute to the system by adding the records necessary to complete the database for that recording.

This meant that quickly, all but the most obscure music was entered into this large cooperative database. And this database itself then became a product that otherwise would not have been available generally.

Each of these new products grows out of the different economics of digital production and the ability of innovators to add value at the edge of the network. Some surprise; others are obvious extensions; and still others are ideas that are timeless but possible only in this time. But regardless of their character, they were enabled by the environment of innovation of the original Net.

NEW MARKETS

NEW PRODUCTS beget new markets. And new modes of distribution (including the removal of barriers to distribution) induce the creation of new markets for existing products as well.

Consider just one example: the production of poetry. The market for poetry is extremely small; the burden in getting poems published is exceptionally great. These real-space constraints translate into an extraordinarily difficult market for poets.

But using both the cheap distribution of the Internet and tools for better structuring the delivery of content, the market for poetry on the Internet has taken off. There has been an explosion of sites dedicated to producing and distributing poetry. Poetry Daily, for example, launched in 1997, receives over 150,000 visitors a month. At peak usage, 12,000 users come to the site per day. And over 16,000 subscribe to a regular content newsletter.[9]

These sites are not simply tools for delivering poems more cheaply. Their technology also enables better control over how that content is consumed. Some sites have technologies for guiding the reading of poetry—thereby making it accessible to or understandable by a much wider audience.[10] Others enable the audio reading of poetry, similarly enabling a market for the blind that otherwise would have been restricted.[11] These tools in turn expand the reach of this form of creativity to people who otherwise would not consume this poetry.

NEW MEANS OF DISTRIBUTION

THE MOST dramatic potential for affecting creativity is, as Coase described earlier, the lowering of the transaction costs of distribution, and hence the expansion of the extent of the market. Here there are a number of well-known examples that we will consider again when we examine changes in copyright law and their effects on the Net.

My.MP3

THE COMPRESSION technique of MP3 is "free" in the sense I have described it: anyone is allowed to develop technologies that use it.[12] And through the 1990s, thousands of such technologies developed. It was extremely easy to find a program on the Net that would "rip" the contents of your CDs—meaning copy the music in an MP3 format so that you could store the music on your machine. And many MP3 players were offered for free or for sale.

But though MP3 files were small relative to their original data file, they were still quite large to be sent across the Internet. While a fast connection could chomp through an MP3 song in a few seconds, on a standard telephone connection it could take twenty to thirty minutes.

This restriction in bandwidth gave birth to an important industry of streaming technologies. The idea was quite simple: Rather than downloading the full copy of music and then playing it, streaming technologies allow the user to stream the desired content and play it at the same time. No copies of the file must be made first, which means the user need not waste time waiting for the music to be delivered.

RealAudio was the innovator here, though its idea was soon mimicked by Microsoft and Apple. RealAudio sold tuners that enabled people to tune in to audio, and then video, content. That content was compressed and streamed across the Net.

MP3.com took this idea further. Started in 1997, MP3.com has no real relation to the technology MP3. It didn't invent the technology, and it had no exclusive license. Nor did its founder, Michael Robertson, have any real relation to the music industry. Robertson was simply an entrepreneur who saw the Internet as a great new opportunity. MP3.com was started to find new ways to use the technology to produce and distribute music.

MP3.com pushed production by encouraging artists to produce and distribute music across its site. This was not unique to MP3.com. It was the business model of companies like EMusic.com as well.

But more interesting were MP3.com's new ideas about how to push distribution. The existing labels had a clear idea about how the business worked. Their business, Robertson explains, "is making a bet. They make big bets on a small number of acts, hoping that one of them is the lottery ticket and pays off."[13] And to help make sure their bets paid off, as artist Courtney Love explains, "record companies controlled the proportion and the marketing; only they had the ability to get lots of radio play, and get records into the big chain stores."[14]

When representatives from the existing labels spoke to Robertson, they tried to convince him to follow the same model. "They were all about, okay, we gotta find the next U2 or Backstreet Boys, or whatever. . . . Try to find that one, and promote the heck out of him, and hope we break even." Owning the artist is key to this model; the traditional labels thus demand exclusivity.

But Robertson's model was different.

> I just said, that's not our model. Why don't we let somebody else make the music and produce the music and do whatever they do in the creative process? And we'll just pick up after that creation is already done, and worry about the delivery.[15]

So MP3.com rejected exclusivity (Robertson: "Exclusivity is a very bad thing for content owners") and worked instead on technologies to make it easier for customers to get access to music. And using subscriptions and advertising, the company expected to make this way of getting content pay.

A core feature of this technology was an "automatic" way for popular content to find its way to the top. As Robertson describes it, the key is collecting good data. For "data changes the balance of power." Consumers "listen to the good music, and we'll make sure the good music floats to the top."[16]

The floating follows the listening. The more users listen and download music, the more the music "floats"; and the more the system learns the patterns of who likes what, the more the system can make sure that the music *you* like is likely to float to the top of *your* screen.

MP3.com thus conceives of itself as a "service bureau."

> [Artists] can come and go as they please. . . . You don't even have to agree to exclusively give it to us. It defies all logic in the music industry. I can't tell you how many people came into my office and said, "You don't get it. You don't get the business. I don't know why you're not forcing these guys to give you a piece of their intellectual property. Because you're gonna make the next Madonna, and you're not gonna own the next Madonna."[17]

There was one innovation, however, that earned MP3.com more than the sucker scorn about Madonna. This was the My.MP3 service, launched in January 2000. Using this service, consumers could get access to their music in two different ways. First, through cooperating sites, they could purchase music. Those cooperating sites would then send a CD to the customer but immediately make the music purchased by the customer available in the customer's MP3 account. Once available in a user's account, the customer would be able to stream that music to his or her computer, wherever the customer was. MP3 would then keep a collection of music stored in that account, and give the customer access to it wherever he or she had access to the Web.

The second aspect of My.MP3 was a bit bolder. MP3.com released a program called Beam-it. If you (the customer) had Beam-it installed on your machine, you could insert a CD into the computer, and the MP3.com service would then identify what the CD was. If MP3.com had that CD in its library, it would make that music available to you. Thus, you could take all the CDs you had at home, "beam" them to the MP3 server, and subsequently get access to your music anywhere else you happened to connect to the Web.

Plainly, consumers could do much of this without MP3.com's help. My former colleague at Harvard Jonathan Zittrain was an early on-line music fanatic. He bought a basic computer from Dell Corporation with a large hard drive, and proceeded to copy all his CDs onto the computer. He then connected the computer to his cable modem and designed the system so that wherever he was (and mainly in his office) he could listen to his music. Zittrain thus built a music server like MP3.com which distributed his music on demand.

The difference with MP3.com was that you didn't need to be Zittrain to get your music. Nor did you have to waste the time that Zittrain wasted to copy all of your music. The Beam-it service would recognize your disk in less than ten seconds; you would have access to your music after a few seconds more. There was no need for a large disk drive to store all your music. All the music was stored at MP3.com's servers.

This service by MP3.com made it easier for consumers to get access to the music they had purchased. It was not a service for giving people free access to music. Of course, people could borrow other people's CDs and hence "steal" the content of those CDs if they wanted. But that was possible before MP3.com came along. MP3.com's aim was simply to make it easier to use what you'd already bought.

Napster

NO DOUBT the most famous story of musical "innovation" has been the explosion called Napster—a technology simplifying file sharing for MP3 files. The idea was the brainchild of Shawn Fanning and Sean Parker—in the eyes of many, children themselves.

Fanning and Parker's idea was just this: Individuals had music stored on their computers—think again about the hoarder Zittrain. Others would want copies of that music. Fanning devised a way to engineer a "meeting" between the copies and those wanting them. His system, Napster, would collect a database of who had what. And when someone searched for a particular song, the database would produce a list of who had that song and was on the line at that moment. The user could then select the copy he or she wanted to copy, and the computer would establish a connection between the user and the computer with the copy. The system would function as a kind of music matchmaking service—responsible for finding the links, but not responsible for what happened after that.

Napster is an "ah-ha" technology: you don't quite get its significance until you use it. The experience of opening a Napster search window, rummaging through your memories for songs you'd like to hear, and then, within a few seconds, finding and hearing those songs is extraordinary. As with the lyric database, you can easily find what is almost impossible to locate; as with the MP3 server, you can then hear what you want almost immediately. Music exchanged on Napster is free—in the sense of costing nothing. And at any particular moment, literally thousands of songs are available.

The innovation excited an immediate legal reaction. The Recording Industry Association of America (RIAA) immediately filed suit against Napster for facilitating copyright violation. That may have been a mistake. At the time the RIAA filed suit, the number of Napster users was under two hundred thousand; after the suit hit the press, the number of users grew to fifty-seven million.

In chapter 11, we will consider in some depth the legal questions that Napster raised. Focus for the moment just on the innovation. For what Fanning had done was to find a way to use the dark matter of the Internet—the personal computers connecting the Net. Rather than depending upon content located on a server somewhere—in this strict hierarchical client/server model of computing—Fanning turned to the many individual computers that are linked to the Net. They could be the place where content resides. Using the protocols of the code layer, he was able to find an underutilized asset at the physical layer. Hence the importance of these centralized servers would be reduced.

Many believe the central motivation behind Napster was to find a way to avoid "the copyright police." For some content (but not streaming content), centralized servers are more efficient places for storage. But they are also more efficient places to harbor illegal content. And if it is illegal content that is being stored, the efficiency of the storage gets outweighed by the risk of getting caught.

But if the content is located on many machines set up individually, then the content is hard to find and it becomes difficult to prosecute those harboring it. So Napster imagined that individuals would put up content that would be available for others, but the individuals holding the content would not be so regular as to be targets of prosecution.

These groups, however, would serve a separate function as well. They would induce the exchange of information about preferences among members of these groups. That information would induce an expansion of demand by consumers of this music. And that demand in turn could be satisfied by music from Napster or from the ordinary channels of distribution.

To the extent you view Napster as nothing more than a device for facilitating the theft of content, there is little usefulness in this new mode of distribution. But the extraordinary feature of Napster was not so much the ability to steal content as it is the range of content that Napster makes available. The important fact is not that a user can get Madonna's latest songs for free; it is that one can *find* a recording of New Orleans jazz drummer Jason Marsalis's band playing "There's a Thing Called Rhythm."

This ability competes with the labels, but it doesn't really substitute for the demand they serve. A significant portion of the content served by Napster is music that is no longer sold by the labels.[18] This mode of distribution—whatever copyright problems it has—gives the world access to a range of music that has not existed in the history of music production.

Once you taste this world of almost limitless access to content, it is hard to imagine going back. What Napster did more effectively than any other technology was to demonstrate what a fully enabled "celestial jukebox" might be.[19] Not just for the music that distributors want to push at any particular moment; not just for the music that a large market would demand; but also for practically any recording with any fans using the service anywhere, the music was available.

This represents the end of the progression that began when broadcast

channels started multiplying. When television, for example, is just a few stations, then the producers of television have a great deal of power to guide
the audience as the program director chooses. As the channels multiply,
each channel becomes a competitor of all others. At any one time, the number of competitors for attention has increased, and the effective choice is
much greater.

Napster represents the extreme of this trend. Channels here no longer
channel consumers. Consumers have the broadest range of choices possible. Thus, just as it is for an avid reader in a very large library, the content of
music becomes available for individuals to choose rather than available as
disc jockeys choose.

NEW DEMAND

IN THE stories so far, the Internet affects the content and the applications
that meet existing demand. But this is only one part of how the Net is different from real space and ultimately, I believe, the less interesting part. Far
more important is how the Net changes how people learn what they want
and how these wants might be changed.

Consider here the bright part of Amazon.com. There are many who are
concerned by the emergence of this powerful bookseller. Shifting book sales
to the superstore can't help but reduce sales in the smaller shops.

But to stop here in the analysis is to make the story a zero-sum game when
it is far too soon to know the net effect. The emergence of Amazon.com and
the like has created a boom in demand that could not be built in real space.

The reason is the complexity of our preferences and how hard it is for others to speak to them. Media observers looking at real-space media doubt this
complexity; most media to them look extremely homogeneous. But a
speaker may utter a general message either because he or she wants to say
something bland or because the costs of saying something more specific are
too high. And these costs can be too high either because the message can't
be targeted or because the costs of knowing what each person would want
to hear are prohibitive.

Focus on the last point first—knowing what someone wants to hear. You
all have friends; some of you have more friends than others; some of your
friends are closer than others. But I doubt any of your friends knows your
tastes in music and books as well as Amazon knows mine. After a three-year
relationship, dutifully remembered by Amazon's data-mining engine, Ama-

zon can recommend to me things that I ought to buy. It *advertises* to me, but its advertisements—unlike 99 percent of the ads I see in real space—actually speak to me. They actually say something that I want to hear. And because they speak to me, I listen.

It is technology that makes this possible. There is no editor at Amazon who decides who should read what. There is just a machine. Preference-matching engines are constantly gathering data about what I buy and what others buy; Amazon adds to that data preferences that I express. It has a handy way for me to signal how much I liked something I bought or whether it should exclude something I bought from its data review. And when it lists recommendations, it lets me tell it that I own what it recommends or that I would never buy what it recommends. Amazon knows, based on real data.

This technology for preference matching was not born at Amazon. A company called Firefly first deployed the technology.[20] But the idea spread quickly. And every successful on-line merchant now competes to understand what its customer wants. As Michael Robertson of MP3.com said, "Data changes everything." With the kind of data that can be collected, the Web can deliver a kind of service that would otherwise be impossible.

This technology is in its infancy, but it is old enough for us to catch a glimpse of where it is going. As it matures, the technology (unless stopped) will increasingly be able to predict what you, as an individual, will want; it will increasingly waste less of your time on what you don't want. And this will increase your demand for the things the Net sells.

From the start, there have been skeptics about these technologies. Some fear the loss of privacy resulting from these systems of perpetual monitoring.[21] Others fear that these systems for giving you just what you want will result in increasingly isolated individuals.[22] Noise, the argument goes, helps build communities. My ability to perfectly select what I hear and what I read may help me, but it may harm society. Increasingly isolated individuals are not the stuff that communities are made of.

Both concerns may prove to be true, but I want to put both aside for the moment and focus on the positive consequences of this emerging technology. The most direct effect of this technology is to make data about people's preferences much more usable—usable, that is, in informing others about individual preferences.

These data are a social resource that the architectures of social life have made hard to collect so far. We've had ways of collecting how many people bought DVD X, or book Y, but no good way of collecting how many who bought book X also bought book Y. And just as the invention of a new machine can in turn reduce the cost of some production process, the ability to capture and use this new resource will reduce the costs of advertising dramatically. Rather than technologies that produce 0.5 percent return,[23] these technologies will produce a much greater return at a lower cost.[24]

Thus the architecture of the Net enables a resource otherwise unavailable. And through this resource, a barrier to entry is reduced. For if one of the hardest parts of breaking into music is the cost of promotion, then as long as these data mines remain competitive, lowering the cost of promotion will make it easier to break into music. The same is true with books or any other content. By increasing the demand for a diverse selection of content, and by enabling the cheaper identification of that demand, the Net widens the range of potential contributors.

NEW PARTICIPATION: P2P

FINALLY, CONSIDER an innovation that enables a new kind of participation that many have called the next great revolution for the Internet, and that in light of our discussion of e2e will be quite familiar: the emergence of peer-to-peer (P2P) networks.[25]

A peer-to-peer network is one where the content is being served not by a single central server, but by equal, or "peer," machines linked across the network. Formally, "p2p is a class of applications that take advantage of resources—storage, cycles, content, human presence—available at the edges of the Internet."[26] In the sense I've described, this was the architecture of the original computers on the Internet—there wasn't a set of central servers that the machines connected to; instead, there was a set of e2e protocols that enabled data to be shared among the machines.

But as commerce came to the Net, the character of this architecture changed. As the World Wide Web became more popular, Web servers became dominant. And as servers grew, the equal peer-to-peer structure of the Internet was replaced by the hierarchical structures of client and server.

This was not intended. When Berners-Lee invented the World Wide Web, he didn't really have in mind centralized Web servers broadcasting tons of content to the many; from the very start, he tried to push developers of browsers to develop them as two-way devices—allowing both the viewing and the writing of HTML code. Berners-Lee wanted a peer-to-peer Web, and his technology enabled that. But in the first generation of its deployment, that wasn't how it was deployed.[27] To large ISPs like AOL, the ends are important only in the way customers in a mall are important—they consume the commerce but don't participate in its design.

More recently, however, a change in the Net's architecture has occurred. As machines have become more powerful, and as they have become more reliably and permanently connected to the Net, the possibility of using peers to process and forward data on the Net has increased. Peer-to-peer services are returning to the Internet as machines mature and are persistently on the Net. The character of what can happen is changing, and the potential—if left free to develop—is extraordinary.

Napster is the most famous peer-to-peer technology, even though it is not exactly peer-to-peer. (There is a central server that keeps a database of who has what; the music itself is kept on other people's machines.) But Napster is the horse and buggy in this transportation system. It is only the beginning.

Consider the SETI project. SETI—the Search for Extraterrestrial Intelligence—scans the radio waves for evidence of intelligent life somewhere else in the universe. It does this by recording the noise of the radio spectrum that we receive on planet Earth. This noise is then analyzed by computers, looking for telltale signs of something unexplained.[28]

Who cares about wandering X-Files types?, you might ask. Is this really it? But the point is the potential that SETI evinces. The computation involved in the SETI project is immense, and they soon discovered that the cost of renting computers to process these recorded radio waves was increasingly prohibitive. So researchers at Berkeley had an idea: Facilitate the distribution of chunks of this recorded data to machines across the Net, then enable these machines across the Net to do the computation required on this data. A package of data would be delivered to the participating computer along with a program to be run; that program would run on the data and send it back to the mother ship.

When the SETI@home project first began, within ten days it had 350,000 participants in 203 countries. In four months, it broke a million users. The service grew so fast that it had to stop processing data for a while. The speed at which data was being collected had surpassed the processing speed.

In mid-2000, the system could boast the equivalent of 280,000 years of processing time devoted to the SETI mission.[29]

Just as Napster had latched on to unused disk space, SETI@home had latched on to unused computer cycles living at the edge of the Net. Idle machines could be turned to large-scale cooperative projects.

Others had seen the same point. Before SETI, in response to a challenge by RSA Labs, distributed.net deployed a technology that would enable computers linked to the Net around the world to help distributed.net crack a DES (digital encryption standard)-encrypted message. The first successful crack of a DES-encrypted message was in 1997, by Rocke Verser. His group cracked the message in ninety-six days. By 1999, distributed.net had improved this "distributed technology" (meaning software that ran remotely on a large number of independent machines) sufficiently that one hundred thousand computers around the world—using idle computer time—were able to crack an encrypted message in just twenty-four hours. The government had estimated this cracking would take many years. distributed.net proved the government wrong.

These examples suggest a future that many companies are scrambling to adopt. Large computing projects can be carved into manageable bites and then shipped to cooperating computers everywhere on the Net. The computers simply process the data as instructed by the organizing machine, and the processed data is then shipped back to the organizing machine. From the user's perspective, the nature of the data being processed could be completely obscure. The point is that the idle time of the machine could be harnessed to the end of getting something done.[30] As Howard Rheingold describes it:

> At its most basic level, distributed processing is a way of harvesting a resource that until now has been squandered on a massive scale: unused CPU cycles. Even if you type two characters per second on your keyboard, you're using only a fraction of your machine's power. [Distributed computing bands together millions of computers] on the Net to create, with their downtime, ad hoc supercomputers.[31]

The potential of peer-to-peer technologies reaches far beyond simple file transfer or the sharing of processing cycles. Indeed, as researchers are coming to understand, the most important peer-to-peer technologies could be more efficient caching technologies. A "cache" is simply a copy of content kept close to the user, so that less time is needed to get access to that content. P2P caching solutions imagine using computers at the edge to more efficiently store data. A user might be paid by a network, for example, to reserve 1 gigabyte of his or her hard disk for the network to do with as it wants. The network could then store content on that disk and keep it closer to the users in the customer's region. By sharing space at the edge of the network, these caching systems can deliver content more efficiently—more cheaply and more quickly. The speed and reliability of streaming technology using peer-to-peer technologies are significantly increased.

So too is the intelligence. Consider Gnutella. Gnutella is best known as an alternative to Napster. Rather than relying upon a centralized server to keep the list of which users have which files, Gnutella uses a peer-to-peer querying algorithm, which makes the central server unnecessary. This means that it is much harder to control the content that gets exchanged in a Gnutella system. And this means in turn that Gnutella so far has been used to facilitate the exchange of a wide range of content too dangerous to post on the Web.

But the real value to Gnutella is not this ability to exchange questionable content. The real potential is for Gnutella to expand the power of searching technologies beyond their presently limited scope. Search engines today miss an increasingly large proportion of the Internet. The engines were initially designed to index static Web pages. As more and more of the Net becomes dynamic (meaning the content displayed is generated each time a Web page request is made), the search engines miss this content.

The Gnutella technology suggests a way around this limitation. By enabling a more sophisticated language with which to relay requests to end devices, Gnutella would make it possible for a search to be launched on the Internet, in which individual machines within the Gnutella network process that search however they think best. As Andy Oram describes it:

> Gnutella offers the path forward. It governs how sites exchange information, but says nothing about what each site does with the information. A site can plug the user's search string into a database query or perform any other processing it finds useful. Search engines adapted to use Gnutella would thus become the union of all searches provided by all sites. A merger of the most advanced technologies available (standard formats like XML for data exchange, database-driven content provision, and distributed computing) could take the Internet to new levels.[32]

This is innovation at the edge of the Internet that implicates its core functionality. It would radically advance the function of the Net, moving the Net from its costly, centralized server architecture to a more distributed and flexible architecture.

These peer-to-peer innovations are enabled by the commons at the code layer. And indeed, the strongest complaint against them is that some of these technologies tend to suck up all available bandwidth. Napster—at least while threatened with extinction—was an example of this use. University systems were overburdened as student accounts became public servers. There is some fear that a generalized Gnutella system would similarly consume bandwidth.

But for this technical problem there are technical solutions. And better-implemented peer-to-peer technologies should better balance demand and supply. What is certain, however, is that they provide a kind of innovation that would not have been possible without the commons of the Net.

IN EACH of these stories the lesson is the same. The platform of the Internet removes real-space barriers; removing these barriers enables individuals with ideas to deploy those ideas. The architecture is different; the innovation it encourages is therefore different.

This encouragement comes from a number of sources. First: Because of the commons at the code layer, there is no cop on the block. The Net does not enable control; in this sense, it therefore encourages those ideas that would have been blocked by a system of control. Where many people have to sign on before a project gets going, the opportunity for irrational vetoes becomes quite great (corporations protecting their vision of the market; management restricting how much they want their departments to change).

Second: Because access to the physical layer is so inexpensive, the market linked to this commons is vast. The market for solar-powered Beanie Babies might be quite small in relative terms. But if the market is the whole world, then the Net would encourage what otherwise could not be sustained.

Third: Because of the character of the code layer, there is an opportunity to exploit a resource that is prohibitively expensive in real space, save for the very large organization—data. Top-down advertising is replaced by bottom-up marketing, which in turn makes it easier for creators without great backing to enter the channel of distribution.[33]

The innovations that I have described flow from the environment the Net is. The environment is a mix of control and freedom. It is sensitive to changes in that mix. If the constraints on the content layer are increased, innovation that depends upon free content will be restricted. If the access guaranteed by a commons at the code layer becomes conditioned or restricted, then innovation that depends upon this access will be threatened.

The environment balances the free against the controlled. Thus, preserving this environment means preserving this balance.

But nothing guarantees that this mix will remain as it is. There is no "nature" of the Internet that will assure a continued commons at the code layer, no strong protections limiting Congress to ensure that adequate resources remain free at the content layer. And most troubling in this environment, there is an increasing pressure to use contracts to muck about with the freedoms enabled at the physical layer—to retrofit those technologies, that is, to ensure that they don't threaten existing interests (as we'll see more of in chapter 10).

This mix constitutes an environment for innovation; this environment enables the new against the old. But the old have an interest in undermining this environment, to the extent it threatens the old. And the means to pollute this environment are well within reach. This requires environmentalism in the Internet era.[34]

A crude economics is skeptical of this dynamic of the old versus the new—not skeptical that the old have an interest in resisting the new, but skeptical that they have the means.[35] If the new represent a more efficient technology, then, over time, that efficiency will drive out the old. There may be struggles in the meantime, and these struggles will no doubt waste resources. But the question is not just whether the old will interfere, but whether intervention to protect the new won't itself be more costly.

At any particular moment, this question of trade-offs will be important. But the issue as I've presented it is not the question of trade-off. The issue is not which technology we can expect to win in the long run. It is, instead, what architecture for innovation best speeds us along the path to the long run. Which architectures encourage experimentation? Which permit the old to protect themselves against the new? Which permit the new the most freedom to question the old?

This raises again precisely the issues that Christensen describes in his *Innovator's Dilemma*. As I've said, Christensen's argument doesn't depend upon stupidity. He is not identifying a failure in the market; he's identifying a feature of successful companies' perspective. The problem is not that the decision maker is irrational; the problem is that innovation is controlled by the wrong decision maker.

The solution is to architect the system to vest the power to innovate in a more decentralized manner. Or, put a different way, the solution is to architect innovation to be free rather than controlled. The lesson that the failure of the Soviet East teaches is that innovation controlled by the state fails. The lesson that Christensen and others teach is that innovation controlled by the most successful in the market will be systematically blind to new forms of creativity. This is the same lesson that the Internet teaches.

LET'S TAKE stock: The architecture of the original Internet minimized the opportunity for control, and that environment of minimal control encourages innovation. In this sense the argument is linked to an argument about the source of liberty on the original Internet. At its birth, the Internet gave individuals great freedoms of speech and privacy. This was because it was hard, under its original design, for behavior on the Net to be monitored or controlled. And the consequence of its being hard was that control was rarely exercised. Freedom was purchased by the high price of control, just as innovation is assured by the high prices of control.

But the story about liberty on the original Net had a sequel: what the architecture could give, the architecture could take away. The inability to control was not fixed in nature. It was a function of the architecture. And as that architecture changed, the ability to control would change as well.

In *Code*, I argued that the original architecture of cyberspace was changing, as governments and commerce increased the ability to control behavior in cyberspace. Technologies were being deployed to better monitor and control behavior, with the consequence, for better or worse, of limiting the liberty of the space. As the architecture changed, the freedom of the space would change, and change it did.

In the balance of this book, I argue that a similar change is occurring with respect to innovation. Here, too, the architecture of the space is changing, interfering with the features that made innovation so rich. And the consequence again will be a decrease in this value that we thought defined the original Net.

But here, the change in architecture is both a change in the architecture in a technical sense and a change in the legal architecture within which cyberspace exists. Much more significant than in the story I told about liberty, the emphasis here is on the interaction between changes in law and changes in code that together will undermine innovation.

Or at least innovation of a certain kind. The story I want to tell is not about the death of innovation generally; it is about the relocation of innovation from the diverse, decentralized Internet back to the institutions that policed innovation before. The story is about the bureaucratization and capture of the innovation process—relocating it back to where it was—as a response to the structures originally enabled by the Internet itself.

Put differently, this is a story about changes in code, both East Coast (by lawmakers in Washington) and West Coast (by software writers in Silicon Valley) code, which will restore some of the power of the old against some of the threat of the new.

My claim is not that therefore no change will occur. Obviously, the world will be different when it is Internet enabled from how it was before the Internet. But it will not be as different as the platform promised, and the changes back to the model of the dark ages are not supported, or justified, by the economics that justified the dark ages. Instead, the power that is created here is importantly artificial—the product of legal rights created in the air and defended with the vigor of courts and code.

PART

III

///

DOT.CONTROL

Old vs. New

PICTURE THE Soviet Union during its final days. Think about the most powerful within that system. These were not inherently evil people, though no doubt, especially during the Stalinist era, there were plenty of psychopaths hanging about. They were quite ordinary in many ways; if you met them at a party, many would strike you as quite liberal and sensible. They were not terribly rich, though some were. And they didn't live in a flourishing society, though they were promised just this as they grew up in the USSR. But by the late 1980s, everyone knew the system had failed. Yet very few were willing to take steps to free that society from state control.

Why? Why wouldn't these "leaders" try to move their society to a better place? Why wouldn't they voluntarily push for a different system of control?

It doesn't take a deep understanding of human psychology to answer this question. Things may have been bad, but how would these leaders know that for them and their families, things would be better under any other system? What incentive was there to release the reins of control, when the resulting system could promise so little that was certain? Like the management of a successful company, they could see the marginal improvements that were possible if they stayed on course. But they could not be confident of improvement if they jumped the other way.

(Here the story of the malevolent giant begins to make more sense. One could well believe the leaders of the Soviet Union expected their society as a whole would be better off under freedom but also believed they would not be able to extract enough of that social gain to make them individually as well off.)

Now picture the leaders of dominant industries, faced with a disruptive technology. What is their rational response? Is it any different?

The perfect marketeers presume these actors would behave differently from the Soviets. They presume the leaders of dinosaur firms would spin those firms on a dime, to become something radically different.

But why would one believe that? Faced with a disruptive technology that threatens their way of life—their mode of doing business, their vision of the market—why would these leaders voluntarily step down from their place and enter a different market with uncertain returns? Why instead isn't the story that Christensen tells—like all deep truth—obvious, once we see it?

And even more obvious, why wouldn't we expect these leaders of existing dominant industries to use whatever power they have to protect themselves? Rather than yielding to the new technology, wouldn't they take steps to protect the old against the new?

What steps would these be? In the story I have told, there are any number of levers that the old Soviets might use. Most obviously, they could use the force of law to stifle innovation that challenges their power. Or they could use market power to chill the willingness of innovators to challenge their position. Or they could use norms to stigmatize the deviants. Or they could use architecture to hinder the opportunity for innovators to innovate. Any one of these techniques could help strengthen the power of the existing Soviets; any one could be deployed to weaken the opportunity of a challenger.

The balance of this book is a story about how our "old Soviets" are doing precisely this with the Internet. "Soviets" is an unfair term, I know, but the image is precise even if unfair. Changes threaten the power of those now in power; they will work in turn to protect themselves from the changes. In the balance of this book, I want to detail their work to change the Internet, and the legal culture surrounding it, to better protect themselves. Some of these changes are legal; some are technical; and some use the power of the market. But all are driven by the desire to assure that this revolution doesn't muck things up—for them.

There's nothing immoral in this desire. This is not a battle between good and evil. Stockholders demand that management maximize its income; we shouldn't expect management to do anything different.

But even if this is "only business" to them, that does not mean it should be "just business" for us. We need not stand by idly as the Internet is changed. They have their interests; we have ours. And for those who believe that the environment of creativity that the Internet produced was worth something, there is reason to resist the changes that I will describe.

Controlling the Wires

(and Hence the Code Layer)

I N CHAPTER 3, I described an architectural principle that I said helped build an innovation commons: end-to-end. I also described the struggle to assure that *in effect* that principle would govern on the telephone lines. Keeping those channels open to enable this commons of innovation was an important, if forgotten, part of the history that gave us the Internet.

The lesson from that story was of the power that came from an inability to control: the innovation and creativity that were inspired by a platform that was free.

If there was a time in the past decade when we had learned this lesson, the story of this chapter is that we have now forgotten it. The changes that I will describe in the pages that follow are all examples of the network being rearchitected for control. I have called the inability to discriminate a feature of the original Net's design. But to many—and especially those building out what the network called the Internet will become—this "feature" is a bug. The power to discriminate is increasingly the norm; building a Net to enable it is the aim.

THE INTERNET was born on networks linking universities, but it took its first step when it came to the phones. It was when ordinary individuals could dial up an Internet connection that the Internet came alive.

Long before people started dialing into the Internet, however, many were already members of on-line services and on-line communities. Compu-Serve and Prodigy were early market players. America Online came a bit later. These services were born serving content of their own. They were not Internet portals. There was indeed no way to move from their proprietary system to the nonproprietary Internet.

By the mid-1990s, all this changed as the attraction of the Internet grew, and as the competitive threat of ISPs increased. As more and more saw the Internet as an attractive alternative to the edited content of the existing service providers, they pressed their service providers to provide access to the Internet.

As I've suggested, the part of this story that is too often missed is the role that the telephone company played in the birth of the Net or, more accurately, the role the telephone company did not play. For what is striking about the birth of this different mode of communication is how little the telephone companies did in response. As their wires were being used for this new and different purpose, they did not balk. They instead stood by as the Internet was served across their wires.

This was no slight change. When telephones are used for talking, the average usage at a particular house is quite small. Calls are ordinarily short, so the number of circuits needed in a particular region is few.

But when phones began to be used to link to the Internet, this usage changed dramatically. Calls no longer lasted a few minutes on average. People were dialing in and hanging on, and the burden placed on the telephone system was great. The average voice call typically lasts only three to five minutes; the average Internet "call" lasts seventeen to twenty minutes.[1]

Ordinarily, one imagines that telephone companies would be quick to respond to this change in usage. They would either be quick to increase rates for calls over a certain length or they might restrict usage to certain kinds of telephone numbers (such as those to the ISPs). And we might imagine that telephone companies, if they were creative, would decide to become their own Internet service providers, offering better rates internally than they did to other Internet service providers. In short, there are any number of games telephone companies might play to respond to this demand for Internet services.

Phone companies, however, did not play these games, because they were not allowed to. And they were not allowed to because regulators stopped them.[2]

As we saw in chapter 3, the telephone company had become a disfavored monopoly. Its power over its wires had first been limited in 1968, in the *Carterfone* decision,[3] and then after growing resistance by Congress and the FCC, most dramatically by the Justice Department in the early 1980s. In

1984, a decree breaking up AT&T was entered, and over the next ten years, Congress and the FCC struggled to find a model under which the Bells created by the breakup would be regulated.

The model finally fixed upon—and ratified by a statute of Congress in 1996—imposed an obligation on the Baby Bells to be neutral about how their lines would be used. The Baby Bells were required to unbundle the services they offered and make it possible for others to compete directly with them. If you wanted to start an ISP, you could connect your service into the telephone company's office. Their wires in a sense became your wires. The important point was preserving and defending neutrality.[4]

This imposed neutrality had an unintended effect on the Internet and its growth, because while the regulators imagined creating competition in the telephone service, they did not have in their head the idea that this might create a kind of competition *with* telephone service. They did not imagine the birth of the Internet as a product of their accidental regulation. But that is precisely what their regulation produced. This imposed neutrality about how the wires would be used left the field open for others to use the wires in ways no one ever expected. The Internet was one such way.

THE END-TO-END IN TELEPHONES

AS I described in chapter 3, the end-to-end argument says intelligence in a network should be located at the edge, or ends, of the network, and that the network itself should remain simple. Only those functions that must be placed in the network are placed in the network. Other functions—other intelligence—are left to the applications that run on the network.

The TCP/IP Internet was designed as an end-to-end network. The protocols of TCP/IP simply enable data to be sent across the network. They regulate how data is to be divided and how the resulting packets are shipped. They don't at all care about what is built into the data or how that built-in part works.

Not all networks are end-to-end in this sense. A contrasting network design is, for example, an asynchronous transfer mode (ATM) design. Under the ATM design, the network first establishes a virtual circuit between two endpoints in the network; it then ships data along that circuit. The virtual circuit means the network can control quality of service. But the virtual circuit also means the network is more "intelligent" than another network.[5] The circuit could be programmed to be compliant with the end-to-end character of the original network design. But it need not be; it can be much more (intelligent) and hence much less.

These differences make it sound as if there is a fairly technical way to describe whether a network complies with "end-to-end" principles. They suggest that the question of whether a network is end-to-end is simply a question to be answered by technologists.

But let's step back from the technical aspects and look more broadly at the types of control there might be over a network. For if value comes from the absence of control architected into a network, then that value may be compromised by other techniques of control.[6]

The point should be obvious, but it bears emphasis. In principle, a network could be architected such that each application must "register" itself with the network before that application will run on the network. A program would then send a request to the network—"May I run X?"—and the network would give it a digital token as permission to run. Such a network would not comply with the end-to-end argument. It would be a control-centered network that requires permission before computer resources are used. The permission this network would require is negotiated technically. The machine does the negotiating, and if you don't get a token, your code doesn't run.

Notice, however, that the very same control could be implemented through other means. The network, for example, could have a rule—imposed through contract—that before your computer ran any program, you would have to register that program with the network administrator. This rule would not be enforced through code—you could cheat and sometimes get away with it. But you might expect the network administrator to have code to detect whether you are cheating. And if it finds that you are cheating, it might force you off the network.

Or we might imagine a community network, where there is an understanding about the kinds of applications that would be run on the network and the kinds of applications that would not be run. Roommates might have a network, and to keep it running fast, they might have an understanding not to use the network to download MP3s. Or better yet, the network news protocol that enables USENET to function might include a norm that the system would not be used to distribute commercial advertisements.

Finally, we could imagine a pricing system for controlling how a network is used. The code could charge users based on the bandwidth used or on the amount of time connected. This was the technique, for example, of AOL for many years. It is the technique of many on-line service providers today.

These different techniques—whether architecture, or rules, or norms, or the market—all effect control over what gets used on a network. Control through architecture is just one kind. And since these techniques could overlap, a network could technically be end-to-end, at least from the perspective of the network architect, but because of other rules imposed through these different techniques, it would deviate from the values protected by end-to-end. If rules, norms, or the market vested control in the center, then the values of a decentralized, end-to-end architecture could be lost.

In this sense, the rules governing a network, whether through laws, contract, or norms, can function as a kind of intelligence in the network. This intelligence can be advantageous or not, just as architectural intelligence can be advantageous or not. But whether or not beneficial, my point so far to see is the change they effect over a network where resources are free.

FAT PIPE

INTERNET ACCESS across telephone lines is slow, even though modem technology has improved dramatically. When I first connected with a modem, I was happy to get a speed of 300 baud. My laptop modem now sends and receives data at up to 56,000 bits per second. But still, that speed is far too slow for the kinds of work people do on the network today. One can't surf the Internet quickly at even 56K; nor can one share large files quickly.

This limitation has pushed the market to supply faster and faster ways of getting access to the Net. And the most important new technology for getting fast access to the Net—at least in the immediate term—is "broadband" through cable lines.[7]

Cable technology was developed in the 1960s as a way of giving remote communities access to television.[8] CATV stood for "community access television," and the very first installations simply placed an antenna on a mountain and ran a cable line down to a community in a valley. When it was first built, cable television was essentially an end-to-end system—there was little intelligence in the network; all the power was provided by the broadcaster and the TV; and both could be conceived to be at the ends. It was also essentially one-way, analog content. Television broadcasts were piped to TVs. There was no way for TVs to talk back.

Congress liked cable TV. The idea of spreading television to many was attractive to many politicians. So in the early 1970s, Congress and the FCC began providing incentives for cable networks to be built. And among these incentives was a particularly lucrative asset—monopoly control.

The argument of the cable industry in favor of monopoly was simple: We need, they argued, incentives to risk the investment to build out cable TV. That build-out would be worth it to us only if we could be certain to recover our investment. This certainty would be adequately provided if we had complete control over the programming on our network. If we get to pick and choose the shows we run, and we get protected monopoly status in the local markets we run cable for, then we will have sufficient incentive to build out cable to secure our needs.

Not a bad deal, if you can get it. And even though "every major policy study on how cable should be regulated recommended that cable operators be required to provide at least some degree of non-discriminatory access to unaffiliated program suppliers,"[9] Congress and the FCC ignored these recommendations. Cable was given control both over the physical infrastructure that built their network and over the code layer that made their network run.

From our perspective, however, there should be something odd about this decision. Telephones and television were both technologies that depended upon wires. Yet just as the nation was resolving to limit the control that the network owner had over one set of wires—telephone—it was increasing the control the network owner would have over a different set of wires—cable. From our perspective, these different policies for the same thing—wires—deserve an explanation, at least.

But at the time, telephones were as different from television as cars are different from buggies. It was not obvious to legislators (or if it was, they didn't let on) why the rules governing one should also govern the other. And even if it was obvious to some, the commercial pressure for exceptionalism was too great to resist. Just at the time America was coming to second-guess its first great network monopoly (telephones), it embraced and supported the construction of a second with the potential to be just as powerful.

So cable entered its golden years, which were brightened in the late 1970s only by the innovations of Ted Turner. Turner looked at cable and saw a waste of wires. Cable, he felt, could become a competing broadcasting network, not simply the supplicant to television broadcasters. So Turner bought access to a satellite and started broadcasting content across the satellite to cable stations everywhere. Cable thus became a content provider as well as a conduit for other people's content.[10]

By the early 1990s, cable was the dominant mode of accessing television in America.[11] It had gone from the farms to the centers of the largest cities. The number of stations increased dramatically, as the technology enabled hundreds of channels. And the range of channels exploded with the decrease in the number of viewers needed to make any particular channel succeed. When channels multiplied, the opportunity cost for each new channel fell; when opportunity costs fell, then uses of the networks increased.

Cable was about to hit a number of bumps in the road, however. Some were of its own creation—perceived "price gouging" led Congress twice to regulate the prices of cable services. But some it did not control.[12] Satellite TV was the first of these; the Internet was the second.

Satellite TV offered competition to cable in the same way that cable had offered competition to TV. Services like DirecTV provided access to many more channels of television than cable, as well as the possibility to sell TV on a pay-per-view basis. Yet because it used no wires, the costs of providing this service were relatively low—at least when compared to cable. Thus, satellite provided a great challenge to the monopoly that cable was.

To respond to this competitive threat, cable needed to upgrade its systems to make it easier to supply two-way communication. Two-way communication was needed so consumers could make pay-per-view selections for television; fatter pipe would make it possible for cable to provide a wider range of content.

But while upgrading to compete with satellite, cable soon realized that it could also upgrade to provide two-way Internet service. And if it upgraded to provide Internet service, then cable could also be used to provide telephony. Thus the upgrade could secure cable in its primary market, while solidifying cable in these two new and growing markets.

AT&T CABLE

TO UPGRADE, however, would require a great deal of investment and, more significantly, technological development. First, there was no standard for enabling Internet across cable. Second, there was a great deal of poor-quality cable that needed to be upgraded. Some was quite old. And even the cable that was not old would require new technologies to make two-way cable work. So the cable companies formed an independent company— Cable Labs—to develop an open standard for serving cable. This standard— called the DOCSIS standard—would then be usable by modem providers that wanted to build cable modems to serve the growing Internet community.[13] And those with low-quality cable lines began replacing their lines with newer technology.

At first, and quite slowly, a number of local cable companies began to experiment with Internet access. An Internet access service provider, @Home, and Road Runner helped the cable systems come on-line. But soon the push for this change in technology came from an entity quite familiar with national communications networks: AT&T.

AT&T was looking for a way to get into the Internet market. In 1995, the Internet had just taken off; AT&T's president, C. Michael Armstrong, decided AT&T had to be a part of the future. So AT&T devised a plan whereby it would purchase an interest in as many cable ventures as possible and slowly combine these cable systems under a single network enabled for broadband content. These networks, in turn, would be supported by selected ISPs—either @Home or Road Runner. Thus the design AT&T envisioned was of an Internet service network that would be supported by a limited number of Internet service providers—namely, those that it would control.

AT&T's reasons for restricting its network to just two ISPs were many, and over time the reasons changed. The essence of its argument was that exclusive dealing with a small number of ISPs was "necessary." At one point, they said it was "technically necessary"—claiming that it would be technically infeasible for AT&T to connect other Internet service providers to the AT&T network. But later, when other cable systems demonstrated how it might be done, AT&T claimed it was "economically necessary"—to give it adequate incentive to develop broadband cable.[14]

AT&T had eaten a bunch of cable monopolies and was now beginning to prove that you are what you eat: like the cable monopolies in the 1970s (and like AT&T in the 1920s), AT&T claimed a protected network was needed if broadband was to develop.

CABLE WAS not, and is not, the only broadband game in town. Wireless, as I suggested in chapter 5, in principle could become an important competitor. And in many communities, cable has a competitor serving broadband across the telephone lines—DSL.

DSL (digital subscriber line) was developed many years ago.[15] It is a way of transmitting data over a telephone line that is also being used for voice. The data is modulated above the frequency where voice service flows, so it doesn't interfere with the telephone conversation. And in tests inside DSL laboratories, there is some hope that it could transmit data at an extraordinarily high rate—52 megabits per second, by some estimates.[16]

But DSL faces many hurdles, much like the hurdles that handicap cable. For a DSL connection to work, the copper wires in the local loop must be reasonably clean. This requires extensive work by telephone companies to find usable wires at the local loop. And it requires installing new routers no more than two miles from DSL customers. The cost of this upgrade to the copper wire world is huge, though some estimates that I have seen demonstrate that the per customer cost is the same for cable and DSL.

DSL does not have the option, however, of running a closed network. DSL is deployed by telephone companies. Telephone companies (by which I mean local Bells) are regulated to be open.[17] That means that telephone companies must give ISPs the right to run their own DSL networks across the telephone companies' wires. And that means that the telephone companies' networks cannot exercise any real power over the kind of Internet service made available across their wires.

It might strike you as odd that the law would require one kind of broadband service—DSL—to remain open to other competitors, while allowing another broadband service—cable—to build the Internet of the future the way cable and telephones were built in the past. Why would the government permit control over the Internet in one case but require open competition in the other?

The answer is that there is no good reason for this inconsistency. It is solely a product of regulatory accident. The regulations governing telephones and all "telecommunications services" are found under Title II of the Communications Act of 1934. The regulations governing cable and all "cable services" are found under Title VI of the Communications Act. Title II requires open access to telecommunications services; Title VI does not. The telephone company is stuck with the position that DSL is a kind of telecommunications service. The cable companies have vigorously argued that broadband cable is not. And so far, though the battles are many, the law is in favor of cable. Cable companies have been allowed to limit the range of ISPs that use their wires, while the telephone company has been required to permit any number of ISPs to have access to its wires.

BUT FORGET what the law is for a moment. Which should it be? Should the lines be kept open, or should cable companies, and phone companies, be allowed to close the lines? Should the government do nothing to protect openness in either case? Or should it consistently demand openness where closed systems reign?

Well, let's first be clear about what's at stake. Recall what end-to-end ensured: that the network would remain simple, and that it would be unable to discriminate against content or applications it didn't like, so that innovations—including those the network didn't like—would be possible on this network. That value is threatened if end-to-end *on the Internet* is compromised—either technically, by building control into the network (in ways that will become clear later on), or effectively, by layering onto the network rules or requirements that replicate this control. Whatever other closed and proprietary networks there might be, polluting the Internet with these systems of control is a certain way to undermine the innovation it inspires.

This is precisely what is happening on the cable networks right now. While the networks are being architected to be technically consistent with the principle of end-to-end, by requiring that everyone who gets access to cable do so through a small number of controlled ISPs, the cable companies will reserve to themselves the power to control what access they get— in particular, the power to decide whether some content will be favored over other content, whether some sites surf faster, and whether certain kinds of applications are permitted.[18]

And on the assumption that this control will be allowed, technology firms such as Cisco are developing technologies to enable this control. Rather than a neutral, nondiscriminatory Internet, they are deploying technologies to enable the "walled garden" Internet. The network is built to prefer content and applications within the garden; access to content and applications outside the garden is "disfavored." "Policy-based routing" replaces the neutral "best efforts" rule. The content favored by the policy becomes the content that flows most easily.[19]

Already cable has exercised this power to decide which kinds of applications should be permitted and which kinds not. As Jerome Saltzer, one of the coauthors of the "end-to-end" argument, describes, cable networks have already begun to be gatekeepers on the Net. As he writes:

Here are five examples of gatekeeping that have been reported by Internet customers of cable companies . . . :

1. Video limits. Some access providers limit the number of minutes that a customer may use a "streaming video" connection. . . . The

technical excuse for this restriction is that the provider doesn't have enough capacity for all customers to use streaming video at the same time. But cable companies have a conflict of interest—they are restricting a service that will someday directly compete with cable TV.

2. Server restrictions. While advertising the benefits of being "always on" the Internet, some providers impose an "acceptable use" contract that forbids customers from operating an Internet service, such as a Web site. The technical excuse is that Web sites tend to attract lots of traffic, and the provider doesn't have enough capacity. But again the access provider has a conflict of interest, because it also offers a Web site hosting service. . . . (Some providers have adopted a more subtle approach: they refuse to assign a stable Internet address to home computers, thereby making it hard for the customer to offer an Internet service that others can reliably find. And some access providers have placed an artificial bottleneck on outbound data rates to discourage people from running Internet services.)

3. Fixed backbone choice. Access providers choose where they attach to a long distance carrier for the Internet, known as a "backbone provider." The route to the backbone provider and the choice of the backbone provider are important decisions, bundled with the access service. . . .

4. Filtering. Data is carried on the Internet in batches called packets, and every Internet packet contains a number, called the destination port, that gives a rough indication of what this packet is for: e-mail, a Web page, a name lookup, a remote login, or file sharing. Several access providers have begun to examine every packet that they carry, and discard those with certain purposes, particularly those used for file sharing. The technical excuse for this filtering is that many users don't realize that their computer allows sharing of files, and filtering prevents other customers from misusing that feature. But some access providers have imposed filtering on every customer, including those who want to share files. . . . And again, there can be a conflict of interest—the access provider has an incentive to find a technical or political excuse to filter out services that compete with the entertainment or Internet services it also offers.

5. No home network. An increasing number of homes have two or more computers interconnected by a home network, and as time

goes on we are likely to find that this home network connects television sets, household appliances, and many other things. Some access providers have suggested that they aren't technically prepared to
attach home networks, but the technology for doing it was developed
in the 1970's. In refusing to attach home networks, providers are actually protecting their ability to assign the network address of the customer. By refusing to carry traffic to Internet addresses they didn't
assign, the access provider can prevent the customer from contracting for simultaneous service with any other Internet access
provider.[20]

The most telling of these limits is video. Cable companies make a lot of
money streaming video to television sets. The Internet, in the view of some,
could become a competitor to cable, by streaming video to computers.
Under @Home rules, users were not permitted to stream more than ten
minutes of video to their computers.[21] And though AT&T offers congestion
as a reason for this limitation, at times it is a bit more forthcoming. As AT&T
executive Daniel Somers is reported to have said, when asked whether
AT&T would permit the streaming of video to computers, "[W]e didn't
spend $56 billion on a cable network to have the blood sucked out of our
veins."[22]

Cable's intent to exercise control is clear; it has already exercised control.
And if the business model that Cisco sells is as attractive as Cisco sells
it to be, then we should expect that cable will continue to exercise control
in the future. It will architect and enforce a network where the kinds of uses
and content that run on the network are as the network chooses—which is
to say, it will build a network just the opposite of the network the Internet
originally was.

The evidence of this intent to discriminate was strongest at AT&T's
@Home media. As François Bar reports, "[T]he @Home 1998 annual report is very clear" on the strategy of discrimination.[23] It proposed to steer its
customers, unknowingly, toward merchants that partnered with @Home. It
would do this through code and marketing—through placement of ads, as
well as through "how do I" wizards that would direct customers to selected
sites. Their reports "explain how they will provide superior quality performance to partnering merchants."[24] In this respect, Bar argues, "@Home is
acting very much like Microsoft, using its control of the operating system's
architecture to favor some applications over others."[25] This closed-access
control would allow cable owners to pursue only the exploration and devel-

opment of new technologies that directly benefit them. "This is not to say that no innovation will take place," Bar argues, "simply that only the technology trajectories that line up with their interest will be pursued."[26]

ONE CHOICE about these trajectories is particularly important to highlight. Recall from chapter 8 my description of the emerging technologies of peer-to-peer. These technologies presume "peers"—that is, machines that are roughly equal. And though connection speeds on narrowband connections were slow, they were equal upstream and downstream.

Not so with the emerging technologies of broadband. Most of these technologies are faster downstream than they are upstream. Most broadcast more quickly than they receive.

Given the way the Internet is used right now, this imbalance makes good sense. E-mail and Web clicks going up take far less bandwidth than streaming video going down. Hence this structure makes sense of the uses of today—it is optimized, that is, for the uses of today.

But as with any optimization, what's good for today is not necessarily good for tomorrow. More important, how we optimize the network today will affect what good is possible tomorrow. Thus, as we optimize the network for this broadcasting mode, it becomes harder for the peer-to-peer structures to evolve. A world where users are servers doesn't scale well when the connection to the Internet is biased in favor of servers at the center.

Ordinarily, we don't have to worry much about this sort of thing in advance. The original PC market didn't care much about design; Apple Computer then changed that preference. The early PCs didn't have much capacity for sound. Later innovation created an incentive for the early PCs to change. The reason in both cases is the power of the market: as long as the market is free and competitive, these new uses will evolve as consumers want them.

In the context of broadband, however, there may well be a reason to be more skeptical about the market. If the concentrations in ownership continue as they have in the past few years (recently encouraged by an FCC that wants to take a more hands-off approach), then at a certain point there may be a strategic reason for these networks to resist the peer-to-peer way. By architecting networks to enable peer-to-peer, broadband providers will be reducing the power they have to direct users as they wish.

Here's an analogy that might suggest the point: Imagine you're a cable company serving twenty channels in your market. A new technology comes along that would open up two hundred more channels on your cable system. This technology is, let's assume, relatively cheap, and with it you could be certain to increase your communications capability ten times over. But the catch is that the content on these two hundred channels will be provided by your customers. Would you, as the cable company, adopt this technology?

The answer is that it depends. If the cable company could charge its customers differently because they used these different channels—if they could make up for the loss they suffered because fewer were watching the twenty channels by charging something for the use of the two hundred channels—then the cable company in principle should have no problem with the new technology. Prices would be adjusted to assure that the revenues the cable company received were as high as they were before.

But there are three problems with this happy assumption as applied to the Net. First, customers don't notice that they are living within a closed system. If a travel site comes up slowly because it is not a favored site, the user is likely to consider this congestion, not something owing to the network. Second, the business model of some networks is based on "owning" the customer, not on charges for access. The last thing these business models can accept is an architecture that opens more channels. But third, and more important, even if there's a price at which the cable company would be willing to allow this new innovation, that price may be too high to inspire investment in this new form of innovation. The innovation that gets devoted to a free, neutral platform is different from the innovation that gets devoted to a platform where the platform owner can, down the road, simply change its mind.

We've seen this lesson before, and we're at a point where we can state a general claim: Where a disruptive technology emerges, there may be good reason not to extend the power of existing interests into power over that technology. That doesn't mean the new technology should be allowed to defeat the old or, at least, defeat the old for free. For example, no doubt the customers who use the "two hundred new channels" technology on the cable system should have to pay something for this new capacity. But the price they pay should not necessarily be within the control of the dinosaurs. Instead, while compensation is justified, control is not required. Or, better, separating control from compensation may well be a way to induce more innovation.

* * *

MY CLAIM so far can be summarized like this: When the Internet was first born, both norms (among core network facilities) and law (restricting the telephone company) effected an end-to-end environment. This created the initial neutral platform. But as the Internet moves to broadband platforms, neither norms nor the law require network providers to preserve the same innovation environment. The trend instead is toward control—toward layering onto the original code layer of the Internet new technologies that facilitate greater discrimination, and hence control, over the content and applications that can run on the Internet. The Net is thereby moving from the principle of end-to-end that defined its birth to something very different.[27]

MANY RESIST the view that this control is anything to worry about. Cable is just one of a number of broadband technologies. DSL, as I have noted, is not free to be closed. In many contexts, DSL competes with cable. Hence if consumers value openness, then they can choose DSL over cable. And if they choose DSL because DSL is open, then cable will be pressed to be open as well.[28] Thus competitive forces will force the network to open up, even if cable desires to be closed.

I agree with this claim, as far as it goes. To the extent consumers prefer open to closed, they will put pressure on the closed providers to be open. But to move from that claim to the conclusion that therefore there is nothing to worry about is, in my view, premature. There are plenty of reasons to worry that the closed character of cable won't correct itself.

First, there is the issue of numbers, and numbers of two sorts—the number of people on cable broadband, and the number and character of other broadband providers. Cable now has a great lead over DSL in subscribers to the cable system. There were 5 million cable broadband customers and 1.8 million DSL customers in 2000.[29] Some predictions suggest that DSL may close in on cable by 2002,[30] especially in nonresidential areas where cable does not now exist. But there are just as many who predict that cable will continue to lead.

But second, there is the number of different broadband providers and the character of their business models. For cable is not the only closed system. Wireless—the great hope from chapter 5—is being deployed now in a way that is primarily closed. The architecture for wireless broadband uses the same specifications that cable does—DOCSIS.[31] DOCSIS, as you'll remember, doesn't yet provide for simple open access. Thus the future is not cable vs. DSL, but DSL vs. a scad of providers, all of which are closed.

Third, while DSL will be a strong competitor to simple Internet access, cable access provides the opportunity to mix television content with Internet content. And while DSL presses its limits to serve Internet as fast as cable does, cable has a great deal of bandwidth that it can use to supply Internet-related content. Right now cable provides 10 percent of its bandwidth to be used for Internet service. It could easily multiply the number of channels supplying Internet service and become a much more attractive option. Thus, while openness might be on DSL's side, the value of openness to the consumer may be outweighed by the ability to bundle cable more effectively with other video content.

But fourth, and most important, consumers' preferences might not be enough to motivate the market. This is the point we have seen both in chapter 3's discussion of the value of e2e and in chapter 4's discussion of neutral platforms: A closed network creates an externality on innovation generally. It increases the cost of innovation by increasing the range of actors that must license any new innovation. That cost is not borne directly by the consumer. In the long run, of course, if it is a cost, it is borne by the consumer. But in the short run, the consumer doesn't notice the innovation that the closed model chills. Thus the consumer does not completely internalize the costs imposed by a closed system. And hence the pressure the consumer puts on closed systems to open themselves up is not equal to the costs that such closed systems impose on innovation generally.

These are good reasons, I believe, for being skeptical about whether the invisible hand will solve the problem of closed networks. The observation that never in the history of telecommunications has a network voluntarily been opened after being closed is another reason to be skeptical. Finally, the interest of those who own these networks to keep control within the network is huge, and a huge reason to be skeptical about their control.

To see this part of the story, however, we need to shift to a different battle about open architectures—AOL.

AMERICA ONLINE was born far from the Internet. Its birth was as an online service that gave members access to other members. While other services were focused on how to sell product, AOL understood from the very beginning that networks are built by communities.

AOL's community was built by making computers easy and access simple.

The company "carpet-bombed" America with AOL disks; it made sign-up simple and access cheap. Quickly AOL built a following that was extraordinary for on-line services.[32]

The AOL network was not really end-to-end. Lots of intelligence was built into the software with which one connected to AOL. AOL made that intelligence work to assure ease of access as well as control where control was needed. The service held the user's hand, but it required some intelligence to know where the hands were. It was a preprogrammed world, which users took as they found it. No one built additions to AOL or added functionality to AOL without AOL's permission.

That wasn't the case with all on-line communities. MUDs (multi-user domains), for example, were on-line communities where people were free to develop new parts of the on-line, virtual, text-based world.[33] If you wanted to add a room to an existing MUD, you simply wrote the code to add the room and submitted it. The space that got built was as the members built it.

In AOL, the only building was that approved by the town planner—AOL. And AOL succeeded in building an extraordinarily popular place.

When the Internet came along, many thought AOL would die. Why pay to get access to preselected content when you could get access much more cheaply to the Internet as a whole? But AOL responded to this challenge by doing what it does best: by building its service to make it easy for users to find their way onto the Internet. The Internet was one place AOL users could go, but then there was also the content on AOL. Both would be available to AOL customers; only the Internet was available to others.

AOL then became another Internet service provider, but with something extra that came from the content it served. It was an ISP plus, because it also had its own content. But many simply used the service to get easy access to the Internet. And AOL then was subject to the fierce competition that every ISP faced. With some five thousand ISPs across America, there was only so much power any one ISP had—even if that ISP had a very large number of customers.

AOL WAS built on narrowband telephone lines. When broadband came along, AOL faced a critical threat. If broadband service was reserved to just two ISPs, and if it was far superior to the service one could get across the telephone lines, then AOL faced a great challenge from this emerging Internet opportunity. If AOL was barred from broadband, then AOL would be history.

AOL thus joined many who were pushing the FCC as well as local governments to require that broadband cable lines be kept open for competition. This was the "open access" movement; AOL was a key player. In 1999, AOL argued to the city of San Francisco during its open access implementation hearings:

> AOL applauds the City for taking this critical step in the implementation of the Board of Supervisors' open access resolution, which wisely supports consumers' freedom to choose their Internet service provider and to access any content they desire — unimpeded by the cable operator.[34]

AOL had made the same arguments in favor of governmental intervention to the FCC.[35] In this campaign, AOL's allies were many. Indeed, before AT&T started buying cable lines, AT&T too was an ally. In Canada, AT&T argued to the Canadian government that access to cable in Canada should be regulated to be open.

> AT&T Canada LDS submits that the application of the Commission's forbearance test to the two separate markets for broadband access and information services supports a finding that there is insufficient competition in the market for broadband access services and the market for information services to warrant forbearance at this time from the regulation of services when they are provided by broadcast carriers. As noted above, these carriers have the ability to exercise market power by controlling access to bottleneck facilities required by other service providers. It would appear, therefore, that if these services were deregulated at this time, it would likely impair the development of competition in this market as well as in upstream markets for which such services are essential inputs.[36]

Vertically integrated cable and telephone facility owners, AT&T had argued, possessed market power and had to be prevented from engaging in anticompetitive practices.[37]

But when AT&T bought its own cable lines, its story changed. No longer did it believe that cable should be regulated. Instead, AT&T began to argue that the market should regulate cable, and the government should stand aside.

This would become a familiar pattern.

In January 2000, AOL and Time Warner announced to a startled world that they had agreed to merge. Time Warner owned many cable companies;

these cable companies would serve AOL content at high speed. AOL had many Internet customers. These customers would be able to get access to Time Warner content. The merger was an ideal opportunity, both companies argued, for synergy in this market. The old and the new would form together one of the most important media companies in the world.

At the same time, AOL announced its policy on open access had changed. It, like AT&T, no longer believed that the government should regulate access. It, like AT&T, believed that the market should regulate itself.[38]

I'M NOT sure why people are surprised by flips in corporate policy, any more than we are surprised by flips of politicians. Corporations have a duty to their shareholders. Their job is to make money. If the opportunities present themselves, they will, and should, change their views. They are not institutions of public policy. And they don't deserve the attack that would befall an institution of public policy that so radically, and transparently, switched sides.

But the other side of this obvious point is that we should not treat what corporations say is good public policy as what is good public policy. We should treat them as statements by individuals who are required by law to be self-serving. This is not just "bias"—this is legally mandated bias.

Thus, I discount both AOL's support and AOL's opposition to government regulations to support open access as evidence about whether open access is good policy. The question is not what AOL believes is good for AOL. The question is what is good for the Internet.

And here again we return to the question, What trend should we expect? The opponents of any governmental role here argue that the market will take care of itself. I think that's true—the market will take care of *itself*. AOL/TW will build itself to maximize its market power. The question is what shape that building will take.

THE DANGER is what economists would call the problems of vertical integration—where one provider controls the full range of services across the layers I described—content, logical, and physical.[39] Outside the Internet, the danger of vertical integration is less.[40] But within a network, the danger grows. Such integration, a report by the National Research Council has concluded, "could, if successful, cause a change in the Internet market,

with innovation and creativity becoming more the province of vertically integrated corporations."[41] It would, Web founder Tim Berners-Lee worries,
be dangerous for innovation generally. "Keeping the medium and the content separate," Berners-Lee writes, "is a good rule in most media. When I
turn on the television, I don't expect it to deliberately jump to a particular
channel, or to give a better picture when I choose a channel that has the
'right' commercials. I expect my television to be an impartial box. I also expect the same neutrality of software."[42]

The danger with the AOL–Time Warner merger is the danger that this
vertical integration will induce AOL/TW to engage in discrimination—
both discrimination in conduits (favoring their own lines over others) and
discrimination in content (favoring their own content over others).

This danger is real. As economists Daniel Rubinfeld and Hal Singer have
concluded, given the existing concentration in cable broadband, AOL/TW
will have a significant incentive to engage in both forms of discrimination.[43]
And by mid-2001, AOL Time Warner had begun to prohibit advertisements
on their sites for competing Internet access providers.[44] Discrimination was
threatened; discrimination is being realized.

AS THE Clinton administration came to an end, one of the last acts of the
(by statute, at least, neutral) Federal Trade Commission (FTC) was a sign of
some hope. After a long and extensive investigation into the risks of the proposed AOL–Time Warner merger, the FTC, led by its chairman, Robert
Pitofsky, conditioned the merger of AOL and Time Warner upon the essential elements of open access. Access to the cable broadband pipes must
be kept open, the FTC insisted. Nonaffiliated content must flow without
hindrance from AOL or Time Warner. And this unhindered access must include access to Internet-active TV.[45]

This decision by the FTC was an important breakthrough in the attitude
of the government. Until this point, the government's view had been that
the market here had to take care of itself. The problem, as the increasing
mergers and restrictive access conditions demonstrated, was that the market
was taking care of itself. The market was building a protection into the architecture that could change the commons for innovation dramatically.

But this decision is just a first round. (And as I describe in chapter 11, this
first round may well be overturned by the courts.) As cable gets built out, as
an administration emerges that is more open to allowing the market rather
than rules to regulate, as other modes of broadband are built, the constant

pressure will be to allow this founding principle of neutrality to itself be neutralized.

And then the question becomes this: If the original Internet architected an innovation space that was free, if it built that space by creating an environment where innovations would not be checked, if it was defined by a code layer that, in Benkler's terms, was open, then as the Internet moves onto fat pipes, will the same principle govern the code layer of the Net? Will broadband respect the principle of end-to-end as narrowband has? And if it doesn't, will the government do anything to resist the change?

WHAT'S AT stake here are two models for organizing a communications network, and the choice for us is which model will prevail. On the one hand, there is the model of the perfectly controlled cable provider—owning and controlling the physical, logical, and content layers of its network. On the other hand, there is the model of the Internet—which exerts no control over a physical layer beyond the decision to include equipment or not, and which enables the free exchange of content over a code layer that remains open.

As the Internet moves from the telephone wires to cable, which model should govern? When you buy a book from Amazon.com, you don't expect AOL to demand a cut. When you run a search at Yahoo!, you don't expect your MSN network to slow down anti-Microsoft sites. You don't expect that because the norm of neutrality on the Internet is so strong. Providers provide access to a network that is neutral. That's the essence of what the Internet means.

But the same neutrality does not guide our thinking about cable. If the cable companies prefer some content over others, that's the natural image of a cable provider. If your provider declines to show certain stations, that's the sort of freedom we imagine it should have. Discrimination and choice are at the core of what a cable monopoly does; neutrality here seems silly.

So which model should govern when the Internet moves to cable? Freedom or control?

NOT EVERY increase in control violates the principle of end-to-end. Obviously the ends are free, as far as this principle is concerned, to do what they want with their machines, and while some would resist calling the cable networks an "end," they could well argue that they are just a private network connected to the Internet. To link to the network is not to commit your hard disk to the use of anyone. The physical layer remains controlled, even if the code layer is free.

Here we see the source of the compromise that this chapter is all about. For in an important sense, the cable network is simply asserting the same rights with "its" equipment that I assert over my machine when connected to the Internet. My machine is mine; I'm not required to make it open to the world. To the extent I leave it open, good for the world. But nothing compels me to support it.

Leaving the ends free to choose, then, creates an opportunity for them to choose *control* where the norm of the Internet has been *freedom*. And control will be exercised when control is in the interest of the ends. When it benefits the ends to restrict access, when it benefits the ends to discriminate, then the ends will restrict and discriminate *regardless of the effect on others*.

Here, then, we have the beginnings of a classic "tragedy of the commons."[46] For if keeping the network as a commons provides a benefit to all, yet closing individual links in the network provides a benefit to individuals, then by the logic that Garrett Hardin describes in chapter 2 above, we should expect the network "naturally" to slide from dot.commons to dot.control. We should expect these private incentives for control to displace the public benefit of neutrality.[47]

The closing of the network by the cable companies at the code layer is one example of this slide. If DSL providers were given the choice, they too would do the same. Wireless providers are implementing essentially the same sort of control. AOL Time Warner is insisting that code using its network be code that it controls.

In all these cases, the pressure to exert control is strong; each step makes sense for each company. The effect on innovation is nowhere reckoned. The value of the innovation commons that dot.commons produces is whittled away as the dot.coms rebuild the assumptions of the original Net.

Consider another example of this tragedy in play:

The World Wide Web is crawling with spiders. These spiders capture content and carry it back to a home site. The most common kind of spider is one that indexes the contents of a site. The spider will come to a Web page, index the words on that Web page, and then follow the links on the Web page to other sites. And by following this process as far as the links go, these spiders index the Web.

This index, then, is what you use when you run a search on the Web.

There are many Web search engines, each with a slightly different technique. But they all rely upon the ability to spider the Web and gather the data the Web makes available.

These "spiders" are also called "bots." A bot is simply a computer program that runs remotely on another machine. Searching is just one example of the kinds of things computer "bots" do to one another on the Web. Some of those other things are awful: "denial of service attack" is an event where either one or a number of coordinating computers sends repeated requests to a Web page, ultimately overwhelming the server for that page. But in the main, these "things computers do to each other" have been productive and extraordinarily creative.

One example of this creativity comes in the context of auction sites. Auction sites make products available to real-time, wide-scale auctions. eBay is the most famous, but not the only one. eBay opened in 1995 as a place where individuals could offer their stuff in an auction to others. The idea caught on, and competing sites started offering the same service. Amazon.com has its own auction site, as does Yahoo!.

But then customers interested in auctions faced another "metaproblem." If they had things they were watching on many different sites, they had the hassle of traipsing through all those sites to find what they wanted to watch. So where there was a problem, the market quickly provided a response. Bidder's Edge, among others, began to offer a site that did the surfing for you. On one page you could see the status of all your auctions. And Bidder's Edge promised to update this information regularly.

In each case, the innovation is the same. The Web is an open architecture; it begs for people to discover new ways to combine the resources it makes available. In each of these cases, someone did discover a new way of combining resources. And this discovery then produced a new kind of market. Search engines were a defining feature of the original World Wide Web. And the opportunity to quickly compare prices was one of the early promises for competition on the Web.

But in each case, too, there is this undeniable fact: When a search engine spiders the Web, it uses resources of others to build its index. When Best Book Buys enters Amazon.com, it collects the price Amazon offers by using Amazon's servers. In a sense, then, we could say that each of these bots *trespasses* on the servers of other sites.

To many, this idea of trespassing bots will seem bizarre. But it did not seem too bizarre to the lawyers at eBay. For eBay didn't want bots that created competitors to eBay. And it had imposed a NO-BOT policy on access to its Web site. That is, it indicated in the code of its site that it did not want unlicensed bots to enter its site.

Bidder's Edge ignored that sign. It continued to gather data even though the eBay lawyers told it not to. And eventually it found itself in court, in a lawsuit brought by eBay charging Bidder's Edge with "trespass."

In one sense, of course, the lawsuit was completely right. In the virtual sense in which one "goes" to a Web site, Bidder's Edge's bot was "entering" a computer without the permission of its owner. And "entering" without permission is the classic definition of "trespass."

But in another sense, the claim seemed bizarre. The Web was built on a norm of open access; this was a community that kept its doors unlocked. No one forced eBay to open itself to the World Wide Web. But if it did, it should live by the norm. And if the norm was openness, then it was eBay that committed the offense.

Both sides brought in lawyers to argue their respective points of view. On the side of eBay was an outspoken, and famous, law professor from the University of Chicago—Richard Epstein. Epstein pushed the law-focused answer: Trespass law made perfect sense in the Internet context. Indeed, it made more sense here than in real space. It was simple to establish signs that stated the conditions under which entry was permitted; those signs could be easily read by bots. If a site wanted to restrict access to all save those who pay, then that was perfectly permissible, Epstein argued. The site, after all, "owned" the equipment. Control over the property one owns is perfectly ordinary.[48]

On the other side was a lawyer who was a bit more careful with the legal tradition. Law professor Dan Burk argued that the law had been strict only when it came to "land." Other property was protected against unauthorized use. But that protection was not absolute. To support a lawsuit based on trespass to property other than land, the plaintiff would have to demonstrate some sort of harm. But in the Bidder's Edge case, no harm had been pleaded. Thus, under traditional trespass doctrine, eBay should lose.

Both sides had a point, and while my bias is with Burk, I don't mean to deny the plausibility of a different regime. What I do deny, however, is that the answer to this question is obvious. What is most damaging about the submission made by Epstein is its obliviousness to any issue on the other side.

For no doubt we could move to a world where every use of data on the Web had to be licensed. We could generalize from the control everyone has over "his" machine to the power to deny the neutrality of the network generally.

But there are costs to that world. Closing access based on this argument grounded in the physical layer of the Net increases the costs of innovation for the Net generally. If to deploy a technology the innovator must first license its use, this legal requirement then functions as a kind of tax on innovation on the Net.

This is especially true with bot technologies. These devices—the next generation after the spiders that gather data from the Net—would enable agent-driven, fluid marketplaces on the Net. These bots could search out prices, negotiate contracts, and schedule delivery in a way that is far more efficient than any of the existing markets.[49]

The response to this is that we don't want rules that force people to devote their resources to something they don't want to support. Bidder's Edge didn't pay the servers that it used when it linked to eBay's data. Why should eBay be forced to subsidize a competitor?

But this story could be told both ways around. eBay benefits greatly from a network that is open and where access is free. It is this general feature of the Net that makes the Net so valuable to users and a source of great innovation. And to the extent that individual sites begin to impose their own rules of exclusion, the value of the network as a network declines. If machines must negotiate before entering any individual site, then the costs of using the network climb.

As I said at the start, this closing of sites selectively changes the character of the Net, but not necessarily its compliance with end-to-end. As it increases, however, it does change the commons of the Internet into something different. To the extent that this ability—to select the uses that access to the Net permits—grows, then this permission changes the character of the commons the Internet creates.

THIS DISCRIMINATION is growing in other contexts as well. Sometimes it happens for innocent reasons, sometimes less innocently. An innocent case is the emergence of a technology called "network address translations" (NATs). NATs are devices for multiplying IP addresses. Every machine on the Internet needs a unique IP address—that's how the Net knows where to send the packets. But NATs make it so many machines can share the same IP address.

NATs were created initially because of an expected shortage of IP addresses. The technology has subsequently grown simply because of the difficulty in coordinating devices in many contexts. Apple, for example, uses NATs to connect machines to its AirPort wireless server. You can plug an AirPort into your cable or DSL modem and then an unspecified number of machines can share the very same IP address.

The problem with NATs is that the techniques used to share IP addresses are not standard. The NAT inserts points of control into the network. Data passing onto a NAT-controlled network must pass through the NAT before the NAT permits it to pass to the end user. If the NAT is unaware of how to process the data from that particular application (either because the NAT was unaware of that application or because it was coded to ignore data of that type), then that application won't function on that NAT-empowered network. Developers of technologies that need to be certain they are talking to a particular machine must therefore survey the world of NATs to make certain their systems will work on all the major brands. This in turn increases the costs of development and, on the margin, may reduce innovation.

No one thinks NAT boxes are part of a conspiracy. This compromise of end-to-end is innocent in the sense that we don't imagine it is implemented for strategic purposes. Nonetheless, it reduces the flexibility of the Internet as a whole.

But there is a solution to the problem that NATs were initially designed to solve—and again, it is to increase capacity. The name space for the Internet (IPv4) is in the process of being upgraded (to IPv6). That will have a practically endless number of addresses,[50] thereby eliminating the need for NATs. With endless address space, technologies for "conserving" addresses become unnecessary at best. Thus, rather than imposing this high-coordination cost on technologists developing technology for the Net, increasing the name space would remove the initial reason for the compromise.

Other compromises with end-to-end are less benign. Consider firewalls, for example. A firewall is a technology for controlling interaction between a local network and the Internet. Like the NAT, it is a technology that adds a point of control within the network that could block everything that has not explicitly been admitted by the local network manager. Unforeseen applications thus again pay a heavy price.

Firewall technology, for example, no doubt serves a legitimate purpose in many cases. Sometimes, however, its purpose is expressly to impose a policy on the Net. Many universities, for example, forbid the use of Napster technologies. They enforce this ban by telling their firewalls to block Napster content. This in turn produces something of an arms race, as developers shift their systems to channels that will never be filtered by a firewall. But that shift will only make it harder to use those channels in different applications efficiently.[51]

Here too there is a solution that could solve the problem that firewalls answer, but without compromising end-to-end. A technology called IPSec could enable better control over access consistent with end-to-end.[52]

In each of these cases, then, there are two issues at stake. As technologies for facilitating discrimination increase, one question is where these technologies get located in the Net—on the Net or at the edge. A second question is the effect such discrimination will have, even if it is located at the ends. The end-to-end principle counsels that we locate such discrimination at the ends rather than in the network; but even when it is located at the ends, a widespread pattern of certain types of discrimination could weaken the commons the network now provides.

There are reasons not to worry so much about this kind of discrimination. Where concentration is slight and many different services are available, the risk that any particular concentration will harm innovation is slight as well. Some ends may be Christian Right; as long as they don't interfere with access to the Christian Left, innovation for the Christian Left will not be harmed. The key is to preserve user autonomy; the danger is a technology that might undermine autonomy.

The danger is discrimination engaged in by concentrated actors. Here again we return to the story of concentrating cable. For if we were in a world where there was significant competition in broadband services, with many different suppliers each essentially open—and hence, each not discriminating in the kind of access that is provided—then the danger from closed access in one channel would be greatly reduced. The value of the commons in the highway is not lost simply because some roads become private. But when there isn't a great deal of competition in access, when a small number of companies can set the rules for the whole system, then the dangers in discrimination return. When a few can make decisions about what kinds of innovation will be permitted, the innovation promised by an end-to-end architecture is lost.

The danger of the changes that I have described in this chapter is that just this concentration is occurring. And the dangers in this concentration include the fear that an opportunity for innovation will be lost. We will have used architecture and rules to shift control over how the network can be used, from the many ends that constituted the Internet originally, to a few that own the wires. Control will have been returned to this medium born free.

THERE IS another side to the stories I have told. Not every increase in control is driven by a desire to lessen competition; not every increase will have the effect of undermining innovation.

Indeed, some increase in control may well be necessary if investment to build a network is to proceed. Just as cable companies argued initially that control over their cable lines was essential if there were to be a sufficient return from laying cable, so too cable companies today may rightly argue that control is needed if the return is to be enough.

The cable companies may be right. And striking a monopoly deal with a provider is a strategy that governments have employed since the start of governments. My argument cannot begin to resolve the question of whether or not the cable companies are right in their defense. If this infrastructure is to be built without public support, then protected monopoly may well be necessary.

My argument is meant simply to highlight a cost that may well run with a benefit. The Internet is not a community antenna. It is not simply a system for delivering a given kind of content more efficiently. The critical feature of the Internet that sets it apart from every other network before it is that it could be a platform upon which a whole world of activity might be built. The Internet is not a fancy cable television system; the Internet is the highway system, or the system of public roads, carrying bits rather than trucks, but carrying them in ways no one can predict.

When the United States built its highway system, we might have imagined that rather than fund the highways through public resources, the government might have turned to Detroit and said, Build it as you wish, and we will protect your right to build it to benefit you. We might then imagine roads over which only American cars can run efficiently, or exits and entrances that tilt against anything built outside Detroit. Or we could imagine Detroit then auctioning rights to use its network to the highest bidder, or excluding Coke trucks because of an exclusive contract with Pepsi.

This power in Detroit might well have been necessary if Detroit were to have had sufficient incentive to build the highways. But it does not follow that Detroit should be given this power. For however much the state may gain by not having to fund roads on its own, society would lose in the aggregate if the open commons of transportation were lost.

That loss is even more pronounced in the context of the Internet. Roads have many uses, but "many" is still not infinite. Any kind of commerce gets to use the roads: trucks as well as VW bugs; campers as well as pickups. But the physical nature of roads limits the possible "many" uses. Lots are possible, but "the possible" is constrained.

The constraints on the Internet—properly architected—are far fewer. The range of uses is far less constrained. The Internet could be a platform for innovation across the full range of social and political life. Its possible uses are, even this far into its growth, unknowable.

We may gain something by giving network owners power over the network. I don't question that. But we will lose something as well. To the extent we chill innovation that threatens disruption, disruption will be slower in coming. That slowness is a cost that society must account for. We may gain something from the "free" infrastructure monopoly builds. But we lose something with the "controlled" infrastructure that monopoly inevitably wants.

Even more significant, we have no good way to make sure that the gains outweigh the losses. To the extent that the code layer builds an innovation commons, changes at the code layer threaten to exhaust that commons. Changes imposed by broadband providers weaken the value of the neutral platform; changes effected through NATs or firewalls similarly weaken the innovation potential of the Net. All these changes are effected locally, but they also have a global effect. Each may make sense locally, but there's no obvious way to be certain that their effect globally will also make sense.

In this way, changes at the code layer create their own *tragedy of the innovation commons*. As we might paraphrase Hardin:

> Therein is the tragedy. Each [firm] is locked into a system that compels [it] to increase [its control] without limit—in a world that is limited. *Ruin is the destination toward which all [firms] rush, each pursuing [its] own best interest in a society that believes in the freedom of the commons. Freedom in a commons brings ruin to all.*[53]

"Ruin" is a strong word, I'll concede. But the dynamic is the same nonetheless: the incentive is for companies to layer control onto the Net; that has been the history of the past five years. But the effect of that incentive is felt by the Net as a whole. Yet its effect on the innovation commons is almost completely ignored.

Against this trend, some rightly argue that government has a role to play to assure that ISPs continue to offer "open IP service." As a recent National Research Council report put it:

> [C]oncerns about the vertical integration of the data transport and content businesses and about content control, as seen in recent debates about access to cable broadband Internet systems, could be eased if ISPs committed to providing their customers with open IP service. From this standpoint, the continued delivery of open IP service would be an enlightened move in the long-term interest of the industry.[54]

Just the sort of wisdom that finds its way into NRC reports and is ignored almost everywhere else.

THE CHANGE that is happening in the context of wires has a particular form. We are in the midst of a radical change in technology; that change threatens existing interests; those interests have an interest in minimizing the threat that this change presents; they can minimize that threat by reestablishing choke points on the system that emerges. They can, in the words of Gerald Faulhaber, use the architecture to regain strategic control.[55]

This is precisely the change that is happening. As Charles Platt put it in a recent article in *Wired*, "Everyone knows that the broadband era will breed a new generation of online services, but this is only half the story. Like any innovation, broadband will inflict major changes on its environment. *It will destroy, once and for all, the egalitarian vision of the Internet.*"[56]

Dinosaurs should die. This lesson we have learned over and over again. And innovators should resist efforts by dinosaurs to keep control. Not because dinosaurs are evil; not because they can't change; but because the greatest innovation will come from those outside these old institutions. Whatever the scientists at Bell Labs understood, AT&T didn't get it. Some may offer a theory to explain why AT&T wouldn't get it. But this is a point most understand without needing to invoke a fancy theory.

Because the Internet is inherently mixed—because it is a commons built upon a layer that is controlled—this tension between the free and the controlled is perpetual. The need for balance is likewise perpetual. But the value of balance is not always seen. This value we need to keep in focus.

Controlling the Wired

(and Hence the Content Layer)

I n the last chapter, I argued that there is a tension between control at the physical layer and freedom at the code layer, and that this tension affects the incentives for innovation. The original freedom built a commons; more control can undermine that commons; the tragedy is our forgetting the value of the free in our race to perfect control.

The same tension exists at the content layer. Some content the law treats as "owned"—copyright and patents are "intellectual property," owned by individuals and corporations. Other content can't be owned—either content that has fallen into the public domain or content that is outside the scope of Congress's power under the copyright and patent clause of the Constitution. Here, too, balance is important. Yet here, too, the owned chases out the unowned. The pressure to protect the controlled is increasingly undermining the scope for the free.

My aim in this chapter is to describe this dynamic and to suggest how changes that we are seeing right now will affect this dynamic. By the time this book is published, I fear the struggle I am describing will be finished. The courts will have resolved these questions, and the politicians will have no courage to interfere with this resolve. Already the endgame is clear; already property has queered the balance. Hence, already the value of this freedom will have been lost.

THIS CHAPTER is meant to mirror chapter 4, "Commons Among Wired." Yet it is not directly about the people I spoke of in chapter 4. The "wired" who are affected by the changes I am describing here are not exactly the same "wired" who built the open source and free software movements that I spoke about there.

But in a critical sense, they are the same. Both innovate by building on the content that has gone before. Both therefore reveal how much creativity depends upon the creativity that has gone before. Both show, that is, innovation as adding something to the work of others.

In some cases, the restrictions I describe in this chapter apply directly to the innovators of chapter 4. Patent law, for example, poses one of the most significant threats to the open code movement that there is. But in general, the changes I describe in this chapter are aimed at controlling a new generation of "wired" folks—those who see the platform of the Internet as an opportunity for a different way of producing and distributing content and those who see the content on the Net as a resource for making better and different content. The changes in this chapter are changes that reestablish control over this class of potentially wired souls.

WHEN THE Net emerged into the popular press, there was an anxiety among many about what the Net would make possible. People could do things *there* that we had discouraged or made illegal *here*.

Pornography was the most dramatic example of this anxiety. The freedom of the Net meant, the world quickly learned, the freedom of anyone—regardless of age—to read the obscene. The news was filled with instances of kids getting access to material deemed "harmful to minors." The demand of many was that Congress do something to respond.

In 1996, Congress did respond, by passing the Communications Decency Act (CDA).[1] Its aim was to protect children from "indecent content" in cyberspace. The act was stupidly drafted, practically impaling itself upon the First Amendment, but its aim was nothing new. Laws have long been used to protect children from material deemed "harmful to minors." Congress was attempting to extend that protection here.

Congress failed. It failed because the CDA was overbroad, regulating speech that could not be regulated constitutionally. And it failed because it had not properly considered the burden this regulation would impose upon activity in cyberspace. The statute required adult IDs before adult content could be made available. But to require sites to keep and run ID machines was to burden Internet speech too severely. Congress would have to guarantee that the burden it was imposing on the Internet generally was no greater than necessary to advance its legitimate state interest—protecting children.

In 1998, Congress tried again. This time it focused on clearly regulable speech—speech that was "harmful to minors." And it was much more forgiving about the technology that would permissibly block kids from "harmful to minors" speech. Still, federal courts struck down the law on the ground that the burden it would impose on the Internet generally was just too great.[2]

These cases evince a distinctive attitude. Though the state's interest in protecting children is compelling, courts have insisted that this compelling state interest be pursued with care. In effect, a demonstration that the regulation won't harm the Net too broadly is required before this state interest can be promoted. Facts, and patient review, are the rule in this area of the law of cyberspace.

Keep this picture in mind as we work through the examples that follow. For the meaning of *Reno* v. *ACLU* is not that porn is okay for kids or that the state's interest in enabling parents to protect their kids from porn is outdated. The Court in *Reno* was quite explicit: Protecting children from speech harmful to minors is a "compelling" state interest. But this compelling interest must be advanced in ways that are consistent with the other free speech values. The state was free to advance its compelling state interest; but it was required, in so doing, not to kill the rest of the Net.

ABOUT THE same time that parents were panicking about porn on the Net, copyright holders were panicking about copyright on the Net. Just as parents worried that there was no way to keep control over their kids, copyright holders worried that there was no way to keep control over copyrighted content. The same features of the Internet that made it hard to keep kids from porn also made it hard to keep copyrights under control.

Both forms of panicking were premature. While it is true that the Net as it was originally built made it hard to control content (by either keeping it from kids or keeping it from being copied by kids), the Net as it was originally built is not the Net as it must be. Code made the Net as it was; that code could change. And the real issue for policy makers should be whether we can expect code to be developed that would solve this problem of control.

In *Code* I argued that in the context of copyright, we should certainly expect such code to be developed.[3] And if it were developed as its architects described, then the real danger, I argued, is not that copyrighted material would be uncontrolled: the real danger is that copyrighted material would be *too perfectly* controlled. That the technologies that were possible and that were being deployed would give content owners more control over copyrighted material than the law of copyright ever intended.

This is precisely what we have seen in the past two years, but with a twist that I never expected. Content providers have been eager to deploy code to protect content; that much I and others expected. But now, not only Congress but also the courts have been doubly eager to back up their protections with law.

This part I didn't predict. And indeed, in light of *Reno* v. *ACLU*, one would be justified in not predicting it. If parents must go slowly before demanding that the law protect their kids, why would we expect Hollywood to get expedited service?

The answer to that question is best left until after we have surveyed the field. So consider the work of the courts, legislatures, and code writers in their crusade to expand the protections for a kind of "property" called IP.

INCREASING CONTROL

Copyright Bots

IN DORM rooms around the country, there are taped copies of old LPs. Taped to the windows, there are posters of rock stars. Books borrowed from friends are on the shelves in some of these rooms. Photocopies of class material, or chapters from assigned texts, are strewn across the floor. In some of these rooms, *fans* live; they have lyrics to favorite songs scribbled on notepads; they may have pictures of favorite cartoon characters pinned to the wall. Their computer may have icons based on characters from *The Simpsons*.

The content in these dorm rooms is being used without direct compensation to the original creator. No doubt, no permission was granted for the taping of the LPs. Posters displayed to the public are not displayed with the permission of the poster producers. Books may have been purchased, but there was no contract forbidding passing them to other friends. Photocopying goes on without anyone knowing what gets copied. The lyrics from songs copied down from a recording are not copied with the permission of the original author. Cartoon characters, the exclusive right of their authors, are not copied and posted, on walls or on computer desktops, with the permission of anyone.

All these *uses* occur without the express permission of the copyright holder. They are unlicensed and uncompensated ways in which copyrighted works get used.

Not all of these uses are impermissible uses. Many are protected by exceptions built into the Copyright Act. When you buy a book, you are free to loan it to someone else. You are free to copy a small section of the book and give it to a friend. Under the Audio Home Recording Act, you are free to copy music from one medium to another. Taped recordings of records are therefore quite legal.

But some of these uses of copyrighted works may well be illegal. To post the poster may be a public display of the poster not authorized by the purchase.[4] To use icons on your computer of *Simpsons* cartoons is said by Fox to violate its rights. And if too much of an assigned text has simply been copied by the student, then that copying may well exceed the scope of "fair use."

The reality of dorm rooms, however—and, for that matter, most private space in real space—is that these violations, if they are violations, don't matter much. Whether or not the law technically gives a student the right to have a *Simpsons* cartoon on his desktop, there is no practical way for Fox Broadcasting Company to enforce its rights against overeager fans. The friction of real space sets the law of real space. And that friction means that for most of these "violations," there is no meaningful violation at all.

Now imagine all this activity moved to cyberspace. Rather than a dorm room, imagine that a student builds a home page. Rather than taped LPs, imagine he produces MP3 translations of the original records. *The Simpsons* cartoon is no longer just on his desktop; imagine it is also on his Web server. And likewise with the poster: the rock star, we can imagine, is now scanned into an image file and introduces this student's Web page.

How have things changed?

Well, in one sense, one might say the change is quite dramatic. Now, rather than simply posting this content to a few friends who might pass through the dorm room, this student is making this content available to millions around the world. After all, pages on the World Wide Web are available anywhere in the world. Millions use the World Wide Web. Millions can now, for free, download the content that this student posted.

But there's a gap in this logic. There are millions who use the World

Wide Web. But there are billions of Web pages. The chances that anyone will stumble across this student's page are quite slight. Search engines balance this point, though that depends upon what's on a particular page. Most Web pages are not even seen by the author's mother. The World Wide Web has amazing potential for publishing; but a potential is not a million-hit site.

Thus, in reality, this page is effectively the same as the student's dorm room. Probably more people view the poster on the dorm room window than will wade through the student's Web page. In terms of exposure, then, moving to cyberspace doesn't change much.

But in terms of the capacity for monitoring the use of this copyrighted material, the change in the move from real space to cyberspace is quite significant. The dorm room in cyberspace is subject to a kind of monitoring that the dorm room in real space is not. Bots, or computer programs, can scan the Web and find content that the bot author wants to flag. The bot author can then collect links to that content and follow through however it seems most sensible.

Consider the story of fans of *The Simpsons* who find themselves summoned to court when their *Simpsons* fan pages are discovered by a bot hired by the television network Fox. The fans are not allowed, Fox said, to collect friends and strangers around these images of Bart Simpson and his dad. These images are "owned" by Fox, and Fox has the right to exercise perfect control.[5] Though "[t]he sites are the Internet equivalent of taping posters of favorite actors to a bedroom wall,"[6] they are not permitted by copyright law.

Fan sites are not the only examples here. Dunkin' Donuts used the threat of a copyright lawsuit to force a site devoted to criticism of the nationwide chain to sell the site to the company. The company claimed it could "more effectively capture the comments and inquiries" if it owned the site.[7] Maybe, but it is also certainly true that it could more effectively edit the content the site made public.

A more telling example is the history of OLGA—an on-line guitar archive started by James Bender at the University of Nevada, Las Vegas. As the Web site describes it:

OLGA is a library of files that show you how to play songs on guitar. The files come from other Internet guitar enthusiasts like yourself, who took the time to write down chords or tablature and send them to the archive or to the newsgroups rec.music.makers.guitar.tablature and alt.guitar.tab. Since they come from amateur contributors, the files vary greatly in quality, but they should all give you somewhere to start in trying to play your favorite tunes.[8]

In 1996, the University of Nevada, Las Vegas, was contacted by EMI Publishing, which alleged that the site violated EMI's copyright. The university shut the site down. The then-current archivist, cathal woods, moved the archive to another host. Then in 1998, OLGA was contacted again, this time by the Harry Fox Agency, which, like EMI, complained of copyright violations without specifying precisely what was being infringed. OLGA closed the archive in that year and then began a long (and as yet unresolved) campaign to establish the right of hobbyists to exchange chord sequences.

The pattern here is extremely common. Copyright holders vaguely allege copyright violations; a hosting site, fearing liability and seeking safe harbor, immediately shuts down the site. The examples could be multiplied thousands of times over, and only then would you begin to have a sense of the regime of control that is slowly emerging over content posted by ordinary individuals in cyberspace. Yahoo!, MSN, and AOL have whole departments devoted to the task of taking down "copyrighted" content from any Web site, however popular, simply because the copyright holder demands it.[9] Machines find this content; ISPs are ordered to remove it; fearing liability, and encouraged by a federal law that gives them immunity if they remove the content quickly,[10] they move quickly to take down the content.

This is the second side of the effect that cyberspace will have on copyright. Copyright interests obsess about the ability for content to be "stolen"; but we must also keep in view the potential for use to be more perfectly controlled. And the pattern so far has tracked that potential. Increasingly, as activity that would be permitted in real space (either because the law protects it or because the costs of tracking it are too high) moves to cyberspace, control over that activity has increased.

This is not a picture of copyrights imperfectly protected; this is a picture of copyright control out of control. As millions move their life to cyberspace, the power of copyright owners to monitor and police the use of "their" content only increases. This increase, in turn, benefits the copyright holders, but with what benefit to society and with what cost to ordinary users? Is it progress if every use must be licensed? If control is maximized?

CPHack

THERE'S LOTS of junk on the World Wide Web. And there's lots that's worse than junk. Some of the stuff, for some people, is offensive or worse. The worse includes material deemed obscene or, and this is a very different category, "harmful to minors"—aka pornography.

As I've described, there's a long and tedious history of Congress's efforts to regulate porn in cyberspace.[11] I'm not interested in that story here. I'm interested here in the efforts of companies to regulate porn in cyberspace by producing code that filters content.

The code I mean is referred to affectionately as "censorware." Censorware is a class of technology intended to block access to Internet content by forbidding a Web browser to link to the blocked sites. Censorware companies make it their job to skim the Web looking for content that is objectionable, and they then add the link to that content to their list. Their list of banned books is then sold to parents who want to protect their kids.

There is obviously nothing wrong with parents exercising judgment over what their kids get to see. And obviously, if the choice is no Internet or a filtered Internet, it is better that kids have access to the Internet.

But this does not mean that censorware is untroubling. For often the sites blocked by censorware systems are themselves completely unobjectionable. Worse, sites often are blocked merely because they oppose the technology of censorware. In December 2000, free speech activists at the civil rights group Peacefire reported that a number of censorware systems had begun to block Web sites affiliated with Amnesty International.[12] This is just the latest in an endless series of similar cases. They all point to a technology that is fundamentally at odds with the openness and free access of the original Net.

In 1999, Eddy Jansson of Sweden and Matthew Skala of Canada decided they wanted to test out one instance of censorware—a product called Cyber Patrol. They therefore wrote a program, CPHack, with which a user could disable Cyber Patrol and then see which sites Cyber Patrol banned. The code thus made it easier, for example, for a number of sites to complain about the censorious practices of Cyber Patrol.

The owner of Cyber Patrol was not happy about CPHack. So like most owners unhappy with what others do, it raced into federal court. In March, Mattel brought suit against the authors and Peacefire, demanding it stop distributing its code for liberating the CP list.

Its claim was copyright violation. These coders, Mattel argued, had violated Mattel's copyright by reverse engineering the code for Cyber Patrol—contrary to the license under which Cyber Patrol was sold. Because their use of Cyber Patrol was unlicensed, it was illegal.

There is something very odd about the claim that Mattel was making. Copyright's core is to protect authors from the theft of others. It is to protect Mattel, in other words, from someone who would steal Cyber Patrol and use it without paying for the program. Copyright is not ordinarily aimed at protecting authors from criticism. It doesn't "promote progress" to forbid criticism of what has happened before. But this is exactly how the law was being used in this case. By claiming that a contract that was attached to the copyrighted code banned a user from criticizing the code, the law was being used to restrict criticism.

Within two weeks, Mattel had received a worldwide injunction against the distribution of CPHack.[13] The injunction was not just against the authors of the program; it also extended to those who linked to the program's site or who merely posted the program. These secondary posters believed they had a fairly strong right to post the code for CPHack. The code stated it was "GPL'ed," which meant that anyone was free to take it and post it as he wished. But all these "conspirators" (as the law had to call them to justify this extraordinary federal action) were now bound by this emergency injunction of a U.S. court. And Mattel then moved quickly to perfect and make permanent this force of law.

Yet here, cracks in the case began to show. First there was the problem of jurisdiction. The authors of CPHack were not citizens of the United States, and their work was not done in the United States. Copyright law, in the main, is national. Just because these two people somewhere in the world did something that would constitute a violation of copyright law in the United States does not show they violated United States copyright law.[14]

But even if there had been jurisdiction, there was a much more fundamental flaw. What exactly was the wrong that these defendants were said to have committed? Mattel said they had "reverse engineered" Cyber Patrol. Reverse engineering is ordinarily a permissible "fair use" under copyright law—copyright law has no incentive to make it impossibly difficult for others to compete with software programs.[15] But, Mattel said, the license that Cyber Patrol was sold under did not give the purchasers any right to reverse engineer. Indeed, it expressly waived the right of the purchaser to reverse engineer the product.

The contract Mattel was speaking of was the sort of shrink-wrapped license that comes with most software today. When you install Cyber Patrol, you are said to have agreed with everything on that license. Now whether such a license in general is enforceable is a hard question. The strongest case in the United States supporting its enforcement is a decision by Judge Frank Easterbrook in the Seventh Circuit Court of Appeals. But Easterbrook is clear that the restrictions beyond copyright law depend upon there being a contract. As he said, "Someone who found a copy of [a copyrighted work] on the street would not be affected by the shrink-wrap license—though the federal copyright laws of their own force would limit the finder's ability to copy or transmit the application program."[16] Thus, to demonstrate that the authors violated the law, you would have to demonstrate they had purchased the product in a way that would have made them liable under the contract.

All that was going to be very hard to prove. But just at the moment the case was to come to trial, Mattel had a surprise. It had purchased the rights to CPHack from the original authors, and now it was simply enforcing the rights it was purchasing. No one, Mattel said, was free to distribute this code, because this code was now Mattel's.

There was a squabble at this point about whether in fact the code was Mattel's. The code had been distributed in a form that indicated it was governed by the GPL. The GPL made it impossible to sell the product in a way that would revoke that license—at least to those down the chain of distribution. The original sellers—who received nothing except the promise that this gaggle of American lawyers would go home—were quick then to deny that they had released the program under the GPL. But that denial rang hollow. The Mattel lawyers had apparently informed them that if Mattel had been tricked, they would be guilty of fraud. And while that would have been an idle threat (at least if the authors had simply agreed to transfer whatever rights they had), it was apparently threat enough to get the authors to deny that CPHack was in fact under the GPL.

Armed with this purchase, Mattel was able to convert the temporary injunction into something permanent. And the judge forbade others who had apparently been restricted by the injunction from intervening to challenge the injunction. As the case settled, and was affirmed by a court of appeals in Boston, Mattel had the rights to CPHack; no one else could distribute it, even if the purpose was simply to criticize the company, Mattel.

The first two centuries of copyright's history were two centuries of censorship.[17] Copyright was the censor's tool: the only things that could be printed were those things printed by authorized presses; the only authorized presses were those cooperating with the Crown.

Here history has repeated itself, though the protected is not the Crown, but commerce. The law has become a tool for effectively disabling the ability of others to criticize a corporation. Coders can release code that censors the Net, and efforts to release the list of censors are censored by the law.

DeCSS

THE LAWYERS for Mattel relied directly upon copyright law. But there was another tack they might have taken—one that will prove much more important as time goes on.

In 1998, Congress passed the Digital Millennium Copyright Act (DMCA).[18] That act strengthened copyright in a number of ways, but one way was particularly troubling. This was its "anticircumvention" provision.

The anticircumvention provision regulates code that cracks code that is intended to protect copyrighted material. There are two parts to the provision—one that restricts the cracking of code that protects copyrighted material, and one that forbids the creation of code that cracks code that protects copyrighted material. In both cases, the aim of the law is to lend legal support to the tools that copyright holders deploy to protect their copyrighted material.[19]

In the ordinary case—with ordinary property—there can be little in this to complain about. It is a crime to steal my car. But obviously, that isn't enough to stop car theft. So many people install a burglar alarm in their car to further inhibit car theft. But obviously again, that too isn't enough. So if a legislature, wanting to reduce the risk of theft even more, passes a law that makes it a crime to disable burglar alarms, or to sell tools whose sole purpose is to disable burglar alarms, there can't be any complaint about these rules, either. If it is wrong to steal a car, and permissible for people to protect their property, it is wrong to crack technology designed to protect the property.

But this story about real property doesn't map directly onto intellectual property. For as I have described, intellectual property is a balanced form of property protection. I don't have the right to fair use of your car; I do have the right to fair use of your book. Your right to your car is perpetual; your right to a copyright is for a limited term. The law protecting my copyright protects it in a more limited way than the law protecting my car.

This limitation is not just laziness on the part of Congress. The limits on the law's power to protect copyright are inherent in the clause granting Congress power to regulate copyright, and in the First Amendment's restrictions on Congress's power. Copyright law, for example, cannot protect ideas; it can protect only expression. The law's protection can extend only for limited times. And fair use of copyrighted works is understood to be constitutionally required.

These limitations distinguish copyright as property from ordinary property. And that distinction suggests the trouble with direct analogy from laws protecting burglar alarms to laws protecting code protecting copyrighted work. If copyright law must protect fair use — meaning the law cannot protect copyrighted material without leaving space for fair use — then laws protecting code protecting copyrighted material should also leave room for fair use. You can't do indirectly (protect fair-use-denying-code protecting copyright) what you can't do directly (protect copyright without protecting fair use).

I am not arguing that it is illegal or somehow unconstitutional for individuals to deploy code that protects copyrighted material more than the law does. There are troubles with this, and I don't think the law can ignore them. But there is ordinarily no constitutional problem unless the law has actually done something.

But in the case I've described, the law has done something. The anticircumvention provision is law that protects code that protects copyrighted material. And my claim is simply that that law must be subject to the same limitations that a law protecting copyrighted material directly is.

How does all this relate to Mattel?

Well, Mattel released a product that was copyrighted. Arguably, at least, its compilation of sites is copyrighted. It protected this copyrighted material using code. This code is what CPHack hacked. Thus, arguably, CPHack violated the anticircumvention provision of the DMCA.

Mattel didn't bring this case, though I wish it had. Had it claimed the anticircumvention provision protected it, then the courts would have had a clear shot at the question of whether or not there are constitutional limitations on the power of Congress to protect code protecting copyright. The Cyber Patrol case would have been a perfect case to raise that claim. If cracking code to demonstrate that the code is censoring speech isn't fair use, then I'm not sure what would be.

Instead, this question of fair use was raised in a very different case.

In 1994, Hollywood started releasing movies on DVD disks. These movies were extremely high fidelity and relatively compact. The disks fit in an ordinary CD-ROM-size drive. And very quickly, manufacturers started producing drives that would read DVD disks.

To protect the movies on these disks, the industry developed an encryption system. This system was named CSS—Content Scramble System. CSS would make it difficult for a user to play back DVD content unless the user was using a machine that could properly decode the CSS routines.

The machines were DVD players that had been licensed to decrypt CSS-encrypted content. These licenses were issued by the consortium that developed and deployed CSS. And they were granted initially to companies that produced Windows- and Macintosh-compatible machines. Those running Windows, or those using a Mac, could play DVD movies on their machines.

Let's be clear first about what CSS did. CSS was not like those early software protection systems. It didn't interfere with the ability to copy DVD disks. If you wanted to pirate a DVD disk, all you needed to do was copy the contents from one disk to another. There was no need to decrypt the system in order to copy it.

So CSS didn't disable copying. All it did was limit the range of machines that DVD disks could be played on. And that in turn was the limitation that gave rise to the need for a crack.

For—surprise, surprise!—Macintosh and Windows are not the only operating systems out there. In addition, there are Linux PCs, among others. These machines could not play DVD movies. And owners of these machines were not happy about this limitation. So a number of them decided to develop a program that would crack CSS, so that DVDs could be played on other machines. And when open source coders developed such a program, they called it DeCSS.

DeCSS disabled the encryption system on a DVD disk. It turned out that CSS itself was a terribly poor encryption technology. And once the system had been cracked, it became possible to play DVD content on other computers. With DeCSS, DVD disks could be played on any machine.

Now again, DeCSS didn't make it any easier to copy DVDs than before. There's no reason you can't simply copy a CSS-protected movie and ship it to your friends. All that CSS did was ensure that you played the movie on a properly licensed machine. Thus, DeCSS didn't increase the likelihood of piracy.[20] All that DeCSS did was (1) reveal how bad an existing encryption system was; and (2) enable disks presumptively legally purchased to be played on Linux (and other) computers.

But upon the release of DeCSS, the industry went nuts. Within six weeks, four lawsuits had been filed in four separate jurisdictions, seeking under many legal theories the quashing of this code.[21] Within three weeks of the filing of the suits, two injunctions had been entered against people who posted DeCSS code and even against journalists who linked to DeCSS.[22] Once again, as with CPHack, the legal system had been fired up to silence this dangerous code.

The core case here was tried in New York. The defendants were many. Some had linked to the sites carrying DeCSS. Others had written articles about the sites and had linked to the links. And others were active distributors of DeCSS. None of these defendants was in the business of selling pirated movies. And at no time in the case did the plaintiffs demonstrate that any movies had been pirated because of DeCSS.

Instead, the sole claim in the case was that these defendants were in the business of distributing code that cracked an encryption system, and hence, these defendants were in violation of the anticircumvention provisions of the DMCA.

The district court judge in the New York case issued an immediate injunction stopping the distribution of DeCSS. After a long trial, he issued an opinion making permanent that injunction. The opinion making the injunction permanent rejected the argument that "fair use" entitled the defendants to produce or distribute this code. Fair use, the court concluded, was something copyright law must allow. This was a law regulating code, not a copyright. The court concluded that Congress had the power to allow private actors to pile on protection on top of the copyright law. No First Amendment interests were violated.

This case was appealed to the circuit court. At the time of this writing, that appeal has not been resolved. But the importance of the case is not how it ends; the importance is the signal that Hollywood sends: any system that threatens its control will be threatened with an army of Hollywood lawyers.

iCraveTV

iCraveTV was a site that streamed television content over the Internet.[23] The site was located in Canada, where Canadian broadcasting law made such streaming legal. Under Canadian law, anyone has the right to rebroadcast television content, as long as he doesn't change the content in any way. iCraveTV wanted to take advantage of that right to give computer users access to TV.

The problem was that though TV was free in Canada, it was not free in the United States. To rebroadcast content in the United States requires the permission of the original broadcaster. So behavior legal in Canada would be illegal in the United States.

But then where was iCraveTV? In one obvious sense, it was in Canada. But when it made itself available on the Internet, it was also, simultaneously, everywhere. That has been the character of the Internet since its birth—to be on the site at any place is to be on the site in every place.

iCraveTV took some steps to limit itself to one place. It tried to block non-Canadians from the site. But when it began this process, the technologies for blocking were not strong. iCraveTV asked for a telephone number, but of course it had no easy way to verify that the telephone number you gave it was your telephone number.

Soon after iCraveTV went on-line, copyright holders in the United States brought suit to shut it down. The theory? By setting up an Internet service to broadcast TV, iCraveTV was broadcasting TV into the United States. It was therefore violating U.S. copyright law (by "publicly performing" what iCraveTV streamed to American viewers). Until it could "guarantee," as the Hollywood lawyers put it, that no United States citizen would get access to this free Canadian TV, the Canadian site had to be shut down.

There was a significant dispute about how hard iCraveTV was working to keep non-Canadians out of its site. The Hollywood lawyers hired Harvard Law School Berkman Center's boy genius Ben Edelman to demonstrate just how easy it was to hack the iCraveTV site. But whether easy or not, the significant issue about the case is this: How much should someone in one country have to be burdened by the laws of another country?

For example: Imagine the Chinese government telling the American site China Online[24] that it must shut down until it is able to block out all Chinese citizens, since the content on China Online is illegal in China. Or imagine a German court telling Amazon.com that it must stop its selling of *Mein Kampf* until it can guarantee that no German citizen will be able to get access to that book—since that book is illegal in Germany. Or imagine a French court telling Yahoo! that it has to block French citizens from purchasing Nazi paraphernalia, since that is illegal in France. (Oops, no need to imagine. A French court did just this.[25])

In all these cases, we are likely to think that the action of these foreign governments is somehow illicit. That the free exchange of the Net tilts us in favor of open and regular access. That steps to shut down foreign sites because of local laws are the very essence of what the Internet was designed to avoid.

But when it comes to copyright law, we become like the Chinese, or Germans, or French. With respect to law, we too want to insist upon local control—especially because local law here is so strong. So with respect to copyright law, we push local control. And the result is the birth of technologies that will facilitate better local control.

iCraveTV, for example, promised the court that it would develop technology to make it possible to block out everyone except Canadians. Jack Goldsmith and Alan Sykes have described the growing collection of technologies that will achieve the same end.[26] These suggest that the future will be very much like the past: life on the future Internet will be regulated locally, just as life before the Internet was regulated locally.

How we will get to that future world was one point of Code and Other Laws of Cyberspace. But for now, the significance of iCraveTV is again the attitude it evinces. Though there was no proof that any revenue would be lost by virtue of people streaming content through their TV, and though Canadian law was assumed to protect this behavior in Canada, the control industry raced to court to shut down the alternative. The courts complied.[27]

MP3

IN CHAPTER 8, I told the story of My.MP3—an innovative new service whose users could "beam" the content of their CD collection to a Web site and then get access to their music at that Web site. This service was provided by the company MP3.com. To provide access to this music, MP3.com had to purchase a very large collection of CDs. It then copied those CDs into its computer database. When a user of My.MP3 placed a CD into the Beam-it program, the system identified whether that CD was in MP3.com's library. If it was, then that user account got access to the content of that CD whenever he or she accessed the account.

Ten days after launching the service, MP3.com received a letter from RIAA attorneys.[28] Its service was a "blatant" violation of copyright laws, said the letter, and MP3.com should take the service down immediately. MP3.com refused, and the lawyers did what lawyers do when someone refuses: they filed suit in U.S. district court, asking for over $100 million in damages.[29]

The RIAA lawyers had a point, if you looked at the statute quite literally. MP3.com may have purchased a bunch of CDs, but it had clearly "copied" these CDs when it created its single, massive database. There was, on its face, then, an unauthorized copy of each of these CDs, and the question became whether or not this copy was nonetheless fair use.

Applying the ordinary standard for fair use, the RIAA argued that it was clearly not. This was for a commercial purpose. Thus, fair use was not a defense, and the blatant and willful copying was then a prosecutable offense.

When lawyers have such a clean, slam-dunk case, they get very, very sure of themselves. And the papers in the My.MP3 case are filled with outrage and certainty.

But when you stand back from the outrage and ask, "What's really going on here?," this case looks a lot different. First, as should be clear, My.MP3 was not facilitating the theft of any music. You had to insert a real CD into your computer before you could get access to the copy on MP3.com's server. Of course, you could borrow someone else's CD and hence trick the system into thinking you were the rightful owner of the CD. But you could borrow someone else's CD and copy it anyway. The existing system permits theft; My.MP3 didn't add to that.

Second, it should be fairly clear that this service would increase the value of any given CD. Using this technology, a consumer could listen to his or her CD in many different places. Once the system recognized your rights to the music on the CD, the system gave you those rights whenever you were at a browser. That means that the same piece of plastic is now more valuable. That increase in value should only increase the number of CDs that are purchased. And that increase would benefit the sellers of CDs.

Third, it is also fairly clear that exactly the sort of thing that MP3.com was doing could easily have been done by the consumers themselves. Any number of companies have created free disk space on the Internet. Anyone could "rip" his or her CDs and then post them to this site. This ripped content could then be downloaded from any computer. And this download could be "streamed" to be just like the service MP3.com was providing.

The difference is simply that users don't have to upload their CDs. On a slow connection, that could take hours; on a fast connection, it still can be quite tedious. And a second difference is that the duplication that would be necessary for everyone to have his or her CDs on-line would be much less. Ironically, by shutting down MP3.com, the RIAA was inducing the production of many more copies of the very same music.

Thus the battle here was between two ways of viewing the law—one very strict and formal and the other much more sensitive to the consequences of one outcome over the other. And the claim of MP3.com was simply that the court should consider the facts in the case before it shut down this innovative structure for distributing content. MP3.com was arguing for a right to "space-shift" content, so that a user's content could be accessible anywhere.

But the court had no patience for MP3.com's innovation. In a stunning decision, the court not only found MP3.com guilty of copyright violation, it also found the violation "willful." And rather than giving nominal or minimal damages for this violation, the court imposed $110 million in damages. For experimenting with a different way to give consumers access to their data, MP3.com was severely punished.

Napster

I DESCRIBED the technology that is Napster in chapter 8. The essence was this: Napster enables individuals to identify and transfer music from other individuals. It enables *peers*, that is, to get music from *peers*. It does this not through a completely peer-to-peer architecture—there is a centralized database of who has what, and who, at any particular moment, is on-line. But the effect is peer-to-peer. Once the service identifies that X has the song that Y wants, it transfers control to the clients of X and Y, and these clients oversee the transfer. The Napster server has just made the link.[30]

But that was enough in the eyes of the recording industry. And with predictably lightning speed, it filed suit here as well. Napster was just a system for stealing copyrighted material. It should, the RIAA demanded, be shut down.

Against the background of MP3.com, Napster does look a bit dicey. After all, the service at issue in MP3.com was a service to give individuals access to content that they presumptively had purchased. On Napster, the presumption is the opposite. There seems little reason for me to download music I already own.

But even that is not quite correct. I've been a Napster user, though I am not an imaginative user, and I am generally quite lazy. I know exactly what I want to hear, and I know that because I own the music already. But it is easier simply to download and play the music I own on Napster than it is for me to go through the CDs I own (most of which are at home, anyway) and insert the one I want in a player. Thus, while I won't say that none of the music I have listened to on Napster is music I don't own, probably only 5 percent is.

That the user owned the music, however, didn't stop the court in the

MP3.com case. And the assurance that users were only downloading music they already owned was not likely to satisfy the RIAA. Most people, the RIAA argued, used Napster's technology to "steal" copyrighted work. It was a technology designed to enable stealing; it should be banned like burglar's tools.

Copyright law is not new to a technology said to be designed solely to facilitate theft. Think of the VCR. The VCR records content from television sets. It is designed to record content from television sets. The designers could well have chosen to disable the record button when the input was from a TV. They could, that is, have permitted recording when the input was from a camera and not a TV. But instead, they designed it so that television content could be copied for free.

No one in the television industry gave individuals the right to copy television content. The television industry instead insisted that copying television content was a crime. The industry launched a massive legal action against producers of VCRs, claiming that it was a technology designed to enable stealing and that it should be banned like burglar's tools. As Motion Picture Association of America president Jack Valenti testified, the VCR was the "Boston Strangler" of the American film industry.[31]

This legal campaign ended up in the courtroom of Judge Warren Ferguson.[32] After "three years of litigation, five weeks of trial and careful consideration of extensive briefing by both sides,"[33] the trial court judge found that the use of VCRs should be considered "fair use" under the copyright act. The court of appeals quickly reversed, but the important work had been done in the trial court. The judge had listened to the facts. Sony was permitted weeks of testimony to demonstrate that, in fact, the VCR would not harm the industry. Sony was permitted, in other words, to show how this technology should be influenced by the law.

These findings were critical in the appellate review of the case. And when the case finally reached the Supreme Court, it gave the Supreme Court sufficient ground to understand matters in a balanced and reasonable way. Though the VCR was designed to steal, the Court concluded that it could not be banned as an infringing technology unless there was no "potential" for a "substantial noninfringing use."

Potential. For a *substantial* noninfringing use. Notice what this standard does not say. It does not require that a majority of the uses of the technology be noninfringing. It requires only that a "substantial" portion be noninfringing. And it does not require that this noninfringement be proven today. It requires only that there be a potential for this noninfringing use. As long as one can demonstrate how the technology could be used in a way that was legitimate, the technology would not be banned by a court.

The Supreme Court's test is rightly permissive. The tradition of American law is not to ban technologies, but to punish infringing use. And that test should have had an obvious answer in the context of the Napster case. Here there are no doubt lots of infringing uses. But there are also lots that under any fair estimation constitute fair or noninfringing use. Music that has been released to the Net to be freely distributed is freely distributed through Napster. That use is clearly noninfringing and is substantial. Music that has fallen into the public domain is available on Napster. That use is clearly noninfringing, and is substantial. And lots of recordings that are not music—lectures, for example—can be made available on Napster. The Electronic Frontier Foundation has a series of lectures that are traded on Napster; they are offered as content that is free.

But when this claim was made to Judge Marilyn Hall Patel in California, she, unlike Judge Ferguson in the Sony case, had no patience for the argument. Without a trial, and with barely contained contempt, she ordered the site shut down.

Within thirty-six hours, Napster attorney David Boies had received a stay of that order from the Ninth Circuit Court of Appeals. And after hearing arguments in the case, that court affirmed much in the injunction of Judge Patel.[34] The court did, however, make one important modification: Napster was not responsible for contributory infringement unless the copyright holder made Napster aware of the violation. Napster therefore wasn't closed down by the court; it wasn't required to become the copyright police. But it was required to remove music posted contrary to the copyright holder's wish. So, like the circuits of the computer Hal in the movie *2001*, the music in the memory of the Napster system will be slowly turned off, as copyright holders will demand the right to control the sharing of their content.

Eldred

RECALL THE story of Eric Eldred's HTML book library from chapter 8. As I described there, Eldred has a passion for producing HTML books from public domain works. As the Framers of our Constitution plainly envisioned, after a limited time, copyrights expire, and the work previously protected then falls into the public's hands without restraint. Eldred takes those public domain works and turns them into freely accessible on-line texts.

But in recent years, Congress has changed the rules. In 1998, Congress extended the term of existing copyrights by twenty years. As I've said, this was simply the latest extension in a pattern that began forty years ago. While Congress changed the term of copyright just once in the first hundred years of copyright, and once again in the next fifty years, it has extended the term of subsisting copyrights eleven times in the past forty years.

This latest extension meant that works that were to fall into the public domain in 1999 would now not be "free" until the year 2019. Thus, works that Eldred had prepared to be released were now bottled up for another generation.

This latest change outraged many, and especially Eric Eldred. Eldred threatened civil disobedience—promising to publish a series of Robert Frost poems that would have fallen into the public domain. After some of us convinced him that that was a very dangerous strategy, Eldred chose instead to challenge the statute in court. In January 1999, in a federal court in Washington, D.C., Eldred filed his complaint.

Eldred's claims were simple. If the Constitution permits Congress to grant authors an exclusive right "for limited times," then the Framers of that power clearly intended that that exclusive right must come to an end. Permitting Congress the power to perpetually extend copyrights would defeat the purpose of the express limitation.

This was Eldred's claim based on the language of the copyright clause of the Constitution. He also raised an argument based on the First Amendment. The First Amendment says that Congress "shall make no law . . . abridging the freedom of speech, or of the press." Copyright is a law that certainly limits Eric Eldred's HTML press. So how are these two provisions of the Constitution—one granting Congress the power to issue copyrights, and the other limiting Congress's power to "abridge" the freedom of the press—to be reconciled?

The Supreme Court has explained how the two coexist. Copyright, the Court has written, is an "engine of free expression."[35] Because of the incentives that copyright law provides, work gets created that otherwise would not have been produced. This means that copyright law both *increases* speech and restricts it. And a fairly balanced copyright law can, in principle, at least, increase more than it restricts. That means that copyright law does not necessarily "abridge" speech; and hence the copyright clause does not necessarily conflict with the guarantees of the First Amendment.

But as Eldred argued, this rationale cannot justify extending the terms for existing copyrights. Existing copyrights protect work that is already created; extending the terms for this work restricts speech without any promise of future creativity. The one thing we know about incentives, Eldred argued, is that incentives are prospective. Whatever we promise Hawthorne, he isn't going to produce any more work.

Both claims appealed to the Framers' sense of balance in establishing the copyright power. As Justice Joseph Story described it, the power gave authors exclusive control for a "short interval"; after that interval, the work was to fall into the public's hands "without restraint."[36] At the time Story wrote that, a "short interval" was an initial term of fourteen years. Today, that "short interval" can easily reach ten times that term.

The courts, however, had little patience for the Framers' sense of balance. Both the District Court and the Court of Appeals for the D.C. Circuit held that the copyright clause did not constrain Congress to a single "limited time." It was free to grant extensions, as long as the extensions themselves were limited. (As Professor Peter Jaszi described it, Congress is therefore free to grant a perpetual term "on the installment plan.")[37] And more dramatically, in rejecting the First Amendment claim, the court of appeals held that "copyrights are categorically immune from First Amendment scrutiny."[38]

The meaning of these two holdings together is that the ability to propertize culture in America is essentially unlimited by the Constitution—even though the plain text of the Constitution speaks volumes against such expansive control. And the consequence of this power to propertize was perhaps best exemplified by a lawsuit to stop the publication of what many considered a sequel to Margaret Mitchell's *Gone with the Wind.*

Gone with the Wind was published in 1936. Under the law as it existed then, Mitchell's copyright would have expired at the end of 1992. But because of the extensions that Eldred was fighting, that copyright now extends until 2031. Until then (or later, if Congress extends the term again), the Mitchell estate has exclusive rights over the story, as well as over other stories that are sufficiently close to the original to be called "derivative."

In 2001, Alice Randall tried to publish a work called *The Wind Done Gone.* While she called it a parody of *Gone with the Wind,* that was her lawyers speaking more than Randall. The work is clearly based on Mitchell's work; in telling the story of *Gone with the Wind* from the perspective of the African slaves, it clearly relies upon Mitchell's work in an intimate and extensive manner. The Mitchell estate called the work a sequel and brought a federal lawsuit to stop its publication. This story, the Mitchell estate essentially argued, was theirs to control well into the twenty-first century.

To most people, this is plainly absurd. *Gone with the Wind* is an extraordinarily important part of American culture; at some point, the story should be free for others to take and criticize in whatever way they want. It should be free, that is, not only for the academic, who would certainly be allowed to quote the book in a critical essay; it should be free as well for authors like Alice Randall as well as film directors or playwrights to adapt or attack as they wish. That's the meaning of a free society, and whatever compromise on that freedom copyright law creates, at some point that compromise should end.

The *Gone with the Wind* case, as well as Eldred's case, is still working its way through the courts. But both tell a similar story: The freedom to build upon and create new works is increasingly, and almost perpetually, restricted under existing law. To a degree unimaginable by the Framers of our Constitution, that control has been concentrated in the hands of the holders of copyrights—increasingly, large media companies.

CONSEQUENCES OF CONTROL

THE INTERNET in its nature shocks real-space law. That's often great; it is sometimes awful. The question policy makers must face is how to respond to this shock.

Courts are policy makers, and they too must ask how best to respond. Should they respond by intervening immediately to remedy the "wrong" said to exist? Or should they wait to allow the system to mature and to see just what harm there is?

In the context of porn, as I have already argued, the courts' response is to wait and see. And indeed, this is the response of the government in many different contexts. Porn, privacy, taxation: in each case, courts and the government have insisted we should wait to see how the network develops.

In the context of copyright, the response has been different. Pushed by an army of high-powered lawyers, greased with piles of money from PACs, Congress and the courts have jumped into action to defend the old against the new. They have legislated, and litigated, quickly to assure that control of the old is not completely undermined by the new.

Ordinary people might find these priorities a bit odd. After all, the recording industry continues to grow at an astounding rate. Annual CD sales have tripled in the past ten years.[39] Yet the law races to support the recording industry, without any showing of harm. (Indeed, possibly the opposite: when

Napster usage fell after the court restricted access, album sales fell as well. Napster may indeed have helped sales rather than hurt them.)[40]

At the same time, it can't be denied that the Net has reduced the ability that parents have to protect their children. Yet the law says, "Wait and see, let's make sure we don't harm the growth of the Net." In one case—where the harm is the least—the law is most active; and in the other—where the harm is most pronounced—the law stands back.

Indeed, the contrast is even stronger than this, and it is this that gets to the heart of the matter.

The Internet exposes much more copyrighted content to theft than in the world that existed before the Internet. This much of the content holders' claim is plainly true.

But as I've argued, the Internet does two other things as well. First, the Internet makes it possible (if the proper code is deployed) to control the use of copyrighted material much more fully than in the world before the Internet. And second, the Internet opens up a range of technologies for production and distribution that threaten the existing concentrations of media power.

In responding to the shock that the Internet presents to copyright law, it is of course important to account for the increased exposure to theft. But the law must also draw a balance to assure that this proper response to an increased risk of theft does not simultaneously erase the important range of access and use rights traditionally protected under copyright law. If the Net creates an initial imbalance, the response by Congress should not create an equal and opposite imbalance, where traditional rights are lost in the name of perfect control by content holders.

That was my argument in *Code*. But now we should add a second concern to that same story: The response by Congress should also not be such as to permit this concentrated industry of today to leverage its control from the old world into the new. Artists deserve compensation. But their right to compensation should not translate into the industry's right to control how innovation in a new industry should develop.

Control, however, is precisely Hollywood's and the recording labels' objective. In the context of copyright law, the industry has been very clear: Its aim, as RIAA president Hilary Rosen has described it, is to assure that no venture capitalist invests in a start-up that aims to distribute content unless that start-up has the approval of the recording industry.[41] This industry thus demands the right to veto new innovation, and it invokes the law to support its veto right.[42]

Michael Robertson of MP3.com agrees that this is the aim and effect. "[T]his litigation," Robertson told me, "is as much about straddling the competition as anything else."[43] And it has had its effect.

[W]hat they've done very successfully is dried up the capital markets for any digital music company. [W]e went public a little over a year ago [and] raise[d] $400 million from going public. Today, if you took a digital music company business plan, you couldn't get a buck and a half from a venture capital company.[44]

This is the reality that the current law has produced. In the name of protecting original copyright holders against the loss of income they never expected, we have established a regime where the future will be as the copyright industry permits. This puny part of the American economy has grabbed a veto on how creative distribution will occur.

One could quibble about whether current law is properly interpreted to give existing interests this control. Some see these cases (in particular the MP3.com and Napster cases) as simple; I find them very hard. But whether they are simple or hard, the underlying law is not unchangeable. Congress could play a role in making sure that the power of the old does not trump innovation in the new. It could, that is, intervene to strike a balance between the right of copyright holders to be compensated and the right of innovators to innovate.

The model for this intervention is something we've already seen: the compulsory license.[45] For recall, as I described in chapter 4, the first real Napster-type case: cable television. It, like Napster, made its money by "stealing" the content of others. Congress in remedying this theft required that the cable companies pay content holders compensation. But at the same time, Congress gave cable television companies the right to license broadcasting content, whether or not the copyright holder wanted to.

Congress's aim in part was to assure that the cable industry could develop free of the influence of the broadcasters. The broadcasters were a powerful industry; Congress felt (rightly) that cable would grow more quickly and innovate more broadly if it was not beholden to the power of broadcasters. So Congress cut any dependency that the cable industry might have, by assuring it could get access to content without yielding control.

Compensation without control.[46]

The same solution is available today. But the recording industry is doing everything it can to keep Congress far from this solution.[47] For it knows that if it has the absolute right to veto distribution that it can't control, then it can strike deals with companies offering distribution that won't threaten the labels' power. The courts, whether rightly or not, have handed the labels this veto power; Congress, if it weren't flustered by the emotion of the recording industry, could well intervene to strike a very different balance.

We find that balance by looking for a balance—not by giving copyright interests a veto over how new technologies will develop. We discover what best serves both interests by allowing experimentation and alternatives.

But this is not how the law is treating copyright interests just now. Instead, they are in effect getting more control over copyright in cyberspace than they had in real space, even though the need for more control is less clear. We are locking down the content layer and handing over the keys to Hollywood.

The costs of this lockdown are great enough without the Internet; the Internet makes them much more significant. Before the Internet, as I described in chapter 7, production was concentrated in the hands of the few. With the Internet, this production could be widespread. But to the extent that content remains controlled, to the extent the Alice Randalls or Eric Eldreds must seek permission to use or build upon other aspects of our culture, these controls create barriers to new creativity. They block the potential for innovation, by adding protections for existing interests.

OKAY, TIME for a politics check. I know what you're thinking: These are just the ravings of a rampant leftist. But as writer Siva Vaidhyanathan argues, "There is no 'left' or 'right' in debates over copyright. There are those who favor 'thick' protection and those who prefer 'thin.' "[48] The argument in favor of balance is not a liberal vs. conservative argument. The argument is old vs. new.

The credentials of at least some conservatives in this debate cannot be questioned. Circuit judge Richard Posner—father of much in law and economics, and perhaps the most prolific and influential judge of the last hundred years—has written persuasively about the complexity in finding balance in copyright law. As I've described, the property right of copyright is incomplete. As Posner writes:

> Since the property right is incomplete, one might suppose that literature is being underproduced and therefore copyright protection should be ex-

panded in both scope and duration—perhaps made comprehensive and perpetual. The matter is not so simple.[49]

Not simple—indeed, quite complex. The complexity is just what we've been considering throughout this book. Intellectual property is both an input and an output in the creative process; increasing the "costs" of intellectual property thus increases both the cost of production and the incentives to produce. Which side outweighs the other can't be known a priori. "An expansion of copyright protection," Posner argues, "might . . . reduce the output of literature . . . by increasing the royalty expense of writers."[50] Thus the ideal mix cannot be found simply by increasing the power of copyright holders to control.

Other conservatives are a bit more colorful about the point. Consider, for example, one of the brightest stars of the Ninth Circuit Court of Appeals, Judge Alex Kozinski.

Kozinski is an immigrant. His family suffered at the hands of Romanian communism; they fled Romania when he was twelve.[51] In 1985, he was appointed by President Reagan to the federal bench. He has since then been the darling of the Federalist Right. He is an extraordinarily talented and insightful judge, who has little patience for the paternalism of the liberal Left.

But the extremes of copyright drive him mad, and there is no better an opinion describing his view of limited copyright terms than a dissent he wrote to an opinion upholding the right of Vanna White to control the use of images that would remind the public of her.

At issue in the Vanna White case was whether intellectual property law—in particular, a state-created right of publicity—would permit Vanna White of *Wheel of Fortune* fame to control all images that suggest her, including in this case any advertisement that "evoke[s] the celebrity's image in the public's mind."[52]

The Court of Appeals for the Ninth Circuit—or, as that circuit includes California, the Court of Appeals for the Hollywood Circuit, as Kozinski puts it[53]—upheld White's right to control the use of this image. Kozinski sharply dissented. As he wrote:

> Something very dangerous is going on here. Private property, including intellectual property, is essential to our way of life. It provides an incentive for investment and innovation; it stimulates the flourishing of our culture; it protects the moral entitlements of people to the fruits of their labors. But reducing too much to private property can be bad medicine.[54]

Why? For the same reasons we've been tracking throughout this book.

Private land . . . is far more useful if separated from other private land by public streets, roads and highways. Public parks, utility rights-of-way and sewers reduce the amount of land in private hands, but vastly enhance the value of the property that remains.[55]

The state must therefore find a balance, and this balance will be struck between overly strong and overly weak protection.

Overprotecting intellectual property is as harmful as underprotecting it. Creativity is impossible without a rich public domain.[56]

But is that unfair? Is it unfair that someone gets to profit off the ideas of someone else? Says Kozinski, No.

Intellectual property law assures authors the right to their original expression, but encourages others to build freely on the ideas that underlie it. This result is neither unfair nor unfortunate: It is the means by which intellectual property law advances the progress of science and art. We give authors certain exclusive rights, but in exchange we get a richer public domain.[57]

This balance reflects something important about this kind of creativity: that it is always building on something else.

Nothing today, likely nothing since we tamed fire, is genuinely new: Culture, like science and technology, grows by accretion, each new creator building on the works of those who came before. Overprotection stifles the very creative forces it's supposed to nurture.[58]

This balance is necessary, Kozinski insists, "to maintain a free environment in which creative genius can flourish."[59] Not because "flourish[ing]" innovation is the darling of the Left, but because innovation and creativity were the ideals of our founding republic.

MY STORY so far has been about copyright and, indirectly, its cousin, trademark law.[60] I have argued that these two bodies of rights will together be used by the old to protect themselves against the threat of the new. This protection is not necessary; there is nothing in our tradition that compels it. But it is pushed not by those with the most to lose, but by those without the most to win. And I have argued that we should be skeptical about just this sort of protectionism.

But now I want to describe a second form of protectionism—perhaps more threatening to the promise of the Internet's future. This threat too is the product of state intervention into Internet space. And this intervention is even harder to justify.[61]

THE ISSUE here is patent law.[62] A patent is a form of governmental regulation. It is a state-backed monopoly granting exclusive rights to an "inventor" for an invention deemed useful, novel, and nonobvious.

The argument favoring patents is as old as the hills. If an inventor can't get a patent, then he will have less incentive to invent. Without a patent, his idea could simply be taken. If his idea could simply be taken, then others could benefit from his invention without the cost. They could, in other words, free-ride off the work of the inventor. If people could so easily free-ride, fewer would be inventors. And if fewer were inventors, then we would have less progress in "science and useful arts."

Getting more progress is the constitutional aim of patents. So the question that must always be asked of any patent regime is whether we have good reason to believe that patents have that effect. As Harvard law professor Stephen Shavell has written, "there is no necessity to marry the incentive to innovate to conferral of monopoly power in innovations."[63] So is there any evidence that it does any good?

In some cases, the evidence is good.[64] For some kinds of innovations, patents are extremely likely to induce more innovation. In particular, in theory, where innovation is independent, or noncumulative (meaning one invention is essentially separate from another), then economists predict that patents will clearly benefit innovation.[65] Likewise, even where innovation is cumulative, if the use of the patent is clear, then in principle, the original patent holder will have a strong incentive to license a patent to follow-on innovators.[66] But here, economists have an important qualification: If we don't know which direction an improvement is likely to take, then licensing may not occur, and patents here may actually do harm.[67] Thus, for economists, at least, the theory suggests contexts in which innovation will be helped by patents as well as contexts where it will be harmed.[68]

The empirical evidence is less encouraging.[69] The strongest conclusion one can draw is that whatever benefit patents provide (except in industries such as pharmaceutics),[70] it is small. As economist Adam Jaffe concludes, "[T]he value of patent rights might still be too small relative to overall costs and returns to have a measurable impact on innovative behavior."[71] And as he concludes more broadly:

> There is a widespread unease that the costs of stronger patent protection may exceed the benefits. Both theoretical and, to a lesser extent, empirical research suggest this possibility. Economists have long understood that, at a theoretical level, technological competition can lead to a socially excessive level of resources devoted to innovation. The empirical literature is convincing that, for the research process itself, the externalities are clearly positive on balance (Griliches, 1992). But to the extent that firms' attention and resources are, at the margin, diverted from innovation itself towards the acquisition, defense and assertion against others of property rights, the social return to the endeavor as a whole is likely to fall.[72]

Other commentators increasingly agree. As *The Economist* recently summarized a broad range of research: "Do firms become more innovative when they increase their patenting activity? Studies of the most patent-conscious business of all—the semiconductor industry—suggest they do not."[73]

This skepticism has been with us from the start of the patent system. Ben Franklin thought patents immoral.[74] Some of the greatest inventors of our history have refused to patent most of their inventions.[75] Science has traditionally resisted patents.[76] And even Bill Gates, no patsy when it comes to intellectual property protections, expressed skepticism about software patents. As he wrote in a memo to Microsoft executives in 1991:

> If people had understood how patents would be granted when most of today's ideas were invented and had taken out patents, the industry would be at a complete standstill today.[77]

The first patent commissioner himself—Thomas Jefferson—was also extremely skeptical about these forms of monopoly. Commenting upon the proposed Constitution, with its proposed provision for granting monopolies to cover writings and inventions, Jefferson wrote that he wished the draft would be amended to eliminate any monopolies. As he wrote:

I sincerely rejoice at the acceptance of our new constitution by nine states. It is a good canvas, on which some strokes only want retouching. What these are, I think are sufficiently manifested by the general voice from north to south which calls for a bill of rights. It seems pretty generally understood that this should go to juries, habeas corpus, standing armies, printing, religion and monopolies. . . . The saying there shall be no monopolies lessens the incitement to ingenuity, which is spurred on by the hope of a monopoly for a limited time, as of 14 years; but the benefit even of limited monopolies is too doubtful to be opposed to that of their general suppression.[78]

Jefferson's views about patents were not his alone. From the beginning of the Supreme Court's interpretation of the law of patent, it has affirmed that patents are no natural right; that the scope of patent rights is just as far as Congress extends it. And Congress should extend it only when Congress has reason to believe the monopolies it extends will do some good.

IN THE first two hundred–plus years after Congress first enacted a patent statute, the duration and scope of patent law were fairly stable. The Framers set a term of four years; they quickly extended that to fourteen; and that term is close to the current term of twenty. And from the start, patents were not granted for just anything; invention was required. So too today, when an invention must be novel, nonobvious, and useful.[79]

But in the past twenty years, an important shift has occurred. The limits to the reach of patent law have been eroded by a number of expansions in patent law doctrine. "These changes," Adam Jaffe writes, "were not brought about primarily by Congressional action, but rather by the . . . Patent Office."[80]

The expansions I want to focus on here are those relating to cyberspace. And these include the patenting of software inventions and business methods.

Before the 1980s, software inventions in the United States were not subject to patent protection. The reasons were tied to the nature of programming (programs were considered algorithms, and algorithms were traditionally not protected), but the arguments in favor of not making software patentable were more pragmatic. Since software is often distributed without its source, it is often extremely hard to understand how it is in fact achieving its effect. On the surface, functions could be implemented in any number of ways. When you sort a list of addresses within an address book program, in principle, the algorithm that sorts the list could be one of a million such programs. (There's more than one way to skin a cat.) When you display a picture, how the picture is displayed is nothing that is obvious to the developer or user.

But beginning in the 1980s, courts started recognizing software inventions as patentable inventions. And by the early 1990s, these patents had taken off. Patent applications for software-related patents went from 250 in 1980 to 21,000 in 1999, and the number granted has increased eight- or ninefold.[81]

What was most striking about this explosion of law regulating innovation was that the putative beneficiaries of this regulation—coders—were fairly uniformly against it. As Richard Stallman put it, "We did not ask for the change that was imposed upon us."[82] And this attitude was not limited to free software advocates. When the U.S. Patent Office began explaining this new benefit it would be providing software developers, key developers from a range of software industries were frantic in avoiding the benefit. As Douglas Brotz from Adobe Corporation said in 1994:

> I believe that software per se should not be allowed patent protection. I take this position as the creator of software and as the beneficiary of the rewards that innovative software can bring in the marketplace. . . . [Adobe and I] take this position because it is the best policy for maintaining a healthy software industry, where innovation can prosper.[83]

Oracle took the same position.[84] The system wasn't broken, these coders said. It certainly didn't need Washington to fix it.

But Washington was not to be deterred, and the push for software patents did not go away. Quite the opposite. Over time, the push was for even broader patent protection—this time to cover business processes as well as software inventions.

A software-implemented business process patent is a patent for a process of doing business, sufficiently novel and nonobvious to earn the U.S. Patent and Trademark Office's favor.[85] Most thought such processes beyond the reach of patent law. This was not because patent law never covered processes—it plainly did. But the expectation was that it would not cover business processes because adequate return from the process itself would create a sufficient incentive to invent.[86]

In 1998, however, the United States Court of Appeals for the Federal Circuit put this idea to rest. The patent law reached business processes just as any other, and patents for business methods were, the court held, not invalid because of the subject matter.[87]

The case in which this issue arose was one where a financial services company had developed a new kind of mutual fund service, one that would manage a pool of mutual funds through a software-based technology. The court upheld both the software patent and the patent on the business method. Both, the court said, were inventions that the patent law could reach. This decision, in turn, gave birth to an explosion of business method patent applications. And by 1999, many were beginning to be approved in a way that surprised the industry. Applications for computer-related business methods jumped from about 1,000 in 1997 to over 2,500 in 1999.[88] High on that list was the Amazon 1-Click patent, but also on the list were Priceline.com's reverse auction patent, and British Telecom's claim that it owned the invention of hypertext links (and hence the World Wide Web!).[89]

In all these cases, the question the monopoly-granting body asked was simply this: Was this sort of "invention" sufficiently like others that were the subject of patents? If so, then the patent was granted for this field of innovation.

Economists, however, are likely to ask a much different question. While it is clear that patents spur innovation in many important fields, it is also clear that for some fields of innovation, patents may do more harm than good.[90] While increasing the incentives to innovate, patents also increase the costs of innovation. And when the costs outweigh the benefits, patents make little sense.

How could this be? The answer links to an argument we've seen in many different contexts before. The ordinary argument for a strong patent right is a kind of prospecting theory. First advanced by Edward Kitch, the prospect theory says there is good reason to hand out broad, strong patents because then others will know with whom they should negotiate if they want to build upon a certain innovation.[91] This in turn will create incentives for people to invent, and as information is a by-product of invention, it will induce "progress" in the "useful arts."[92]

The problem with this theory, however, is its very strong assumption (in some contexts, at least) that the parties will know enough to properly license the initial foundational invention, or that other issues won't muck up the incentives to license.[93]

Both limitations on the ability to license are what economists would call transaction costs.[94] The transaction cost from ignorance is similar to the insight the founders of the Net had when they embraced an end-to-end architecture: rather than architecting a system of control from which changes could be negotiated, they were driven by humility to a system of noncontrol to induce many others to experiment with ways of using the technology that the experts wouldn't get.[95]

The transaction cost affecting incentives to license is in part a problem of ignorance, but in part the problem of strategic behavior that we've seen in many different contexts. It is the problem Christensen is discussing in *The Innovator's Dilemma*: the problem of nonneutral platforms that guided my review in chapter 4 of open code projects.

My claim is not that these transaction costs are so high as to make patents unadvisable in the Internet context. My point is simply that these considerations, supported as they have been,[96] at least raise a question.

So given this complexity, you might think that policy makers would be eager to know whether the fields covered by software and business method patents are the sorts where innovation is helped by patents or harmed. You might think—given the extraordinary importance that these markets have played in the recent economic boom—that before the government tries to fix something through monopolies, it would check to see if anything is broken.

I had the chance to ask the government just this. In a debate in Washington, I was on a panel with Q. Todd Dickinson, patent commissioner in the last days of the Clinton administration. In my part of the opening presentation, I suggested that it would be important to know whether patents will help in these fields or harm.

Dickinson was impatient with the suggestion. As he said:

Some days I wish I was the professor and only had to think about these things and not do the work. But I got an office to run. And I've got 1,500 applications coming in this year and I have to figure out what to do with them. I don't have the luxury to wait for five years for Congress to figure out whether they will change the law or not.

Publisher and Net guru Tim O'Reilly was on the same panel. He had a quick and devastating response. The head of the U.S. Patent Office, O'Reilly said, has two roles in the administration. One is, as Dickinson had just said, to run the office. But the other is to advise the administration about what policy made sense. And where, O'Reilly asked, following up on my own question, was the policy analysis that justified this extraordinary change in regulation?

I remember thinking, Where are the Republicans when you need them? Here was critical new regulation that would significantly affect innovation in cyberspace. Where was the regulatory impact statement? Here was a government official overseeing a radical expansion in patent regulation, within a field that had been the most important component of growth in the United States' economy in the past twenty years. Yet the government didn't have time to learn whether its patent policy would do any harm or good? Regulate first, ask questions later.

There's good reason to wonder whether patents are necessary in a field such as this. Patent law is designed to create a barrier against idea theft, so that inventors have an incentive to invent and use their ideas. The term of this protection is not to be overly long: patents are monopolies; monopolies raise prices. The term should be long enough to give enough incentive, without being so long as to raise prices unnecessarily.

But a patent isn't the only device that might protect the innovator against inefficient copying. Being first to market in a network economy creates a first-mover advantage without imposing the costs of a patent.

And other incentives are often sufficient to induce innovation without a patent. Jeff Bezos, for example, said of the 1-Click patent that Amazon.com would have developed the 1-Click technology whether or not there was a patent system.[97] The reason is obvious: The system helps sell more books, and the profit from those additional sales of books is enough of an incentive for the invention of new technology.

Either one of these reasons, plus a host of others suggested by legal and economic scholars, would lead a rational policy maker to ask whether monopoly is needed here.[98] But this question has not been asked about patents affecting cyberspace.

SO WHY is Washington doing it? What reason could there be for the government to allow this launch of regulation to occur without even a hearing about whether the regulation will do any good?[99]

The answer is obscure, but we can identify a number of causes. First is the patent bar itself. Dickinson is not an evil man; his heart is certainly in the right place. But he is a political figure, who feels the pressure of the interest group that is most affected by the decisions of his department. That interest group is the patent bar—a group of lawyers who like a world where their market increases dramatically. What interest do they have asking whether this increased regulation does any good?

Second is our general way of thinking about patents. Most of us don't think about patents as a form of regulation. Most consider patents property in the same sense that my car is property. In that same debate, patent king Jay Walker was also on the panel. He argued that the question in this debate about patents was whether you were for property or against it—and in his view, the pro-property view was "beyond reproach."[100]

But again, this is just silly. Patents are no more (and no less) "property" than welfare is property. Granting patents may make sense, as providing welfare certainly makes sense. But the idea that there is a right to a patent is just absurd. From the very beginning, our tradition has self-consciously understood that the only question guiding whether to issue a patent or not is whether or not patents will do *society* any good. As conservative economist Friedrich von Hayek put it:

> It seems to me beyond doubt that in [the fields of patent and copyright] a
> slavish application of the concept of property as it has been developed for
> material things has done a great deal to foster the growth of monopoly and
> that here drastic reforms may be required if competition is to be made to
> work.[101]

Rather than reason, what governs the current patent debate is bias—bias in favor of a system that seems right just because it seems old.[102] But the relevant system is not old—it is being expanded in ways that would shock lawyers of a generation ago. And something is right not because it is old, but only if it does some good. But we will never know whether or not it does any good if we accept this never-ending expansion without limit. We will never know what benefit this regulation provides until we begin to demand that the regulation prove itself.

For the harms from this regulation are not hard to identify, and for the cynical, or conspiratorial, the harms are not surprising. (On the margin, the costs of a patent system will harm small inventors more than large; negotiating a patent system is easier for IBM than for the garage inventor.)[103] And the harms from an expanded American patent system will harm foreign inventors more than American. (It is easier to hire American law firms locally than from a distance.) Thus this expansion in patent protection will shift the competitive field away from the small, non-American inventor in favor of the large, American inventor.[104]

The harms are even more pronounced, however, for open code projects. Tim Berners-Lee has noticed its effect on Web development already. ("Developers are stalling their efforts in a given direction when they hear rumors that some company may have a patent that may involve the technology."[105] One example is the development of P3P, which may enable better protection of privacy on the Web.) And open code proponents—like software developers generally—have been among the strongest opponents to patents in this field. As Richard Stallman writes, "The worst threat we face comes from software patents, which can put . . . features off-limits to free software for up to twenty years."[106] Red Hat chairman Bob Young thinks much the same: "[S]oftware patents [are] an evil, or at least [a] very damaging encroachment on the efficacy of the software programming industry."[107]

The reason patents harm open code in particular is not hard to see. Think about the mechanics of licensing a patent when you are licensing for anyone working on an open code project. Who knows who they are? How many users need to be sanctioned? As Peter Wayner writes, "[T]hese questions are much easier to answer if you're a corporation charging customers to buy a product."[108] Thus patents tilt the process to harm open code developers.

The problem is exacerbated with software patents because though the patent system was designed to induce inventors to reveal their invention to the public, there is no obligation that a software inventor reveal his source code to get a patent. "The single most revealing symptom" of the failure of the existing system, Professor Brian Kahin writes, "is that the software professionals do not read patents."[109] As Bob Young analogizes it, "It's like that ceramic guy, producing a new kind of ceramic and [patenting it] without ever telling anyone how he made the extra hard ceramic. So in software you're saying 'I'm patenting software that has this look and feel, but I don't actually have to tell people how I achieved that look and feel.' The source code remains a secret."[110]

And then there is the expense of patents, which is borne more sharply by smaller inventors than larger. The costs include the costs of securing a patent, but those in the end are trivial. The real costs are borne by those who would challenge a patent. If the U.S. Patent Office makes a mistake, and a patent is granted that shouldn't be granted, then it costs on average $1.5 million (for each side) to take a patent dispute to trial.[111]

Finally, there is the obvious "hold-up" problem—where an innovator is about to release a product and is discovered to be violating a patent. As Berkeley economist Carl Shapiro describes it:

> The hold-up problem is worst in industries where hundreds if not thousands of patents, some already issued, others pending, can potentially read on a given product. In these industries, the danger that a manufacturer will "step on a land mine" is all too real. The result will be that some companies avoid the minefield altogether, i.e., refrain from introducing certain products for fear of hold-up. Other companies will lose their corporate legs, i.e., will be forced to pay royalties on patents that they could easily have invented around at an earlier stage, had they merely been aware that such a patent either existed or was pending.[112]

As Shapiro concludes, "[T]his 'hold-up' problem is very real today, and . . . should [be considered] a problem of first-order significance in the years ahead."[113]

This may be an unintended consequence of this recent expansion in protection. I am, for example, quite certain this would not have motivated the different courts that have contributed to this expansion. But it may well explain why there is little passion from those who fund lobbyists to find a way to cut back on the expansion. By letting things go as they are, this change may well give them a competitive advantage over the innovator who can't fund a legal team or isn't from the United States. Again, as Bill Gates of Microsoft told his senior management:

> A future start-up with no patents of its own will be forced to pay whatever price the giants choose to impose. That price might be high: *Established companies have an interest in excluding future competitors.*[114]

THIS STORY about the potential danger of patents in a field where innovation is sequential and complementary (where one builds on another, and the second complements the value of the first) gets additional support from an ingenious argument that Michigan law professor Michael Heller initially made and that economist James Buchanan has now followed up on.[115] Heller introduces the concept of an "anticommons." If a commons is a resource where everyone has a right to use the resource (and therefore sometimes overuse the resource), an anticommons is a resource where many have the right to *block* the use of a resource by others (and therefore many more underuse the resource). Heller gives the example of formerly state-owned buildings in post-Soviet Russia: Because of the many claims that could be made on them, the buildings were never developed. Too many bureaucrats could veto any project, and thus insufficient effort at innovating in the use of these buildings was made.

Nobel Prize–winning economist James Buchanan has expanded this idea to the problem of regulation generally.[116] He points to the problem of patents in particular as an example where multiple and overlapping patent protection may create an anticommons, where innovators are afraid to innovate in a field because too many people have the right to veto the use of a particular resource or idea. This potential for strategic behavior by these many rights holders makes it irrational for an innovator to develop a particular idea, just as the possibility of veto by many bureaucrats may leave a particular piece of real property underdeveloped.

These ideas map directly onto the argument we've considered in this book. Control, when complex, can often increase the costs of using a resource; increasing those costs can easily chill innovation. Recall the extreme of AT&T's control over innovation in the telecommunications system: Who would waste his or her time developing for that system, when any development would require convincing so many quasi bureaucrats before it could even be tried?

The complexity in these rights to exclude creates this anticommons problem. And the more severe the problem, the more it will stifle new innovation.

I'VE TOLD a story about intellectual property in two critical competitive contexts.[117] In both contexts, the emerging regime will have a significant regulatory effect. In both contexts, the regime will shift protection from the new to the old. The law in both cases will, on the margin, protect the old against the new. RIAA president Hilary Rosen was clear about this objective in the context of copyright law: No new ideas should be allowed unless the old system of distribution okays it. And this will be the certain, if unintended, consequence of the patent system as well. Those most likely to be displaced by new innovation will have the power, through these government-backed monopolies, to check or inhibit this innovation.

This power is the product of government-backed monopolies that in the ordinary case raise little trouble. I am not against copyright law (I agree with Hollywood: if you have simply copied the whole of this book, you are a thief); in the ordinary case, the scope of its monopoly ought to be respected.

But when we, as a society, undergo a radical technological shift—which the Internet revolution certainly is—then we should reexamine the scope of the monopoly power we extend and ask once again whether that power makes any sense. Is it necessary? Is there reason to believe it will do some good?

The tradition before the Internet had favored massive increase in the scope of copyright law and a significant increase in the reach of patents. Essentially anything you could attribute to a creative work, you had to respect by getting the permission of this creative work before using it.

In a world like the world I described as the dark ages, this may not be a terrible thing. When all publishers are largish corporations, who really cares if creative energies must be licensed? The licensing process is an ordinary cost of doing business, just like paying sales tax or filing statements with the SEC. It may, on the margin, inhibit a bit, but not a terribly significant amount.

But when the world of creativity shifts outside the largish corporation— when individuals and smaller groups are much more enabled to do this creative activity—then this system of exclusive licenses for every derivative use of a creative work begins to tax the creative process significantly. The opportunity cost, as economists would describe it, of this system of control is higher when, without this system of control, much more creative activity would go on.

Thus, when we have a massive shift in opportunity, we should be reevaluating how necessary these systems of control are. We should be asking whether control is necessary, or at least how far control is required. And if we don't have a good reason for extending these systems of government-backed control, then we shouldn't. If we have no good reason to believe a government-backed monopoly will help, then we have no good reason to establish government-backed monopolies.

AT THE end of chapter 7, I argued that the control of media in the dark ages may well be a product of economic constraints. That as long as economics constrains, then this system of concentration and control may be inevitable. The constraints I identified are not to be imagined or ignored away. They are real and unavoidable.

But the constraints that I have described in this chapter are different. They are not "real" in the same sense. The constraints of IP are constraints we build. We create regimes of IP, and then the regimes we have built yield the control I have identified. No doubt these regimes are in large measure justified. No doubt in the main they promote progress. But often (in copyright for sure, and possibly with patents as well) the regime expands beyond its initial justification. The restrictions it imposes are artificial, in the sense that they don't promote progress; they simply benefit one person at the expense of another.

This then presses the fundamental question of this book: If the extremes of these constraints are not necessary, if there is no good showing that they do any good, if they limit the range of creativity by virtue of the system of control they erect, why do we have them?

For this is a change. The content layer—the ability to use content and ideas—is closing. It is closing without a clear showing of the benefit this closing will provide and with a fairly clear showing of the harms it will impose. Like the closing of the code layer described in chapter 10, this closing of the content layer is control without any showing of a return. Mindless locking up of resources that spur innovation. Control without reason.

This closing will not be without cost. Making it harder for innovations to enter, making resources more universally controlled—this will drive new competitors off the field, leaving the field once again safe for the old.

And more important, this closing does not occur without a purpose. As I suggested at the end of the last chapter, our greatest fear should be of dinosaurs stopping evolution. More precisely, we should be most concerned when existing interests use the legal system to protect themselves against innovation that might threaten them. The commitment of a society open to innovation must be to let the old die young. The law should resist becoming a tool to defend against the new; when change is on the horizon, it should allow the market to bring about that change.

This is just what is not happening in the field of intellectual property. The state is being pushed to defend expanded intellectual property rights in the name of protecting the way the world was.

As in chapter 10, we are allowing an idea about "property" to overrun the balance that grants access. Because we don't see that balance, or don't see the place for balance, we are quick to follow the arguments that favor control.

Again, this idea in the background—the sanctity of perfect control—blinds us. We in turn render blind the opportunities for innovation. When the only innovation that will be allowed is what Hollywood permits, we will not see innovation. That lesson, at least, we have already seen.

Controlling Wire-less

(and Hence the Physical Layer)

IN THE wall in my office is a multicolored poster. The poster is large (maybe 30 by 42 inches), and it is titled, in beautifully retro typewriter font, "United States Frequency Allocations—The Radio Spectrum." To the left are thirty-three colored boxes, listing the legends for the poster. Thirty list "radio services." Three list "activity codes." Among the activity codes are "government exclusive," "government/non-government shared," and "nongovernmental exclusive." (Appropriately enough, government exclusive is red, while nongovernmental exclusive is green.)

If you could tilt this poster and give it a bit of a 3D look, it might remind you of the famous *New Yorker* cartoon maps, where everything close is detailed and significant, while everything far is wide open and unimportant. So it is with spectrum as well. At the highest frequency (30–300 gigahertz), the allocations are a patchwork of tiny colored boxes, sometimes four deep; but as you move down the frequency range, the allocations get wider and less precise. The largest swath is AM radio.

This map, however, doesn't mark out any physical space. It marks the allocation of radio spectrum. The map says what kind of use will be permitted at what range of radio spectrum in any particular part of the territorial United States. It does not say by whom.

As I described in chapter 5, the "by whom" part is determined by a complex set of federal regulations. The FCC makes a decision about who gets to use what spectrum when, and under what conditions. These "licenses" are not really licenses to spectrum. As Thomas Hazlett describes them, they are simply permissions to use certain kinds of equipment at certain times for certain purposes. Their effect is therefore not so much to regulate a resource (spectrum) as it is to determine who has the rights to engage in certain kinds of businesses, where. To say that company X has an FCC license is to say that the government has given company X the right to engage in a certain kind of business (say, radio broadcasting) using certain equipment tuned to certain radio frequencies.[1]

The manner in which this allocation of rights to use spectrum is made has changed, and it changes still. As Eli Noam describes, in the first era of spectrum use, spectrum was allocated on a first come, first served basis. This was before the federal government entered the field. After 1912, Noam's "second era," it was the government that chose who got what spectrum. This invited predictable biases: existing owners bought the favor of regulators, and regulators in turn protected them. The examples are many, and extraordinary (at least to those who live outside D.C.): Hazlett has cataloged the cases where favored interests have succeeded in using their power over regulators to resist new technologies;[2] as Noam writes, "[I]n the early 1950s, only newspaper companies that had editorially endorsed Eisenhower for President had a chance at getting a TV license."[3]

In the third era (now), the right to use spectrum is increasingly allocated through auctions. The government sells the right to the highest bidder (subject to a scad of typically governmentlike, mainly silly, conditions). That bidder uses the spectrum as the auction specifies or, in a small set of cases, the bidder is then free to reassign the right to others.

Politicians from the Left and the Right just love auctions. For the Left, auctions promise more money for the government to spend; for the Right, auctions sound like markets, and markets are always good.

But as we saw in chapter 5, both auctions and government assignments ignore a fundamentally different way to "allocate" spectrum—namely, not allocating it or, more realistically, not allocating all of it. Rather than assigning rights to use the spectrum resource ex ante, this alternative would allow users to share the resource when the need to use it arose. This sharing would be policed either by a market (in Noam's conception) or by other technological devices designed to deal with congestion.[4] Like the Internet, on this latter model, the system would find a technological means to deal with undercapacity. Spectrum could then be shared, and a range of different technologies says how.

How much? How completely? Could shared spectrum govern everywhere?

The optimists in this story say that shared spectrum could service all of our spectrum needs: that we could replace allocated spectrum in one fell swoop and free spectrum for the use of all.[5] Others argue that shared spectrum could serve only a small part of our spectrum needs and that we will always need to have some spectrum that is allocated or controlled through a market.[6]

Whether all or not, however, it is clear that shared spectrum could serve a great deal of our spectrum needs, which means that not all spectrum needs to be allocated for spectrum to be usable. Even under the most conservative estimates of what shared spectrum might offer, shared spectrum could serve a large and important part of our spectrum demand.

Which raises an important question that by now will have become familiar: To the extent spectrum could be shared, what justifies the extent of spectrum allocation that we now see?

TO BUREAUCRATS and legislators, this kind of question will seem odd. What *justifies* it? "What justifies it is that we've always done it like this. Any change must be as we permit." Thus, the FCC is moving slowly to open the spectrum that it can, just as fast as it believes is right in the face of any lobbying or opposition we might see.

But to courts, the question of justification is at the core of what they do. And when one asks what justifies a particular system of allocation, "We've always done it like this" is not an answer. The answer is that it is justified only if it is.

So is this system of allocation justified?

When the government allocates a speech resource like spectrum, its decisions are tested according to a well-defined standard. The question is not whether the regulation meets strict scrutiny—as would a regulation that said, for example, that only Republicans may use the spectrum. The question instead is whether the regulation meets intermediate scrutiny— whether "[1] it advances important governmental interests unrelated to the suppression of free speech and [2] does not burden substantially more speech than necessary to further those interests."[7]

If a court addressed that question now, my sense is that it would clearly decide that the FCC's system for allocating spectrum is just fine. But it would decide that mainly because the alternatives are not yet developed or understood. We don't have many great examples of how spectrum could otherwise be regulated. Most of the mature examples of how spectrum can be used are examples that rely upon this system of allocated spectrum.

But the catch-22 is that the ability of these alternatives to demonstrate their success depends upon the FCC's opening up spectrum for alternative use. The more it opens, and leaves to private market experimentation, the easier it will be to demonstrate that the shared spectrum model works. And likewise with the contrary. The less the FCC leaves open for experimentation, the fewer incentives there will be in the market for innovators to develop new innovation. Thus, the critical need right now is a broad range of spectrum where these alternative uses might demonstrate themselves.

In a sense, this is the telephone network all over again, though this time the wires are ether, and the control is imposed through law alone rather than through the law backing up the control of AT&T's technology. Until innovators are free to use a communications resource (now spectrum, before the wires), innovation will be slowed. Yet in this case, one would expect, the claim to free use is even stronger than with the wires. No investor or corporation built the radio spectrum. This resource was given to us prebuilt by Mother Nature. Thus, the claim to free access is simply a claim that the government not get in the way of experimentation by innovators.

AT THE very minimum, this possibility suggests a strategy for government regulators (if those regulators were not effectively captured by existing spectrum users). The strategy builds on what we know: that government control over spectrum use has stifled innovation; that it will continue to stifle innovation as long as existing users have a political channel through which they can defend their existing privilege. We therefore should move—as quickly as possible—to a regime where the right to innovate does not depend upon the permission of someone else.

Essentially, two such regimes are possible. As I described in chapter 5, one follows Coase, and the other is a commons. Under the first, spectrum would be propertized and sold on a market. The buyer would be free to manage his spectrum however he saw fit. "Band managers" would control the chunks of spectrum that they own; users wanting to "use" that spectrum would license that right from a wide array of spectrum owners. Assuming the supply of spectrum would be great and the number of competitors large, this system would produce a strong competition in spectrum supply. No single supplier could control innovation any more than a single supplier of paper can control what books get written.

Under the second regime, spectrum is held in a commons and shared in real time by smart technologies for sharing. The rights are not allocated up front; as with the Internet, the demand is managed by protocols as it arises. Here, too, assuming the supply of spectrum is great and the protocols neutral, there would be no one who could stymie innovation. As with the Internet, the system would have no intelligence to discriminate against one form of spectrum use in favor of another.

There are advantages and disadvantages to both regimes. The property regime would produce great competition in spectrum use, and if competition were sufficiently "perfect," then, as I've noted before, the regime would produce the feature of the commons that is most salient here: that strategic action by the resource owner would not be possible. The only costs to the property regime are the burdens of any property regime—the costs imposed on the market by the need to negotiate and secure rights to access.[8] And if the ability to "share" spectrum becomes central to efficient spectrum management, then the costs of securing this right to "share" through private contract could become quite prohibitive.

The commons regime, too, would produce great competition in spectrum use. But the danger with the commons is overuse: that the free resource of spectrum would produce more demand than supply; and that important uses of spectrum would be shut down by congestion.

But in this choice between regimes, the mistake is to assume that a single solution is necessary. There is no reason to embrace *either* the market *or* the commons completely. Instead, the best strategy for now would be to embrace both solutions vigorously—to mark off significant chunks of spectrum for sale, while leaving significant chunks of spectrum open in a commons. Alongside auctioned space, we should have broad swaths of unowned space. And the government should then assure innovators that the unowned would remain so for a good long time—say, the length of a patent or, better yet, a single copyright (just to get some political energy on the side of reducing the term of copyright).[9]

This way the market could experiment with technologies and different spectrum uses. Some spectrum uses may need reserved space; let the market provide that. Other spectrum uses may be more flexible—as use of the Internet today is. But the opportunity for broad and creative use of the spectrum would inspire many to develop technologies that they wouldn't otherwise build. As entrepreneur Alex Lightman puts it:

> We need to have some slack in the system. We need to have a certain amount of the spectrum not be in the category where it's owned.[10]

This proposal is relatively neutral. It doesn't take sides in the technology of the future; it instead structures the competitive environment to allow a range of technologies to flourish. It acknowledges that many different solutions are possible; it recognizes the radical change in technologies for using spectrum that we are already seeing; and it simply embraces a strategy for getting the most out of these innovations. But it does say that for the moment, "these things need to be held in common, and they need to be held for the future. Because we don't know what the future will hold."[11]

SO IS this proposal anything close to what the government is actually doing? The answer is yes in words, but no in reality. At the level of high theory, the government remains committed to developing these alternative uses. But the devil is in the details, and the dungeons of Washington are well detailed.

If there is one thing that is certain about governments and innovation, it is that those who are threatened by new innovation will turn first to the government for help. Spectrum policy is not, and has never been, different. Every new idea is a threat to those who depend upon old ways of doing business. As David Hughes puts it, "[B]ig corporations have always marched to government to lock in their profits."[12] So we might well expect that those whose way of doing business depends upon the comfortable life of government-backed monopolies over spectrum will do what they can to make sure that those monopolies are not threatened by this new, free way of using spectrum.

We might expect it, and if we look at what's happening at the FCC, we would also observe it. For as quickly as innovators can develop new ways of using spectrum, incumbents are finding ways to make this innovation harder.

As I've already argued, this is nothing new. The surprise is how blatantly this protectionism continues. Consider, for example, the effort of former FCC chairman William Kennard to license low-power FM radio stations. This was a good move from the standpoint of increasing competition and diversity in speech. Kennard was committed to finding a way to free spectrum resources to enable a broader range of speakers. And there was very good technical evidence that these low-power radio stations—which might support a community action center or a local school—would create no technical interference with existing radio stations.[13]

The aim of the FCC was to enable local community broadcasts while assuring the broadcasts would not interfere with existing radio stations. The technical staff of the FCC conducted tests to determine how low-power the stations would have to be to assure no interference; the rules the FCC eventually proposed were more conservative than the technical staff recommended. "As a result of the FCC's conservatism, community groups in large urban centers with many incumbent broadcasters would find it difficult, if not impossible, to operate. But it would have enabled over 1,000 community organizations, churches, and schools to create a new medium for local discourse."[14]

But the existing stations balked. At first they complained to the FCC. When the FCC concluded that their evidence of interference was not substantiated, the broadcasters went to Congress. Congress didn't care much about these low-power stations (not many campaign dollars, after all, come from them). It did care about the broadcasters who were threatened. So Congress passed a law to restrict low-power broadcasters.[15] Large FM stations were protected from increased competition; that protection was effected through a law that silenced other speakers. So much for the First Amendment's demand that "Congress shall make no law . . . abridging the freedom of speech."

An example closer to the technology at the core of this chapter is the case of "AirPorts" in "airports." The AirPort is a wireless device sold by Apple Computer. It uses the 802.11b protocol to enable a computer to connect to a network at very fast speeds—11 megabits per second is the maximum for 802.11b, which is about twice the current DSL or cable speed. The device uses spread spectrum technology within one of the three swaths of spectrum that the FCC has allocated for "unlicensed use" for data.

Apple was a pioneer in pushing this form of technology. But the AirPort connects not just Apples. Any computer with an 802.11b wireless card can connect to an AirPort. And other companies, too, are building the equivalent of AirPort modems. Indeed, a whole sector is growing up around this possibility of wireless network access.

Some got the idea of putting AirPorts (or their equivalent) in airports—enabling travelers to connect to their Internet while sitting in an airport lounge. But soon local airport authorities started to complain: wireless modems, they argued, would interfere with air traffic controllers. They would also reduce the usage of pay phones.[16]

Now, I don't doubt that interference is possible for some of these new technologies. It is important that we be certain that new technologies don't damage important pieces of the existing infrastructure—at least those parts that we want to keep. But this complaint about air traffic was just silly. There is more interference caused by a hair dryer than by an Apple AirPort modem. And the notion that airport authorities should be able to stop progress to protect their telephone revenue is absurd.[17]

What's needed in contexts like this is a balanced way to evaluate these claims of interference to resolve whether they are real or just pretext. More generally, what's needed is a commitment to progress in the use of spectrum resources.

Instead the politicians have done just the opposite. Claims of technical interference are not credibly evaluated. Indeed, the FCC has placed the burden on new technologies not to harm existing use at all.[18] As Hazlett puts it, the "system is booby-trapped against new rivals, an irresistible 'attractive nuisance' to anticompetitive constituencies."[19] Thus, for example, amateur radio operators are allowed to veto new spectrum uses if they interfere *at all* with existing ham operations. And this pork is not just because of a special favor to amateur operators. Any new use that interferes with any old use must step aside.[20]

These restrictions on the use of amateur radio spectrum are particularly ironic. The Amateur Radio Service (ARS) defines a range of spectrum that is allocated to amateurs, but the members of the service "share" the spectrum in a commons mode. Any amateur can use any portion of that spectrum at any time and with just about any modulation technique now known. Within the prime "beachfront" spectrum property (from 30 megahertz to 3 gigahertz) there is a great deal allocated to the ARS. But armed with the FCC's veto rule, amateurs are effectively able to veto new and different users of "their" spectrum—despite the obligation imposed by the FCC's regulation to enhance "the value . . . to the public as a voluntary noncommercial communication service."[21]

These are technical rules that protect the old from the new. So too are there political rules that achieve the same end. Among these, none is more significant than the commitment and eagerness of the government to sell rights to spectrum, in the way spectrum rights are sold now.[22] This form of auction essentially entrenches the use of spectrum for particular businesses. The license "does not yield the right to deploy spectrum in alternative uses."[23] It entrenches a way of speaking of spectrum that is resistant to modern sharing technologies: that the spectrum is "my property." Once that property is established, it will be harder to deploy technologies that "share" other people's "property." (This despite the fact that an applicant for an

FCC license must first certify that it will not assert any propertied interest in radio spectrum.)[24] As Dave Hughes has asked:

> [W]hy should AT&T, who is offering a wireless service, . . . consent to competitors in their own area? . . . [I]t's not just a question of interference now. Now it becomes . . . opening the door by their consent to competition. And the last damn thing big companies want is competition.[25]

THE DANGER in selling spectrum or, more precisely, in not experimenting broadly with unlicensed spectrum is that existing spectrum users will be able to use purchased spectrum to resist changes in spectrum policy that might threaten their business models.[26] By selling spectrum now, before alternative uses can be developed, we create a world where the resources for these new alternatives are held by those *with the strongest incentive to stop them.* As Eli Noam puts it, it is like "having the old AT&T auction off the right to compete against it. Under such a system, MCI would not have emerged."[27]

The concern is not just about spectrum owners; it is also about the nature of the existing spectrum uses. The dominant and fastest-growing spectrum use right now is mobile telephone systems. These systems are architected in just the way the old telephone network was—intelligence is located not at the ends, but instead in the network itself. The cellular phone companies retain control over how the cellular technology develops; if you want a new application for your (increasingly powerful) phone, you will get it only if the telephone company wants you to.

This architecture for a wireless system creates the obvious protectionist risks. And as Charmed Technologies CEO Alex Lightman puts it, we are already seeing these risks mature into protectionist practices.

> [T]here is a nice little cozy ménage à trois between the companies that are providing infrastructure and the companies that provide the handsets, and the monopoly carriers or the oligopoly carriers.[28]

By selling the spectrum, the carriers have a strong incentive to assure returns sufficient to recover the investment in spectrum. These returns are best assured (or at least it seems to the companies that are best assured) if the companies husband the market power that is carried over from the noncompetitive telephone world (recall: much of the action here is international, where competitive phone systems don't yet exist). Thus, the willingness of the existing players to open up their spectrum to a wildly different form of use—one that would be much more competitive—is unlikely at best. Recall the words of AT&T executive Jack Osterman in 1964: "[W]e'll be damned if we allow the creation of a competitor to ourselves."[29]

A policy from the FCC that does not create a strong opportunity for an alternative to develop is designed to protect existing interests. To not encourage or permit wide-scale experimentation, to not set aside much broader unlicensed spectrum, to protect existing uses against *any* interference— these are policies designed to preserve the old against the new. They are just what we would expect from government regulation of spectrum; they are much less than we should demand after the experience of the Internet.

The government's role should be to induce investment where there is a great deal of social value to be created. This is precisely the opportunity with unlicensed spectrum.[30]

OPPONENTS OF this mixed strategy are of two sorts: those who think it is unnecessary—that the market will get us to the right answer without the experiments with open spectrum; and those who think it unwise—that open spectrum is a terrible way to allocate spectrum resources.

The first group thinks that the market has a sufficient incentive to find the optimal use of spectrum. As with any resource, these market mavens argue, privatization will give owners the strongest incentive to commit the resources that they hold to the highest and best use. Thus, if there is an innovative new way to use spectrum, then someone who owns the spectrum has the best incentive to find it and deploy it. Markets deal best with scarcity and choice about innovation. Hence we should be pushing to strengthen the market.

Peter Huber is a good example of this kind of optimist. Huber is a brilliant polymath who, while working full-time as a lawyer, has written some of the most important policy and academic work about government regulation in general and telecommunications policy in particular.[31] In his book *Law and Disorder in Cyberspace*, Huber describes both the market model for allocating spectrum—where spectrum rights are auctioned off up front—and the commons model for allocating spectrum, promoted most strongly by an ally of Huber's, George Gilder. As I described in chapter 5, Gilder argues strongly that we should allocate spectrum as a commons. Auctions, Gilder argues, will simply entrench existing uses; free or common spectrum would create a strong incentive for new uses.

Huber does not reject Gilder's predications. He argues instead that we could get to Gilder's world of spectrum as a commons by first auctioning off all the spectrum and then allowing the market to "reassemble" the rights if that proves efficient.

Markets find ways of reassembling private pieces into public spaces when that is the most profitable thing to do. They may take more time than an omniscient central authority, but finding omniscient central authority takes even longer. For now, the thing to do is to get the spectrum out of government hands, however it can be done, and leave it to the market to re-create the public commons. It will, if the economics are there.[32]

This is an empirical claim that begs for some evidence. I doubt there is a single example of "private pieces" "reassembling" into "public spaces." Certainly there are examples of small landowners selling their land to developers; and we might imagine developers selling their land to other developers. But I can't begin to imagine the process by which this buying and selling of rights eventually leads to the spectrum commons that Gilder has described. There are too many sirens of strategic behavior on the way to imagine the private property system working itself pure.

If Huber's model were correct, we should expect that at least in some places the construction of commons has been left solely to a market. But at least within our tradition, however distasteful this is to strong libertarians, the most important commons have been supported by state intervention. Not the intervention of nationalization—these are commons, not state property. Instead, the intervention of a legal system that protects certain resources as open and neutral. Roads are not built through the "reassembling of private pieces" into a national highway grid. They are built by self-conscious commons constructions.[33]

Even if one were optimistic in the way Huber is, a more obvious question is this: Why start with the burdens of establishing a property system if there is good reason to believe that the better solution would be a commons? Why not start the other way around—with a commons that might, in certain circumstances, be privatized where needed?

This default of a commons gains support when one considers the kind of spectrum use that is increasingly preferred by researchers. To the extent research shows that a more efficient manner of organizing spectrum is not to narrow the bandwidth allocated while increasing the power of the transmitter, but instead to broaden the bandwidth used with much less power, the model of propertized spectrum makes much less sense.[34]

It is here that the open spectrum model confronts a different critic—one who argues that a spectrum commons would be a wildly inefficient method of allocating spectrum. And here, Thomas Hazlett is again the strongest voice. In a recent paper addressing this idea of the spectrum commons, Hazlett rightly ties the idea to the Internet. Writes Hazlett:

> The spectrum commons idea is motivated by analogy to the Internet. Yet the architecture of the Internet ... seriously misallocates scarce bandwidth. Because data cannot easily be prioritized, or billed, within the existing Internet protocols, tragedy of the commons appears frequently. High value communications are jammed in congested arteries with massive volumes of data of only marginal significance. Classically, the brain surgeon cannot read the life-or-death CT-scan because the Internet backbone is clogged with junk e-mail.[35]

But the response to Hazlett's example is not to criticize the Internet. The response is to ask who is this "brain surgeon" reading a CT scan over the Internet? And how does *her* ability to use the Net determine whether the Net "seriously misallocates" resources? Hazlett offers no data to support the claim that the "tragedy of the commons appears frequently." In fact, capacity has consistently outstripped demand.[36]

More significant, Hazlett ignores the advantages to innovation that I have identified throughout this book. Let's assume that the Internet "misallocates" bandwidth relative to the model Hazlett has. Does Hazlett really believe that the very same innovation (or better) would have been realized had the Internet been architected to "properly allocate" bandwidth from the start?

For there is no conceptual reason why we couldn't have auctioned off the Internet's resources at the start of the Internet. We could easily have imagined protocols to charge and prioritize being implemented from the very start. If we had, would we have produced the same kind of innovation? Across the same range? Had the network been architected to give the network owners control, would we have produced the Internet that we did?

Clearly, in my view, the answer is no. But I'm just a lawyer; I haven't the skill to model this counterfactual. My point is simply the part that Hazlett has not yet accounted for. He must at least show us why the oppor-

tunity for innovation that the original Net created was not actually beneficial. And he must likewise show that it would not be beneficial in spectrum,
either.

Hazlett has his biases; I have mine. He's enamored of perfect pricing and
perfect control; I'm still surprised (lawyer that I am) by the extraordinary innovation that comes from imperfect pricing and leaky control. If we had to
take a poll among neutrals—people biased neither as I am nor as Hazlett
is—I suspect most would be skeptical about whether a control architecture
in the Internet would have produced the same innovation that the commons architecture did. But whatever a poll would indicate, it is here that the
debate should occur. Given the creativity and innovation that the original
Internet produced, and given how different that innovation is relative to
other computer networks and other telecommunications systems, my bet for
spectrum would be that an architecture modeled on the Internet would not
be so bad.

THE IDEAL mix in the short term would be a regime that had both a commons and a property component, with the property component subject to
an important caveat. There would be broad swaths of spectrum left in the
commons; there would be broad swaths that would be sold as Hazlett proposes. But in light of the emerging technologies for sharing, even the spectrum sold as property would be subject to an important qualification: Other
users would be free to "share" that spectrum if they followed a "listen first"
protocol—the technology would listen to see whether a certain chunk of
spectrum were being used at a particular time, and if it weren't, it would be
free for the taking.

I recognize that idea is jarring—that "my property" would be free for the
taking just because I was not using it. But do you recognize why the idea is
jarring? The assumption that fuels the dissonance about property "free for
the taking" is that the taken property is exhaustible. I may not be using my
car at the moment, but that doesn't mean you should have the right to take
it, since your use of my car will, to some degree, deplete the property I have.
Cars are exhaustible resources.

Spectrum is not. When I use a bit of spectrum at a particular moment in
time, that spectrum is just as good after I'm finished as it was before. My use
in no way exhausts the resource. And more important, when spectrum is not
used, its value as a resource is not saved. Unused spectrum, like an empty
seat on an airplane, is a resource that is lost forever.

Thus, if we adjust our intuitions about what spectrum *is*—recognizing that even if under some protocols spectrum is *rivalrous* (in some sense, we both can't use the "same" spectrum at exactly the same time), it is *inexhaustible*—then a property rule that presumes an opportunity for sharing begins to make sense. The implicit "use it or lose it" requirement, while costly for some sorts of rights, is not costly where the social consequence of not using a particular resource is that that resource is lost forever.

Wouldn't there still be a conflict if I'm "sharing" your spectrum and you then decide you want to use it? In principle, but not in practice. For the "sharing" rule would require that the sharer use the spectrum for an extremely short period of time. Thus, the owner may be delayed, but the delay would not be significant.

This compromise simply recognizes an important limitation in current understanding of how spectrum might optimally be used.[37] It may well be that the market model makes most sense, and that in the long run, a market for spectrum will govern all spectrum. But that doesn't mean we need to embrace the market fully now. For as Eli Noam has demonstrated, a market structure could be layered onto open spectrum without embracing the ex ante allocation that auctions envision.[38] Like the Ethernet network described in chapter 5, at the time the system needs it, the system would make a request for a reservation. The only addition would be a system for charging for that token of reservation. Noam likens that system to the subway's method of charging for ridership.

The advantage of Noam's solution is that it keeps the cost of spectrum use down. As Noam writes, an auction is simply "a tax on the communications sector and its users."[39] Given the size of the bids currently being offered for this resource, it will tend, as Noam argues, to encourage oligopoly. "An auction payment that must be paid in advance is a barrier to entry, unless capital markets are perfect, which they are not."[40]

We are far from the moment, however, when it would make sense to layer this market onto open spectrum. Just as the National Park Service began charging entrance fees late in its life, so too should we begin without entrance fees and layer them on, neutrally, as needed. This mode of regulating a large chunk of the resource of spectrum would inspire the widest range of spectrum use. And a strong commitment by the government to support open spectrum would convince venture capitalists to invest in this alternative use.

*   *   *

BUT WHILE theorists favoring the market fight theorists pushing the commons, our government is pursuing neither policy well. Instead, our government pursues policies that are precisely contrary to freeing the spectrum, either through the competition of a well-functioning market or through a commons. It gets pushed by politicians, so it pushes to sell off rights to spectrum without fully embracing the property model. The reason is not ideal spectrum policy. The reason is that it auctions off this form to best protect existing businesses. As Gilder puts it, this push to sell off spectrum is simply a "legal infrastructure and protectionist program for information smokestacks and gas guzzlers."[41] The effect won't be to inspire new ways of using spectrum; instead, the effect will be to entrench the old ways against new uses.

While auctions "seem preferable to the agency's previous policy of simply giving [spectrum] away to 'worthy' applicants," they will not inspire new uses, and they may tend, Gilder argues, "to produce a winner's curse."[42] The expected revenue from these sales will exceed $50 billion; that revenue will put pressure on the incumbents to earn supracompetitive returns. The best way to earn supracompetitive returns is to continue the noncompetitive architecture in broadcasting that has earned them profits in the past. Selling spectrum will give the incumbents the means and the motive to make certain that the spectrum does not become (as we as a society should want) a commodity product—constrained by strong and broad competition.

GILDER'S ARGUMENT assumes a kind of irrationality within firms that economists are quick to attack. The money spent on spectrum is a "sunk cost." The rational business would ignore the sunk costs already spent and focus instead on the optimal way to get a return from the assets it has.

But Gilder's fear is not just a result of irrationality; the fear is that powerful actors can work to slow innovation that harms them. The long-run advantages of FM radio didn't stop AM broadcasters from working to kill FM.[43] The technical arguments in FM's favor, powerful and unrefuted, were impotent in the face of existing broadcasting interests. And the same danger continues to exist about spectrum management policies. There are too many places for the devil to find details that will effectively kill important new technologies.[44]

There is an opportunity here for a crucial layer of the communicative architecture to be opened and made free. Opening it would reduce the pressure on other channels of Internet access. Keeping it free would encourage a wide range of innovation around how that resource is used. But instead of encouraging the use of this resource, instead of expanding it broadly, we are quickly whittling away the opportunity this commons would create. Without justification beyond the knee-jerk bias of our day, we are swallowing the idea that control is better than freedom.

HERE AGAIN, an idea about property is doing all the work—but this time the idea is at its most attenuated. We don't yet have a full property regime for allocating and controlling spectrum. Yet we are still being driven to embrace this single view. We are racing to deny the opportunity for balance, pushed (as we always are) by those who have the least to gain from a world of balance. The possibility of a commons at the physical layer is ignored; even the chance to experiment with the commons is denied. Instead, policy makers on the Right and on the Left race to embrace a system of perfect control.

So strong is this idea of property, so unbalanced is our understanding of its tradition, that we embrace it fully, without limitation, even when it doesn't yet exist, and *even when the asset being assigned a property right is not*—like the wires of AT&T's cable or the creative genius behind Disney's Mickey Mouse—*something anyone has created*. We are racing to assign property rights in the air, because we can't imagine that balance could do better.

13

W h a t ' s   H a p p e n i n g   H e r e ?

N THE early 1970s, RCA was experimenting with a new technology for distributing film on magnetic tape—what we would come to call video. Researchers were keen not only to find a technology that could reproduce film with high fidelity; they were also keen to find a way to control the use of the technology. Their aim was a technology that could control the use of film distributed on video, so that the owner of the film might maximize its return from the distribution.

The technology eventually chosen was relatively simple. A video would play once, and when finished, the film would lock into place. If a renter of the video wanted to play the video again, he or she would have to return the video to the video store and have the tape unlocked. In this way, the owner of the film could assure that it was being compensated for every use of the copyrighted material.

RCA presented this technology to the Disney Corporation in the early 1970s. In a room with just five of the senior executives from Disney, a young RCA executive, Pat Feely, demonstrated RCA's device. The executives were horrified. They would "never," Feely reports their saying, permit their content to be distributed in this form. For the content, however clever the self-locking tape player was, was still insufficiently controlled. "How could they know," a Disney executive asked Feely, "how many people are going to be sitting there watching" a film? "What's to stop someone else coming in and watching for free?"[1]

＊　＊　＊

AS THE cost of digital filmmaking falls, educators are experimenting with filmmaking as a way of learning. There's something different about expression in film. As John Seely Brown, chief scientist at Xerox PARC, describes it:

> [As] you move into the role of film . . . you get something that most people overlook. [I]n text we can always add the parenthetical comment: Paren, dot, dot, dot, comma, if, sorta. . . . And so you string qualifier after qualifier. [But w]hen you do a sketch of an idea there are no qualifiers. . . . [Q]ualifiers don't hold. You've got to decide what the kernel idea is and then you sketch that idea.[2]

This means learning through filmmaking is different. And in a group of California schools, a number of filmmakers have been experimenting with giving students the tools to make film as a kind of writing. These experiments let the students draw upon a wide range of existing film, which they recombine in new and creative ways and then supplement with new scenes that the students shoot on their own.

This "changes the thinking process," Brown describes. It produces a "completely different experience from writing an essay." And though these educators are just at the start of this experiment, they have already seen the changes it can make in the students it touches. This is a new kind of thinking, enabled by this emerging digital technology.

The product of this creativity, however, can't be displayed publicly. The films these students produce are housed on a private, password-protected network. Lawyers for the university supporting this work have advised the educators that putting the content on the Web would subject the teachers to liability. Thus this creativity is bottled up in a private network, unavailable for other students to view or learn from. The lesson the students learn is that sharing this creativity is not to be allowed.

But why? John Seely Brown asks.

> To me, this is where education . . . is going. [This is how] students who grow up digital think and want to learn. [But] we are building a [legal] system that completely suppresses the natural tendencies of today's digital students.

The law says that their creation can't be shared and the technologies that we've seen in chapter 11 will take away the very ability to draw upon film content and mix it with something different.

Here we have an educational crisis in our country and we have this incredible platform where these students are discovering on their own. [But this platform] is progressively going to be closed down instead of opened up.

"Technology makes it possible," Brown concluded, "but the law is going to come in . . . and knock it out."

THE STORY of this part is easy to summarize. In one sense, each of the changes I describe in these three chapters is very different. Modifications to the broadband environment are different from modifications to patent law; changes in spectrum rules don't quite track the motives of Hollywood.

Yet in another sense, each of these examples is motivated by a common idea or common attitude. In each, an attitude of control, perfected by an idea about property, is in tension with a system that protects a commons. And in each, the idea about property prevails. We race to empower networks to discriminate (after all, they are "their computers"); we race to empower owners of copyright to control new modes of distribution; we race to develop property in the air. Our single, overriding view of the world is that only property matters; our systematic blindness is to the lesson of our tradition—that property flourishes best in an environment of freedom, both freedom from state control and freedom from private control. That a commons can have value greater than the same assets would if enclosed.

The consequence in each of these contexts is a change in the environment within which innovation occurs. That change has been, or threatens to be, a shift from a world where the commons dominates to a world where control has been reclaimed. The shift is away from the open resources that defined the early Internet to a world where a smaller number get to control how resources in this space are deployed.

This change will have consequences. It will entrench the old against the new. It will centralize and commercialize the kinds of creativity that the Net permits. And it will stifle creativity that is outside the picture of the world that those with control prefer.

If there were a reason why this change was necessary—if there were a reason to believe the Net could not advance without it or would be harmed without it—then I would support this shift, however reluctantly.

But no good *reason* has been given. We are marching backward, undoing the architecture—both the legal and the technical—of the original Net without anyone demonstrating why this change is needed. We are moving resources from the commons into a system of control without an argument about why control will help or why the commons will fail. We are jumping in the name of an ideology without any consideration of the facts of these past ten years.

So why are we making these changes?

In part, there is a dark story to be told. Change threatens existing interests. Channeling change is often the best strategy for preserving that threatened power. Those whose position is threatened by the change the Internet represents have a strong interest in trying to channel that change.

So, too, do they have the means. It is an iron law of politics that the organized beat the unorganized and that the vested have interests that get organized over the unknown. In Washington, decisions are made by representatives conferring with people whose interests are affected by changes in the Net. But who represents the innovations not yet made? Who demands that the platform be kept open for them?

No one. Some of those interests can't afford the negotiation with existing interests; some interests don't even yet exist.

The result is that the pressure in the existing system is biased in favor of the old. Policies get made to favor the old; the interest of the new simply has no voice.

But the larger story here is not about dark forces. It is about a blindness that affects our political culture generally. We have been so captured by the ideals of property and control that we don't even see the benefits from resources not perfectly controlled. Resistance to property is read as an endorsement of the state. The challenge to extreme propertization is read as the endorsement of nationalization.

In the context of intellectual property, the general problem is magnified by another blindness, the error induced by thinking of intellectual property as property. By simplifying the nature of the rights that IP law protects, by speaking of it as property, just like the ordinary property of cars and homes, our thinking is guided in a very particular way. When it is viewed as property, we see endless arguments for strengthening IP and few for resisting that increase.

This is not conspiracy. It is a cultural blindness. We have forgotten what the Framers of the American Constitution knew about the nature of IP, and hence we have lost the balance our Framers had in protecting IP.

The consequence of these three stories is a massive push in cyberspace right now to reestablish systems of control. This push is happening at all three of Benkler's communications layers: it is happening at the physical layer—as the architecture for wired access gets pushed to an architecture of control and as the spectrum carrying wireless content gets sold into a system of control; it is happening at the code layer, as the legal system through patents favors closed code over open and as content providers build the architecture that will enable them to have more perfect control over content on the Net; and it is happening at the content layer, as the rules, both technical and legal, for facilitating distribution of content increasingly favor control of that distribution over the free flow of the original Net.

This shift is a step back, to a system of creativity and distribution that is largely within the control of large commercial actors. But this time, this system of control does not have the relatively neutral justification of economics behind it. The constraints that make this control necessary are not the constraints built into the nature of real-space scarcity. Here, instead, the scarcity is largely artificial. The expansion of IP rights creates a certain scarcity, but to the extent that expansion is beyond what is needed to induce progress, it is an unnecessary and unjustified handout to existing interests. To the extent the architecture gets built to reestablish the power to control distribution, and thereby innovation, it is a constraint that is not demanded by economics. It is a constraint that simply favors some interests over others.

Because our bias is to ignore the choice between the free and the controlled, we ignore the costs of a system of control over a system that remains free. We fail to see the benefits from freedom because we assume that freedom is not possible. We assume that creativity and innovation and growth will occur only where property and markets function most strongly.

Against this ideology, I offer the Internet. Against this bias, I submit a tradition that has understood balance better. The past decade has demonstrated the value of the free; that freedom came from the Net's architecture. The changes we are now seeing simply ignore the value of the free; they get implemented by changing the architecture of the original Net.

In *Code*, I argued that the original Net protected fundamental aspects of liberty—free speech, privacy, access to content, freedom from excessive regulation; I argued that those freedoms flowed from the architecture of the Net; but, I argued, that architecture was not fixed; nothing guaranteed it would survive unchanged; and, in fact, this architecture was being changed in ways that took away some of these fundamental liberties.

I've now told the same story about innovation and the Net. The original Net protected fundamental aspects of innovation. End-to-end meant new ideas were protected; open code meant innovation would not be attacked;

free distribution meant new ways of connecting would be assured. These protections were largely architectural. This architecture is now changing. And as it changes, as with the threats to liberty, there is a threat here to innovation.

In both cases, the conclusion is the same. We can architect this space in any number of ways. Some architectures protect liberty, others do not. Some architectures protect innovation, others do not. But nothing assures that the first version of the Net's architecture will survive through its maturity. Indeed, in both cases, there is all the pressure in the world to say that the first version will not survive.

As the old Net gets replaced by the new, as old interests succeed in protecting themselves against the new, we face a fundamental choice. We can embrace this return to the architecture of creativity that has defined modern American life—perpetual control by homogeneous corporations of a system for creativity focused primarily on a mass audience. Or we can embrace the architecture the Net was. This is a choice we cannot avoid, and in the next chapter, I offer points of resistance to the trend we now see.

14

Alt.Commons

HERE ARE changes that could be made. This march backward is neither necessary nor complete. We still have the time to point policy in a different direction. The question is whether we have the will. Are we willing to set principles that will guide the next stage of the Internet's evolution, or will we allow those who have interests inconsistent with those principles to exercise their control?

My aim in this chapter is to outline some of these changes. My list is neither complete nor certain. But it should be a start of a conversation about returning the Net to the conditions that let innovation flourish.

I divide these proposals into the frame of Benkler's three layers. Changes in some might make changes elsewhere unnecessary, but changes in all of them would make the situation much better.

THE PHYSICAL LAYER

THE PHYSICAL layer would seem the least likely for reform, since this layer lives within real space only, and as I've argued, the constraints of real space are, well, real.

But there are a number of places where a change might do some good. And the most important follows from the argument considered in chapter 12.

Free Spectrum

THE PHYSICAL layer includes technology upon which, or in which, or over which the network lives. It includes the computers that connect to the Net, the wires they connect to, the routers that feed those wires, and the spectrum that substitutes for the wires.

As I have described, most of these elements are owned—and with one exception, I think properly so. Computers are private property, whether the government's (in the NSA or libraries) or individuals'. The wires, whether copper or fiber, linking these computers to routers to other computers are privately owned. Massive investment laid them; even greater investment has been needed to bring them up to date.

These private investments deserve the reward of private property. With one qualification that I will offer in the next section, the owners of this property should be free to use it as they wish. No one should have the right to sit at my machine. Access to my machine, and the wires of AT&T, should not be free. If it were free, then those who buy the machines and those who lay the wires would lose lots of the reason to buy the machines and lay the wires. If access were free, the incentives to build the Net out would largely be lost.

But the same virtues from control can't be said of spectrum. Or at least they can't be asserted with the same confidence. No one builds spectrum; no investment from AT&T has made it possible. No entitlement justifies special control over spectrum, and the owners of Ryder Truck Rental and Leasing should not have a monopoly right to control the highways just because they purchased expensive equipment to use it. Thus, any monopoly control over spectrum should be allowed only if it can be shown that monopoly control is needed.

My argument is not that exclusive control is not needed. It may well be that Hazlett is right. The congestion in the airwaves may push us to build out a property system. Spectrum auctions—either in advance or in real time—may turn out to be needed to use the spectrum in the best possible way.

But we don't know that yet, and we certainly don't know enough yet to know how spectrum will be used. Thus, rather than architecting the space exclusively for control, we should begin, as much as possible, as we began with the Internet: by building a regime that by design leaves a significant part of these resources in the commons. And once we see how that commons gets used, we can then change how that commons gets controlled.

This argues for a dual strategy. We should be setting aside broad swaths of spectrum as a commons, intermixed with spectrum as property. The market should be assured that both models will survive for the next chunk of time. And regulators should assure that the devices using the commons are smart enough not to spoil the space.[1]

What would this idea look like in detail? First, spectrum is not all the same. The spectrum the AM radio uses can't do what the spectrum that radio astronomy uses does. Thus, we can't simply carve off a single chunk of spectrum for open, unlicensed use. We must instead set off significant bands at each spectrum level, to assure that innovation for different uses of spectrum would be possible.

Second, we should force the government to give up its obscenely wasteful hoarding of spectrum. When radios were stupid and clear channels were necessary, this hoarding made sense. But the government is not using this spectrum with stupid radios. The most advanced work being done in "software-defined radios"—radios that would, like chameleons, change their character to fit the protocol in the context that works best—is being done by the same group that gave us the Internet—the Defense Advanced Research Projects Agency (DARPA). DARPA is researching software-defined radios that share spectrum smartly. It is, in other words, building the Internet in the air.[2]

I'm a great fan of DARPA's work, but I don't believe the government should have a monopoly on innovation around networks. A sensible policy would divide spectrum into many swaths, some controlled, some free. Users of the spectrum—meaning the machines that use the spectrum—would then decide which chunks work best for them. Indeed, with software-defined radios, they could make that decision many times over. Out on the highway, a cell phone could connect to a network in the best of several different ways. Some of those ways might use the free space of unlicensed spectrum. Some might log on to controlled spectrum property. But the decision would be a function of which choice made most sense at the moment.

Third, there is no doubt that a sensible spectrum policy for the future will require changes in the way spectrum is used today. Steel mills didn't get a permanent waiver from pollution laws just because their technology was old.[3] And pollution is precisely the way we should think about old uses of spectrum: large and stupid towers billow overly powerful broadcasts into the ether, making it impossible for smaller, quieter, more efficient uses of spectrum to flourish. Why should these smokestack technologies get protection, when the steel mills did not? Why not force them to improve their technology—to reduce the pollution they spew forth into the ether—so that others could innovate in yet unimagined ways?

These changes may well force familiar uses of the spectrum off of spectrum completely. Broadcast television, for example, is an extraordinary spectrum guzzler; in most contexts it would be best moved from the air to wires. This is just another instance of what has been called "the Negroponte switch"—that everything that used wireless spectrum would move to wires, and everything using wires would move to the air. Such movement will impose costs on some—just as rebuilding smokestacks imposed costs on Pittsburgh. But these costs in the short run would be easily outweighed by benefits in the long run. By establishing a dual system of free and controlled spectrum, each with an equivalent opportunity to demonstrate its own success, we could ensure future spectrum innovation.

Existing spectrum users will resist these changes. It is unfair, they will argue, to change the rules now. They paid good money, they will insist, for the monopoly control they have purchased. It is wrong for the government to go back on promises it made.

But this argument is absurd. First, technically, this change would not breach any promise. From the very beginning of spectrum allocation, the recipients have been required to affirm that they asserted no property interest in the spectrum rights they got.[4] From the very beginning, the express understanding has been that the licenses granted were limited in time and that the risk that spectrum would be allocated differently was a risk these businesses should take into account. For corporations now to claim that, these statements notwithstanding, they expected to have their monopolies in perpetuity is just absurd.

That this argument is being made, however, does signal the importance of the government's acting soon. Rather than racing to auction off more spectrum in the way it has to date, and thereby increasing the sense of entitlement that these spectrum hoarders claim, the government should be marking off much wider areas of spectrum that will be dedicated, for a significant period, to the commons. The government could free existing holders of spectrum to sell their leaseholds to others—thereby facilitating the market that Hazlett wants. But before it puts any more of this resource into a system of control, it should assure that the commons in spectrum is properly secured.

Finally, the FCC should free up greater access to existing unlicensed bands, including the Amateur Radio Service bands. Existing users here too should not have the power to veto something new simply because it is a late-comer.[5]

If there were a rich and developed physical layer of free spectrum access—permitting many competitors to offer Internet access using this final link of free spectrum—then the need for the government to worry about other modes of access to the Net would be lessened. If a rich and powerful channel is kept open and kept in the commons, then what owners of other channels, not left in the commons, do is less of a concern. The key is balance, but our practice now is at the extreme.

Free Highways

OPENING CHANNELS of spectrum would be one important expansion of the commons. It isn't, however, the only possible change. There are other steps the government might take to open access at the physical layer—not by becoming network owners, but by clearing the way for others to develop and run networks.

The model here is the highway system. While we have grown skeptical about the state's role in many aspects of our life, there remains a strong belief that the state has a place in the provision of basic services like roads. The government has funded the construction of highways and local roads; these highways are then used either "for free" or with the payment of a toll. In either case, the highway functions as a commons.

In some cases there has been a move to privatize highways. Los Angeles, for example, has experimented with private roads, promising lower congestion in exchange. But these experiments exist alongside open, public roads. The two go together, and where only one road is available, it is a public one.

This is a sensible use of public resources. It builds a resource for exchange that all have access to. It balances resources controlled privately; it sets a baseline against which private resources compete.

In my view, the same attitude should guide government policy with respect to the physical infrastructure supporting the Net—in particular, the fiber infrastructure and rights-of-way to deploy alternative access. Just as the state has spent resources on building highways, so too might it need to spend resources on building out the information superhighway.[6]

Many cities are already picking up on the idea. Chicago, for example, has started funding the deployment of "dark fiber"—meaning simply fiber optic cable that is not immediately connected to any particular service.[7] The city does not get into the business of wiring the links or running the routers; the city's job is simply to fund the laying of the cable and let competitors connect to the fiber to sell Internet access.[8]

The advantage in this way of building the basic physical infrastructure upon which the network is built is that there is no need to strike a bargain with the monopoly devil to finance the deployment of this fiber. But with cable, the government decided to fund the build-out with the grant of monopolies to the cable owners. That strategy proved costly, as the cable owners became invested with eagerness to defend their monopoly. The aim of a monopolist is always to protect his monopoly, and if he's rational, he's willing to spend the net present value of his monopoly to defend it.

But if the state were funding the building of at least some of this basic infrastructure, and if it were kept far from the content that gets played across this infrastructure, then there would be no actor in this system with an incentive to discriminate. Government would lay the pipes; private industry would use the pipes to serve access to local customers.

This point would not stop with dark fiber. Right now the most expensive part of the connection is the "last mile" to the consumer's home. That's expensive in part because the technology for converting from glass to electronics is itself expensive and in part because of the cost of trenches. If every house had to be rewired (or fibered), the cost of running fast Internet to every house would be very high.

One alternative would be to run the fiber to a wireless broadcasting station that then would beam Internet service to many users in the neighborhood. (This would be the inverse of the system that gave us cable TV.) But to do this, providers would have to have access to telephone poles or other places where broadcasting stations might be built.

Here again the state could play a role—either by granting access to state property or by purchasing access to private property. This access would amount to permission for a private company to build a broadcasting service; it would not be an invitation for the state to get into the ISP business. And because the capacity of these fibers is so great, the potential for a bottleneck would be much less.

In both cases, the role the state plays is to assure that bottlenecks not become opportunities for exercising market power. The state builds a competitive environment where there is incentive to behave *as a competitor*. This commitment will require resources; it would be less pressing if the

FCC freed spectrum generally. But it is an appropriately translated role for the state when superhighways carry bits rather than trucks.

THE CODE LAYER

THE CODE layer is the heart of the Internet; its particular architecture is what was special. It would make no sense, however, to say that we should fix ourselves to the particular architecture of the network at any one time. The point is not a blind originalism; the point instead is to preserve the values expressed by that original architecture. Some ways to do that are considered here.

Neutral Platforms

THE CRITICAL layer to protect if we are to protect innovation on the Net is the code layer—the space where code decides how content and applications flow, and where code could control how innovation develops. It is at this layer that the Internet originally embraced the principle of end-to-end. That principle assured that control was bottom up; that what would succeed would succeed because users demanded it; and that what users demanded would be free to flow to them.

It is the compromise of this principle that threatens the greatest harm to innovation. And the pressure to compromise comes from those who would use their power over architecture to protect a legacy monopoly. The danger exists when control over the platform can translate into the power to protect against new innovation.

We've seen this power in two different contexts. The claims the government made against Microsoft were the clearest example of this danger: Microsoft, the government argued, used its power over the Windows platform to protect the Windows platform from innovation that would threaten it. Likewise in the context of broadband cable: the danger was that by restricting the number of ISPs, the network owner could exercise control over the ISPs to assure that its content, or business model, would not be threatened by certain uses of the Net.

This power, whether exercised over the operating system or over the network within which Internet traffic flows, threatens innovation. The risk of a strategic response by the platform owner reduces the expected benefit from innovating in certain status quo–threatening ways. Thus, if innovation is our goal, our policy should be to minimize the threat of this strategic be-havior. A number of strategies to that end are obvious.

First, the government should encourage the development of open code. Open code, as I've argued, risks none of the dangers of strategic behavior that closed code, or controlled networks, do. If open code is used strategi-cally, then the resources to counter that strategic action are always available. Innovators can rely upon the promise of open code in their innovations. They need not worry that what they develop will be swallowed by the plat-form they develop for.

This encouragement should not be coercive. There's no reason to ban or punish proprietary providers. People should be free to develop code how-ever they wish. But a government has its own interests, and closing its re-sources to others is not one of them. If the federal government develops a system to handle welfare claims, what reason does it have for hiding the code for that system from the states? Why not let the states take that code and build upon it? And if the states, then so, too, with the universities. In each case, the aim should be to expand the reach of these powerful and valuable resources, not to contract and hoard them when no value to the hoarding exists.

Likewise with the government's choice of operating systems. What reason does the government have for supporting closed code, when open code is as powerful and the externalities from using open code would benefit oth-ers? If the PCs that the government owned ran something other than Win-dows, then the market for these alternative platforms would be wildly expanded. And if the market for alternatives were strong, then the benefits from building for these alternatives would be strong as well.

Again, such a strategy does not flow from animus against proprietary providers. Any environment is richer when built upon a diversity of life. As the various viruses that have plagued the Internet have shown, we are in-creasingly vulnerable the more concentrated the strain. Opening the code that constitutes cyberspace in as many contexts as possible will enable a flourishing of innovation that need not depend upon a single platform. Microsoft may not like this, but a policy favoring this diversity is not a policy against Microsoft.[9]

Second, the government should continue to ensure that no major player in the Internet space is able to architect the Internet space to empower its own strategic behavior. If the cable companies want to build a cable tele-vision system where they have complete control over the content that flows across their cable, more power to them. Control has been at the core of the cable system from the start. But if cable wants to carry TCP/IP, then the values of the Internet should trump the control of cable. Any major network that wants to piggyback on the Internet's success should piggyback with the values of the Internet kept in mind.

How best can the government carry this role into effect? Historically, the most successful strategy has been banishment. When the government, for example, banished the telephone company from the game of providing computer services, then the telephone company had little interest in playing games among different providers of computer service. If it were simply in the business of selling access to pipe, then those buying that access would have an equal playing field for competing in providing network services.

Since the 1996 Telecommunications Act, the strategy has been different. The government has required the telephone company to compete against ISPs. The telephone company, for example, is permitted to sell you DSL, but it must permit competitor DSL providers to offer you DSL service as well. This is the "open access" requirement. Competition is assured by regulating the Bell companies and by requiring them to unbundle local access services. And this unbundling in turn assures that the telephone company can't play any games.

In this way, the regulation assures that competitive pressures will exist for every mode of broadband access, so that broadband providers won't have the incentive to exercise control in a strategic way. And until enough competitors are on the competitive field, this may well be the best strategy for keeping access to the Internet open.[10]

Alternatively, we might imagine a simpler regulatory strategy. If the concern at stake is that network providers will leverage control over the network into some control over content—if the concern is that they will have an incentive to compromise the principle of end-to-end—then rather than requiring unbundling of services, the government could adopt a more direct regulatory strategy: if you provide Internet services, then you must provide them consistent with the principle of end-to-end.[11]

It is hard in the abstract to game that alternative. DSL would compete with cable, fiber, and wireless service in providing Internet traffic. The latter would not be required to facilitate competition on their own facilities, but the competition among facilities might be enough in most places to ensure that prices are kept low. As long as discrimination is not enabled (the consequence of preserving end-to-end), the essential elements of a commons would be preserved as well.

My bias is in favor of the least invasive regulatory response, but it is also a bias in favor of a guarantee of a regulatory response if regulation is needed. The trends have not been toward fast networks that promise uncontrolled access. The trends have been toward control.

One useful point of comparison here is our neighbor to the north, Canada. The Canadians have required open access for broadband providers, and a recent *Report of the National Broadband Task Force* has endorsed a "bill of rights" for broadband users that assures continued consumer choice for any build-out of a network employing government funds. This choice of policy has apparently not harmed Canadian access. According to a recent OECD report, broadband connections are twice as common in Canada per capita as in the United States.[12]

Finally, and at a minimum, regulators should begin to evaluate changes to the network in terms of the neutrality of end-to-end. We should begin to think about the trade-offs between control and neutrality explicitly—not because every trade-off would be a sin, but because otherwise, the loss will be invisible.

THE CONTENT LAYER

THE CHANGES at the physical and code layers are significant. They will require a commitment that I am skeptical our politicians are capable of giving. But they are nothing compared with the changes that are required at the content layer. For it is here that we have moved the furthest from sensible policy, and here where there is the strongest political power to resist.

The core idea that we, as a culture, must recapture is that control over content is not to be perfect. Ideas and expression must to some degree be free. That was the aim of copyright law initially—the balance between control and freedom. It was, "even twenty years ago . . . an article of faith [that it] offer only circumscribed, porous protection."[13] But these balanced laws now have an ally that threatens to destroy the balance: code.

Technology, tied to law, now promises almost perfect control over content and its distribution. And it is this perfect control that threatens to undermine the potential for innovation that the Internet promises.

To resist this threat, we need specific changes to reestablish a balance between control and creativity. Our aim should be a system of sufficient control to give artists enough incentive to produce, while leaving free as much as we can for others to build upon and create.

In setting this balance, there are a few ideas to keep in mind. First, we live in a world with "free" content, and this freedom is not an imperfection. We listen to the radio without paying for the songs we hear; we hear friends humming tunes that they have not licensed. We refer to plots in movies to tell jokes without the permission of the director. We read books to our children borrowed from a library without any payment for performance rights to the original copyright holder. The fact that content at any particular time is free tells us nothing about whether using that content is "theft." Similarly, an argument for increasing control by content owners needs more than "they didn't pay for this use" to back it up.

Second, and related, the reason perfect control is not our aim is that creation is always the building upon something else. There is no art that doesn't reuse. And there will be less art if every reuse is taxed by the earlier appropriator. Monopoly controls have been the exception in free society; they have been the rule in closed societies.

Finally, while control is needed, and perfectly justifiable, our bias should be clear up front: Monopolies are not justified by theory; they should be permitted only when justified by facts. If there is no solid basis for extending a certain monopoly protection, then we should not extend that protection. This does not mean that every copyright must prove its value up front. That would be a far too cumbersome system of control. But it does mean that every system or category of copyright or patent should prove its value up front. Before the monopoly should be permitted, there should be reason to believe it will do some good—*for society*, and not just for monopoly holders.

With these ideals in mind, here are some first steps to freeing culture:

Copyright

THE TREND in copyright law has been to increase copyright's scope and duration, while making the right easier to secure and keep. While the original copyright statutes put a great burden on copyright owners to register their work, make deposits of their work to the government, and renew the copyright after an initial term, now copyright affixes automatically, it extends for the life of the author plus seventy years without any effort by the copyright owner, and the copyright owner need make no effort at all to continue to enjoy this government-granted monopoly.

This shift is bizarre. We have been pushed to this "no effort" monopoly handout by the view that "technical" requirements should not interfere with the right of an author to his or her copyright. That argument sounds good until one considers the other side of the bargain—the public. Copyright owners should not be denied legitimate copyright protection for technicalities, no doubt; but assuring that the reach of state-backed monopolies over speech is not broader than necessary is not a "technicality." If welfare recipients can be denied their benefits because they fail to complete a benefits form properly, then I can't see the unfairness in requiring those who demand state support to defend their monopoly similarly by filling out a registration form.

I would go even further.[14]

FIVE-YEAR RENEWABLE TERMS

AUTHORS AND creators deserve to receive the benefits of their creation. But when those benefits stop, what they create should fall into the public domain. It does not do so now. Every creative act reduced to a tangible medium is protected for upward of 150 years, whether or not the protection benefits the author. This work thus falls into a copyright black hole, unfree for over a century.

The solution to this black hole of copyright is to force those who benefit from copyright to take steps to protect their state-backed benefit. And in the age of the Internet, those steps could be extremely simple.

Work that an author "publishes" should be protected for a term of five years once registered, and that registration can be renewed fifteen times. If the registration is not renewed, then the work falls into the public domain.

Registration need not be difficult. The U.S. Copyright Office could run a simple Web site where authors could register their work. That Web site could be funded by charges for copyright renewals. When an author wants to renew the copyright, the system could charge the author a renewal fee. That fee might increase over time or depend upon the nature of the work.

This registration site could also take deposits of certain kinds of work. For archive purposes, the site could collect digital copies of all the works copyrighted. And for certain kinds of work—software in particular—those deposits would be required for the protection to be secured. Given how easy the Net has made such transfers, these costs would be relatively small.

"Unpublished works" would be different. If I write an e-mail and send it to a group of my friends, that creativity should be treated differently from the creativity of a published book or recorded song. The e-mail should be protected for privacy reasons, the song and book protected as a quid pro quo for a government-backed monopoly. Thus, for private, unpublished correspondence, I think the current protection is perfectly sensible: the life of the

author plus seventy years, automatically created, with no registration or renewal requirements.

One of the strongest reasons that the copyright industry has raised for the
elimination of this renewal requirement is the injustice that comes from a
family's or author's losing copyright protection merely because of a technicality. If "technicality" means something like the registration was lost in the
mail or was delivered two hours late, then the complaint is a good one.
There is no reason to punish authors for slips. But the remedy for an overly
strict system is a more relaxed system, not no system at all. If a registration is
lost or a deadline missed by a short period of time, the U.S. Copyright Office should have the power to forgive.

A change in the copyright term would have no effect on the incentives for
authors to produce work today. There is no author who decides whether or
not to write a book depending upon whether he or his estate will receive
money three-quarters of a century from now. The same with a film producer: Hollywood studios forecast revenues a few years into the future, not
ninety-five. The effect on expected income from this change would therefore be tiny.

But the benefit for creativity from more works falling into the commons
would be large. If a copyright isn't worth it to an author to renew for a modest
fee, then it isn't worth it to society to support—through an array of criminal
and civil statutes—the monopoly protected. But the same work that the original author might not value could well be used by other creators in society.

Even more significant, this repository of data about what work is protected would lower the costs of licensing copyrighted works significantly.
Because the database would be relatively fresh—with a requirement that
contact information be kept current—creators who want to license other
creators' work would have a simple tool to do so.

SOFTWARE COPYRIGHT

SOFTWARE IS a special case. The current protection for software is the life
of an author plus seventy years or, if a corporation, ninety-five years. This is
a parody of the Constitution's requirement that copyright be for "limited
times." When Apple Macintosh's operating system falls into the public domain, there will be no machine that could possibly run it. The term of
copyright for software is effectively unlimited.

Worse, the copyright system protects software without getting any new
knowledge in return. When the system protects Hemingway, we at least get

to see how Hemingway writes. We get to learn about his style and the tricks he uses to make his work succeed. We can see this because it is the nature of creative writing that the writing is public. There is no such thing as language that doesn't simultaneously transmit its words.

Software is different. As I've described, software is compiled; the compiled code is essentially unreadable; but to copyright software, the author need not reveal the source code. Thus, while an English Department gets to analyze Virginia Woolf's novels to train writers in better writing, the Computer Science Department doesn't get to examine Microsoft's operating system to train its students in better coding.

The harm from this system of protecting creativity is greater than this loss to computer science education. While the creative works from the sixteenth century can still be accessed and used by others, the data used by software programs from the 1990s are already inaccessible. Once a company producing a certain product goes out of business, there is no simple way to uncover how its products encoded data. The data are thus lost, and the software is unusable. Knowledge has been destroyed.

The reason copyright law doesn't require the production of source code is that it is believed that that would make the software unprotectable. The open code movement might throw that view into doubt, but even if one believes it, the remedy (no source code) is worse than the harm. There are plenty of ways for software to be protected without the protection of law. Copy protection systems, for example, give the copyright holder plenty of control over how and when the software is copied.

If society is to give software producers more protection than they otherwise would get through technology, then we should get something in return. And one thing we could get would be access to the source code after the copyright expires. Thus, I would protect software for a term of five years, renewable once. But that protection would be granted only if the author submitted a copy of the source code to be held in escrow while the work was protected. Once the copyright expired, that escrowed copy would be publicly available from the U.S. Copyright Office server.[15]

PROTECTING INNOVATION

THE SINGLE most striking feature of copyright law is its ability to give owners the power to control innovation in the context of the Net. The power to issue injunctions against technologies for distributing content is an extraordinary power for controlling what new technologies can be created.

This is the power that Hollywood has used to control the development of new distribution technologies. Without any showing of harm, the industry has been able to exercise control over new modes of distribution.

No one industry should have the power to veto the Net's development. No single set of interests should be able to decide what innovations are best. This is especially true when no showing of harm is necessary for this veto to be imposed. And this is precisely the reality with respect to copyright and the Net.

Congress should limit this reactive character of copyright law. While in the ordinary case the copyright holder should not have to prove harm before enforcing a copyright, in a context of significant technological change, a defendant should at least have the opportunity to show that the copyright holder will suffer no harm.[16]

PROTECTING MUSIC

THE NET has created a world where content is free. Napster is the most salient example of this world, but it is not the only one. At any time a user can select the channel of music he or she wants. A song from your childhood? Search on the lyrics and find a recording. Within seconds you can hear any music you want.

This freedom the recording industry calls theft. But they don't call it theft when I hear an old favorite of mine on the radio. They don't call it theft when they are recording takeoffs of prior recorded music. And they don't call it theft when they make a new version of "Jingle Bells." They don't, in other words, call it theft when *they* are using music for free in ways that have been defined by the copyright system as fair and appropriate uses.

The issue we must confront is whether this free distribution should continue to be free. And the solution to that question is to keep an important distinction in mind: As we've seen, there is a distinction between music being "free" and music being available at zero cost. Artists should be paid, but it doesn't follow that selling music like chewing gum is the only possible way.[17]

Here, too, a bit of history helps. As I have described, there have been many contexts where Congress had to balance the rights of free access against the rights of control. When the courts said piano rolls were not "copies" of sheet music, Congress balanced the rights of composers against the rights to mechanically reproduce what was composed. It balanced these rights through a compulsory license that enabled payment to artists while assuring free access to the work produced. The same is true in the context of cable TV. As we saw in chapter 7, the Supreme Court twice said that cable TV providers had a right, under existing law, to free TV. Congress finally changed those rights, but again, in a balanced and sensible way. Cable providers got access to television broadcasts, but broadcasters and copyright holders had a right to compensation for that access. This compensation again was set by a compulsory licensing term. Congress protected the author, but not through a *property* right.

The same solution is possible in the context of music on the Net.[18] But here, rather than balance, the rhetoric is about "theft" and "crime." But was it "theft" when cable TV took television broadcasts?

Congress should empower file sharing by recognizing a similar system of compulsory licenses. These fees should not be set by an industry intent on killing this new mode of distribution. They should be set, as they have always been set, by a policy maker keen on striking a balance. If only such a policy maker were somewhere to be found.

REBUILDING THE CREATIVE COMMONS

THESE CHANGES would affect works produced in the future. They would have no effect on works already produced and protected by these extensive terms. Nor could these changes affect works already produced—the Constitution limits Congress's power to take away property already granted, as well it should.

But there are other ways that Congress might act to create an incentive to build out the creative commons. One way would be to create incentives for holders of copyright to donate their holdings into a public conservancy. I've worked with others to build such a conservancy, but ours is not the only possible one. If Congress gave tax benefits to donors of IP to parallel the tax benefits given to donors of art, then there would be a much greater incentive to donate works to the general weal.[19]

One context in particular where incentives could do some good is that of orphaned software. Companies often decide that the costs of developing or maintaining software are higher than the benefits. They therefore orphan the software, by neither selling it nor supporting it. They have little reason, however, to make the source code for that software available to others. The code therefore simply disappears, and the products become useless.

If Congress created an incentive for these companies to donate their code to a conservancy, then others could build on the earlier work to produce updated or altered versions. This in turn could improve the software available by avoiding the loss of knowledge that was built into the original code. Orphans could be adopted by others who saw their special benefit.

There are other steps that Congress could take as well. One problem that often plagues creators is the claim that a work is copyrighted when it is not. It is a common practice for publishers, for example, to claim copyright when under the law they plainly do not have such a right. Sheet music publishers, for example, will often put copyright notices on public domain works.

This practice is in violation of existing copyright law. It is a crime to say something is copyrighted when in fact it is not. But the only punishment that the law provides for this crime is an action brought by a U.S. attorney. Not surprisingly, U.S. attorneys have better things to do; no one has ever been prosecuted for violations of this.[20]

This is a perfect claim for private attorneys general. Professor David Lange suggests that "claims . . . so extravagant in relation to the reality from which . . . they . . . spring . . . ought to be made the subject of a serious counterclaim for punitive damages rooted in some sort of tort . . . to be termed 'unconscionable overreaching.'"[21] Congress could authorize private citizens to bring suits against false copyright claims. If successful, the plaintiffs in these suits should earn a bounty, plus their costs. And if publicized, such suits should change the behavior of publishers.

LIMITS ON CODE

AS I'VE described, the interests that copyright law protects can be protected by technology as well as law. As the DVD case discussed in chapter 11 makes clear, this protection by technology can often reach far beyond the protection of law. Copyright protection systems can limit fair use or extend the term of protection beyond the copyright term. If there is a reason for the balance in copyright law, then there is a reason to be concerned about the imbalance created by this code.

How one thinks about the code on its own is a hard legal question. We don't ordinarily think that there is an affirmative wrong in these private systems of protection. But where the law backs up this code, then there is clear reason to be concerned. Then the protection that the copyright gets is not just the private protection of code; it is also the protection of law. So here, in my view, there is a clear reason to limit the protections of law. Congress should expressly require that any law protecting copyright protection systems not protect those systems beyond the reach of copyright law itself. Only those code protection systems, in other words, that preserve adequate room for fair use would get the protection of Congress's law. (This is a version of what has been called the "Cohen Theorem," named after law professor Julie Cohen: that one has a right to hack copyright protection systems in order to secure fair use.)

LIMITS ON CONTRACT

THE SAME point can be made about contract. Often a copyrighted work is sold or licensed subject to a set of terms imposed in a license. Sometimes the terms imposed by the license are inconsistent with the balance that copyright law aims for. If the balance in copyright law is important, then it should not be undermined by a different kind of law—contract law. While not every license is in conflict with copyright law, many licenses are in conflict with the limited protection copyright law is to give.

State laws in particular that give copyright holders greater power than the balance copyright law was to set should be resisted. Among these, the most troubling is a uniform law making its way through the states called the "Uniform Computer Information Transactions Act"—or UCITA.

UCITA is designed to facilitate transactions in computer information. Its aim is to make on-line contracting easier. But as many have argued (quite convincingly, in my view), the balance that UCITA strikes between the seller and the consumer is not adequate to protect the balance the law intends between copyright and the commons.[22]

The opposition to UCITA has been strong; the need to adopt a uniform code right now has not been demonstrated. We have very little understanding of what on-line contracts could be. Yet UCITA is marching across the states with the aim to settle a range of issues up front.

This is a mistake. The premise of state uniform laws is that they are to reflect and codify mature and settled understandings of the law. They are not to be leaders; they are simply to clarify and to make uniform where uniformity matters. In this case, the law has been used to expand the rights of one side of a deal relative to another. The process has been captured. The proper response to this capture is to reject the proposal now and wait to see what's needed later.

LIMIT COMMERCIAL EXPLOITATION

PROFESSOR JESSICA Litman has taken these recommendations one step further. As she rightly observes, following the work of Professor L. Ray Patterson,[23] copyright was originally simply a restriction on commercial entities. It regulated "publishers" and those who "vend" "maps, charts, and books." Because the law slipped into using the term *copy* in 1909, it has now extended its reach to every act of duplication, by printing press or computer memory. It now therefore covers actions far beyond the "commercial" exploitation of anything.

Litman therefore argues that we take copyright back to its roots. "[W]hy not," she writes, "start by recasting copyright as an exclusive right of commercial exploitation? Making money (or trying to) from someone else's work without permission would be infringement, as would large scale interference with the copyright holders' opportunities to do so."[24] Thus, she argues, we should redraw the border between commercial and noncommercial exploitation, giving authors strong control over the "pirating" of their work by commercial entities, but leaving noncommercial actions outside the reach of the law.

There is a great merit to this idea and, in my view, good reason to explore it extensively. The strongest reason to be skeptical is that the Net itself has now erased any effective distinction between commercial and noncommercial. Napster no doubt is a commercial activity, though the sharing that Napster enables is not. The law might well regulate Napster, but then subsequent p2p technologies would enable the same sort of sharing, just without commercial links. If there were a harm from Napster (and I'm not certain there is), it's not clear what benefit we gain from merely pushing the control underground.

This line-drawing problem reinforces my own view that the better solution is simply to go back to the Framers' notion of limited terms. The great benefit of a technology such as Napster is the ability to get access to music that is no longer made available commercially—songs from the 1930s or 1940s, for example, that still hang in copyright, but that the copyright holders don't make available commercially. If copyright were returned to a meaningfully "limited time," then we wouldn't need to worry so much about drawing commercial vs. noncommercial distinctions. For five or maybe ten years, commercial entities would hold these rights exclusively. Beyond that, the music, like culture generally, would be freely available.

Litman's suggestion does hint at a different limitation on the copyright.

We might call this the "use it or lose it" restriction.[25] Once a work is published, if a holder of a copyright does not continue to make it available commercially, then others should have the right to exploit the work. Technically, we could accomplish this balance by giving anyone a right, after a brief period of exclusive control, to license the work under compulsory terms. The terms of such licenses can't be set here. Which would work best depends upon lots of things we can't know in the abstract. But the basic idea is that once a limited monopoly right has been granted, there is no further reason to allow a rights holder to hold up the content. This, like the need to renew, would assure that work was quickly pushed into the public domain.

Patents

THE URGENCY in the field of patents is even greater. Here again, patents are not evil per se; they are evil only if they do no *social* good. They do no *social* good if they benefit certain companies at the expense of innovation generally. And as many have argued convincingly, that's just what many patents today do.

Our response should be empirical. Congress should demand of the U.S. Patent Office that it perform a regulatory review of its patent regulation and produce from that review a regulatory impact statement. In particular, it should be required to perform an economic study to justify the most controversial extensions of patent right now—business method and software patents. If these forms of innovation regulation can't at least meet the burden of demonstrating that they are more likely to aid innovation than harm it, then Congress should withdraw this form of monopoly protection.

In the meantime, there are smaller changes that Congress might make, all designed to lessen the harm patents generally, and bad patents in particular, might cause.

MORATORIUM

CONGRESS SHOULD enact a moratorium on the offensive use of these questionable patents until this review is complete. While this study occurs, innovators should be free to file for these patents. If someone tries to enforce a patent, then a company should be allowed to defend against that enforcement with patents secured in the ordinary way. But until there is a showing of the good this system does, we should allow the courts to intervene in the regulatory process.

DAMAGES

THE GREATEST harm that patents create may well be independent of the patents; the greatest harm may well be the harm caused by its enforcement. The real power a patent holder has—whether he or she holds a valid or invalid patent—is the threat of an injunction to stop the use of the patented technology, when damages would be an adequate remedy. Ordinarily, the use of someone else's "property" without negotiation is deemed adequate justification for an injunction; but there is no reason we should have to conceive of patents in this context as "property." Inventors could get an adequate return from the guarantee of reasonable royalties; users of patents could be assured that their innovation would not be blocked by a guarantee of a compulsory license.

This is not an easy idea to sketch briefly. To the extent that technologies are rightfully patented, granting only a compulsory right can, in many contexts, defeat the important incentives that patents produce. Thus, it would be a mistake to give up property protections for patents in all cases.

But you don't have to give up property protections for patents in all cases for it to make sense to adjust patents in the context of the Net. Here, where innovation is sequential and complementary, giving users greater flexibility would reduce the hold-up problem created by patent law.[26]

REFORM

FINALLY, THERE'S a range of reform that has been pushed on the U.S. Patent Office, much of it extremely valuable.[27] Software patents are (relatively speaking) new. At least, they are newer than software itself. For many years, software could not be patented, which means that, for many years, the U.S. Patent Office did not collect data about prior art in patents.

This fact combines with another to make patents in this field particularly uncertain. When a person seeking a patent files the patent application, he or she is to include in the application a list of known "prior art"—earlier inventions that might be related to the invention for which a patent is sought. As the rules are now, however, the applicant need report only what the applicant actually knows. This creates an ostrich incentive: if you're responsible only for what you know, then you have an incentive to do very little research.[28]

The law deals with problems like this in many contexts. The ordinary response is a "negligence standard": the applicant must file what he or she knows *or should have known*. This creates a strong incentive for the applicant to discover relevant prior art. And it would help the U.S. Patent Office make a judgment about whether a patent should be granted.

If Congress determines that business method patents are justified, it should also consider the proposals of Jeff Bezos and Tim O'Reilly to grant patent protection for business methods for only a very short period. Bezos proposes five years, but an even shorter period may make sense.[29] Network technologies move so quickly that a longer period of protection is never really needed; and whatever distortions this system might produce, they could be minimized by shorting the period of protection.

Congress should also, and most obviously, radically improve funding for the U.S. Patent Office and mandate fundamental improvements in the functioning of that office.[30]

Finally, Congress should consider the proposals of Congressman Berman to deny patents to business methods that are simply translations from real-space inventions to cyberspace.[31] Scholars at first thought these inventions would be denied patent protection because of lack of inventiveness.[32] But a clear rule marking the lack of inventiveness has not been shown. [33]

THESE CHANGES are just beginnings, but they would be significant beginnings if done. They would together go a great distance in assuring that the space for innovation remains open and that the resources for innovation remain free. They would commit us to an environment that would preserve the innovation we have seen.

What Orrin Understands

RRIN HATCH is a conservative. The senior senator from Utah, former chair of the Judiciary Committee, he is a critical force in practically every sphere of the Senate. He was a candidate for president in 2000. And he is admired by most, especially on the Right, as a principled politician and a decent man.

But there's something funny about Hatch. He betrays "policy anomalies"—positions that can't quite be explained on a simple left/right scale. Some of the things that he believes in most are puzzles to many conservatives. And puzzles in a politician are trouble. Unpredictability is not an asset in a political world where results cost lobbyists millions to buy.

Two of Hatch's anomalies are at the core of this book. The first is his concern about the market power and behavior of the Microsoft Corporation. And the second is his affection for emerging technologies like Napster. Hatch was a strong supporter of the Justice Department's investigation into Microsoft's behavior; he is a strong skeptic of the power that music labels have over innovation in the arts.

The pundits think they have an explanation for Hatch's resistance to Microsoft: Corel Corporation, which purchased WordPerfect. WordPerfect had been the dominant word processor. It was a Utah-based company. As with many leading technologies, WordPerfect fumbled the move to GUI interfaces. Microsoft picked up the ball and ran far. Many attribute Hatch's skepticism about Microsoft to these sour grapes.

Hatch's views on Napster are explained in a different way. Hatch is a musician. He has written and recorded many Christian songs. But you don't find the senator's CDs in record stores; the recording labels were not much interested in recruiting the senator from Utah. Thus, Hatch again may have a motive to resent the labels. Therefore, when a new technology comes along that threatens the power of the labels, it is Schadenfreude, not concern, that drives the senator.

It is hard to believe that any politician does what he does for a reason of principle. We live in an era when principled politicians are characters in TV dramas; real politicians are something very different. Thus, the idea that a successful senator would do something that might harm him politically because of *ideals* strikes us as a fantasy. The stuff of Hollywood, perhaps, but not of Washington, D.C.

But as this book has made clear, there is a principle that would explain Hatch's stand. And while I am no friend of Hatch's, or of many of the policies that he has pushed, I do believe that what pushes Hatch to both positions is a matter of principle. Concentrations of power worry conservatives like Hatch; and in both of these anomalies, concentration of power is at stake.

In the Microsoft case, the fear is that this dominant controller of the platform will be able to use its power to direct evolution. Power over the platform will mean the ability to direct how the platform develops. And the ability to direct how the platform develops is a dangerous power for any single company to hold. It would be awful for the FCC to decide what technologies should look like in the future, then force those technologies on us through the power of law. But likewise, while it wouldn't be *as awful*, it is still fairly bad that any single company, whether by virtue of the law or because of its control over a platform, could control how technology should develop. Hatch is a believer in the diverse, decentralized market that allows consumers to choose the future. Thus, though he is among the oldest members of the Senate, his spirit is among the closest to what makes the Net run.

The same can be said about the production of culture. Obviously, the government has no legitimate role in controlling how our culture should evolve. What music people listen to and what art they find compelling are matters of private, not public, choice. But even if not *as bad* as it has been, the world we now have controlling media in our country is worse than the world that Hatch would want. The concentration of power that Hollywood has permits Hollywood a power that Hatch would rather it not have. A better system is less concentrated, less controlled, more diverse and decentralized. As Hatch has written:

> [I]f those digital pipes through which the new music will be delivered are significantly narrowed by gatekeepers who limit access to or divert fans to preferred content, a unique opportunity will be lost for both the creators of music and their fans. That is why I think it is crucial that policymakers be vigilant in keeping the pipes wide open.[1]

As I have argued throughout this book, the architecture that keeps the "pipes wide open" is simply the original architecture of the Net. And a commitment to keeping these pipes open is a commitment to preserving the Net.

In both of these contexts, the senator sees something that ideologues miss: that the greatest lesson of our history is the strength that comes from our economic and cultural diversity. That concentration in either threatens innovation in both—not because concentration alone is necessarily bad, but because concentration gives the concentrated the power to steer evolution as it benefits them.

That power is not within our tradition. It is not what has built the America we admire. And whether you're from the Right or the Left, there is a lesson in what this conservative preaches. We make choices, Hatch shows us, that affect how easily the concentrated can direct the future. We should make choices, Hatch insists, that make it less easy for the future to be directed. Decentralized, diverse, nominated: this is the tradition that Hatch defends; this is the architecture of the original Net.

AS I write the last pages of this book, the threat to those values grows. A court has just effectively shut down Napster, thereby assuring that the recording industry gets to choose what kind of innovation in the distribution of content will be allowed. Another court has ruled against Eric Eldred's challenge to copyright's bloating, finding that "copyrights are categorically immune from challenges under the First Amendment."[2] Though the Constitution speaks of "limited times," Congress is free to give Hollywood "perpetual copyright on the installment plan."[3] And streaming across my computer as I write these final paragraphs, judges from the D.C. Circuit Court of Appeals are asking skeptical questions of lawyers for the government defending the judgment against Microsoft. Commenting on the government's defense of Java technologies, one judge has just said, "We are going to replace one monopoly with another . . . right?"[4]

Though we've seen the new only when it has been freed from the old, that lesson is lost on the Napster court. And though our Framers saw as clearly as we can today that free content fuels innovation, that lesson was forgotten by the court that decided Eric Eldred's case. And though the clearest lesson of the past twenty years is that innovation flourishes best when it flourishes freely on a neutral platform, the judges deciding the Microsoft case cannot even imagine the value of a neutral platform. Is one monopoly really just as good as another?

Alexander Hamilton promised that the judiciary would be "the least dangerous branch." The early history of the Net confirmed Hamilton's predictions. The Court in *Reno* v. *ACLU* spoke of the values in a free Net. It resisted the popular efforts by Congress to regulate it quickly, even if Congress was regulating in the name of important social values.

But the most significant governmental actions affecting the Net in the twenty-first century so far are instances of judges intervening to protect the old against the new. Rather than "wait and see," the law has become the willing tool of those who would protect what they have against the innovation the Net could promise. The law is the instrument through which a technological revolution is undone. And since we barely understand how the technologists built this revolution, we don't even see when the lawyers take it away. As activist and technologist John Gilmore has put it, in a line that captures the puzzle of this book: "[W]e have invented the technology to eliminate scarcity, but we are deliberately throwing it away to benefit those who profit from scarcity. . . . I think," Gilmore continues, "we should embrace the era of plenty, and work out how to mutually live in it."[5]

LATE IN the afternoon of one of California's inevitably beautiful days, Marc Andreessen was driving along one of California's inevitably overcrowded highways. More fitting the traffic than the weather, Andreessen's mood was dark. He was a twenty-nine-year-old computer science graduate who had become one of the most successful entrepreneurs of his generation. Coauthor of an early browser for the World Wide Web (Mosaic), founder of the first company to make the World Wide Web go (Netscape), Andreessen was nonetheless down on the future.

"Innovation," in Andreessen's mind, is what the Web produced. As he told me:

When I came to Silicon Valley, everybody said . . . there's no way in hell that you could ever fund another desktop software company. That's just over. And then in 1995, 1996, 1997, and 1998, all those developers who previously worked on desktop software said, Ah-hah, we're upgrading to a brand-new platform not controlled . . . by anybody—the Internet. [A]ll of a sudden there was an explosion of innovation, a huge number of applications, and [a] huge number [of] companies.[6]

Innovation "resumed" just at the time when the platform for innovation was neutral and, in the sense that I've described, free: when many different actors were able to bring new ideas to the Net; when they knew that this neutrality meant the old could not control how the new would behave; when the new could behave however the market demanded.

But this innovation, Andreessen said, "is slowing once again. . . . Application lock-in . . . [has] actually gotten stronger." The opportunity to innovate outside of the dominant players has again evaporated. We are back to where we were before this revolution began. As control shifts back to the large, the powerful, and the old, and as that control is ratified by the judges in black robes, the opportunity that drew Andreessen from cold but trafficless Illinois disappears. The chance for something different is lost. The innovation age, Andreessen says, "is over." And we are back to a world where innovation proceeds as the dominant players choose.

Andreessen's story is the fear of this book. An "explosion" of innovation grew upon a neutral platform; that explosion is burning out quickly as the platform is increasingly controlled.[7] Whether through changes in the physical, or code, or content layers, the change Andreessen worries about is the shift that I have described.

There is little to stop the transformation that worries Andreessen; there is everything to push it along as fast as it can go. This book will be published just as Microsoft's .NET and Hailstorm initiatives hit the network. They promise to integrate an extraordinary range of functionality into the core operating system that Microsoft owns. Emboldened by an expected victory at the court of appeals, Microsoft has expanded the bundling that the government attacked to include a range of services never imagined by government prosecutors. Authentication, instant messaging, e-mail, Web services—all these will be bundled into the core operating system of the next generation of Windows. Anyone who wants to compete in the provision of these services will face as strong a barrier as Netscape faced against a bundled Internet Explorer.

Microsoft is simply responding to another, very different nonneutral platform—the emerging and dominant platform of America Online. After its merger with Time Warner, AOL and its loyal members are another huge and powerful force influencing the future of the Internet. AOL is not an operating system, but for almost a majority of those who use the Internet, it is in effect an operating system. Functionality is served in the AOL suite of software; functionality beyond that is not.

These two companies—AOL Time Warner and Microsoft—will define the next five years of the Internet's life. Neither company has committed itself to a neutral and open platform.[8] Hence, the next five years will be radically different from the past ten. Innovation in content and applications will be as these platform owners permit. Additions that benefit either company will be encouraged; additions that don't, won't. We will have re-created the network of old AT&T, but now on the platform of the Internet. Content and access will once again be controlled; the innovation commons will have been carved up and sold.

This is the future of ideas. It could be different, but my sense is that it won't be. If we were more like Hatch, more skeptical of "gatekeepers," whether private or public; if we were less like Jay Walker, eager to view every government-granted privilege as a God-given property right; if we were more like Richard Stallman, committed to a principle of freedom in knowledge and to a practice that assures that the power to control is minimized; if there weren't so few Paul Barans, willing to struggle for many years to force a monopoly to face itself—if all this were so, there would be reason for hope.

But we are not. We are a democracy increasingly ruled by judges. We elect a Congress that is increasingly chained by lobbyists. And we are a culture that deep down believes in this counterrevolution: that strangely thinks that this increase in control makes sense.

As commentator Gordon Cook writes:

The Internet revolution has come and gone. It has created a tremendous burst of innovation[—a] burst that now looks to have been mismanaged. . . . [T]he people who did the least to advance the new technologies seem most likely to control them. We are left not with the edge-controlled intelligence of the [end-to-end] network but with the central authoritarian control of the likes of AOL Time Warner.[9]

The irony astounds. We win the political struggle against state control so as to reentrench control in the name of the market. We fight battles in the name of free speech, only to have those tools turned over to the arsenal of those who would control speech. We defend the ideal of property and then forget its limits, and extend its reach to a space none of our Founders would ever have imagined.

We move through this moment of an architecture of innovation to, once again, embrace an architecture of control—without noticing, without resistance, without so much as a question. Those threatened by this technology of freedom have learned how to turn the technology off. The switch is now being thrown. We are doing nothing about it.

Notes

NOTE: All URLs given as citations are subject to change.

PREFACE

[1] Andrew L. Shapiro, *The Control Revolution: How the Internet Is Putting Individuals in Charge and Changing the World We Know* (New York: PublicAffairs, 1999).

CHAPTER 1

[1] Telephone interview with Davis Guggenheim, November 15, 2000. The law on the books in this area (as distinct from what directors and lawyers working for directors think) is "by no means certain." See Melville B. Nimmer and David Nimmer, "Nimmer on Copyright," §13.05[D][3], at 13-222 (2001).

[2] For these cases and others, see the extraordinarily helpful site http://www.benedict.com/visual/visual.htm. See also Daniel B. Wood, "Hollywood Loves an Original Idea," *Christian Science Monitor*, December 15, 1997, http://www.csmonitor.com/durable/1997/12/15/us/us.4.html; *Woods* v. *Universal City Studios, Inc.*, 920 F. Supp. 62 (SDNY 1996) (*12 Monkeys*).

[3] See Matthew C. Lucas, "The De Minimis Dilemma: A Bedeviling Problem of Definitions and a New Proposal for a Notice Rule," *Journal of Technology Law & Policy* 4, no. 3 (2000): 2 (http://journal.law.ufl.edu/~techlaw/4-3/lucas.html).

[4] Jessica Litman, *Digital Copyright* (Amherst, N.Y.: Prometheus Books, 2001), 244–45.

[5] Telephone interview with Davis Guggenheim.

[6] Niccolò Machiavelli, *The Prince*, 2nd ed. (London and New York: W. W. Norton, 1992), 17.

[7] In 1710, the English Parliament passed the Statute of Anne, which, to the horror of its original supporters, was amended to limit the term of copyright to twenty-eight years. In 1774, the House of Lords finally upheld the limit, permitting the works of Shakespeare to fall into the public domain for the first time. *Donaldson* v. *Becket, English Reports* 98 (House of Lords, 1774), 251, overturning *Millar* v. *Taylor, Burroughs* 4 (1769): 2303, 2308. See Mark Rose, *Authors and Owners* (Cambridge, Mass.: Harvard Univer-

sity Press, 1993), 97. Had the work of Shakespeare not fallen into the public domain, it would not have been protected in the United States, because foreign copyrights were not protected in the United States until 1891. T. Bender and D. Sampliner, "Poets, Pirates, and the Creation of American Literature," *New York University Journal of International Law & Politics* 29 (1997): 255. Americans were free to copy English works without the permission of English authors and were free to translate foreign works without the permission of foreign copyright holders.

8 For an introduction, see "The Future of Digital Entertainment" (Special Report), *Scientific American* 283 (2000): 47.

9 Apple, of course, means something a bit narrower by the term *mix*. See http://www. apple.com/imac/digitalmusic.html: "Because iTunes is really about freedom. The freedom, first and foremost, to play songs in the order you want, not the order they were first recorded on CD. The freedom to mix and match artists and musical categories as it suits you. The freedom to create your own music CDs. And the freedom to put more than a hundred MP3 songs on a single CD."

10 The relationship to low-cost production is no accident with some modern music. As John Leland describes it, "The digital sampling device has changed not only the sound of pop music, but also the mythology. It has done what punk rock threatened to do: made everybody into a potential musician, bridged the gap between performer and audience." Siva Vaidhyanathan, *Copyrights and Copywrongs: The Rise of Intellectual Property and How It Threatens Creativity* (New York: New York University Press, 2001), 138. By keeping the cost low, and hence the distance between creator and consumer short, the genre aspires to keep the range of creators as broad as possible. That aspiration for music could, I argue in this book, become an aspiration for creativity more generally.

11 This is the character of Caribbean music as well. "Every new version will slightly modify the original tune," but then, obviously, draw upon and copy it. Ibid., 136.

12 Richard Stallman has been likened to the Moses of what I will call the "open code" movement. The likeness is indeed striking. As I describe in chapter 4, below, Stallman began the movement to build a free operating system. But as with Moses, it was another leader, Linus Torvalds, who finally carried the movement into the promised land by facilitating the development of the final part of the OS puzzle. Like Moses, too, Stallman is both respected and reviled by allies within the movement. He is an unforgiving, and hence for many inspiring, leader of a critically important aspect of modern culture. I have deep respect for the principle and commitment of this extraordinary individual, though I also have great respect for those who are courageous enough to question his thinking and then sustain his wrath.

Stallman insists that those who would advance the values of the free software movement must adopt the language "free" rather than "open." This seems to me an unproductive debate. To the extent Stallman believes that people dilute the insights of the free software movement by minimizing its connection to fundamental values, he is correct. The importance of free and open source software is much more than business, or efficient code. But the remedy to narrowness is not magic words — especially when the magic words tend to confuse rather than clarify. I am partial to the term *open* — as in open society; I believe it is properly a reference to values as well as the licenses under which code is distributed; and by "open code" I mean to refer to the values across both technical and legal contexts that promote a world where governing structures — code — are fundamentally free.

For an exceptional study of free and open source software, and the incentives that are behind it, see Working Group on Libre Software, "Free Software/Open Source: Information Society Opportunities for Europe?," Version 1.2 (April 2000), http://eu. conecta.it/paper.pdf.

[13] In the terms of legal theory, there are two distinct ways in which a resource could be "free" in the sense I mean. Either no one would have any entitlement to the resource, or if someone did have an entitlement, the resource would be protected by a liability rather than a property rule. See Guido Calabresi and Douglas Melamed, "Property Rules, Liability Rules, and Inalienability: One View of the Cathedral," *Harvard Law Review* 85 (1972): 1089. See also Robert P. Merges, "Institutions for Intellectual Property Transactions: The Case of Patent Pools," in *Expanding the Boundaries of Intellectual Property*, Rochelle Cooper Dreyfuss and Diane Leenheer Zimmerman, eds. (Oxford: Oxford University Press, 2001), 123, 131 ("The essence of this Framework is this: Calabresi and Melamed assign all legal entitlements to one of two rules, 'property rules' and 'liability rules.' The former are best described as 'absolute permission rules': one cannot take these entitlements without prior permission of the owner. The rightholder, acting individually, thus sets the price. Most real estate fits this description. By contrast, liability rules are best described as 'take now, pay later.' They allow for nonowners to take the entitlement without permission of the owner, so long as they adequately compensate the owner later. In the Calabresi-Melamed Framework, ex post adequate compensation is deemed 'collective valuation.' ").

[14] Carol Rose, "The Comedy of the Commons: Custom, Commerce, and Inherently Public Property," *University of Chicago Law Review* 53 (1986): 711, 712 .

[15] I don't mean that all such barriers will be properly considered "neutral." Sometimes barriers are merely a tool for raising rivals' costs. Some of those nonneutral barriers will be remedied through antitrust law. But I'm assuming the general case is benign in real space.

CHAPTER 2

[1] For useful analyses of "the commons," see generally *Anarchy and the Environment: The International Relations of Common Pool Resources*, J. Samuel Barkin and George E. Shambaugh, eds. (Albany: State University of New York Press, 1999); *Managing the Commons*, 2nd ed., John A. Baden and Douglas S. Noonan, eds. (Bloomington, Ind.: Indiana University Press, 1998); Susan J. Buck, *The Global Commons: An Introduction* (Washington, D.C.: Island Press, 1998); *Privatizing Nature: Political Struggles for the Global Commons*, Michael Goldman, ed. (London: Pluto Press, in association with Transnational Institute, 1998); *Local Commons and Global Interdependence: Heterogeneity and Cooperation in Two Domains*, Robert O. Keohane and Elinor Ostrom, eds. (London and Thousand Oaks, Calif.: Sage Publications, 1995); *The Political Economy of Customs and Culture: Informal Solutions to the Commons Problem*, Terry L. Anderson and Randy T. Simmons, eds. (Savage, Md.: Rowman and Littlefield Publishers, 1993); *Making the Commons Work: Theory, Practice and Policy*, Daniel W. Bromley, ed. (San Francisco: ICS Press, 1992); *Commons Without Tragedy: Protecting the Environment from Overpopulation—A New Approach*, Robert V. Anderson, ed. (London: Shepheard-Walwyn; Savage, Md.: Barnes & Noble, 1991); Glenn G. Stevenson, *Common Property Economics: A General Theory and Land Use Applications* (Cambridge, England, and New York: Cambridge University Press, 1991); Elinor Ostrom, *Governing the Commons: The Evolution of Institutions for Collective Action* (Cambridge, England, and New York: Cambridge University Press, 1990).

The traditional commons is distinct from what Henry Smith calls a "semicommons." See Henry E. Smith, "Semicommon Property Rights and Scattering in the Open Fields," *Journal of Legal Studies* 29 (2000): 131 (defining a semicommons as a mix of common and private rights where both are significant and interact).

While the standard view is that a commons induces overuse, some argue that it may inspire underuse. Compare Richard A. Posner, *Economic Analysis of Law*, 4th ed. (Boston: Little, Brown, 1992), 32, with Frank I. Michelman, "Ethics, Economics and the Law of Property," in *Ethics, Economics, and the Law*, J. Roland Pennock and John W. Chapman, eds. (New York: New York University Press, Nomos XXIV [series], 1982), 25–27.

[2] The OED was compiled from the volunteer efforts of thousands of people sending examples of usage to editors. See Simon Winchester, *The Professor and the Madman: A Tale of Murder, Insanity, and the Making of the Oxford English Dictionary* (New York: HarperCollins Publishers, 1998).

[3] *The Oxford English Dictionary*, 2nd ed., vol. 3, prepared by J. A. Simpson and E. S. C. Weiner (Oxford: Clarendon Press; New York: Oxford University Press, 1989), 567.

[4] The observant will notice that a resource offered in conditions of perfect competition comes close to the conditions that I described obtain with a commons, even though the resource is "owned." Perfect competition constrains the owner in similar ways, though the right not to sell at all distinguishes the two sets of constraints.

[5] This is the essence of an entitlement protected by a property rule. See Guido Calabresi and Douglas Melamed, "Property Rules, Liability Rules, and Inalienability: One View of the Cathedral," *Harvard Law Review* 85 (1972): 1089, 1092. Not all liability rule cases will eliminate this core of discretion. But the system is structured to avoid it.

[6] Virgil, *Virgil in English Rhythm*, 2nd ed., Robert Corbet Singleton, trans. (London: Bell and Daldy [imprint], 1871), iii–iv ("There is a common of language to which both poetry and prose have the freest access.").

[7] Garrett Hardin, "The Tragedy of the Commons," *Science* 162 (1968): 1243. The idea of congestion externalities of course predates Hardin. See Posner, "Economic Analysis of Law," 32–34, citing Frank H. Knight, "Some Fallacies in the Interpretation of Social Cost," *Quarterly Journal of Economics* 38 (1924): 582.

[8] Hardin, 1244 (emphasis added).

[9] Ostrom, ch. 3; Robert C. Ellickson, *Order Without Law: How Neighbors Settle Disputes* (Cambridge, Mass.: Harvard University Press, 1991). See also *Making the Commons Work: Theory, Practice and Policy*, Daniel W. Bromley, ed. (San Francisco: ICS Press, 1992), part 2 (describing case studies).

[10] Elinor Ostrom has been the most effective in demonstrating the "fallacy" of the "tragedy of the commons." As she writes:

> What makes these models so dangerous—when they are used metaphorically as the foundation for policy—is that the constraints that are assumed to be fixed for the purpose of analysis are taken on faith as being fixed in empirical settings, unless some external authorities change them.

Ostrom, 6–7. For example, in an article in 1988, *The Economist* asserts about fisheries that "left to their own devices, fishermen will overexploit stocks" and that "to avoid disaster, managers must have effective hegemony over them." Ibid., 8. But that assumption cannot be made. It depends upon the social system within which the commons exist; often, as Ostrom has demonstrated, control is possible without either state intervention or a system of private property.

[11] Obviously, many have noticed the "commonslike" character of the Internet. See, e.g., Douglas S. Noonan, "Internet Decentralization, Feedback, and Self-Organization," 188–89, in *Managing the Commons*, 2nd ed., John A. Baden and Douglas S. Noonan, eds. (Bloomington, Ind.: Indiana University Press, 1998) ("The Internet is a commons [or several commons]. . . ."). See also James Boyle, "A Politics of Intellectual Property: Environmentalism for the Net?," *Duke Law Journal* 47 (1997): 87. Not all have been as convinced that its commons nature accounts for its innovation. See, e.g., Noonan, "Internet Decentralization," 198 ("In spite of its commons nature, or perhaps because of it").

[12] See Yochai Benkler, "From Consumers to Users: Shifting the Deeper Structures of Regulation," *Federal Communications Law Journal* 52 (2000): 561, 562–63 ("These choices occur at all levels of the information environment: the physical infrastructure layer—wires, cable, radio frequency spectrum—the logical infrastructure layer—software—and the content layer. . . .").

[13] I'm simplifying vastly from both the OSI seven-layer model of network design, see Douglas E. Comer, *Internetworking with TCP/IP*, 4th ed. (Upper Saddle River, N.J.: Prentice-Hall, 2000), 181–95; Pete Loshin, *TCP/IP Clearly Explained*, 2nd ed. (Boston: AP Professional, 1997), 12–18; and Berners-Lee's four-layer description (transmission, computer, software, and content) in Tim Berners-Lee, *Weaving the Web: The Original Design and Ultimate Destiny of the World Wide Web by Its Inventor* (San Francisco: HarperSanFrancisco, 1999), 129–30.

[14] Certain speech has always been regulated on the telephone. For example, in 1883, a local telephone company terminated a subscriber's service for using the word *damned* with an operator. The company's contract prohibited "profane, indecent or rude language." An Ohio court upheld the company's actions, and the Supreme Court Commission later affirmed the court's decision. For this and other examples, see Peter W. Huber, Michael K. Kellogg, and John Thorne, *Federal Telecommunications Law*, 2nd ed. (Gaithersburg, Md.: Aspen Law & Business, 1999), 1275–76, 1288–92.

CHAPTER 3

[1] Milton Mueller, *Universal Service: Competition, Interconnection, and Monopoly in the Making of the American Telephone System* (Cambridge, Mass.: MIT Press; Washington, D.C.: AEI Press, 1997), 180. For other useful histories, see *A History of Computing Research at Bell Laboratories (1937–1975)*, Bernard D. Holbrook and W. Stanley Brown, eds. (New York: The Laboratories, 1982); *A History of Engineering and Science in the Bell System*, M. D. Fagen, ed. (New York: The Laboratories, prepared by members of the technical staff, Bell Telephone Laboratories, 1975–85); Robert W. Garnet, *The Telephone Enterprise: The Evolution of the Bell System's Horizontal Structure, 1876–1909* (Baltimore: Johns Hopkins University Press, 1985); Alvin Von Auw, *Heritage and Destiny: Reflections on the Bell System in Transition* (New York: Praeger, 1983); John Brooks, *Telephone: The First Hundred Years* (New York: Harper & Row, 1976); George David Smith, *The Anatomy of a Business Strategy: Bell, Western Electric, and the Origins of the American Telephone Industry* (Baltimore: Johns Hopkins University Press, 1985); Edwin M. Asmann, *The Telegraph and the Telephone: Their Development and Role in the Economic History of the United States: The First Century, 1844–1944* (Lake Forest: Lake Forest College, 1980); Amy Friedlander, *Natural Monopoly and Universal Service: Telephones and Telegraphs in the U.S. Communications Infrastructure, 1837–1940* (Reston, Va.: Corporation for National Research Initiatives, 1995); John Patrick Phillips, *Ma Bell's Millions* (New York: Vantage Press, 1970).

[2] Mueller, 7.

[3] Ibid., 148.

[4] Ibid., 188–89.

[5] Ibid., 104–13.

[6] Ibid., 180–81. See also David F. Weiman and Richard C. Levin, "Preying for Monopoly? The Case of Southern Bell Telephone Company, 1894–1912," *Journal of the Political Economy* 102 (1994): 103 (proposing a "modified version of the predation hypothesis" that shores up Mueller's work).

[7] Mueller, 51, 78–79.

[8] The alternative, modern meaning for "universal service" is that every household has access to the network. Mueller argues convincingly this was not the original meaning; ibid., 163. For an argument that the funding obligations that support universal service should be extended to ISPs, see Robert M. Frieden, "Universal Service: When Technologies Converge and Regulatory Models Diverge," *Harvard Journal of Law & Technology* 13 (2000): 395.

[9] Peter W. Huber, Michael K. Kellogg, and John Thorne, *Federal Telecommunications Law,* 2nd ed. (Gaithersburg, Md.: Aspen Law & Business, 1999), 17.

[10] Ibid.

[11] Ibid.

[12] Ibid.

[13] Mueller, 162.

[14] Interview with Paul Baran in Stanford, California, November 14, 2000. For other interviews of Baran, see Stewart Brand, "Founding Father," *Wired* (March 2001), available at http://www.wired.com/wired/archive/9.03/baran_pr.html; interview by David Hochfelder with Paul Baran, electrical engineer, Newark, New Jersey (October 24, 1999), available at http://ieee.org/organizations/history_center/oral_histories/transcripts/baran.html; interview by J. O'Neill with Paul Baran, Menlo Park, California (March 5, 1990); George Gilder, "Inventing the Internet Again," *Forbes* (June 2, 1997), 106 (lengthy article about Baran); Katie Hafner and Matthew Lyon, "Casting the Net," *The Sciences* (September 1, 1996), 32.

[15] American Telephone & Telegraphy Co., *Telephone Almanac,* foreword (1941).

[16] Interview with Paul Baran.

[17] Ibid.

[18] Peter Huber, *Orwell's Revenge: The 1984 Palimpsest* (New York: Free Press; Toronto: Maxwell Macmillan Canada; New York: Maxwell Macmillan International, 1994), 268–69; Huber, Kellogg, and Thorne, 416.

[19] And the decision was reversed by the D.C. circuit. *Hush-a-Phone Corp.* v. *United States,* 238 F. 2d 266 (D.C. Cir., 1956).

[20] The idea is developed in Kleinrock's dissertation: Leonard Kleinrock, *Message Delay in Communication Nets with Storage* (1962, unpublished Ph.D. dissertation, Massachusetts Institute of Technology), which was later published in a modified form. See Leonard Kleinrock, *Communication Nets: Stochastic Message Flow and Delay* (New York: McGraw-Hill, 1964). See also John Naughton, *A Brief History of the Future: The Origins of the Internet* (London: Weidenfeld & Nicolson, 1999), 92, 118–19 (discussing other earlier contributors to the Internet).

[21] Baran attributes to him the discovery of the term. Interview with Paul Baran ("The term 'packet switching' was first used by Donald Davies of the National Physical Laboratory in England, who independently came up with the same general concept in November 1965.").

[22] Baran confirmed this history to me in an interview. "So the first level of objections was about technology—that I didn't understand how the telephone system worked, [and] that what I'm proposing could not possibly work." Interview with Paul Baran.

[23] Naughton, 107. Authors Katie Hafner and Matthew Lyon recount a similar resistance in *Where Wizards Stay Up Late: The Origins of the Internet* (New York: Simon & Schuster, 1996), 62–64.

[24] Interview with Paul Baran.

[25] Ibid.

[26] See Steve Bickerstaff, "Shackles on the Giant: How the Federal Government Created Microsoft, Personal Computers, and the Internet," *Texas Law Review* 78 (1999): 1, 60–61 (explaining that "restrictions on the Bell System helped the personal computer market to develop through diverse competition and innovation"); Peter W. Huber, *Law and Disorder in Cyberspace: Abolish the FCC and Let Common Law Rule the Telecosm* (Oxford and New York: Oxford University Press, 1997).

[27] Naughton, 108–9.

[28] Interview with Paul Baran.

[29] See J. H. Saltzer et al., "End-to-End Arguments in System Design," available at http://web.mit.edu/Saltzer/www/publications/endtoend/endtoend.pdf; David P. Reed et al., "Active Networking in End-to-End Arguments," available at http://Web.mit.edu/Saltzer/www/publications/endtoend/ANe2ecomment.html. For treatment of e2e, see Cameron R. Graham, "Cable TV Law 2001: Competition in Video, Internet and Telephony," *Practicing Law Institute: PLI Order No. G0–00LY*, 642 (2001): 486; Rob Frieden, "Does a Hierarchical Internet Necessitate Multilateral Intervention?," *North Carolina Journal of International Law and Commercial Regulation* 26 (2001): 361; Robert M. Kossick Jr., "The Internet in Latin America: New Opportunities, Developments and Challenges," *Cyberspace Lawyer* 6, no. 1 (2001): 11 (noting the use of end-to-end principles in Brazil and Mexico); and Lawrence Lessig, foreword, "Cyberspace and Privacy: A New Legal Paradigm?," *Stanford Law Review* 52 (2000): 987.

[30] National Research Council, *The Internet's Coming of Age* (Washington, D.C.: National Academy Press, 2000), 30.

[31] Telephone interview with David P. Reed (February 7, 2001), who contributed to the early design of the Internet protocols—TCP/IP—while a graduate student at MIT.

[32] As I describe in this paragraph, the importance of architecture to the character of the Internet was a theme of the early activism of Mitch Kapor. But the author who first focused the importance of architecture on the issues I describe in this book is Kevin Werbach. As Werbach wrote in *Release 1.0*:

> Architecture matters. For the most part, today's Net is open, decentralized and competitive. It fosters innovation because it is a standards-based general-purpose platform.... [But t]he people building the next generation of high-speed access pipes are trying to change this model.

Kevin Werbach, "The Architecture of Internet 2.0," *Release 1.0* (February 19, 1999). As François Bar puts it, describing the electronic marketplace: "The most fundamental transformation of commercial activities [from cyberspace] is not primarily about efficiency, but has to do with the market and industry structure. It is about architecture." François Bar, "The Construction of Marketplace Architecture," *Brookings & Internet Policy Institute* (forthcoming 2001): 12.

[33] Lawrence Lessig, *Code and Other Laws of Cyberspace* (New York: Basic Books, 1999), 243, note 19 (citing Kapor).

[34] To computer scientists, my use of the term *architecture* is a bit misleading. Computer scientists typically use "architecture" to refer to "the visible characteristics of only the element actually performing instructions, that is, the processor of a computer system"; Harold Lorin, *Introduction to Computer Architecture and Organization*, 2nd ed. (New York: Wiley, 1989), 10, and analogously for a network. IBM's System/360 is said to be the first computer system to have had an "architecture." According to its architects, "the term *architecture* [means] the attributes of a system as seen by the programmer, i.e., the conceptual structure and functional behavior, as distinct from the organization of the data flow and controls, the logical design and the physical implementation." Carliss Y. Baldwin and Kim B. Clark, *Design Rules*, vol. 1 (Cambridge, Mass.: MIT Press, 2000), 215.

I mean the term to be far more general—to refer to "both the Internet's technical protocols (e.g., TCP/IP) and its entrenched structures of governance and social patterns of usage that themselves are not easily changeable, at least not without coordinated action by many parties." Lawrence Lessig and Paul Resnick, "Zoning Internet Speech," *Michigan Law Review* 98 (1999): 395.

[35] Network Working Group, "Request for Comments: 1958, Architectural Principles of the Internet," Brian E. Carpenter, ed. (1996), available at http://www.ietf.org/rfc/rfc1958.txt.

[36] Ibid., §2.1.

[37] Ibid.

[38] Tim Berners-Lee, *Weaving the Web: The Original Design and Ultimate Destiny of the World Wide Web by Its Inventor* (San Francisco: HarperSanFrancisco, 1999), 99.

[39] As background, see Peter Cukor and Lee McKnight, "Knowledge Networks, the Internet, and Development," *Fletcher Forum of World Affairs* (Winter 2001): 43, 46; George Gilder, *Telecosm: How Infinite Bandwidth Will Revolutionize Our World* (New York: Free Press, 2000), 70–71.

[40] Telephone interview with David Isenberg, February 14, 2001.

[41] Or at least this is an ideal. See Roger Feldman, "e2e vs. General Edison OnLine," *PMA OnLine Magazine*, http://www.retailenergy.com/feldman/0007flmn.htm.

[42] Telephone interview with David Reed.

[43] Berners-Lee, 208.

[44] National Research Council, 138.

[45] Ibid., 107.

[46] Ibid., 36–37.

[47] Ibid., 37.

[48] Douglas E. Comer, *Internetworking with TCP/IP*, 4th ed., vol. 1 (Upper Saddle River, N.J.: Prentice-Hall, 2000), 691 (HTTP stands for "hypertext transfer protocol" and is "[t]he protocol used to transfer Web documents from a server to a browser"), 713 (TCP stands for "transmission control protocol"), and 694 (IP stands for "Internet protocol"). Together, TCP and IP allow data delivery between machines on the Internet. "The entire protocol suite is often referred to as TCP/IP because TCP and IP are the two fundamental protocols.").

[49] Berners-Lee, 35.

[50] See, e.g., Paul E. Ceruzzi, *A History of Modern Computing* (Cambridge, Mass.: MIT Press, 1998), 301–2 (describing hypertext "inventor" Ted Nelson's debt to Vannevar Bush, quoting Bush: "The human mind . . . operates by association. With one item in its grasp, it snaps instantly to the next that is suggested by the association of thoughts, in accordance with some intricate web of trails carried by the cells of the brain.").

[51] See Robert M. Fano, "On the Social Role of Computer Communications," *Proceedings of the IEEE* 60 (September 1972): 1249.

[52] Berners-Lee, 46. See also James Gillies, *How the Web Was Born: The Story of the World Wide Web* (Oxford and New York: Oxford University Press, 2000); Hafner and Lyon, *Internet Dreams: Archetypes, Myths, and Metaphors*, Mark J. Stefik and Vinton G. Cerf, eds. (Cambridge, Mass.: MIT Press, 1997).

[53] Berners-Lee, 40 (describing Gopher and WAIS growing faster).

[54] Ibid. (interconnect).

[55] Ibid., 72–73.

[56] Ibid.

[57] Ibid., 74.

[58] Ibid., 99.

[59] See Barbara Esbin, "Internet over Cable: Defining the Future in Terms of the Past," *Communications Law Conspectus* (Winter 1999): 37, 46 ("ARPA began to support the development of communications protocols for transferring data and electronic mail [e-mail] between different types of computer networks."); Needham J. Boddie II et al., "A Review of Copyright and the Internet," *Campbell Law Review* 20 (1998): 193, 196 ("Funding for the Internet comes from five federal agencies, various universities and states, and private companies such as IBM and MCI.").

[60] Naughton, 83–85.

[61] Ibid., 84.

[62] See, e.g., http://www.asiapoint.net/insight/asia/countries/myanmar/my_spedev.htm.

[63] Among other restrictions, AT&T was not permitted to get into the computer business. This fact becomes quite important in explaining the birth of Unix. For a comprehensive and balanced account of the effect of these limitations, see Bickerstaff, 14–17.

[64] Bickerstaff, 25.

[65] For more on the history of the FCC's Computer I and Computer II decrees, see ibid., 1–37; Huber, Kellogg, and Thorne, §5.4.

[66] National Research Council, 130–31, n. 18 (describing best efforts as consequences of uniformity).

[67] "Humans can tolerate about 250 msec of latency before it has a noticeable effect," http://www.dialogic.com/solution/Internet/4070Web.htm.

[68] They are described in Mark Gaynor et al., "Theory of Service Architecture: How to Encourage Innovation of Services in Networks" (working paper, 2000, on file with author), 14.

[69] Indeed, George Gilder believes the increasing capacity of optical fiber will render moot this debate about QoS. "Today on the Internet, the consensus claims that QoS will be indispensable for voice and video. But with true bandwidth abundance, QoS complexities are irrelevant—an ATM tax imposed on the vast bandwidth of fiber with its 10 to the minus 15 error rates, far better than the reliability of telephone circuits." Gilder, *Telecosm*, 80.

This point is made expressly with respect to quality of service and end-to-end in an important paper by Barbara van Schewick, "The End-to-End Principle in Network Design, Its Impact on Innovation and Competition in the Internet, and Its Future in the Network Architecture of the Next Generation Internet" (working paper, September 2000, on file with author). Van Schewick distinguishes between two forms of QoS—integrated services architecture and differentiated services architecture (6, 7)—and argues that the former puts more pressure on the end-to-end principle than the latter. She argues that a more general solution to the QoS problem is overprovisioning (7), and motivates that argument with strong evidence of the incentives of network providers to differentiate between different applications. This, she argues, reduces "the incentives for a potential innovator to develop new applications." Ibid., 7.

Van Schewick is the first researcher I know of to link QoS, overprovisioning, and end-to-end, and I have drawn heavily upon her understanding in this context and throughout this book.

Others are skeptical of the overprovisioning solution. For overprovisioning to work, they argue, overprovisioning must exist at every point of the network. But that requires coordinated action that is impossible in the context of the Internet. Thus, the solution is an ideal without a mechanism to achieve it.

This skepticism is appropriate, but it does suggest another response. If the market "naturally" would not choose overprovisioning, but overprovisioning would nonetheless be a productive response, then we may well have identified a role for government. I describe this a bit more in chapter 12.

70 For examples of QoS technologies, and a discussion of QoS generally, see Joe Lardieri, "Quality of Service: Which Flavor Is Right for You?," *Telecommunications* (August 1999): 53; Dave Kosiur, "Directing Traffic with a Touch of Class," *PC Week* (March 23, 1998): 91; David B. Miller, "Quality of Service: Directing Data Through the Network," *ENT* (October 6, 1999): 22.

71 See Gilder, *Telecosm*, 158–64.

72 The critical change necessary for this "fibered" network to achieve this level of capacity is the emergence of optical routing technologies. The emerging bottleneck in the network is the relatively slow speed of electronic switches. For an introduction, see "The Ultimate Optical Network" (Special Report), *Scientific American* 284 (January 2001): 80.

73 See, e.g., Bill Frezza, "Telecosmic Punditry: The World Through Gilder-Colored Glasses," *Internet Week* (December 4, 2000): 47; Rob Walker, "The Gildercosm," *Slate* magazine (September 11, 2000), available at http://slate.msn.com/code/MoneyBox/ MoneyBox.asp?Show=9/11/2000&idMessage=6030 (Gilder runs "against the current wisdom that sees bandwidth shortage as a problem"); Julian Dibbell, "From Here to Infinity," *Village Voice*, September 5, 2000, 65 ("It takes either profound sloth or transcendent faith to persist in voicing such breathless sentiments."). For a more favorable review, see, e.g., Blair Levin, "Review, TELECOSM: How Infinite Bandwidth Will Revolutionize Our World," *Washington Monthly* (September 1, 2000): 54.

74 E-mail from Timothy Wu to Lawrence Lessig, February 16, 2001.

75 This claim depends upon the assumption that the value of the network activity was higher than the telephone activity it displaced. That assumption about social value therefore has little relation to the actual costs.

CHAPTER 4

1 Technically, some of these functions could be provided if the program simply provided perfectly transparent representations of the "application program interfaces," or APIs. In some contexts this distinction will be important, but I ignore it here. A sufficiently skilled programmer could also learn something about compiled code through reverse engineering. The success of this would depend upon how well structured the original code was.

2 Ceruzzi, *A History of Modern Computing*, 108.

3 For a brief history of Unix, see William Shattuck, "The Meaning of UNIX," in *The*

Unix System Encyclopedia, 2d ed.,Yates Ventures, eds. (Palo Alto, Calif.: Yates Ventures, 1985), 89, 93–94; Peter H. Salus, *A Quarter Century of UNIX* (Reading, Mass.: Addison-Wesley Publishing Company, 1994), 5–61; Ronda Hauben, "The History of UNIX," available at http://www.dei.isep.ipp.pt/docs/unix.html (last visited June 12, 2001).

4 Robert Young and Wendy Goldman Rohm, *Under the Radar: How Red Hat Changed the Software Business — and Took Microsoft by Surprise* (Scottsdale, Ariz.: Coriolis Group Books, 1999), 21; Donald K. Rosenberg, *Open Source: The Unauthorized White Papers* (Foster City, Calif.: Hungry Minds, 2000), 9.

5 Ceruzzi, 94–95.

6 Ibid., 92.

7 Ibid., 283 (The result was that "UNIX was a godsend for university computer science departments").

8 Young and Rohm, 20.

9 See Richard Stallman, "The GNU Operating System and the Free Software Movement," in *Open Sources: Voices from the Open Source Revolution*, Chris DiBona, Sam Ockman, and Mark Stone, eds. (Beijing and Sebastopol: O'Reilly, 1999), 53–54.

10 This commons would be built, in Stallman's ideal world, with nonproprietary code. Stallman is not opposed, however, to commercial software. As he explains, "Commercial software and proprietary software are totally different concepts. 'Commercial' refers to the financial arrangement of the software. 'Proprietary' refers to what the users are permitted to do. Free software must have the freedom to copy, to modify, and to have the source code. So proprietary software is mutually exclusive with free software, but there can be commercial software that [is] free software." Telephone interview by Hiroo Yamagata with Richard M. Stallman, August 8, 1997.

11 Peter Wayner, *Free for All: How Linux and the Free Software Movement Undercut the High-Tech Titans* (New York: HarperBusiness, 2000), 36.

12 For a discussion of Stallman and the history of GNU/Linux, see ibid., 9, 34–36, 67–68; Stallman, 53–66; Mark Leon, "Richard Stallman, GNU/Linux," *InfoWorld* (October 9, 2000): 62.

13 See, e.g., Linus Torvalds and David Diamond, *Just for Fun: The Story of an Accidental Revolutionary* (New York: HarperBusiness, 2001); Pekka Himanen, Manuel Castells (epilogue), and Linus Torvalds (prologue), *The Hacker Ethic and the Spirit of the Information Age* (New York: Random House, 2001); Paula Rooney, "No. 11: The Dark Horse," *Computer Reseller News*, November 15, 1999.

14 Stallman: "Around 1992, combining Linux with the not-quite-complete GNU system resulted in a complete free operating system. (Combining them was a substantial job in itself, of course.) It is due to Linux that we can actually run a version of the GNU system today." Stallman, 65.

What to call this resulting OS — "Linux" or "GNU/Linux" — is a hotly contested issue. Indeed, I've received more heat about this issue than about any other I've discussed in this book. Supporters of the free software movement insist the product is GNU/Linux and object that calling it "Linux" underplays the importance of Stallman and the Free Software Foundation. Others emphasize the other great work that has spread this free OS and insist that "Linux" is enough of a moniker. As Bob Young, chairman of Red Hat, wrote me, "While Linus gets more credit than he deserves for the whole 800 MB OSs that are known by their 16 MB Linux kernel, Richard gets less credit than he deserves. But where Linus gets far more credit than he demands, Richard demands more credit than he deserves (not that he does not deserve a great deal)." E-mail, June 8, 2001.

It is an unfortunate feature of the current debate around open source and free software projects that so much energy is devoted to what things are called—with great fury directed at those who fail to speak properly (using "open" where "free" is to be used; using "closed" where "proprietary" should be used). I'm guilty of some of those language sins in this book, and only sometimes self-consciously. I will refer generally to the Linux OS as "Linux," though sometimes as "GNU/Linux" when the reminder helps. The important point for our purposes is not who gets credit for what, but that the kernel of the Linux OS is licensed under the Free Software Foundation's General Public License (GPL). That is, I believe, a critically important feature of this debate, and one that must be kept clear.

[15] For a recent and compelling history of the birth of Linux, see Glyn Moody, *Rebel Code: Linux and the Open Source Revolution* (Cambridge, Mass.: Perseus Press, 2001).

[16] Linus Torvalds, "The Linux Edge," in *Open Sources: Voices from the Open Source Revolution*, Chris DiBona, Sam Ockman and Mark Stone, eds. (Beijing and Sebastopol: O'Reilly, 1999), 101.

[17] Torvalds, "The Linux Edge," 101.

[18] Moody, *Rebel Code*, 130. See also Dorte Toft, "Open Source Group Forms Nonprofit," *Industry Standard* (July 1, 1999), at http://www.thestandard.com/article/0,1902,5377,00.html (visited on May 27, 2001).

[19] See http://www.isc.org/products/BIND/bind-history.html.

[20] Tim O'Reilly, "Hardware, Software, and Infoware," in *Open Sources: Voices from the Open Source Revolution*, Chris DiBona, Sam Ockman, and Mark Stone, eds. (Beijing and Sebastopol: O'Reilly, 1999) 189, 191.

[21] Wayner, 172.

[22] See Carolyn Duffy Marsan, "Sendmail Adds Admin Console, IPv6 Support; New Unix-Based Tool Can Manage Sendmail-Based E-mail Systems Across a Widespread Organization," *Network World* (February 7, 2000).

[23] Alan Cox, "This Is How Free Software Works," *wideopennews* 5, 8.6, http://www2.usermagnet.com/cox/index.html.

[24] There is a resistance to calling these "exclusive rights" "monopolies." Frank Easterbrook, "Intellectual Property Is Still Property," *Harvard Journal of Law & Public Policy* 13 (1991): 108–09. But technically, of course, they are. That, however, does not entail that a given exclusive right has any monopoly power. There is a purpose, however, in calling these rights "monopolies"—to shift the burden of defending the rights to those who claim they do some good. This was the strategy of Macaulay in the mid–nineteenth century as well. See Siva Vaidhyanathan, *Copyrights and Copywrongs: The Rise of Intellectual Property and How It Threatens Creativity* (New York: New York University Press, 2001), 142.

[25] Letter from Thomas Jefferson to Isaac McPherson (August 13, 1813), in *The Writings of Thomas Jefferson*, vol. 6 (H. A. Washington, ed., 1861), 175, 180.

[26] Though GPL is often referred to as a "copyleft" license, copyleft depends fundamentally upon copyright. Without a copyright, there would be no way to ensure that users of a bit of software code agreed to further obligations imposed upon the code by the GPL. Software dedicated to the public domain, for example, would not have the capacity to ensure that users were bound by GPL. But with copyrighted code offered subject to the terms of GPL, the user either complies with the license or is an infringing user of the code.

As I describe more below, GPL is not the only, or perhaps even the most important, open code license. Other open code licenses differ from GPL by not requiring that subsequent derivative works open up their own code base. For an evaluation of GPL's viability under German law, see Axel Metzger and Till Jaeger, "Open Source Software and German Copyright Law," *International Review of Industrial Property & Copyright Law* 32 (2001):52.

[27] See http://www.fsf.org/copyleft/gpl.html.

[28] Stallman, 56.

[29] See Moody, 168 (describing open source definition).

[30] For a fuller discussion of various open code licenses and their implications, see David McGowan, "Legal Implications of Open Source Software," *University of Illinois Law Review* (2001): 101, 113–19; Patrick K. Bobko, "Can Copyright Keep 'Open Source' Software Free?," *AIPLA Quarterly Journal* 28 (2000): 81; Ira V. Heffan, "Note: Copyleft: Licensing Collaborative Works in the Digital Age," *Stanford Law Review* 49 (1997): 1487; Daniel B. Ravicher, "Facilitating Collaborative Software Development: The Enforceability of Mass-Market Public Software Licenses," *Virginia Journal of Law & Technology* 5 (2000): 11.

[31] Wayner, 260.

[32] The latest operating system from Apple, OS X, includes a portion called Darwin that is licensed under an open source license. See http://www.apple.com/macosx/tour/darwin.html.

[33] For detailed analyses of this case, see Ken Auletta, *World War 3.0: Microsoft and Its Enemies* (New York: Random House, 2001); David Bank, *Breaking Windows: How Bill Gates Fumbled the Future of Microsoft* (New York: Free Press, 2001); John Heilemann, *Pride Before the Fall: The Trials of Bill Gates and the End of the Microsoft Era* (New York: HarperCollins, 2001).

[34] The government isn't the only one to make this allegation. As Red Hat chairman Bob Young describes it, "Microsoft appeared to have gone so far as to dictate how fast other companies could bring out new products—or if they could bring them out at all, for that matter." Young and Rohm, 7.

[35] Some attempts were made at graphical user interface desktop environments before Windows hit pay dirt, including VisiOn (by VisiCalc), Top View (by IBM), GEM (by Digital Research), and Interface Manager (Microsoft's precursor to Windows); none fared well with consumers, however. Ceruzzi, 276.

[36] In a well-known story, the company didn't actually write DOS but simply licensed it from Tim Paterson of Seattle Computer Products. Microsoft paid "about $15,000 for the rights to use Seattle Computer Products's work." Microsoft later paid more for the complete rights. Ibid., 270.

[37] Stan Miastkowski, "A Cure for What Ails DOS," *BYTE* (August 1990): 107.

[38] See *Caldera v. Microsoft*, 72 F. Supp. 2d 1295, 1299 (D. Utah, 1999).

[39] Jim Carlton, *Apple: The Intrigue, Egomania, and Business Blunders That Toppled an American Icon* (New York: Times Books/Random House, 1997), 39–47.

[40] Ibid., 28.

[41] "Strategic behavior arises when two or more individuals interact and each individual's decision turns on what that individual expects the others to do." Douglas G. Baird, Robert H. Gertner, and Randal C. Picker, *Game Theory and the Law* (Cambridge, Mass.: Harvard University Press, 1994), 1. As I use the term, I mean to restrict it to cases where the resulting behavior raises questions under antitrust law.

As David Bank writes, the notion of a competitive strategy to protect Microsoft's base was at the core of Microsoft's product design. This was referred to within Microsoft as the "strategy tax." As Bank writes:

Gates invariably pressed the same point: Be more "strategic." He demanded hooks to lock in customers. The goal was to drive interdependencies between various Microsoft products and thus make it more painful for customers to switch to a competitor for any individual feature.

Bank, 134. Gates placed the need for "strategic advantage" above concern for "customers." As Gates wrote in an e-mail titled "HTML 'Openness' ":

> People were suggesting that Office had to work equally well with all browsers and that we shouldn't force Office users to use our browser. . . . This is wrong and I wanted to correct this.

Ibid., 73–74. Instead, as he went on to instruct, the product should be designed to be "Office/Windows/Microsoft specific." Ibid.

This "strategy tax" was "inherently demoralizing," Bank writes. Ibid., 134. Software teams wanted to "win on the merits," ibid., not based on tricks built into the code. More generally, Bank argues, many within the firm believed the strategy tax would eventually harm Microsoft competitively. As Ben Slivka said to Gates, "I think your focus on 'common code' as a goal in itself has served to stifle innovation." Ibid., 99. Slivka pushed "unfettered innovation," free from "the constraints of the company's historical franchises." Ibid. Another senior executive, Brad Silverberg, wrote, "I simply do not want to spend my life in meetings struggling with the internal issues, getting pissy mail from Billg, [or] hearing from people who want me to do unnatural and losing things to 'protect' Windows." Ibid., 175.

The idea that a company might succeed in this market without proprietary control—without, in other words, a "strategy tax"—might seem counterintuitive. Companies such as Cisco, however, demonstrate that success can come from something other than playing games with platforms. Cisco has flourished despite the fact that the platform it builds upon—the protocols of TCP/IP—are neutral and unowned. No doubt it faces fierce competition, but it has succeeded nonetheless.

As I describe in chapter 14, Bank believes the strategy within Microsoft has now changed to embrace neutral, rather than "taxing," competition.

42 Elizabeth Corcoran, "Microsoft Deal Came Down to a Phone Call," *Washington Post*, July 18, 1994, A1.

43 Ibid.

44 As David Bank writes:

> At 3 am on a rainy Monday in April 1995, Gates declared in an e-mail to his top lieutenants that the "Internet is destroying our position as the setter of standards. . . . [It] is taking away our power every day and will have eroded it irretrievably by the time broadband is pervasive on the course we are on right now.["]

Bank, 26. The core of the threat, Gates believed, was Netscape. "As Netscape's standards became more important than Windows'," Gates wrote, Netscape's browser would "commoditize the underlying operating system." Ibid., 27.

Gates was equally concerned about Microsoft's embrace of Java. As he wrote after reading an analysis that pushed neutral development of Java, "This scares the hell out of me. . . . It's still very unclear to me what our [OSes] will offer to Java that will make them unique enough to preserve our market position." Ibid.

45 The government relied upon extensive evidence from Mr. Gates's own e-mail and statements. See *United States* v. *Microsoft*, 84 F. Supp. 2d 9, 59–60 (D.D.C. 1999).

[46] While it is a mistake to read too much into the loose use of the term *leverage*, it is clear that Microsoft executives believed "leveraging" IE through the use of Windows was the most effective way to gain market share. Bank, 70 (quoting Allchin). "We should think first about an integrated solution—that is our strength." Ibid., 69.

For a careful analysis of current economic thinking about tying and exclusive contracts (at the core of the Microsoft case), see Michael D. Whinston, "Exclusivity and Tying in *United States* v. *Microsoft*: What We Know, and Don't Know," *Journal of Economic Perspectives* 15 (2001): 63.

[47] Ibid., 11, 13.

[48] Ibid., 212.

[49] Ibid., 228.

And obviously, too, it can control more than the pace of innovation. My concern in *Code and Other Laws of Cyberspace* was precisely the regulation that gets effected through code—"Code is Law"—and the concern that the more code controls our life, the more we should care about who the coders are. Denise Caruso has written powerfully on the same idea. As she puts it, "[I]t is still true today that software—written by a team of sleep-deprived programmers in some fusty cubicle—is the code that lays down the absolute law by which we live our digital lives. We are not free to change that code; our choice is to love it or leave it. In the Microsoft trial . . . the battle is really over whose law is to be sovereign, software's or the government's." "The Legacy of Microsoft's Trial," *New York Times*, December 6, 1999, available at http://www.nytimes.com/library/tech/99/12/biztech/articles/06digi.html. She adds, "[C]yberspace is already regulated by software code, which by its nature decides whether and under what circumstances we will have privacy or anonymity and who can or cannot have access and how. Though this fact was not so terrifying when the software running the global Internet was built on open standards, the situation has become significantly more ominous as the code has become commercialized and thus private and not open to public scrutiny. . . . [W]hen commercial code begins to determine the Internet's architecture, it creates a kind of privatized law that must be regulated if the public interest and public values are to be democratically represented." Ibid.

[50] One of the most important Unix clones was a project called BSD—the Berkeley Software Distribution Project. The BSD project was born when Unix was still free. After AT&T reclaimed control of Unix, it demanded that BSD cease its distribution. BSD refused, and lawsuits ensued. After protracted litigation, the right of BSD (with certain code rewritten) to distribute its version of Unix free of AT&T was sustained through a settlement. For more on the BSD lawsuit and BSD generally, see Wayner, 38, 49–54 (discussing AT&T's lawsuit against BSD), and 92–95 (discussing the development of BSD); Cheryl Garber, "*USL* v. *Berkeley*," *UNIX Review* 10 (1992): 32.

BSD gave its code away under a very weak license. Anyone could do anything with the code, as long as he kept the copyright notices clear. But as groups developed to support this free code, divisions among the troops developed as well: from this common base of BSD, the project forked to include FreeBSD, NetBSD, and OpenBSD, among others. Wayner, 98–99.

[51] There is an interesting but unresolved debate about whether GPL (the strictest of the open code licenses) does more to stem the risk of forking than more permissive open code licenses. Compare Young and Rohm, 180 (arguing that GPL minimizes forking), with Wayner, 221 (arguing the contrary).

[52] Ibid., 210.

[53] Eric S. Raymond, *The Cathedral and the Bazaar: Musings on Linux and Open*

Source by an Accidental Revolutionary (Beijing and Sebastopol, Calif.: O'Reilly, 1999), 151.

54 Wayner, 289.

55 "IBM Extends Software Leadership on Linux," IBM Press Release, December 8, 2000.

56 Economists have only begun to examine the incentives that might affect open code projects. Josh Lerner and Jean Tirole have summarized some of the benefits, relative to closed code projects, as follows: (1) lower costs due to (a) familiarity of the code from, e.g., university training, and (b) customization/bug-fixing advantages; and (2) higher benefits, especially due to signaling from (a) better performance measurement (easier to demonstrate skill), (b) "full initiative" (because no supervisory involvement), and (c) greater labor market fluidity. See Josh Lerner and Jean Tirole, "The Simple Economics of Open Source" (NBER Working Paper No. 7600, December 2000).

James Bessen has offered a far more ambitious model of the benefits from open code projects. In a paper not yet published, Bessen argues that open code provision is superior to closed source provision when the public good (i.e., software) is a complex public good. The intuition is that the costs of debugging complex software projects become prohibitively high within a closed code environment. As Bessen writes, "[I]f a product had 100 independent features and each combination took only one second to test, then the job could not be finished before the sun is predicted to swallow the earth even if every human currently alive spent every second until then testing." James Bessen, "Open Source Software: Free Provision of Complex Public Goods" (working version, April 2001), http://researchoninnovation.org. Bessen concludes that "strong property rights . . . may actually limit provision of complex [public goods]," and hence that open code projects have a competitive advantage over closed.

57 This argument is related to a point made by Carl Shapiro and Hal R. Varian in *Information Rules: A Strategic Guide to the Network Economy* (Boston, Mass.: Harvard Business School Press, 1999), 256–59. As they argue there, in a market heavily dependent upon standards, there is often an incentive for competitors to contribute to public standards rather than to make the standard proprietary. The battle over the standard HTML is an example of this. For a while, both Netscape and Microsoft tried to develop extensions to HTML that were peculiar to their own servers and Web development software. Their aim was to split the common standard base to induce the market to follow their own design. Later, however, they both apparently decided that this effort to divide the standard would not be profitable; better if there were more on a common platform than fewer on a proprietary platform. Varian and Shapiro demonstrate the conditions under which that behavior could be rational. See also Varian, "Buying, Sharing, and Renting Information Goods," *Journal of Industrial Economics* 48 (2000): 473. On Microsoft's attitude toward a neutral HTML, see Bank, 74 ("If Microsoft doesn't get to do anything 'proprietary' with HTML in the browser," Gates wrote, then "we have to stop viewing HTML as central to our strategy and get onto another strategy."). See also ibid., 73 (regarding Office). See also Moody, 200. Moody believes that because the Apache server was a dominant server for HTTP, and uncontrolled by any commercial venture, it did not fracture in the same way. See ibid., 149.

58 For articles identifying scenarios in which this proposition fails, see Douglas Lichtman et al., "Shared Information Goods," *Journal of Law & Economics* 42 (1999): 117; Hal R. Varian, "Buying, Sharing, and Renting Information Goods," *Journal of Industrial Economics* 48 (2000): 473; Douglas Lichtman, "Property Rights in Emerging Platform Technologies," *Journal of Legal Studies* 29 (2000): 615.

[59] James Boyle, *Shamans, Software, and Spleens: Law and the Construction of the Information Society* (Cambridge, Mass.: Harvard University Press, 1996), ch. 4.

[60] This is especially the case with embedded systems, which have exploded recently because of the ability to incorporate essential operating system code freely. See "Embedded Linux Basics," http://lw.itworld.com/linuxworld/lw-2000–05/lw-05-embedded_p. html; "Companies Bet on Embedded Linux," http://www.forbes.com/2000/04/07/mu4. html.

CHAPTER 5

[1] See Susan J. Douglas, *Inventing American Broadcasting 1899–1922*, reprint ed. (Baltimore: Johns Hopkins University Press, 1997), 227–28; Eszter Hargittai, "Radio's Lessons for the Internet," *Communications ACM* 43 (2000): 51, 54.

[2] See *National Broadcasting Co. v. U.S.*, 319 U.S. 190, 210 (1943). Radio "broadcasting," however, did not begin until KDKA began its service in Pittsburgh in 1920. See Thomas W. Hazlett, "The Wireless Craze, the Unlimited Bandwidth Myth, the Spectrum Auction Faux Pas, and the Punchline to Ronald Coase's 'Big Joke': An Essay on Airwave Allocation Policy" (Working Paper 01–01, AEI-Brookings Joint Center for Regulatory Studies, January 2001), 95 (*Harvard Journal of Law and Technology*, spring 2001).

[3] See *Red Lion Broadcasting v. FCC*, 395 U.S. 367, fn4 (1969). The statute was the Radio Act of 1927, ch. 169, 44 Stat. 1162 (1927).

[4] For an excellent account of the emergence of broadcasting as we would recognize it, see Douglas, 292–322.

[5] Robert W. McChesney, *Rich Media, Poor Democracy: Communication Politics in Dubious Times* (Urbana: University of Illinois Press, 1999), 192.

[6] Ibid., 194.

[7] Hazlett, "The Wireless Craze," 48.

[8] Edward S. Herman and Robert W. McChesney, *The Global Media: The New Missionaries of Corporate Capitalism* (London and Washington, D.C.: Cassell, 1997), 138.

[9] Erik Barnouw, *A History of Broadcasting in the United States*, vol. 1 (New York: Oxford University Press, 1966–70), 96, 177–78, 243, 262–66.

[10] See Peter W. Huber, Michael K. Kellogg, and John Thorne, *Federal Telecommunications Law*, 2nd ed. (Gaithersburg, Md.: Aspen Law & Business, 1999), 220–21, 865–66.

[11] *NBC v. U.S.*, 213.

[12] Ibid., 228 (Murphy, J., dissenting).

[13] R. H. Coase, "The Federal Communications Commission," *Journal of Law and Economics* 2 (1959): 1.

[14] The idea originated in an article by a University of Chicago law student. See Leo Herzel, " 'Public Interest' and the Market in Color Television Regulation," *University of Chicago Law Review* 18 (1951): 802, 811–12 ("The FCC could lease channels for a stated period to the highest bidder without making any other judgment of the economic or engineering adequacy of the standards to be used by the applicant."). See also Richard A. Posner, *Economic Analysis of Law*, 4th ed. (Boston: Little, Brown, 1992), 673 (saying the Supreme Court's rationale for different spectrum regulation rules "is economic nonsense").

Ronald Coase, however, made the idea famous. See Yochai Benkler, "Overcoming Agoraphobia: Building the Commons of the Digitally Networked Environment," *Harvard Journal of Law & Technology* 11 (1998): 287, 316–17.

[15] As Coase wrote: "But it is a commonplace of economics that almost all resources used in the economic system (and not simply radio and television frequencies) are limited in amount and scarce, in that people would like to use more than exists. Land, labor and capital are all scarce, but this, of itself, does not call for government regulation. It is true that some mechanism has to be employed to decide who, out of the many claimants, should be allowed to use the scarce resource. But the way this is usually done in the American economic system is to employ the price mechanism, and this allocates resources to users without the need for government regulation." R. H. Coase, "The Federal Communications Commission," *Journal of Law & Economics* 2 (1959): 1, 14.

[16] Hazlett has been prolific in advancing this argument. See, e.g., Hazlett and Sosa, "Chilling the Internet? Lessons from FCC Regulation of Radio Broadcasting," *Michigan Telecommunications & Technology Law Review* 4 (1997–98): 35; Hazlett, "Physical Scarcity, Rent Seeking, and the First Amendment," *Columbia Law Review* 97 (1997): 905; Hazlett, "Assigning Property Rights to Radio Spectrum Users: Why Did FCC License Auctions Take 67 Years?," *Journal of Law & Economics* 41 (1998): 529; Hazlett, "Spectrum Flash Dance: Eli Noam's Proposal for 'Open Access' to Radio Waves," *Journal of Law & Economics* 41 (1998): 805; Hazlett and Sosa, "Was the Fairness Doctrine a 'Chilling Effect'? Evidence from the Postderegulation Radio Market," *Journal of Legal Studies* 26 (1997): 279; Hazlett, "The Rationality of U.S. Regulation of the Broadcast Spectrum," *Journal of Law & Economics* 23 (1990): 133.

[17] See, e.g., Hazlett, "Spectrum Flash Dance," 816. ("Profit maximization will force competitive band managers to devise better technical means to increase wireless communications traffic.")

[18] The source of the skepticism is traced, as Yochai Benkler describes, to Claude E. Shannon, "Communication in the Presence of Noise," *Proceedings of the IRE* 37 (1949): 10, and Claude E. Shannon, "A Mathematical Theory of Communication," *Bell System Technology Journal* 27 (1948): 379 and 623 (two-part publication). "These articles lay out the theoretical underpinnings of direct sequencing spread spectrum." Benkler, *Overcoming Agoraphobia*, 323, note 171.

[19] In order to be called "spread spectrum," two conditions must be met: (1) the transmitted signal bandwidth is greater than the minimal information bandwidth needed to successfully transmit the signal; and (2) some function other than the information itself is being employed to determine the resultant transmitted bandwidth. Robert C. Dixon, "Why Spread Spectrum?," *IEEE Communication Society Magazine* (July 1975): 21–25. See also Yochai Benkler, "From Consumers to Users: Shifting the Deeper Structures of Regulation Toward Sustainable Commons and User Access," *Federal Communications Law Journal* 52 (2000): 561, 576–77. For an excellent study that links technological and policy questions, see Stuart Buck et al., "Spread Spectrum: Regulation in Light of Changing Technologies" (1998), http://cyber.law.harvard.edu/ltac98/student-papers.html. See also "The Unwired World" (Special Report), *Scientific American* 278 (1998): 69.

[20] E-mail from David P. Reed to Lawrence Lessig, March 25, 2001.

[21] For an introduction, see http://www.freesoft.org/CIE/Topics/60.htm. (This scheme, one of many that can regulate access to a hardware medium, is referred to as CSMA/CD, an acronym for "carrier sense, multiple access/collision detect.") See also Douglas E. Comer, *Internetworking with TCP/IP*, 4th ed., vol. 1 (Upper Saddle River, N.J.: Prentice-Hall, 2000), 28 (explaining how the Ethernet handles access and collision detection through CSMA/CD).

[22] Hazlett, "Physical Scarcity," 928–29; Hazlett, "The Wireless Craze," 10.

[23] For discussions of the technology, see Benkler, *From Consumers to Users*, 576–77; Benkler, *Overcoming Agoraphobia*, 290 ("Technological developments in digital information processing and wireless communications have made possible an alternative regulatory approach. It is now possible to regulate wireless communications as we do the Internet—with minimal standard protocols—or the highway system—with limited governmentally imposed rules of the road."); ibid., part IV, 322–30 (describing examples of current business models utilizing spread spectrum technologies where unlicensed operations are permitted: proprietary infrastructure cellular network—Metricom's Ricochet wireless network, ad hoc network of equipment owned by users—rooftop networks, and publicly owned infrastructure of unlicensed devices—the NSF field tests).

[24] See Steve Stroh, "Hollywood Star Was a Wireless Pioneer," *CLEC Magazine* (March–April 2000): 20. See also http://www.ncafe.com/chris/pat2/index.html (describing Lamarr's contribution).

[25] Anna Couey, "The Birth of Spread Spectrum: How 'The Bad Boy of Music' and 'The Most Beautiful Girl in the World' Catalyzed a Wireless Revolution—in 1941," http://www.sirius.be/lamarr.htm. Lamarr's work inspired what is known as the "frequency-hopping" form of spread spectrum. "Direct sequence," or CDMA, was developed later.

[26] For more on the technology, see Roger L. Peterson, Rodger E. Ziemer, and David E. Borth, *Introduction to Spread-Spectrum Communications* (Englewood Cliffs, N.J.: Prentice-Hall, 1995); Amer A. Hassan, John E. Hershey, and Gary J. Saulnier, *Perspectives in Spread Spectrum* (Boston and London: Kluwer Academic, 1998).

[27] Telephone interview with Dave Hughes, November 13, 2000.

[28] Ibid.

[29] See http://www.techweek.com/articles/8-23-99/wireless.htm.

[30] See, e.g., U.S. Congress, Office of Technology Assessment, *Telecommunications Technology and Native Americans: Opportunities and Challenges*, OTA-ITC-621 (Washington, D.C.: U.S. Government Printing Office, August 1995). See also statement "FCC Takes Steps to Promote Access to Telecommunications on Tribal Lands" (FCC news release, June 8, 2000).

[31] The FCC has set aside three data bands as "unlicensed," meaning users can deploy devices that rely upon these bands without permission from the FCC or a spectrum owner. The regulations governing this use are found in part 15 of the FCC's rules, and the bands are 915 MHz (902–928 MHz), 2.4 GHz (2,400–2,483.5 MHz), and 5.7 GHz (5,725–5,850 MHz). Part 15 devices may not cause any harmful interference to authorized services and must accept any interference that may be received. C.F.R., 47, §15.5. Operation under these rules was limited to frequency-hopping and direct sequence spread spectrum systems. But the FCC announced its intention to broaden the technologies permitted. See "In the Matter of Amendment of Part 15 of the Commission's Rules Regarding Spread Spectrum Devices" (DA 00–2317) (May 11, 2001); "Operation of Radio Frequency Devices Without an Individual License," 54 Fed. Reg. 17,710 (1989), codified at C.F.R., 47; pt. 2 and pt. 15 (1996). In addition, the FCC has six unlicensed bands for non–spread spectrum use. They are the Citizens Band, the Radio Control Service Band, the Low Power Radio Service Band, the Wireless Telemetry Service Band, the Medical Implant Communications Band, and the Family Radio Service Band.

[32] 802.11b refers to a standard developed by the IEEE. See http://www.manta.ieee.org/groups/802/11/. The standard enables wireless protocols in the unlicensed spectrum in the 2.5 GHz range at 11 Mbps.

[33] See also James Gleick, "The Wireless Age: Theories of Connectivity," *New York Times Magazine*, April 22, 2001 (discussing other wireless technologies).

34 No doubt there are many who are competing to develop technologies for these unlicensed options. For a description of the range of companies, see Amara D. Angelica,
"Wireless Internet Access," *TechWeek*, http://www.techweek.com/articles/8-23-99/wireless.
htm.

35 This does not mean the regulation would necessarily be harmless. Bad regulation at
the device level could well inhibit innovation just as bad regulation at the spectrum level
has inhibited innovation.

36 These "free spectrum" or "open spectrum" advocates are all very different, though
they share a belief that spectrum should be managed differently. The differences among
them boil down to their attitude about scarcity. At one extreme is a group we might call
utopians. These people, such as Dave Hughes, Paul Baran, David Reed, and George
Gilder, believe that it is more likely than not that spectrum, properly used, would in
essence be unlimited. See, e.g., Paul Baran, "Is the UHF Frequency Shortage a Self-
Made Problem?," (paper given at the Marconi Centennial Symposium, Bologna, Italy,
June 23, 1995, on file with the *Columbia Law Review*), 3; Gilder, *Telecosm*, 158–64;
David Hughes and Kambiz Hooshmand, "ABR Stretches ATM Network Resources,"
Data Communications 24, no. 5 (April 1995): 123.

At the other extreme is Eli Noam, who believes that spectrum is scarce and therefore
needs a system for rationing. See Eli Noam, "The Future of Telecommunications Regulation," *NRRI Quarterly Bulletin* 20 (1999): 17; Eli Noam, "Spectrum Auctions: Yesterday's Heresy, Today's Orthodoxy, Tomorrow's Anachronism: Taking the Next Step
to Open Spectrum Access," *Journal of Law & Economics* 41 (1998): 765; Eli Noam,
"Beyond Auctions: Open Spectrum Access," in *Regulators' Revenge: The Future of Telecommunications Deregulation*, Tom W. Bell and Solveig Singleton, eds. (Cato Institute, 1998), 1; Eli Noam, "Will Universal Service and Common Carriage Survive
the Telecommunications Act of 1996?," *Columbia Law Review* 97 (1997): 955; Eli
Noam, "Spectrum and Universal Service," *Telecommunications Policy* 21 (1997); Eli
Noam, "Taking the Next Step Beyond Spectrum Auctions: Open Spectrum Access,"
IEEE Communications Magazine 33 (1995): 66 ; Eli Noam, "The Federal-State Friction
Built into the 1934 Act and Options for Reform," in *American Regulatory Federalism &
Telecommunications Infrastructure*, Paul Teske, ed. (Hillsdale, N.J.: Lawrence Erlbaum
Associates, 1995), 113–14; Eli Noam, "Beyond Liberalization II: The Impending Doom
of Common Carriage," *Telecommunications Policy* 18 (1994): 435; Eli Noam, "A Public
and Private-Choice Model of Broadcasting," *Public Choice* 55 (1987): 163. His system
has the flavor of a market, but it is more the kind of market that controls access to sub-
ways than the ownership of taxis: just as a subway rider purchases a token at the moment
he or she needs to ride the subway, the user of spectrum, in real time, would purchase a
token that would assure his or her right to use spectrum. Unlike subway tokens, however,
these tokens would fluctuate in price as the demand for spectrum changes. During times
of great congestion, the price would go up; during times of low usage, the price would
fall. This market would be competitive, so the prices would be neutral, and hence the
proposal still fits my definition of a commons. But it is different from Gilder's and Reed's
in that it requires money to get access.

In the middle is Yochai Benkler, who is agnostic about the technology but clear about
the constitutional norm. See Yochai Benkler, "Siren Songs and Amish Children: Autonomy, Information, and Law," *New York University Law Review* 76 (2000): 23, 81,
where he talks about constitutionality. If spectrum is effectively unlimited, or if it could
be organized to be effectively unlimited, then it should be structured to permit free ac-

cess. But if congestion is a problem, then we should allocate access to the spectrum to minimize that congestion and possibly, if necessary, adopt a structure like Noam's. See also Benkler, "From Consumers to Users," 561; Benkler, "Viacom-CBS Merger: From Consumers to Users: Shifting the Deeper Structures of Regulation Toward Sustainable Commons and User Access," *Federal Communications Law Journal* 52 (2000): 561; Benkler, "Free as the Air to Common Use: First Amendment Constraints on Enclosure of the Public Domain," *New York University Law Review* 74 (1999): 354; Benkler, "Communications Infrastructure Regulation and the Distribution of Control over Content," *Telecommunications Policy* 22 (1998): 183; Benkler, "Overcoming Agoraphobia," 287.

These are important differences, though in the end they matter in only one sense. No one believes it has been proven that spectrum as it is presently used is unlimited. David Reed points to the research of Tim Shepard and others demonstrating that a wireless network could be structured so that an increase in the number of users actually *increases* total capacity. Tim Shepard, *Decentralized Channel Management in Scalable Multihop Spread-Spectrum Packet Radio Networks*, MIT, EECS thesis, 1995. See also Timothy J. Shepard, "A Channel Access Scheme for Large Dense Packet Radio Networks," at http://www.acm.org/pubs/articles/proceedings/comm/248156/p219-shepard/p219-shepard.pdf. Reed argues that the " 'capacity' of a free space radio network is not fixed, but instead is an increasing function of the density of user 'terminals' in that space." Telephone interview with David Reed, February 7, 2001. This means that as more people enter the shared spectrum space (as the number of terminals, that is, increases), the available spectrum *increases*, not decreases. The more nodes there are on the network, the closer these nodes are; the closer they are, the weaker the signal connecting these nodes must be; the weaker the signal, the more signals there can be. A network of wireless nodes could expand spectrum capacity as the number of nodes increases.

But even without this increasing capacity, Baran and Hughes both argue that given existing capacity, properly deployed, we could fulfill all the need we have for delivering data across the ether without any constraint at all.

The differences between those who see bandwidth as essentially unlimited and those who see it as scarce obscure a more fundamental agreement: All would agree that spectrum use could undergo a radical shift—a paradigm change, in Eli Noam's terms. All would agree that this change would fundamentally alter the nature of our use of spectrum and would lead to an explosion of innovation in the use of spectrum that would not otherwise, under either the government or the market model, exist. Everyone now concedes that state-licensed spectrum has stifled innovation—the most glaring example was the government's stalling, because of the pressure of industry, the development of FM radio. See *Edwin R. Armstrong: A Man and His Invention* (Eli Noam, ed., forthcoming). All agree that the alternative of allowing spectrum to be sold is like "having the old AT&T auction off the right to compete against itself." Noam, "Beyond Spectrum Auctions," 473.

Noam and Benkler have an even stronger (from a legal perspective) argument against the sale of spectrum. In a world where the control of spectrum was not "necessary," as the Supreme Court said it was in the NBC case, why was control of spectrum constitutionally permitted? Spectrum is speech, and the regulation of spectrum is the regulation of speech. The constitutional status of spectrum auctions is rendered problematic by the emergence of this alternative technology. Control is not "necessary" anymore, any more than control of newspapers is necessary. It would certainly be unconstitutional to force newspapers to buy a license to print (the way taxi drivers have to buy a medallion to drive a taxi), so why is it any less unconstitutional to force a newspaper to buy the right to broadcast?

The key to this use of spectrum would be a robust software-defined radio (SDR) technology, meaning a radio whose protocols get set by software, enabling easy switching among different frequencies, carriers, and networks. Just as a modem, for example, can switch among a number of protocols for modulating data transmissions, so too could a SDR switch among protocols for communicating between radios. The switching in SDRs is much greater than in modems, however, as it would include not only protocols, but also power levels and modes of transmitting. But in principle, the system could allow radios to sniff the environment and determine which kind of communication for that environment would work best.

The government is doing some of the most important work in this area. DARPA, which was responsible in part for the birth of the Internet, is experimenting with SDRs that could communicate in battlefield contexts. To make this succeed, however, the government needs "a common architecture so that you're not tied to one particular technology as an implementation of your next-generation radio." Telephone interview with Bill Lane, FCC, November 15, 2000. It is also important, as Intel has argued in comments to the FCC, that the rules unbundle radio control from user application software, so as to facilitate the broadest range of innovation at the software level. As Intel argues, "[A] programmable platform would lower entry costs for the independent third party developers who played a key role in delivering innovative solutions elsewhere." Intel, "Comments of Intel Corporation, In the Matter of Authorization and Use of Software Defined Radios," ET Docket No. 00–47 (Washington), 4.

FCC chairman Michael Powell has a similar intuition about the potential: "[A]dvanced technologies such as spread spectrum have ushered in all sorts of innovative and efficient services. Indeed, rather than being a uniquely scarce resource[], spectrum has the potential to be a bottomless resource, unlike coal, oil, or timber[,] which are more susceptible to depletion. *Perhaps it is uniquely abundant rather than uniquely scarce.*" Michael K. Powell, "Willful Denial and First Amendment Jurisprudence," Remarks Before the Media Institute, April 22, 1998 (transcript available at http://www. fcc.gov/Speeches/Powell/spmkp808.html), 5 (emphasis added).

37 George Gilder, *Telecosm: How Infinite Bandwidth Will Revolutionize Our World* (New York: Free Press, 2000), 160.

CHAPTER 6

1 Carol Rose, "The Comedy of the Commons: Custom, Commerce, and Inherently Public Property," *University of Chicago Law Review* 53 (1986): 711, 713.

2 Ibid., 712.

3 Ibid., 744.

4 See ibid., 752 (describing how "antiholdout" rules historically protected public usage of roads from private actors who might "siphon off its public value"). The development of the highway system has had strong direct (employment) and indirect (productivity) effects on the United States economy. See M. Ishaq Nadiri and Theofanis P. Mamuneas, "Contribution of Highway Capital to Output and Productivity Growth in the U.S. Economy and Industries," Department of Transportation Federal Highway Administration, August 1998, available at http://www.fhwa.dot.gov/policy/gro98cvr.htm; T. A. Heppenheimer, "The Rise of the Interstates," *American Herald of Inventions & Technology* 7 (1991): 8; Mark H. Rose, *Interstate 15–67* (Knoxville: University of Ten-

nessee Press, 1990). See also *The New America That's Coming* (1956) (special report by editors of *Automotive Industries*) (describing effect of "superhighways program on industry, commerce and vehicle design").

To the extent transportation has been privately owned, the dominant regulatory rule has been common carriage. Railroads, for example, were privately owned; but they were also subject to common carrier obligations. The effect of these common carrier regulations was to render the common carrier a commons as well. See, e.g., Andrew A. Nimelman, "Of Common Carriage and Cable Access: Deregulation of Cable Television by the Supreme Court," *Federal Communications Law Journal* 34 (1982): 167, 173; Robert Means and Deborah Cohn, "Common Carriage of Natural Gas," *Tulane Law Review* 59 (1985): 529. As Yochai Benkler writes, however, "after the internal combustion engine was invented, it was not a better system for awarding railroad franchises that was needed, but a well-regulated commons like our national highway system." Yochai Benkler, "The Commons as a Neglected Factor of Information Policy" (paper presented at Telecommunications Policy Research Center conference, October 3–5, 1998), 68. And indeed, the revenue from rail transportation was $28,348,895,000 in 1992, compared with $135,437,000,000 for local and long-haul trucking services. See section 21, "Transportation-Land," of 1997 U.S. Economic Census conducted by U.S. Census Bureau, available at http://www.census.gov/prod/2/gen/96statab/transind.pdf.

[5] Rose, "The Comedy of the Commons," 759, citing *President of Cincinnati* v. *Lessee of White*, 31 U.S. (6 Pet.) 429 (1832) (recognizing an implied dedication of a square for traditional public use). See also Hanoch Dagan and Michael A. Heller, "The Liberal Commons," *Yale Law Journal* 110 (2001): 549; Michael A. Heller, "The Tragedy of the Anticommons: Property in the Transition from Marx to Markets," *Harvard Law Review* 111 (1998): 621, 622–26; Alison Rieser, "Prescriptions for the Commons: Environmental Scholarship and the Fishing Quotas Debate," *Harvard Environmental Law Review* 23 (1999): 393; Elinor Ostrom, *Governing the Commons: The Evolution of Institutions for Collective Action* (Cambridge, England, and New York: Cambridge University Press, 1990), 2–23.

Henry Smith has identified a similar strategic cost in semicommons contexts. See Henry E. Smith, "Semicommon Property Rights and Scattering in the Open Fields," *Journal of Legal Studies* 29 (2000): 131, 161–62.

[6] Rose, "The Comedy of the Commons," 769.

[7] Robert Merges offers a complementing argument, focusing on interoperability and the value brought by individuals' investment in, for example, learning the commands in a program. Robert Merges, "Who Owns the Charles River Bridge? Intellectual Property and Competition in the Software Industry" (working paper, 1999).

[8] The classic text supporting a broad range of open or free resources, building on the work of Joseph Schumpeter, is Richard R. Nelson and Sidney G. Winter, *An Evolutionary Theory of Economic Change* (Cambridge, Mass.: Belknap Press of Harvard University Press, 1982). As they write: "[I]nnovation in the economic system—and indeed the creation of any sort of novelty in art, science, or practical life—consists to a substantial extent of a recombination of conceptual and physical materials that were previously in existence. The vast momentum of scientific, technological, and economic progress in the modern world derives largely from the fact that each new achievement is not merely the answer to a particular problem, but also a new item in the vast storehouse of components that are available for use, in 'new combinations,' in the solution of other problems in the future." Ibid., 130. For a recent work advancing an analytic framework for evaluating "in-

novation policy," see Brett Frischmann, "Innovation and Institutions: Rethinking the Economics of U.S. Science and Technology Policy," *Vermont Law Review* 24 (2000): 347.

[9] See David P. Reed, Jerome H. Saltzer, and David D. Clark, "Comment on Active Networking and End-to-End Arguments," *IEEE Network* 12, no. 3 (May–June 1998): 69–71.

[10] Ostrom too has found that commons problems are best solved as commons where environments are "uncertain and complex." Ostrom, 88–89.

[11] The argument is related to a point made by a number of scholars about patents. Where the use of an invention is unknown, the transaction costs of licensing the invention are high. This can mean that patents over such inventions inhibit, rather than induce, innovation. See Arti Kaur Rai, "Regulating Scientific Research: Intellectual Property Rights and the Norms of Science," *Northwestern University Law Review* 94 (1999): 77, 136–37; James Bessen and Eric Maskin, "Sequential Innovation, Patents, and Imitation" (Cambridge University, Department of Economics, Working Paper 00–01, January 2000).

[12] As David Reed puts the same point:

> In an application of technologies and structure you don't understand, there's a great value in creating the opportunity and framework in which innovators can experiment and build on a platform that allows them [to] do what they want to do.

Telephone interview with David Reed, February 7, 2001.

[13] Mark Gaynor et al., "Theory of Service Architecture," 42. Baldwin and Clark use a similar notion to explain the value of modular design. See Carliss Y. Baldwin and Kim B. Clark, *Design Rules*, vol. 1 (Cambridge, Mass.: MIT Press, 2000), 234–37 ("Modularity creates design options and in so doing can radically change the market value of a given set of designs.").

[14] Telephone interview with David Reed.

[15] Though, as he acknowledges, the idea was first suggested by Dean Kim Clark. See Kim B. Clark, "The Interaction of Design Hierarchies and Market Concepts in Technological Evolution," *Research Policy* 14 (1985): 235–51. For a more recent study adding support to Christensen's thesis, see Richard Foster and Sarah Kaplan, *Creative Destruction: Why Companies That Are Built to Last Underperform the Market—and How to Successfully Transform Them* (New York: Currency/Doubleday, 2001). There is also a link to the work of William Abernathy, who has argued that "as designers worked on the agenda of problems established by the dominant design, the locus of competition between firms would shift from product improvement to cost reduction. A 'productivity dilemma' would then emerge, as the search for lower cost drove out, first, large innovations, and later, all but the most minor innovations." See Baldwin and Clark, 57.

The intuition behind Christensen's work—that an existing firm holds psychological commitments that make it hard for the firm to follow new leads—has support in a wide range of work in innovation economics. See, e.g., Paul Romer, "Thinking and Feeling," *American Economic Review* 90 (2000): 439.

[16] E-mail from David S. Isenberg to Lawrence Lessig, January 29, 2001.

[17] Clayton M. Christensen, *The Innovator's Dilemma: The Revolutionary National Bestseller That Changed the Way We Do Business* (Cambridge, Mass.: Harvard Business School Press, 1997).

[18] Telephone interview with David Reed.

[19] See Jim Carlton, *Apple: The Inside Story of Intrigue, Egomania, and Business Blun-*

ders (New York: Times Books/Random House, 1997), 38–61 (describing Apple's internal licensing debate).

[20] Baldwin and Clark, 11. In Baldwin and Clark's terms, modularity describes an "interdependence within and independence across modules." Carliss Y. Baldwin and Kim B. Clark, *Design Rules*, vol. 1 (Cambridge, Mass.: MIT Press, 2000), 63. Modules are units "whose structural elements are powerfully connected among themselves and relatively weakly connected to elements in other units." They thus depend upon "a framework—and architecture—that allows for both independence of structure and integration of function." Ibid.

"Architecture" is thus fundamental to all modular systems. As Baldwin and Clark describe, "[T]he word is both an evocative term with a rich set of associations, and a technical term, meant to have a precise meaning in a particular context." Ibid., 215. A proper architecture enables parts to be broken into smaller units, with clean and clear interfaces among the smaller modules.

Baldwin and Clark thus advance four "principles of modularity": (1) Create nested, regular, hierarchical structures in a complex system; (2) define independent components within an integrated architecture; (3) establish and maintain rigorous partitions of design information into hidden and visible subsets; (4) invest in clear interfaces and "good" module tests. Ibid., 413. These together "made it possible for human beings of individually limited capacity to design and produce ever more complex machines and programs. [T]he resulting modular designs could change in unpredicted, yet coordinated ways. They could be improved via a decentralized, value-seeking process, which we have called *design evolution*." Ibid.

[21] See Michael Walzer, *Spheres of Justice: A Defense of Pluralism and Equality* (New York: Basic Books, 1984).

[22] See, e.g., Margaret Jane Radin, *Contested Commodities* (Cambridge, Mass.: Harvard University Press, 1996), 132–36.

[23] Letter from Thomas Jefferson to Isaac McPherson (August 13, 1813), in *The Writings of Thomas Jefferson* 6 (H. A. Washington, ed., 1861), 175, 180.

[24] Rose, "The Comedy of the Commons," 742.

[25] Some researchers have suggested that there is a way of organizing access to spectrum that would increase the spectrum as the number of users increases. See Timothy J. Shepard, "A Channel Access Scheme for Large Dense Packet Radio Networks," at http://www.acm.org/pubs/articles/proceedings/comm/248156/p219-shepard/p219-shepard.pdf. See also Rick Boyd-Merritt, "Engineer's Wireless Internet in a Box Draws Interest," EE Times.com, http://www.eetimes.com/story/OEG19981007S0014.

[26] The term is of recent origin. Professor Fisher traces its origins to the late nineteenth century; William W. Fisher III, "The Growth of Intellectual Property: A History of the Ownership of Ideas in the United States" (1999) 2, 8, available at http://cyber.law.harvard.edu/ipcoop/97fish.1.html. The term appears to have been used twice before 1900; *Mitchell* v. *Tilghman*, 86 U.S. 287 (1873) and *Davoll* v. *Brown*, 7 Fed. Cas. 197 (Cir. Ct., D. Mass. 1845). These early usages were essentially translations of European documents, except for *Davoll*, where the court uses the term in exactly its modern sense:

> Only thus can ingenuity and perseverance be encouraged to exert themselves in this way usefully to the community; and only in this way can we protect intellectual property, the labors of the mind, productions and interests as much a man's own, and as much the fruit of his honest industry, as the wheat he cultivates, or the flocks he rears.

Its appearance in federal cases since the turn of the twentieth century has grown dramatically:

Decade	Number of References	Per 100k cases
1900–1919	1	
1920–1929	0	
1930–1939	4	1.163
1940–1949	9	3.399
1950–1959	15	5.038
1960–1969	11	2.827
1970–1979	56	8.213
1980–1989	341	26.42
1990–1999	1721	86.37
2000–2001	466	

I am grateful to Professor Hank Greely for these data.

Of course, in some sense intellectual property is certainly property; see Frank Easterbrook, "Intellectual Property Is Still Property," *Harvard Journal of Law & Public Policy* 13 (1991): 108. But to the untrained, the connotations of the term *property* will not suggest the limited nature this "property" is to have. As Vaidhyanathan argues:

> It is essential to understand that copyright in the American tradition was not meant to be a "property right" as the public generally understands property. It was originally a narrow federal policy that granted a limited trade monopoly in exchange for universal use and access.

Siva Vaidhyanathan, *Copyrights and Copywrongs: The Rise of Intellectual Property and How It Threatens Creativity* (New York: New York University Press, 2001), 21.

27 Jessica Litman, *Digital Copyright* (Amherst, N.Y.: Prometheus Books, 2000), 15.

28 See, e.g., Pamela Samuelson et al., "A Manifesto Concerning the Legal Protection of Computer Programs," *Columbia Law Review* 94 (1994): 2308, 2427; Raymond Shih Ray Ku, "Copyright & Cyberspace: Napster and the New Economics of Digital Technology" (draft on file with author, April 7, 2001), 9 ("[W]hile digital technology facilitates the copyright and distribution of digital information, it also permits greater control over the use and distribution of information.").

CHAPTER 7

1 As Judge Posner writes, distinguishing the rules for land from the rules for copyrighted material:

> One reason [the two are different] is that it is more inefficient to have unowned land lying around (say, as the result of the expiration of a time-limited property right) than to have unowned intellectual property. Ideally, all land should be owned by someone, to prevent the congestion externalities that we discussed in connection with the natural pasture from arising. But . . . there is no parallel problem concerning information and expression. A's use of some piece of information will not make it more costly for B to use the same information.

Richard A. Posner, *Economic Analysis of Law*, 4th ed. (Boston: Little, Brown, 1992), 41.

2 "Works are *not* crafted out of thin air." James Boyle, *Shamans, Software, and Spleens: Law and the Construction of the Information Society* (Cambridge, Mass.: Harvard University Press, 1996), 57.

3 *Feist Publications, Inc. v. Rural Telephone Service Co., Inc.*, 499 U.S. 340, 345–47 (1991).

4 Siva Vaidhyanathan, *Copyrights and Copywrongs: The Rise of Intellectual Property and How It Threatens Creativity* (New York: New York University Press, 2001), 203.

5 The United States finally extended copyright protection to foreign publishers through the International Copyright Act of 1891, ch. 565, §13, 26 Stat. 1110 (1891). Before 1891, "the United States was notorious for its singular and, in many regards, cavalier attitude toward the intellectual property of foreigners." William P. Alford, "Making the World Safe for What? Intellectual Property Rights, Human Rights and Foreign Economic Policy in the Post–European Cold War World," *New York University Journal of International Law & Politics* 29 (1997): 135, 146. See also Jessica Litman, *Digital Copyright* (Amherst, N.Y.: Prometheus Books, 2000), 15.

6 Richard A. Posner, *Law and Literature*, rev. and enlarged ed. (Cambridge, Mass.: Harvard University Press, 1998), 389. The first United States case to decide the question comes in 1853, when a circuit court held that the copyright to *Uncle Tom's Cabin* did not reach a German translation of the same work. Vaidhyanathan, 92–93.

7 John Tebbel, *A History of Book Publishing in the United States: The Creation of an Industry 1630–1865* (New York: R. R. Bowker, 1972), 141.

8 These laws were Pub. L. No. 87-668, 76 Stat. 555 (1962); Pub. L. No. 89-142, 79 Stat. 581 (1965); Pub. L. No. 90-141, 81 Stat. 464 (1967); Pub. L. No. 90-416, 82 Stat. 397 (1968); Pub. L. No. 91-147, 83 Stat. 360 (1969); Pub. L. No. 91-555, 84 Stat. 1441 (1970); Pub. L. No. 92-170, 85 Stat. 490 (1971); Pub. L. No. 92-566, 86 Stat. 1181 (1972); Pub. L. No. 93-573, title I, §104, 88 Stat. 1873 (1974).

9 On books, see Stephen Breyer, "The Uneasy Case for Copyright: A Study of Copyright in Books, Photocopies, and Computer Programs," *Harvard Law Review* 84 (1970): 281 (acknowledging the economic rationale for copyright protection of books and films, but not software). The MPAA estimates that the average cost of a feature film (including studio overhead and capitalized interest) was $51.5 million in 1999. See MPAA, "MPAA Average Negative Costs," slide 14 of 44 (visited June 21, 2001), http://www.mpaa.org/useconomicreview/2000Economic/slide.asp?ref=14.

10 As Yochai Benkler writes, "[M]ainstream economics very clearly negates the superstition that if some property rights in information are good, then more rights in information are even better." Yochai Benkler, "A Political Economy of the Public Domain: Markets in Information Goods Versus the Marketplace of Ideas," in *Expanding the Boundaries of Intellectual Property: Innovation Policy for the Knowledge Society*, Rochelle Cooper Dreyfuss and Diane Leenheer Zimmerman, eds. (Oxford: Oxford University Press, 2001), 267, 271. As Vaidhyanathan argues:

> Through a series of case studies in different media through the 20th Century, it argues for 'thin' copyright protection: just strong enough to encourage and reward aspiring artists, writers, musicians, and entrepreneurs, yet porous enough to allow full and rich democratic speech and the free flow of information.

Vaidhyanathan, 8.

The skepticism among economists about perfect or extremely strong copyright protection is well known. For an expansive economic account, see Richard Watt, *Copyright and Economic Theory: Friends or Foes?* (Cheltenham, England, and Northampton,

Mass.: E. Elgar, 2000). For a rich philosophical survey of justifications for copyright, see Peter Drahos, *A Philosophy of Intellectual Property* (Aldershot, England, and Brookfield, Vt.: Dartmouth Publishing Company, 1996).

11 Posner, *Law and Literature*, 391. A related point is made by Watt, who describes conditions under which piracy of copyrighted work is in fact favorable to the copyright owner. See Richard Watt, *Copyright and Economic Theory: Friends or Foes?* (Cheltenham, England, and Northampton, Mass.: E. Elgar, 2000), 58–67, 201 ("some copyright 'piracy' is highly likely to be socially efficient"). As Watt concludes, economic theory then is guilty of pointing out that there exist cases in which legal copyright protection hampers rather than helps society in general. Perhaps more surprisingly, economists can show that legal copyright protection can also hamper copyright holders and producers of originals themselves. Hence, "economic theory can perhaps best be thought of as throwing out a warning to copyright advocates, that they should take care not to lobby for policy that ends up damaging the interests of copyright holders, or those of the society in general." See ibid., 200.

12 *Twentieth Century Music Corp. et al.* v. *Aiken*, 422 U.S. 151, 154–55 (1975).

13 While Fourneaux is credited with inventing the first player piano, in 1902, Melville Clark was the first to create one with the full eighty-eight-key range of the standard piano. Clark was also one of the first to produce the player and the piano combined in a self-contained unit. See Harvey Roehl, *Player Piano Treasury: The Scrapbook History of the Mechanical Piano in America as Told in Story, Pictures, Trade Journal Articles and Advertising* (Vestal, N.Y.: Vestal Press, 1961); Arthur W. J. G. Ord-Hume, *Pianola: The History of the Self-Playing Piano* (London: George Allen & Unwin, 1984).

14 Edward Samuels, *The Illustrated Story of Copyright* (New York: St. Martin's Press, 2000), 34.

15 *White-Smith Music Publishing Co.* v. *Apollo Co.*, 209 U.S. 1, 21 (1908).

16 Congress's initial statute was Act of March 4, 1909, ch. 320(e), 35 Stat. 1075 (1909), superseded by 17 U.S.C. §115 (1988). See generally Fred H. Cate, "Cable Television and the Compulsory Copyright License," *Federal Communications Law Journal* 42 (1990): 191; C. H. Dobal, "A Proposal to Amend the Cable Compulsory License Provisions of the 1976 Copyright Act," *Southern California Law Review* 61 (1988): 699; Paul Glist, "Cable Copyright: The Role of the Copyright Office," *Emory Law Journal* 35 (1986): 621; Stanley M. Besen, Willard G. Manning Jr., and Bridger M. Mitchell, "Copyright Liability for Cable Television: Compulsory Licensing and the Coase Theorem," *Journal of Law & Economics* 21 (1978): 67.

Robert Merges has argued that compulsory rights do create problems in contexts such as this, and that some property rights will induce the creation of independent institutions that could most cheaply negotiate the rights. See Robert P. Merges, "Contracting into Liability Rules: Intellectual Property Rights and Collective Rights Organizations," *California Law Review* 84 (1996): 1293; Robert P. Merges, "Institutions for Intellectual Property Transactions: The Case of Patent Pools," in *Expanding the Boundaries of Intellectual Property*, Rochelle Cooper Dreyfuss and Diane Leenheer Zimmerman, eds. (Oxford: Oxford University Press, 2001), 131. Ian Ayres and Eric Talley reach a very different conclusion. See Ian Ayres and Eric Talley, "Solomonic Bargaining: Dividing a Legal Entitlement to Facilitate Coasean Trade," *Yale Law Journal* 104 (1995): 1027, 1092–94 (arguing that a liability rule will induce parties to reveal their true valuations and hence is more likely to produce a Coasean trade).

17 See Copyright Act of 1909, ch. 320, §(e), 35 Stat. 1075 (1909), superseded by 17 U.S.C. §115 (1982).

¹⁸ *Fortnightly Corp.* v. *United Artists Television, Inc.*, 392 U.S. 390 (1968), and *Teleprompter Corp.* v. *Columbia Broadcasting System, Inc.*, 415 U.S. 394 (1974).

¹⁹ The compulsory right was incorporated in §111 of the 1976 act. As Paul Goldstein has written, "[M]ore explicitly than any other aspect of the [1976 Act], it commits its operation to assumptions about industry structure and regulation." "Preempted State Doctrines, Involuntary Transfers and Compulsory Licenses: Testing the Limits of Copyright," *U.C.L.A. Law Review* 24 (1977): 1107, 1127–35. See also Melville B. Nimmer and David Nimmer, "Nimmer on Copyright," §8.18[E], 4.

²⁰ See generally Samuels, 181–82. The satellite TV retransmission right was enacted in 1988. See Satellite Home Viewer Act, Act of November 16, 1988, Pub. L. No. 100-667, 102 Stat. 3935, codified at 17 U.S.C. §119 (supp. 1993). Jukeboxes were covered by the 1976 act, 17 U.S.C. §116. That provision was in tension with the Berne Convention, which forbade compulsory licenses for public performances. In 1989, Congress added §116A, which added negotiated agreements between performance rights associations. In 1993, Congress then repealed the original §116 and renamed §116A to §116. See Scott M. Martin, "The Berne Convention and the U.S. Compulsory License for Jukeboxes: Why the Song Could Not Remain the Same," *Journal of the Copyright Society U.S.A.* 37 (1990): 262.

²¹ As Calabresi and Melamed describe, a resource is protected with a liability rule when one using the resources must pay compensation for the use. The resource is protected by a property rule when one using the resource must negotiate for it before it can be taken. Guido Calabresi and Douglas Melamed, "Property Rules, Liability Rules, and Inalienability: One View of the Cathedral," *Harvard Law Review* 85 (1972): 1089, 1092. When a copyright is protected by a liability rule, those wishing to use the resource can take the resource, as long as they pay the liability price. When it is protected by a property rule, taking the resource without paying for it can make one criminally liable. Robert P. Merges, "Institutions for Intellectual Property Transactions: The Case of Patent Pools," in *Expanding the Boundaries of Intellectual Property*, R. Dreyfuss, ed. (Oxford: Oxford University Press, 2001), 131–32.

²² "Chicago school" analysts argued that a monopolist possesses a fixed amount of market power and therefore can extract only a fixed amount of monopoly profit from consumers, whether from one market or several. On this basis, they concluded that leverage of monopoly power from one market into another is impossible. See, e.g., Robert H. Bork, *The Antitrust Paradox: A Policy at War with Itself* (New York: Basic Books, 1978); Richard A. Posner, *Antitrust Law: An Economic Perspective* (Chicago: University of Chicago Press, 1976). More recent economic analyses have demonstrated several mechanisms by which market power in one market can be used to harm competition in another market. As Steven Salop and Craig Romaine put it:

> Post-Chicago economic analysis has suggested that there are a number of limiting assumptions required for this single monopoly profit theory to apply. When these assumptions are relaxed, the theory's strong result and the public policy implications no longer hold. There are a number of common market situations in which integration into a second market may raise anticompetitive concerns. These include markets in which the first monopoly is regulated, markets that are characterized by economies of scale and scope and in which the inputs are not used in fixed proportions, and markets with multiple types of buyers. In such markets, it is possible for a monopolist to profitably extend its power into a second market and harm consumers. (footnote omitted)

Steven C. Salop and R. Craig Romaine, "Preserving Monopoly: Economic Analysis, Legal Standards, and Microsoft," *George Mason Law Review* 7 (1999): 617, 625. See also Michael D. Whinston, "Tying, Foreclosure, and Exclusion," *American Economic Review* 80 (1990): 837 (demonstrating multiple situations in which foreclosure of the tied market can occur, including a case where the monopolist can precommit to the tie through product design or production processes); Janusz A. Ordover, Garth Saloner, and Steven C. Salop, "Equilibrium Vertical Foreclosure," *American Economic Review* 80 (1990): 127 (integration across multiple products permits competitor to exclude unintegrated rival). See also Louis Kaplow, "Extension of Monopoly Power Through Leverage," *Columbia Law Review* 85 (1985): 515 (expressing early skepticism about the Chicago school analysis). See also Dennis W. Carlton and Michael Waldman, "The Strategic Use of Tying to Preserve and Create Market Power in Evolving Industries" (September 1998 working paper) (arguing that tying deters entry in primary tying markets in addition to providing leverage into tied markets).

[23] See Douglas Abell, "Pay-for-Play," *Vanderbilt Journal of Entertainment Law & Practice* 2 (2000): 52.

[24] See 17 U.S.C. §111 (2000). The statute initially set up a Copyright Royalty Tribunal, but that was abolished in favor of private negotiation in 1993. See Robert P. Merges, Peter S. Menell, and Mark A. Lemley, *Intellectual Property in the New Technological Age*, 2nd ed. (Gaithersburg: Aspen Law & Business, 2000), 481.

Congress initially tried to balance this effective control by establishing rules of access such as the "Fairness Doctrine." See Jerry Kang, *Communications Law and Policy: Cases and Materials* (Gaithersburg, Md.: Aspen Law & Business, 2001), 85–86. These rules have been drawn into constitutional doubt—see, for example, *Miami Herald Publishing Co. v. Tornillo*, 418 U.S. 241 (1974), *Huddy v. FCC*, 236 F.3d 720, 723 (D.C. Cir. 2001)—and are generally viewed as a failure. See L. A. Scot Powe, *American Broadcasting and the First Amendment* (Berkeley: University of California Press, 1987), 197–209.

[25] As FCC chairman Powell has described it:

> In 1969, broadcasting consisted of a handful of radio stations in any given market plus two or three television stations affiliated with one of the three major networks. Occasionally, larger markets had an independent station too. Three major networks held more than 90% of the market for video programming. Not so anymore. Not only has the market share of the three largest networks been eroded by cable programming, the last time I looked there were about seven "declared" national television networks. . . . Obviously, things have changed a lot. . . . In our current technological environment, it can reasonably be argued that there is a bounty, not a scarcity of outlets for expressing one's viewpoint. In the traditional broadcasting arena, the numbers are impressive: There are 1,207 commercial TV stations and 367 noncommercial stations. There are also some 5,000 TV translators and 2,000 low-power TV stations. In addition, there are almost 12,500 radio stations.

Michael K. Powell, "Willful Denial and First Amendment Jurisprudence, Remarks Before the Media Institute," April 22, 1998 (transcript available at http://www.fcc.gov/Speeches/Powell/spmkp808.html).

[26] See Robert M. Fano, "On the Social Role of Computer Communications," *Proceedings of the IEEE* 60 (September 1972): 1249.

[27] Simson L. Garfinkel, *Architects of the Information Society: Thirty-Five Years of the Laboratory for Computer Science at MIT* (Cambridge, Mass.: MIT Press, 1999), 8–9.

[28] Ronald Coase, "Looking for Results," interviewed by Thomas W. Hazlett, *Reason* (January 1997).

[29] See Linda Shrieves, "When It's Your Turn, Here's Why You're Served a Chorus of . . . ; The Birthday Song Is Still Copyrighted and Nets Nearly $1 Million a Year in Royalties," *Orlando Sentinel*, February 27, 2001, E1.

[30] Or at least not yet. George Gilder has repeatedly argued that a future infrastructure based on fiber optics would provide "infinite bandwidth." See George Gilder, *Telecosm: How Infinite Bandwidth Will Revolutionize Our World* (New York: Free Press, 2000); George Gilder, "Rulers of the Rainbow: The New Emperors of the Telecosm Will Use the Infinite Spectrum of Light—Visible and Invisible—to Beef up Bandwidth," *Forbes ASAP* (October 1998): 104; and George Gilder, "Into the Fibersphere (Fiber Optics)," *Forbes* (December 1992): 111.

[31] Ben H. Bagdikian, *The Media Monopoly*, 6th ed. (Boston: Beacon Press, 2000), 4.

[32] Robert W. McChesney, *Rich Media, Poor Democracy: Communication Politics in Dubious Times* (Urbana: University of Illinois Press, 1999), 18.

[33] The reasons for this increased concentration are hard to track precisely. There are a number of changes that have certainly occurred. The relaxation of rules on ownership of radio stations, for example, has exploded concentration in radio station ownership. This, in turn, has led to an increase in the modern equivalent of "payola." See Douglas Abell, "Pay-for-Play," *Vanderbilt Journal of Entertainment Law & Practice* 2 (2000): 52. As Boehlert describes it:

> There are 10,000 commercial radio stations in the United States; record companies rely on approximately 1,000 of the largest to create hits and sell records. Each of those 1,000 stations adds roughly three new songs to its playlist each week. The [independents] get paid for every one; $1,000 on average for an "add" at a Top 40 or rock station, but as high as $6,000 or $8,000 under certain circumstances.

Eric Boehlert, "Pay for Play," *Salon*, March 14, 2001, http://www.salon.com/ent/feature/2001/03/14/payola/print.html, 2.

[34] Allyson Lieberman, "Sagging Warner Music out of Tune with AOL TW," *New York Post*, April 19, 2001, 34. See also Charles Mann, "The Heavenly Jukebox," *Atlantic Monthly* (September 2000), 39, 53.

[35] Boehlert, 2.

[36] McChesney, 18.

[37] Ibid., 17.

[38] Ibid., 33.

[39] Ibid., 18.

[40] According to the National Cable Television Association's figures, the top seven "multiple system operators," or MSOs, controlled 90 percent of the national cable television market at the end of 2000. http://www.ncta.com/industry_overview/top50mso.cfm. See also Richard Waters, "Appeals Court Overrules Curbs on Cable TV Ownership in U.S. Federal Rules," *Financial Times*, March 3, 2001, 7. As of March 2001, AOL–Time Warner's cable market share was about 20 percent, while AT&T's share stood at 42 percent (including AT&T's purchase of MediaOne Group and its 25.5 percent stake in Time Warner Entertainment). AT&T's 42 percent market share well exceeds the FCC's cap of 30 percent, leading AT&T to challenge the cap in court as being "arbitrary." See Edmund Sanders and Sallie Hofmeister, "Court Rejects Limits on Cable Ownership; Television: Controversial 30% Cap Is Deemed Unconstitutional, but Consumer Groups Call the Decision 'Devastating,' " *Los Angeles Times*, March 3, 2001, C1.

[41] Bagdikian, 4.

[42] Ibid., x.

[43] See Mike Hoyt, "With 'Strategic Alliances,' the Map Gets Messy," *Columbia Journalism Review* (January–February 2000), at http://www.cjr.org/year/00/1/hoyt.asp; *Global Media Economics: Commercialization, Concentration and Integration of World Media Markets*, Allan B. Albarran and Sylvia M. Chan-Olmsted, eds. (Ames: Iowa State University Press, 1998), 19–31; Dennis W. Mazzocco, *Networks of Power: Corporate T.V.'s Threat to Democracy* (Boston, Mass.: South End Press, 1994), 1–8. Cf. Benjamin M. Compaine, "Distinguishing Between Concentration and Competition," in *Who Owns the Media*, 3rd ed., Benjamin M. Compaine and Douglas Gomery, eds. (Mahwah, N.J.: L. Erlbaum Associates, 2000), 537; Douglas Gomery, "Interpreting Media Ownership," in *Who Owns the Media?*, 3rd ed., Benjamin M. Compaine and Douglas Gomery, eds. (Mahwah, N.J.: L. Erlbaum Associates, 2000), 507.

[44] Bagdikian, 7. There are, of course, many who believe there is no necessary link between the mergers and these features of modern media. See, e.g., Steven Rattner, "A Golden Age of Competition," in *Media Mergers*, Nancy J. Woodhull and Robert W. Snyder, eds. (New Brunswick, N.J.: Transaction Publishers, 1998), 9. See also Bruce M. Owen, *Economics and Freedom of Expression: Media Structure and the First Amendment* (Cambridge, Mass.: Ballinger Publishing Company, 1975).

[45] Andrew Kreig, *Spiked: How Chain Management Corrupted America's Oldest Newspaper* (Old Saybrook, Conn.: Peregrine Press, 1987).

[46] Bagdikian, 30.

[47] McChesney, 245.

[48] Compare Judge Posner's comment: "[T]he management of a large publicly held corporation will have difficulty finding issues on which a partisan stand would not alienate large numbers of shareholders." Posner, *Economic Analysis of Law*, 674.

[49] Bagdikian, 129.

[50] Ibid., 35.

[51] McChesney, 80, 179.

[52] Ibid., 250.

[53] Ibid., 148.

[54] Ibid., 168.

CHAPTER 8

[1] See Lawrence Lessig, *Code and Other Laws of Cyberspace* (New York: Basic Books, 1999).

[2] For examples of on-line mapping services, see MapQuest.com at http://www.mapquest.com; Maps On Us at http://www.mapsonus.com; and MapBlast! at http://www.mapblast.com.

[3] For examples of on-line translation Web sites, see AltaVista World/Translate at http://world.altavista.com; FreeTranslation.com at http://www.freetranslation.com; and From Language to Language at http://www.langtolang.com.

[4] A short list of many examples of on-line dictionaries includes Merriam-Webster OnLine at http://www.m-w.com; Cambridge Dictionaries Online at http://dictionary.cambridge.org; and AllWords.com at http://www.allwords.com. There are also sites that perform aggregate searches through multiple multilingual dictionaries, such as yourDictionary.com at http://www.yourdictionary.com.

[5] As we'll see in chapter 11, this is not a slight constraint. Because his site was noncommercial, Eldred could include only work that had fallen into the public domain.

When Eldred began, the content constraint meant that works published before 1923 were free, works published after 1923 were only possibly free. But in 1998, Congress changed that by passing the Sonny Bono Copyright Term Extension Act. The Bono Act extended the term of existing copyrights by twenty years, meaning work that was to fall into the public domain in 1999 would now not fall into the public domain until 2019. As we'll see, this turned Eldred into an activist.

6 See http://www.apple.com/hotnews/articles/2001/03/imacdirector/.

7 There are skeptics, however, about whether diversity will increase. Le Duc, for example, argues that the real constraint on diversity in films is not the channels of distribution, but rather the limited attention viewers have for stars. There are only so many stars we can like; they are the true constraint on this mode of production; and as long as that limit remains, the range of film will be restricted as well. Don R. Le Duc, *Beyond Broadcasting: Patterns in Policy and Law* (New York: Longman, 1987), 128.

8 On the risk of liability, see JaNet Kornblum, "Lyrics Site Takes Steps to Avoid Napster Woes," *USA Today*, December 12, 2000, available at http://www.usatoday.com/life/cyber/tech/jk121200.htm.

9 Tom Parsons, "World Wide Web Gives Poets, Poetry Room to Grow," *Dallas Morning News*, July 30, 2000, 8J.

10 For example, a Web site devoted to Chaucer uses multiple frames to navigate quickly through *The Canterbury Tales* and define the medieval English terms. See Librarius at http://www.librarius.com/cantales.htm. Another site provides a high-tech multimedia companion to the printed *Anthology of Modern American Poetry*. See Modern American Poetry at http://www.english.uiuc.edu/maps.

11 See Favorite Poem Project at http://www.favoritepoem.org (featuring readings of famous poems read by individual Americans); Internet Poetry Archive at http://www.ibiblio.org/ipa (offering modern poetry readings by the poets); and e-poets.net at http://www.e-poets.net (featuring contemporary audio poetry).

12 Free in the sense that I have defined the term. The technology is offered under a nondiscriminatory license. The underlying technology is patented. See Brad King, "MP3.com Open to Friends," *Wired News*, January 19, 2001, at http://www.wired.com/news/mp3/0,1285,41195,00.html. "Vorbis" is an alternative to MP3 that is royalty free and compresses more than the MP3 format does. Vito Pilieci, "MP3 May Go Way of Eight-Track: Vorbis Audio File Players Would Be Free of Royalty, Patent Fees," *National Post*, June 29, 2000, C8. The licensing does, however, create problems for open code developers. See Wendy C. Freedman, "Open Source Movement Vies with Classic IP Model, Free Software Is Bound to Have a Significant Effect on Patent, Copyright, Trade Secret Suits," *National Law Journal* 22 (March 13, 2000): B14.

13 Telephone interview with Michael Robertson, November 16, 2000.

14 Courtney Love, "Courtney Love Does the Math," *Salon* (June 12, 2000): 5. Love has offered a slightly exaggerated but illustrative description of how the market for music now works:

This story is about a bidding-war band that gets a huge deal with a 20 percent royalty rate and a million-dollar advance. (No bidding-war band ever got a 20 percent royalty, but whatever.) This is my "funny" math based on some reality and I just want to qualify it by saying I'm positive it's better math than what Edgar Bronfman Jr. [the president and CEO of Seagram, which owns Polygram] would provide. What happens to that million dollars? They spend half a million to record their album. That leaves the band with $500,000. They pay $100,000 to their manager for 20 percent commission. They pay

$25,000 each to their lawyer and business manager. That leaves $350,000 for the four band members to split. After $170,000 in taxes, there's $180,000 left. That comes out to $45,000 per person. That's $45,000 to live on for a year until the record gets released. The record is a big hit and sells a million copies. (How a bidding-war band sells a million copies of its debut record is another rant entirely, but it's based on any basic civics-class knowledge that any of us have about cartels. Put simply, the antitrust laws in this country are basically a joke, protecting us just enough to not have to rename our park service the Phillip Morris National Park Service.) So, this band releases two singles and makes two videos. The two videos cost a million dollars to make and 50 percent of the video production costs are recouped out of the band's royalties. The band gets $200,000 in tour support, which is 100 percent recoupable. The record company spends $300,000 on independent radio promotion. You have to pay independent promotion to get your song on the radio; independent promotion is a system where the record companies use middlemen so they can pretend not to know that radio stations — the unified broadcast system — are getting paid to play their records. All of those independent promotion costs are charged to the band. Since the original million-dollar advance is also recoupable, the band owes $2 million to the record company. If all of the million records are sold at full price with no discounts or record clubs, the band earns $2 million in royalties, since their 20 percent royalty works out to $2 a record. Two million dollars in royalties minus $2 million in recoupable expenses equals . . . zero! How much does the record company make? They grossed $11 million. It costs $500,000 to manufacture the CDs and they advanced the band $1 million. Plus there were $1 million in video costs, $300,000 in radio promotion and $200,000 in tour support. The company also paid $750,000 in music publishing royalties. They spent $2.2 million on marketing. That's mostly retail advertising, but marketing also pays for those huge posters of Marilyn Manson in Times Square and the street scouts who drive around in vans handing out black Korn T-shirts and backwards baseball caps. Not to mention trips to Scores and cash for tips for all and sundry. Add it up and the record company has spent about $4.4 million. So their profit is $6.6 million; the band may as well be working at a 7-Eleven.

Ibid. Compare Senator Hatch's very different account of music production outside the control of the labels:

> I will quote him at length, because his experience is instructive. He said: "As a result of doing it on my own, I get about $7 for every CD that sells in a store. And about $10 per CD sold at concerts. In contrast, I've got a friend who is also a performer/songwriter who opted to sign with a . . . label. He recorded a CD that cost about $18,000 to make, which the label paid for. Now, when one of his CDs sells at a store or at a concert, he makes about $1. The rest of the $7–$10 which I make on my CD sales goes to his label. On top of that, he has to pay back the $18,000 it cost to make the CD out of his $1-per-CD cut. In other words, he won't make a dime until he has sold 18,000 CDs. And then, he still won't own the CD, the label will. They maintain the copyright. It's kind of like paying off your mortgage and then having the bank still own your house.

Orrin G. Hatch, "Address of Senator Orrin G. Hatch Before the Future of Music Coalition," Future of Music Coalition, January 10, 2001, 2. Currently, the average album release is under twenty-five thousand per CD. Jon Healey, "Industry Seeks to Justify Huge Overhead on the Price of Compact Disks," *Knight Ridder Tribune Business News*, September 3, 2000.

[15] Telephone interview with Michael Robertson.

[16] Ibid.

[17] Ibid.

[18] See Testimony of the Future of Music Coalition on "Online Music and Copyright Law," submitted to Senate Judiciary Committee, April 3, 2001, 13 ("The fastest-growing demographic segment using Napster are adults over the age of 24. Research reports have confirmed that one of the major reasons that they are doing so is to access commercial recordings that are no longer commercially available.").

[19] See Paul Goldstein, *Copyright's Highway: From Gutenberg to the Celestial Jukebox* (New York: Hill and Wang, 1994). There are two parts to this conception, of course. One is the "celestial" part—emphasizing universal access. The other is the "jukebox" part—emphasizing payment. Napster emphasized the first.

[20] See Scott Kirsner, "Firefly: From the Media Lab to Microsoft," *Wired News*, April 9, 1998, at http://www.wired.com/news/business/0,1367,11585,00.html; Daniel Lyons, "The Buzz About Firefly," *New York Times*, June 29, 1997, section 6, 37. See also Andrew L. Shapiro, *The Control Revolution: How the Internet Is Putting Individuals in Charge and Changing the World We Know* (New York: PublicAffairs, 1999), 84–101.

[21] See Laura J. Gurak, *Persuasion and Privacy in Cyberspace: The Online Protests Over Lotus MarketPlace and the Clipper Chip* (New Haven, Conn., and London: Yale University Press, 1997); Seth Safier, "Between Big Brother and the Bottom Line: Privacy in Cyberspace," *Virginia Journal of Law & Technology* 5 (2000): 6; Andrew Shapiro, "Privacy for Sale: Peddling Data on the Internet," *Nation* (June 23, 1997). The FTC has taken an active role in monitoring the monitors. See "United States Federal Trade Commission, Privacy Online: Fair Information Practices in the Electronic Marketplace: A Federal Trade Commission Report to Congress" (Washington, D.C.: Federal Trade Commission, May 2000), available at http://www.ftc.gov/reports/privacy2000/privacy2000.pdf. For a list of current legislation proposed, see current information on the status of pending privacy bills, available at http://www.epic.org/privacy/bill_track.html.

[22] This is the argument made by Cass Sunstein, in *Republic.com* (Princeton, N.J.: Princeton University Press, 2001). As Sunstein argues, how groups are structured—what their composition is, how they deliberate—affects the results that deliberation produces. Cass Sunstein, *Republic.com*, 65–71.

[23] The success rate of advertising is highly controversial. The general consensus is that direct snail mail advertising response rates are generally in the 1–3 percent range. Directed e-mail advertising campaigns may have response rates in the 10–15 percent range, though some estimates run as high as 25 percent. The click-through rate for banner ads on the Web is much lower, estimated at 0.5 percent. Mark Brownlow for Internet Business Forum, available at www.ibizbasics.com/online040301.htm.

[24] A "lower cost," of course, does not mean no cost. There is still the cost of publishing a book and at least some cost in an initial promotion.

[25] For a summary of peer-to-peer standards in progress, see http://peer-to-peerwg.org. See also http://p2ptracker.com (summarizing current technology); "Business, Bandwidth May Dash Hopes of a Peer-to-Peer Utopia," http://news.cnet.com/news/0-1005-201-3248711-0.html.

[26] Clay Shirky, "Clay Shirky's Writings About the Internet: Economics and Culture, Media and Community, Open Source," November 16, 2000, www.openp2p.com/pub/a/p2p/2000/11/24/shirky1-whatisp2p.html.

[27] See, e.g., Nelson Minar and Marc Hedlund, "A Network of Peers: Peer-to-Peer

Models Throughout the History of the Internet," in *Peer-to-Peer: Harnessing the Benefits of a Disruptive Technology*, Andy Oram, ed. (Beijing and Cambridge, Mass: O'Reilly, 2001), 3–15 (describing how the original Internet was "fundamentally designed as a peer-to-peer system" but became increasingly client/server oriented over time owing to Web browser applications, firewalls, and other factors).

[28] For background on SETI, see "History of SETI," at http://www.seti-inst.edu/general/history.html; Eric Korpela et al., "SETI@home: Massively Distributed Computing for SETI," at http://www.computer.org/cise/articles/seti.htm.

[29] Howard Rheingold, "You Got the Power," *Wired* (August 2001), at http://www.wired.com/wired/archive/8.08/comcomp.html?pg=1&topic=&topic_set=.

[30] For a useful survey of issues related to P2P, see *Peer-to-Peer: Harnessing the Benefits of a Disruptive Technology*, Andrew Oram, ed. (Beijing and Cambridge, Mass.: O'Reilly, 2001). See also http://www.oreillynet.com/p2p/ (collecting articles). Xerox PARC has conducted an interesting study of the free-riding problem with p2p technologies. See Eytan Adar and Bernardo A. Huberman, "Free Riding on Gnutella," *First Monday*, October 2000, 5 at http://www.firstmonday.dk/issues/issue5_10/adar/index.html. For a pessimistic view of the potential for P2P, see Lee Gomes, "P-to-P, B-to-B, RIP?," *Wall Street Journal*, April 4, 2001, B1.

[31] Rheingold, *You Got the Power*.

[32] Andy Oram, "The Value of Gnutella and Freenet," *Webreview* (May 2000), at http://www.webreview.com/pi/2000/05_12_00.shtml.

[33] Again, this is just relative. The claim is not that there is equal access to equally valuable data. Amazon.com is in a better position to market than tinybookseller.com. Likewise, it may well be that scale here makes all the difference. There have been suggestions that these architectures may reduce competition. See Yannis Bakos and Erik Brynjolfsson, "Bundling and Competition on the Internet," *Marketing Science*, January 2000, available at http://ecommerce.mit.edu/erik/bci-final.pdf (finding that "economies of aggregation" for information goods could adversely affect competition). At this stage, however, I don't think we know enough to say.

For a careful analysis mapping the path to concentration in distribution from the nature of IP rights, see Martin Kretschmer, George Michael Klimis, and Roger Wallis, "The Changing Location of Intellectual Property Rights in Music: A Study of Music Publishers, Collecting Societies and Media Conglomerates," *Prometheus* 17 (1999): 163.

[34] James Boyle, "A Politics of Intellectual Property: Environmentalism for the Net?," *Duke Law Journal* 47 (1997): 87. See also Carol Rose, "The Several Futures of Property: Of Cyberspace and Folk Tales, Emission Trades and Ecosystems," *Minnesota Law Review* 83 (1998): 129.

[35] See Carl Shapiro, "Will E-Commerce Erode Liberty?," *Harvard Business Review* (May–June 2000): 189 (book review of Lessig, *Code and Other Laws of Cyberspace* [New York: Basic Books, 1999]).

CHAPTER 10

[1] Peter W. Huber, Michael K. Kellogg, and John Thorne, *Federal Telecommunications Law*, 2nd ed. (Gaithersburg, Md.: Aspen Law & Business, 1999), 164–65.

[2] The regulations that effected this neutrality were many and are described comprehensively in Huber, Kellogg, and Thorne.

[3] In *Carterfone*, the FCC required the Bell system to allow the connection of

customer-provided equipment as long as it did not harm the network. The device at issue in the decision permitted communication between a mobile radio and the landline network. The Bell system declined to permit the connection but could not demonstrate the harm interconnection would create. The FCC ordered the carrier to permit the interconnection, and this requirement, in turn, spurred a great deal of innovation for the telephone network. Ibid., 409.

[4] My emphasis on neutrality does not deny the effect of other regulatory measures. For example, the fact that ISPs enjoyed business rates for their usage—flat rate pricing, rather than metered pricing—effected an important subsidy for Internet service. See Peter W. Huber et al., *Federal Telecommunication Law* (Gaithersburg, Md: Aspen Business & Law, 1999), §11.5, 1030.

[5] On ATM circuits, see Douglas E. Comer, *Computer Networks and Internets*, 2nd ed. (Upper Saddle River, N.J.: Prentice-Hall, 1999), 88, 184. On the link to quality of service, see Paul A. David and Raymond Werle, *The Evolution of Global Networks: Technical, Organizational and Cultural Dimensions* (May 2000), 10.

[6] Likewise, if there are vices in networks that are technically not end-to-end compliant, then we might imagine rules that would balance those vices to better achieve the value of end-to-end. For example, other networks that are not end-to-end compliant—such as ATM networks or multiprotocol label switching (MPLS) networks—may have an aim that respects the values that end-to-end promotes. The TCP/IP network, while not "optimized" for any particular use, in effect is optimized for some uses rather than others. It does well, for example, with applications that do not suffer from network latency (e-mail), but not with applications that do suffer from network latency (voice-over IP). These other networks would better enable these other applications, thus rendering the network as a whole more neutral among applications. If the value of end-to-end inheres in the consequences of this neutrality, then a properly implemented mix might achieve end-to-end values without every part of the network being end-to-end. I am grateful to Tim Wu for making this point to me.

[7] The Telecommunications Act of 1996 does not define broadband. It refers to broadband as a characteristic of "advanced telecommunications capability," which is defined as "high-speed, switched, *broadband* telecommunications capability that enables users to originate and receive high-quality voice, data, graphics, and video telecommunications using any technology." Telecommunications Act of 1996, Pub. L. No. 104–104, §706 (c)(1), 110 Stat. 56 (1996). See also 47 U.S.C. §157 note (2001). The FCC filed its *Section 706 Report to Congress* in 1999 and defined broadband as "the capability of supporting, in both the provider-to-consumer (downstream) and the consumer-to-provider (upstream) directions, a speed (in technical terms, "bandwidth") in excess of 200 kilobits per second (kbps) in the last mile." 14 FCC Rcd. 2398 at 2406 ¶20 (1999). See also http://www.fcc.gov/Bureaus/Cable/Reports/broadbandtoday.pdf.

[8] For an excellent and comprehensive history of and background on broadband issues related to cable, see Kim Maxwell, *Residential Broadband: An Insider's Guide to the Battle for the Last Mile* (New York: John Wiley & Sons, 1999). See also Patrick R. Parsons and Robert M. Frieden, *The Cable and Satellite Television Industries* (Boston: Allyn and Bacon, 1998).

[9] See Mark S. Nadel, "Cablespeech for Whom?," *Cardozo Arts & Entertainment Law Journal* 4 (1985): 51, 70 and n. 104.

[10] See Patrick R. Parsons and Robert M. Frieden, *The Cable and Satellite Television Industries* (Boston: Allyn and Bacon, 1998), chs. 2, 5; Robert W. Crandall and Harold

Furchtgott-Roth, *Cable TV: Regulation or Competition?* (Washington, D.C.: Brookings Institution, 1996), 1–23; Porter Bibb, *It Ain't as Easy as It Looks: Ted Turner's Amazing Story* (New York: Crown Publishers, 1993) (Ted Turner biography).

[11] By 1987, of the 87.5 million homes with TVs, 44.1 million (50.4 percent) were cable subscribers. Currently about 66 percent of TV households in the country use cable. Parsons and Frieden, 3, 121–22.

[12] For a summary, see Jerry Kang, *Communications Law and Policy: Cases and Materials* (Gaithersburg, Md.: Aspen Law & Business, 2001), 154–61.

[13] Mark E. Laubach, David J. Farber, and Stephen D. Dukes, *Delivering Internet Connections over Cable: Breaking the Access Barrier* (New York: John Wiley, 2001), 11–12. For a primer on DOCSIS and its history, see http://www.cablemodem.com/DOCSIS.pdf.

[14] See, e.g., Federal Communications Commission, "In the Matter of Applications for Consent to the Transfer of Control of Licenses and Section 214 Authorizations from Tele-Communications, Inc., Transferor to AT&T Corp., Transferee, CS Docket No. 98–178," February 18, 1999, ¶89, available at http://www.fcc.gov/Bureaus/Cable/Orders/1999/fcc99024.txt ("According to AT&T-TCI, any equal access conditions such as those advocated by opponents to the requested transfers will impose substantial investment costs and expenses on @Home, which will only delay and diminish its deployment of broadband services to residential customers.").

[15] See Thomas Starr, John M. Cioffi, and Peter Silverman, *Understanding Digital Subscriber Line Technology* (Upper Saddle River, N.J.: Prentice-Hall, 1999) (citing 1976).

[16] Comer, *Computer Networks and Internets*, 159.

[17] Throughout this section, by "telephone companies" I am referring to the regional Bell operating companies (the RBOCs). Non-RBOCs are not subject to the same obligations of open access under the statute. See *AT&T Corp.* v. *City of Portland*, 216 F.3d 871, 879 (9th Cir., 2000).

[18] There are more traditional concerns as well. "Over the long term, the cable providers' tying strategy will thus undermine competitive investment in both the broadband transport and portal markets, insulating cable providers from conduit and content competition, and ensuring that the delivery of Internet-based video by competing conduits does not erode cable providers' monopoly power in the market for traditional video programming." Daniel L. Rubinfeld and Hal J. Singer, "Vertical Foreclosure in High Technology Industries: A Case Study of the AOL Time Warner Merger" (Rubinfeld-Singer White Paper), 10. Rubinfeld believes the vertical integration of cable will create an incentive to pursue two foreclosure strategies: (1) conduit discrimination; and (2) content discrimination. Ibid., 29–30.

[19] See, for example, Cisco White Paper, "Controlling Your Network—A Must for Cable Operators" (1999), 5, available at http://www.cptech.org/ecom/openaccess/cisco1.html, describing tools to effect discrimination. As one research report summarizes the problem:

> The situation is analogous to a customer trying to drive to the bookstore of their choice only to find that roadblocks have been established to channel customers to another bookseller, to the exclusion of all other booksellers. Unlike the roadway analogy, in the online world the end user may not be aware that the roadblocks have been placed and may have their behavior influenced without even knowing that the ISP has limited their ability to choose.

AARP, "Tangled Web: The Internet and Broadband Open Access Policy," January 2001, research.aarp.org, 13.

[20] See, e.g., http://web.mit.edu/Saltzer/www/publications/openaccess.html. For Saltzer's model licenses for cable access, see http://web.mit.edu/Saltzer/www/publications/clauses2.html.

[21] See Brock Meeks, "Excite@Home Keeps a Video Collar," *ZDNet News*, November 1, 1999, at http://www.zdnet.com/zdnn/stories/news/0,4586,2385059,00.html. See also Harold Feld, "Whose Line Is It Anyway?: The First Amendment and Cable Open Access," *CommLaw Conspectus* 8 (2000): 23, 34; Mark Cooper, "Transforming the Information Superhighway into a Private Toll Road," *Colorado Law Review* 71 (2000): 1011, 1055. An industry trade journal notes that both Excite@Home and Road Runner limit consumers to ten-minute streaming segments. "PC-TV Convergence Driving Streaming Industry Growth," *Warren's Cable Reg. Monitor*, March 1, 1999, 1999 WL 6825624.

[22] David Lieberman, "Media Giants' Net Change: Major Companies Establish Strong Foothold Online," *USA Today*, December 14, 1999, B2. See also telephone interview with David Isenberg, February 14, 2001 ("They couldn't possibly open up their system so that it would have the capability to do TV over IP. That would be killing themselves.").

[23] Bar et al., 32.

[24] Ibid., 34.

[25] Ibid., 35.

[26] Ibid., 29.

[27] François Bar has a similar assessment. See François Bar, "The Construction of Marketplace Architecture," *Brookings & Internet Policy Institute* 15 (forthcoming 2001), (describing the decline of end-to-end).

[28] This, of course, is assured only if there is no actual or effective tying between cable products and other services that might effectively protect cable from meaningful competition with DSL.

[29] See Joanna Glasner, "DSL Rhymes with Hell," *Wired News*, January 2001, available at http://www.wired.com/news/business/0,1367,41433,00.html (DSL numbers); Roy Mark, "U.S. Scores First Decline in Internet Subscribers," dc.internet.com, May 2, 2001, available at: http://dc.internet.com/news/article/0,1934,2101_756771,00.html (cable numbers).

[30] See Morgan Stanley Dean Witter, *The Broadband Report* (May 2000). See also David Lake, "Strike Up the Broadband," *Industry Standard*, February 2, 2001, at http://www.thestandard.com/article/0,1902,21892,00.html. ("In the fourth quarter of 2000, cable-modem providers watched their subscriber base increase 19 percent to 4.2 million users. Still, the adoption of DSL is happening at a faster pace. At the beginning of last year, the number of cable-modem subscribers outnumbered DSL subscribers 5 to 1. Now that ratio hovers at almost 2 to 1, in favor of cable-modem access. Nevertheless, cable modems are expected to retain an edge. In 2003, 51 percent of broadband subscribers will use cable modems, while DSL is expected to account for only 37 percent of the high-speed market, according to Jupiter Research.")

[31] Laubach, Farber, and Dukes, 238.

[32] The campaign was conceived of by Jan Brandt. "Since Brandt's arrival at AOL in 1993, membership has grown from 250,000 to 8 million [in 1997]." *Upside* magazine said that "Brandt's carpet-bombing techniques have redefined the use of direct mail in the high-tech industry and pioneered the get-something-for-nothing marketing coups copied by Netscape and other Internet underdogs to achieve brand-name recog-

nition in no time flat." http://media.aoltimewarner.com/media/cb_press_view.cfm?
release_num=147.

[33] On the character of these virtual worlds, see Julian Dibbell, *My Tiny Life: Crime and Passion in a Virtual World* (London: Fourth Estate, 1998). See also Lynn Cherny, *Conversation and Community: Chat in a Virtual World* (Stanford, Calif.: CSLI Publications, 1999).

[34] America Online Inc., "Open Access Comments of America Online, Inc." before the Department of Telecommunications and Information Services, San Francisco, October 27, 1999.

[35] Comments of America Online, Inc., "In the Matter of Transfer of Control of FCC Licenses of MediaOne Group, Inc. to AT&T Corporation," Federal Communications Commission, CS Docket No. 99–251, August 23, 1999. As it argued:

> What this merger does offer, however, is the means for a newly "RBOC-icized" cable industry reinforced by interlocking ownership relationships to (1) prevent Internet-based challenge to cable's core video offerings; (2) leverage its control over essential video facilities into broadband Internet access services; (3) extend its control over cable Internet access services into broadband cable Internet content; (4) seek to establish itself as the "electronic national gateway" for the full and growing range of cable communications services.

> To avoid such detrimental results for consumers, the Commission can act to ensure that broadband develops into a communications path that is as accessible and diverse as narrowband. Just as the Commission has often acted to maintain the openness of other last-mile infrastructure, here too it should adopt open cable Internet access as a competitive safeguard—a check against cable's extension of market power over facilities that were first secured through government protection and now, in their broadband form, are being leveraged into cable Internet markets. Affording high-speed Internet subscribers with an effective means to obtain the full range of data, voice and video services available in the marketplace, regardless of the transmission facility used, is a sound and vital policy—both because of the immediate benefit for consumers and because of its longer-range spur to broadband investment and deployment. Here, the Commission need do no more than establish an obligation on the merged entity to provide non-affiliated ISPs connectivity to the cable platform on rates, terms and conditions equal to those accorded to affiliated service providers. (AOL, FCC, 4)

[36] Comments of AT&T Wireless Services, Inc., "In the Matter of Inquiry Regarding Software Defined Radios," Federal Communications Commission, ET Docket No. 00–47, July 14, 2000, 15.

[37] AT&T Canada Long Distance Services, "Comments of AT&T Canada Long Distance Services Company," before the Canadian Radio-television and Telecommunications Commission, Telecom Public Notice CRTC 96–36: "Regulation of Certain Telecommunications Service Offered by Broadcast Carriers," February 4, 1997. For the best analysis of this change in position, see the submission by Mark Cooper of the Consumer Federation of America, Petition to Deny, in re "Application of America Online and Time Warner for Transfers of Control," before the FCC, CS 00–30 (April 26, 2000):

> The dominant and vertically integrated position of cable broadcast carriers requires a number of safeguards to protect against anti-competitive behaviour. These carriers have considerable advantages in the market, particularly with respect to their ability to make

use of their underlying network facilities for the delivery of new services. To grant these carriers unconditional forbearance would provide them with the opportunity to leverage their existing networks to the detriment of other potential service providers. In particular, unconditional forbearance of the broadband access services provided by cable broadcast carriers would create both the incentive and opportunity for these carriers to lessen competition and choice in the provision of broadband service that could be made available to the end customer. Safeguards such as rate regulation for broadband access services will be necessary to prevent instances of below cost and/or excessive pricing, at least in the near term.

Telephone companies also have sources of market power that warrant maintaining safeguards against anti-competitive behaviour. For example, telephone companies are still overwhelmingly dominant in the local telephony market, and until this dominance is diminished, it would not be appropriate to forbear unconditionally from rate regulation of broadband access services. (AT&T, p. 15)

In the opinion of AT&T Canada LDS, both the cable companies and the telephone companies have the incentive and opportunity to engage in these types of anticompetitive activities as a result of their vertically integrated structures. For example, cable companies, as the dominant provider of broadband distribution services, would be in a position to engage in above cost pricing in uncontested markets, unless effective constraints are put in place. On the other hand, the telephone company will likely be the new entrant in broadband access services in most areas, and therefore expected to price at or below the level of cable companies. While this provides some assurances that telephone companies are unlikely to engage in excessive pricing, it does not address the incentive and opportunity to price below cost. Accordingly, floor-pricing tests would be appropriate for services of both cable and telephone companies. (AT&T, 16–17)

Furthermore, in the case of both cable and telephone broadcast carriers, safeguards would also need to be established to prevent other forms of discriminatory behaviour and to ensure that broadband access services are unbundled. (AT&T, 17)

[38] See, e.g., Lisa Bowman, "Will Merger Shut Lid on Open Access?," ZDNet News, January 11, 2000, available at http://www.zdnet.com/zdnn/stories/news/0,4586,2420130,00.html.

[39] My point is not that this is the only threat. For example, as Denise Caruso has argued, the merger of Internet backbone providers might lead to a situation where peering on the Internet (exchanging data between peers neutrally) will cease. In "Mergers Threaten Internet's Informal System of Data Exchange," New York Times, February 14, 2000, available at http://www.nytimes.com/library/tech/00/02/biztech/articles/14digi.html, she writes, "In the early days of the Internet, self-interest forced backbone providers into peering [the free sharing of data between service providers]. . . . But it is scarcely true today. . . . [U]pon completion of the Worldcom-Sprint merger, a single company would control nearly half of the Internet's backbone—making it, literally and figuratively, without peer. Given the furious pace and high stakes of the telecommunications industry today, some fear that it is only a matter of time before one big backbone provider or another refuses to exchange data traffic with one of its peers. What happens then? 'Well, they would have a legitimate excuse,' says Hal Varian, dean of the school of information management at the University of California at Berkeley. 'An ISP could complain, and rightly so, that another ISP was sending them huge amounts of traffic and putting a load on their system. . . . That's an excuse to say, 'We can't handle this guy's packets; we aren't going to connect with him.' " Ibid.

[40] Timothy F. Bresnahan and Garth Saloner, "Large Firms' Demand for Computer Products and Services: Competing Market Models, Inertia, and Enabling Strategic Change," October 1994 (Research Paper No. 1318 in the Stanford Graduate School of Business Jackson Library).

[41] National Research Council, *The Internet's Coming of Age* (Washington, D.C.: National Academy Press, 2000), chapter 3, 24.

[42] Tim Berners-Lee, *Weaving the Web: The Original Design and Ultimate Destiny of the World Wide Web by Its Inventor* (San Francisco: HarperSanFrancisco, 1999), 130.

[43] See Daniel L. Rubinfeld and Hal J. Singer, "Open Access to Broadband Networks: A Case Study of the AOL/Time Warner Merger," *Berkeley Technology Law Journal* 16 (2001): 631, 672 ("Our analysis has shown that a policy of . . . conduit discrimination may be profitable post acquisition [and] that content discrimination is likely to be profitable post-acquisition.").

[44] See Seth Schiesel, "Cable Giants Block Rival Ads in Battle for Internet Customers," *New York Times*, June 8, 2001, A1.

Denise Caruso raised concerns about the free speech aspects of this change eighteen months earlier. As she argued, there is an increasing possibility that most of the Internet's content will be controlled by a few—or perhaps even one—large corporations, raising some very troubling issues. "The reasons for urgency are twofold. First is the issue of how to open privately owned broadband Internet access to all comers. In addition, the free-speech issue arises when any single entity, of any size, controls both a transmission medium and the information that flows over it. Open access is a particular concern. . . . Powerful corporations like AT&T and the proposed AOL Time Warner would have the power to balkanize the broadband Internet for their own purposes, with no legal reason to open their networks to competitors." "Convergence Raises Concerns About Access," *New York Times*, January 31, 2000, available at http://www.nytimes.com/library/tech/00/01/biztech/articles/31digi.html.

[45] See Federal Trade Commission, "FTC Approves AOL/Time Warner Merger with Conditions," December 14, 2000, http://www.ftc.gov/opa/2000/12/aol.htm; Federal Trade Commission, Docket No. C-3989. See also John R. Wilke, "AOL and Time-Warner Pledge Cable Access to Ease FTC Fears," *Wall Street Journal*, December 14, 2000.

[46] Or alternatively, a tragedy of an anticommons. The opportunity for any number of players to interfere with open access to the network could be viewed as an anticommons. See Michael A. Heller, "The Tragedy of the Anticommons," *Harvard Law Review* 111 (1998): 621; James M. Buchanan and Yong J. Yoon, "Symmetric Tragedies: Commons and Anticommons," *Journal of Law & Economics* 43 (2000): 1.

[47] This is not quite the tragedy that Hardin is describing. There is no common physical resource that is being overused. But there is a common virtual resource—the opportunity to innovate freely on the network—that is being misused by restricting the scope of that innovation with respect to one part of the network. That produces an externality, even if it doesn't "overuse" a resource.

[48] See Brief of Amici Curiae, Reed Elsevier Inc. et al., 7–9, *eBay Inc.* v. *Bidder's Edge Inc.*, 100 F. Supp. 2d 1058 (N.D. Cal. 2000) (No. C-99–21200RMW).

[49] See Chip Bayers, "The Bot.com Future," *Wired* (March 2000): 210.

[50] The total number of addresses available under Ipv6 is 10^{38}. That is a huge number: "If the address space of IPv4 is compared to 1 millimeter, the address space of IPv6 would be 80 times the diameter of the galactic system." See http://www.wide.ad.jp/wg/iPv6/index.html.

[51] By forcing more traffic over a single port, this arms race interferes with the opportunity to optimize traffic based on ports.

[52] The functioning of ports is explained in Craig Hunt, *TCP/IP Network Administration*, 2nd ed. (Sebastopol, Calif.: O'Reilly, 1998), 42–47. IPSec is described in a series of RFCs, which are available at http://www.ietf.org/html.charters/ipsec-charter.html. I am not claiming IPSec would necessarily be consistent with end-to-end, but simply that it provides a consistent protocol that could be implemented consistent with end-to-end.

[53] Garrett Hardin, "The Tragedy of the Commons," *Science* 162 (1968): 1243, 1244 (emphasis added).

[54] National Research Council, 24–25.

[55] As Faulhaber put it, "[T]he third view is that, as Adam Smith pointed out, producers are always conspiring about how to fleece the unsuspecting consuming public; it is only the competitive market that keeps their avarice in check. But producers will always search for ways to escape competition, through marketing, customer lock-in, predatory pricing, network effects, etc. AND . . . technological innovation is just a part of this strategic quest for greater profits, perhaps at the consumers' expense." "Faulhaber Comments at E-2-E Workshop," http://www.law.stanford.edu/e2e/papers.html. François Bar has made a similar point: "If the Internet could reduce friction, the same technology can also be deployed to create more of it." François Bar, "The Construction of Marketplace Architecture," 5.

[56] Charles Platt, "The Future Will Be Fast but Not Free," *Wired*, May 2001, available at http://www.wired.com/wired/archive/9.05/broadband_pr.html (emphasis added).

CHAPTER 11

[1] See 47 U.S.C. §223 (Supp. 1996); *ACLU v. Reno*, 521 U.S. 844 (1997).

[2] *ACLU v. Reno*, 217 F. 3d 162 (3d Cir., 2000).

[3] Lawrence Lessig, *Code and Other Laws of Cyberspace* (New York: Basic Books, 1999), 225.

[4] See 17 USCA §106 (2001): "[O]wner of copyright under this title has the exclusive rights . . . (5) in the case of . . . pictorial, graphic, or sculptural works . . . to display the copyrighted work publicly." But the claim would be weak. Except in the most extreme circumstances, the public display of a copyrighted work would be fair use. William Carleton, "Copyright Royalties for Visual Artists: A Display-Based Alternative to the Droit de Suite," *Cornell Law Review* 76 (1991): 510, 525 ("The general principle that section 109(c) observes, however, according to the House Report, is that 'the lawful owner of a copy of a work should be able to put his copy on public display without the consent of the copyright owner' " [quoting 1976 U.S. Code Cong. & Admin. News 5659, 5693]). See also *Ringgold* v. *Black Entertainment Television, Inc.*, 126 F. 3d 70 (2nd Cir., 1997).

[5] See Kevin V. Johnson, "Show's Fan Sites Fight Off 'Demon;' Fox: Production Company Cites Its Copyrights," *USA Today*, December 23, 1999, 4D, available at 1999 WL 6862067; and Aaron Barnhart and Kevin V. Johnson, "Twentieth, the Web Slayer: Studio Shifts Its Crusade to 'Buffy' Fans' Web sites," *Electronic Media*, December 6, 1999, 9, available at 1999 WL 8767348. Fox does not limit itself to the Web. See *Twentieth Century Fox Film Corp. v. 316 W. 49th Street Pub. Corp.*, No. 90 Civ. 6083 (MJL), 1990 WL 165680 (S.D.N.Y., October 23, 1990) (holding that a nightclub could not display images of *The Simpsons* on its wall without Fox's permission). Fox says that it "appreciates" fan sites, but not enough to allow them to exist freely. Johnson, 4D. As Warner Bros. Online president Jim Moloshok says, "We decided that we were going to create a better experience for the fans." Ibid.

⁶ Ibid.

⁷ Fara Warner et al., "Holes in the Net . . . ," *Wall Street Journal*, August 30, 1999, A1.

⁸ See http://www.olga.net/about.

⁹ See, e.g., Siva Vaidhyanathan, *Copyrights and Copywrongs: The Rise of Intellectual Property and How It Threatens Creativity* (New York: New York University Press, 2001), 355 ("In July 1999, journalist Michael Colton posted an Internet parody of *Talk* magazine, which is a partnership between Hearst Magazines and Walt Disney–owned Miramax Films. Miramax lawyers sent a cease-and-desist letter to Earthlink, the Internet company that owned the server on which the parody sat. Earthlink immediately shut down the parody. It only restored the site after *Talk* editor Tina Brown appealed to the Miramax legal department to let the parody stand. Because of widespread misunderstanding of copyright law, cease-and-desist letters carry inordinate cultural power and can chill if not directly censor expression.").

¹⁰ See Digital Millennium Copyright Act, 105 P. L. 304, Sec. 202(c)(1)(iii) (1998).

¹¹ Lessig, 173–75.

¹² See Bennett Haselton, "Amnesty Intercepted," December 12, 2000, http://www.peacefire.org/amnesty-intercepted.

¹³ See *Microsystems Software, Inc.* v. *Scandinavia Online AB*, 98 F. Supp. 2d 74 (D. Mass., 2000), aff'd, 226 F. 3d 35 (1st Cir., 2000) (enjoining "all persons in active concert" with Jansson and Skala from "publishing the software source code and binaries known as [CPHack]").

¹⁴ See http://www.aclu.org/court/cyberpatrol_motion.html.

¹⁵ *Sony Computer Entertainment, Inc.* v. *Connectix Corp*, 203 F. 3d 596 (9th Cir., 2000).

¹⁶ *ProCD, Inc.* v. *Zeidenberg*, 86 F. 3d 1447, 1454 (7th Cir., 1996).

¹⁷ See Paul Goldstein, "Copyright and the First Amendment," *Columbia Law Review* 70 (1970): 983 (describing the ongoing potential of copyright's grant of monopoly over expression as censorship); Pamela Samuelson, "Reviving Zacchini: Analyzing First Amendment Defenses in Right of Publicity and Copyright Cases," *Tulane Law Review* 57 (1983): 836 (same).

¹⁸ For a detailed analysis of the DMCA, see David Nimmer, "A Riff on Fair Use in the Digital Millennium Copyright Act," *University of Pennsylvania Law Review* 148 (2000): 673 (discussing the formulation, adoption, and practical effect of the DMCA).

¹⁹ See Carolyn Andrepont, "Legislative Updates: Digital Millennium Copyright Act: Copyright Protections for the Digital Age," *DePaul-LCA Journal of Art & Entertainment Law* 9 (1999): 397 (characterizing the DMCA as a necessary tool for protecting on-line copyrighted material); and Michelle A. Ravn, Note, "Navigating Terra Incognita: Why the Digital Millennium Copyright Act Was Needed to Chart the Course of Online Service Provider Liability for Copyright Infringement," *Ohio State Law Journal* 60 (1999): 755 (arguing that the DMCA was particularly needed to clarify liability for on-line copyright infringements).

²⁰ Or at least not significantly. It is true that if you could play DVD movies on any machine, there would be more machines that might demand DVD content.

²¹ The MPAA filed suit against four Web site operators in the Southern District of New York and in the District of Connecticut. The DVD Copy Control Association filed suit in California State court against about twenty named defendants and five hundred unnamed ones. For a history of these suits, see Openlaw/DVD: Resources, at http://eon.law.harvard.edu/openlaw/DVD/resources.html (visited April 19, 2001).

²² *Universal City Studios, Inc.* v. *Reimerdes*, 82 F. Supp. 2d 211 (S.D.N.Y., 2000) and

DVD Copy Control Ass'n, Inc. v. *McLaughlin,* No. CV 786804, 2000 WL 48512 (Cal. Superior, January 21, 2000).

23 See Michael A. Geist, "iCraveTV and the New Rules of Internet Broadcasting," *University of Arkansas at Little Rock Law Review* 23 (2000): 223; and John Borland, "Online TV Service May Spark New Net Battle," CNET.com, at http://news.cnet.com/ news/0-1004-200-1477491.html (last visited April 4, 2001) (describing the launch of the iCraveTV.com Web site). For a scholarly analysis of the case, see Howard P. Knopf, "Copyright and the Internet in Canada and Beyond: Convergence, Vision and Division," *European Intellectual Property Review* (2000): 262.

24 China Online (visited April 17, 2001), http://www.chinaonline.com (a U.S.-based English-language news site on China). Or alternatively, Human Rights in China (visited April 17, 2001), http://www.hrichina.org (a New York–based Chinese/English-language Web site chronicling Chinese human rights abuses).

25 See *Association "Union des Étudiants Juifs de France", la "Ligue contre le Racisme et l'Antisémitisme"* v. *Yahoo! Inc. et Yahoo France,* T.G.I. Paris, Ordonnance de référé du 22 mai 2000, available at: http://www.legalis.net/jnet/decisions/responsabilite/ ord_tgi-paris_220500.htm.

26 See Jack L. Goldsmith and Alan O. Sykes, "The Internet and the Dormant Commerce Clause," *Yale Law Journal* 110 (2001): 785. See also Lawrence Lessig and Paul Resnick, "Zoning Speech on the Internet: A Legal and Technical Model," *Michigan Law Review* 98 (1999): 395

27 A very similar point is made by Denise Caruso. See "Case Illustrates Entertainment Industry's Copyright Power," *New York Times,* March 13, 2000, available at http://www. nytimes.com/library/tech/00/03/biztech/articles/13digi.html. As Caruso writes, "The most chilling aspect of the case . . . was [iCraveTV's] response. That is, [it] did not argue the legality of the action against [it], but instead responded by inventing a technology that could stop the discussion dead in its tracks." Caruso continues: "Many people are likely to object strongly to [the site's] balkanized Internet . . . such a system would devolve the Internet into a model very much like the restricted, centralized control of cable television. That is a business model with which the $65 billion media and entertainment industries—the very ones that nearly sued the pants off [of the site]—are quite familiar." Ibid.

28 See Press Release, Recording Industry Association of America, RIAA Statement Concerning MP3.Com's New Services, January 21, 2000, at http://www.riaa.com/ PR_Story.cfm?id=47.

29 The court's ruling in the case determines that the damages are $25,000 per CD. This leads to possible damages of $118 million if the total is determined to be at least 4,700 CDs. *UMG Recordings, Inc.* v. *MP3.Com, Inc.,* No. 00 CIV. 472(JSR), 2000 WL 1262568, at *6 (S.D.N.Y., 2000).

30 See, e.g., Amy Harmon, "Powerful Music Software Has Industry Worried," *New York Times,* March 7, 2000, available at http://www.nytimes.com/library/tech/00/03/biztech/ articles/07net.html; Karl Taro Greenfeld, "The Free Juke Box," *Time* (March 27, 2000), available at http://www.time.com/time/everyone/magazine/sidebar_napster.html; Andy Oram, "Gnutella and Freenet Represent True Technological Innovation," May 12, 2000, at http://www.oreillynet.com/pub/a/network/2000/05/12/magazine/gnutella.html; also *Peer-to-Peer: Harnessing the Benefits of a Disruptive Technology,* Andy Oram, ed. (Beijing and Cambridge, Mass.: O'Reilly, 2000).

31 Home Recording of Copyrighted Works: Hearing on H.R. 4783, H.R. 4794, H.R. 4808, H.R. 5250, H.R. 5488, and H.R. 5750 Before the Subcomm. on Courts, Civil Lib-

erties, and the Admin. of Justice of the Comm. on the Judiciary, 97th Cong. (2nd session), 8 (1983) (testimony of Jack Valenti, president, Motion Picture Association of America, Inc.). See also Sam Costello, "How VCRs May Help Napster's Legal Fight," *Industry Standard*, July 25, 2000, available at http://www.thestandard.com/article/0,1902,17095,00.html.

[32] *Universal City Studios, Inc.* v. *Sony Corp. of Am.*, 480 F. Supp. 429, 432 (C.D. Cal., 1979) (district court opinion by Judge Ferguson).

[33] Ibid., 432.

[34] *A&M Records, Inc.* v. *Napster, Inc.* 239 F. 3d 1004 (9th Cir., 2001).

[35] *Harper & Row Publishers, Inc.* v. *Nation Enterprises*, 471 U.S. 539, 588 (1985).

[36] Joseph Story, "Commentaries on the Constitution of the United States," R. Rotunda and J. Nowak, eds. (1987), §502, 402.

[37] See Testimony of Professor Peter Jaszi, "The Copyright Term Extension Act of 1995: Hearings on S.483 Before the Senate Judiciary Comm.," 104th Cong. (1995), available at 1995 WL 10524355, at *6.

[38] *Eldred* v. *Reno*, 239 F. 3d 372, 375 (D.C. Cir., 2001).

[39] Recording Industry Association of America, 2000 Year-end Statistics (2001), at http://www.riaa.com/pdf/Year_End_2000.pdf.

[40] Jeff Leeds, "Album Sales Test the Napster Effect," *Los Angeles Times*, June 20, 2001, C1.

[41] "This case has always been about sending a message to the technology and venture capital communities that consumers, creators and innovators will best flourish when copyright interests are respected." Jim Hu and Evan Hansen, "Record Label Signs Deal with Napster," October 31, 2000, http://news.cnet.com/news/0-1005-200-3345604.html. See also "Online Entertainment: Coming Soon to a Digital Device Near You: Hearing Before the Senate Comm. on the Judiciary," 107th Cong. (2001) (statement of Hilary Rosen, president and CEO, Recording Industry Association of America), available at http://judiciary.senate.gov/te040301hr.htm; Press Release, Record Industry Association of America, Hilary Rosen Press Conference Statement, February 12, 2001, available at http://www.riaa.com/News_Story.cfm?id=371.

[42] As Yochai Benkler writes, "[I]ncreases in intellectual property rights are likely to lead, over time, to concentration of a greater portion of the information production function in the hands of large commercial organizations that vertically integrate new production with inventory management." Yochai Benkler, "The Commons as a Neglected Factor of Information Policy," October 3–5, 1998, 74.

Likely, and we might add, have. Compare, as David Isenberg points out, the connection to the history of AT&T: "You can see now in the record industry, for example, that the record companies are unwilling to give up this idea of the control of the physical medium even though they could perhaps do a very good job of artist development." Telephone interview with David Isenberg, February 14, 2001.

[43] Telephone interview with Michael Robertson, November 16, 2000.

[44] Ibid.

[45] See also Richard Watt, *Copyright and Economic Theory: Friends or Foes?* (Cheltenham, England, and Northampton, Mass.: E. Elgar, 2000), 161–200 (describing role of cooperatives and collectives). For a more comprehensive analysis of compulsory rights, see generally Marshall Leaffer, *Understanding Copyright Law*, 3rd ed. (New York: M. Bender, 1999), 69–71 (detailing both support for and criticism of compulsory licenses), cited in Michael Freno, note, "Database Protection: Resolving the U.S. Database Dilemma with an Eye Toward International Protection" 34 (2000), *Cornell*

International Law Journal 34: 165, 209 (promoting compulsory licenses in the context of databases); Christopher Scott Harrison, comment, "Protection of Pharmaceuticals as Foreign Policy: The Canada-U.S. Trade Agreement and Bill C-22 Versus the North American Free Trade Agreement and Bill C-91" (2001), *North Carolina Journal of International Law and Communications Regulation* 26: 457, 525 (advocating generally the free distribution of compulsory licenses); Anthony Reese, "Copyright and Internet Music Transmissions: Existing Law, Major Controversies, Possible Solutions" (2001), *University of Miami Law Review* 55: 237, 270 (arguing for the extension of compulsory licenses in the area of music on the Internet); Bess-Carolina Dolmo, note, "Examining Global Access to Essential Pharmaceuticals in the Face of Patent Protection Rights: The South African Experience" (2001), *Buffalo Human Rights Law Review* 7: 137 (explaining the benefits of compulsory licenses for developing countries); Sheldon W. Halpern, "The Digital Threat to the Normative Role of Copyright Law" (2001), *Ohio State Law Journal* 62: 569, 593 (supporting compulsory licensing for digital images); Laura N. Gasaway, "Impasse: Distance Learning and Copyright" (2001), *Ohio State Law Journal* 62: 783 (questioning the practicality of compulsory licenses); Robert P. Merges, "One Hundred Years of Solicitude: Intellectual Property Law, 1900–2000," (2000), *California Law Review* 88: 2187, 2194, n. 15 (criticizing compulsory licenses in one context); Robert P. Merges, "Contracting into Liability Rules: Intellectual Property Rights and Collective Rights Organizations," *California Law Review* 84: 1293, (arguing against compulsory licenses for digital content); Ralph Oman, "The Compulsory License Redux: Will It Survive in a Changing Marketplace?" (1986), *Cardozo Arts & Entertainment Law Journal* 5: 37, 48 (noting that many actors in the area of intellectual property prefer private solutions over compulsory licenses); Scott L. Bach, note, "Music Recording, Publishing, and Compulsory Licenses: Toward a Consistent Copyright Law," *Hofstra Law Review* 14: 379, 398–401 (arguing that compulsory licenses are unfair to many artists, discourage innovation, and may be unconstitutional under the copyright clause).

46 For a similar argument, see Raymond Shih Ray Ku, "Copyright & Cyberspace: Napster and the New Economics of Digital Technology" (draft on file with author, April 7, 2001) ("[C]yberspace and the economics of digital technology require the unbundling of the public's interests in the creation and distribution of digital works.").

47 Christopher Stern, "Napster Copyright Fight Goes to Hill," *Washington Post*, April 4, 2001, E03.

48 Vaidhyanathan, 14.

49 Richard A. Posner, *Law and Literature*, rev. and enlarged ed. (Cambridge, Mass.: Harvard University Press, 1998), 392.

50 Ibid., 396. See also William M. Landes and Richard A. Posner, "An Economic Analysis of Copyright Law," *Journal of Legal Studies* 18 (1989): 325.

51 For the history of Judge Kozinski, see Susan Rice's "Profile," in *Los Angeles Daily Journal*, September 29, 1988, 1. See also *History of the Federal Judiciary* (Washington, D.C.: Federal Judicial Center, 2001) (bio of Alex Kozinski from Federal Judges Biographical Database), at http://air.fjc.gov/history/judges_frm.html.

52 *Vanna White* v. *Samsung Elecs. Am., Inc.*; *David Deutsch Assocs.*, 989 F. 2d 1512, 1514 (1993).

53 Ibid., 34.

54 Ibid., 27.

55 Ibid.

56 Ibid.

57 Ibid., 31.

⁵⁸ Ibid., 27.

⁵⁹ Ibid., 30.

⁶⁰ I do not address the reach of trademark law in this area, but it would only strengthen the argument I am making. Unlike traditional intellectual property, trademarks are perpetual, and their effective power has expanded dramatically. This has become especially significant as the domain name system has had to deal with the conflict between trademarks and domain names. This has tempted the World Intellectual Property Association to build control for trademark interests into the very architecture of the network. See ¶¶23–28, "Executive Summary of the Interim Report of the Second WIPO Internet Domain Name Process," available at http://wipo2.wipo.int.

⁶¹ The origin of modern economic work here is Kenneth Arrow's "Economic Welfare and the Allocation of Resources for Invention," in National Bureau Committee for Economic Research, *The Rate and Direction of Inventive Activity, Economic and Social Factors*, Richard Nelson, ed. (Princeton, N.J.: Princeton University Press, 1962), 609. Harold Demsetz responded to this by arguing in favor of a stronger property-based regime. See Harold Demsetz, "Information and Efficiency: Another Viewpoint," *Journal of Law & Economics* 12 (1969): 1. On the question of optimal protection, see Richard Gilbert and Carl Shapiro, "Optimal Patent Length and Breadth," *RAND Journal of Economics* 21 (1990): 106.

⁶² For a careful account of the Framers' view of the patent power, see Edward C. Walterscheid, "Patents and the Jeffersonian Mythology," *John Marshall Law Review* 29 (1995): 269. Professor Pollack makes a persuasive argument that the conception is limited by Lockean conceptions of the property right. See Malla Pollack, "The Owned Public Domain: The Constitutional Right Not to Be Excluded—or the Supreme Court Chose the Right Breakfast Cereal in *Kellogg* v. *National Biscuit Co.*," *Hastings Communications & Entertainment Law Journal* 22 (2000): 265. For an introduction to the rationale, see Richard A. Posner, *Economic Analysis of Law*, 4th ed. (Boston: Little, Brown, 1992), 38–41.

⁶³ Steven Shavell and Tanguy van Ypersele, "Rewards Versus Intellectual Property Rights" (NBER Working Paper No. 6956, February 1999), 27. Shavell and Ypersele suggest a reward system to replace a patent system. A similar proposal has been made by Michael Kremer, "Patent Buy-Outs: A Mechanism for Encouraging Innovation" (NBER Working Paper No. 6304, December 1997). Chicago professor Douglas Lichtman has a related proposal to subsidize access to patented drugs. See Douglas Lichtman, "Pricing Prozac: Why the Government Should Subsidize the Purchase of Patented Pharmaceuticals," *Harvard Journal of Law & Technology* 11 (1997): 123. For criticism of the reward alternative, see F. Scott Kieff, "Property Rights and Property Rules for Commercializing Inventions," *Minnesota Law Review* 85 (2001): 697, 709–21.

⁶⁴ Though the economic argument about the effect of patents on innovation remain ambiguous at best. See, e.g., Roberto Mazzoleni and Richard R. Nelson, "Economic Theories About the Benefits and Costs of Patents," *Journal of Economic Issues* 32 (December 1998): 1031.

⁶⁵ Adam B. Jaffe, "The U.S. Patent System in Transition: Policy Innovation and the Innovation Process" (NBER Working Paper Series, August 1999), 24–25.

⁶⁶ Ibid., 26.

⁶⁷ Ibid.

⁶⁸ A similar skepticism has been raised about strong property rights where network externalities are strong. See Pamela Samuelson et al., "Manifesto Concerning the Legal Protection of Computer Programs," *Columbia Law Review* 94 (1994): 2308, 2375, citing

Joseph Farrell, "Standardization and Intellectual Property," *Jurimetrics Journal* 30 (1989): 35, 36–38, 45–46 (discussing network effects).

⁶⁹ See, e.g., Josh Lerner, "150 Years of Patent Protection" (NBER Working Paper No. 7477, January 2000) (examines 177 policy changes in the strength of protection across sixty countries, over a 150-year period, and concludes that strengthening patent protection had few positive effects on patent applications in the country making the policy change); Mariko Sakakibara and Lee Branstetter, "Do Stronger Patents Induce More Innovation? Evidence from the 1988 Japanese Patent Law Reforms," *Rand Journal of Economics* 32 (2001): 77 (authors find no evidence of an increase in R&D spending or innovative output). For a long-standing source of skepticism about the effect of strong patents on innovation, see Robert P. Merges and Richard R. Nelson, "On the Complex Economics of Patent Scope," *Columbia Law Review* 90 (1990): 839 (strong patent assertions in electrical lighting, automobiles, airplanes, radio slowed down innovation).

⁷⁰ See, e.g., Jean O. Lanjouw, "The Introduction of Pharmaceutical Product Patents in India: 'Heartless Exploitation of the Poor and Suffering'?" (NBER Working Paper No. 6366, 1998); F. Scott Kieff, "Property Rights and Property Rules for Commercializing Inventions," *Minnesota Law Review* 67 (2001): 727–28. For an excellent and comprehensive account of the actual patenting practice, see John R. Allison and Mark A. Lemley, "Who's Patenting What? An Empirical Exploration of Patent Prosecution," *Vanderbilt Law Review* 53 (2000): 2099, 2146; John R. Allison and Mark A. Lemley, "How Federal Circuit Judges Vote in Patent Validity Cases," *Florida State University Law Review* 27 (2000): 745, 765 (concluding no systematic bias in judges' votes).

⁷¹ Jaffe, 46.

⁷² Ibid., 47. Jaffe's argument here is narrower than the point I am making in this section. His concern is the social costs from too much effort being devoted to the pursuit of patented innovation. My concern is the cost of patents on the innovation process generally.

⁷³ "Patently Absurd?" *The Economist* (June 21, 2001). As the article goes on to report, interviewees from patenting firms indicated that "rather than patenting to win exclusive rights to a valuable new technology, patents were filed more for strategic purposes."

⁷⁴ Benjamin Franklin, "having no desire of profiting by patents myself," cited "a principle which has ever weighed with me . . . [t]hat, as we enjoy great advantages from the inventions of others, we should be glad of an opportunity to serve others by any invention of ours; and this we should do freely and generously." Benjamin Franklin, *The Autobiography of Benjamin Franklin*, Frank Woodworth Pine, ed. (Garden City, N.Y.: Garden City Publishing Co., 1916 ed.; originally published 1793), 215–16.

⁷⁵ George Washington Carver, for example, observed about his inventions that "God gave them to me, how can I sell them to someone else?" "Inventors," *Atlanta Journal & Constitution*, February 12, 1999, A17.

⁷⁶ Robert K. Merton, "A Note on Science and Democracy," *Journal of Law & Political Sociology* 1 (1942): 115, 123. ("Patents proclaim exclusive rights of use and, often, nonuse. The suppression of invention denies the rationale of scientific production and diffusion.") As Professor Arti Rai describes it, "[T]raditional scientific norms promote a public domain of freely available scientific information, independent choice in the selection of research topics, and (perhaps above all) respect for uninhibited scientific invention." Arti Kaur Rai, "Regulating Scientific Research: Intellectual Property Rights and the Norms of Science," *Northwestern University Law Review* 94 (1999): 77, 89–90.

More famously, Merton is known for characterizing "science" as "communistic":

"Communism," in the nontechnical and extended sense of common ownership of goods, is a second integral element of the scientific ethos. The substantive findings of science are a product of social collaboration and are assigned to the community. They constitute a common heritage in which the equity of the individual producer is severely limited. An eponymous law or theory does not enter into the exclusive possession of the discoverer and his heirs, nor do the mores bestow upon them special rights of use and disposition. Property rights in science are whittled down to a bare minimum by the rationale of the scientific ethic. The scientist's claim to "his" intellectual "property" is limited to that of recognition and esteem which, if the institution functions with a modicum of efficiency, is roughly commensurate with the significance of the increments brought to the common fund of knowledge. Eponymy—for example, the Copernican system, Boyle's law—is thus at once a mnemonic and a commemorative device.

Merton, 121.

[77] Fred Warshofsky, *The Patent Wars* (New York: Wiley, 1994), 170. Of course, I don't mean to suggest that Microsoft is against software patents. Indeed, in the same memo, Gates goes on to recommend the Microsoft strategy to respond to this new world of patents:

The solution . . . is patent exchanges . . . and patenting as much as we can. . . . A future start-up with no patents of its own will be forced to pay whatever price the giants choose to impose. That price might be high: *Established companies have an interest in excluding future competitors.*

Ibid., at 170–71 (emphasis added).

[78] Thomas Jefferson, Letter to James Madison, in Julian P. Boyd, ed., *The Papers of Thomas Jefferson* 13 (Princeton, N.J.: Princeton University Press, 1956), 440, 442–43.

[79] To qualify for patent protection, an invention must be novel, 35 U.S.C. §§101, 102 (1982); it must provide utility, ibid.; and it must be nonobvious, ibid., §103. The invention must also be within the list of patentable subject matter, 35 U.S.C. §101 (1982).

[80] Jaffe, 9. The changes have also coincided with an increase in the number of patents. On one account, that increase may be because patents are indeed a spur to innovation. Researchers, however, have concluded differently. Samuel Kortum and Josh Lerner, "Stronger Protection or Technological Revolution: What Is Behind the Recent Surge in Patenting?," *Carnegie-Rochester Conference Series on Public Policy* 48 (1998): 247 (attributing the increase to improvements in the management of research); Bronwyn H. Hall and Rosemarie Ham Ziedonis, "The Patent Paradox Revisited: An Empirical Study of Patenting in the U.S. Semiconductor Industry, 1979–1995," *Rand Journal of Economics* 32 (2001): 101 (attributing the increase to portfolio races).

[81] E-mail from Greg Aharonian, author, Internet Patent News Service, May 28, 2001, on file with author.

Greg Aharonian is perhaps the leading expert on the practice of software and Internet-related patents. While he is a supporter of patents in principle, he has been a strong critic of the U.S. Patent Office. Aharonian estimates the number of software patents in a number of ways. He provided the following data to me:

"TOTAL is the total number of patents issued that year, GREG is my count or estimated count of software patents (using the Greg Aharonian scheme) issued in that year. SOFTWARE is the number of patents in that year that include the word *software* somewhere in the specification, claims, or abstract. 364&395 is the total number of patents issued in these two main computing classes."

YEAR	TOTAL	GREG	SOFTWARE	(364&395)
1999	154,534	21,000 (est.)	17,603	6,410
1998	150,961	17,500 (est.)	16,100	10,571
1997	124,181	13,000 (est.)	10,017	8,190
1996	121,799	9,000	9,104	7,922
1995	113,941	6,142	6,951	6,114
1994	113,706	4,569	6,009	5,745
1993	109,876	2,400	4,929	4,862
1992	107,489	1,624	4,068	4,073
1991	106,831	1,500	3,543	3,817
1990	99,210	1,300	3,046	3,606
1989	102,686	1,600	3,090	3,980
1988	84,433	800	2,053	2,708
1987	89,578	800	2,038	2,766
1986	77,039	600	1,483	2,202
1985	77,268	500	1,324	1,978
1984	72,668	400	1,003	1,857
1983	62,005	350	635	1,517
1982	63,291	300	603	1,446
1981	71,105	300	544	1,257
1980	66,206	250	465	1,239
1979	52,480	200	269	986
1978	70,564	150	299	1,272
1977	69,797	100	300	1,320
1976	70,924	100	208	1,113
1975	72,156	100	188	817
1974	62,342	100	188	838
1973	61,019	150	122	871
1972	58,603	200	110	906
1971	50,904	100	68	896
	2,537,596	33,635	96,360	91,279

[82] Seth Shulman, *Owning the Future* (Boston: Houghton Mifflin, 1999), 69.

[83] Douglas Brotz made this statement at the Public Hearing on Use of the Patent System to Protect Software Related Inventions, January 26, 1994, at the San Jose Convention Center, transcript available at http://lpf.ai.mit.edu/Patents/testimony/statements/adobe.testimony.html.

[84] "Oracle Corporation opposes the patentability of software." Statement available at http://www.base.com/software-patents/statements/oracle.statement.html (visited June 8, 2001).

[85] Patent law has long protected process patents. Mark A. Lemley, "Patent Scope and Innovation in the Software Industry," *California Law Review* 89 (2001): 1, 8.

[86] Rochelle Cooper Dreyfuss, "State Street or Easy Street: Is Patenting Business Methods Good for Business?," *U.S. Intellectual Property: Law & Policy* 6 (2000): 27.

[87] *State St. Bank & Trust Co.* v. *Signature Fin. Group, Inc.*, 149 F. 3d 1368 (Fed. Cir., 1998).

[88] Carl Shapiro, "Navigating the Patent Thicket: Cross Licenses, Patent Pools, and Standard-Setting" (working draft paper presented at National Bureau of Economic Research annual conference, May 2000): 2.

[89] See Laura Rohde, "BT Flexes Muscles Over U.S. Hyperlink Patent," June 21, 2000, available at http://www.idg.net/idgns/2000/06/21/BTFlexesMusclesOverUSHyperlink. shtml. The Amazon patent has received increasingly skeptical review in the courts. After a district court enjoined Barnes & Noble from using a similar technology, *Amazon. com* v. *Barnesandnoble.com*, 73 F. Supp. 2d 1228 (W.D. Wash., 1999), the Court of Appeals for the Federal Circuit reversed the injunction, finding that Barnesandnoble. com had mounted a substantial challenge to the validity of the patent. *Amazon.com* v. *Barnesandnoble.com*, 239 F. 3d 1343 (CAFC, 2001).

[90] James Bessen and Eric Maskin, "Sequential Innovation, Patents, and Imitation," January 2000, available at http://researchoninnovation.org/patent.pdf (visited on June 10, 2001). See also *Patently Absurd*: "[T]he rush to acquire patent portfolios could slow down the generation of new ideas."

[91] See Edmund W. Kitch, "The Nature and Function of the Patent System," *Journal of Law & Economics* 20 (1977): 265 (advocating prospect theory). See also Merges and Nelson, 839 (propounding a race-to-invent theory; lethargy in patent development will lead to a problem of "under-fishing"; thus, where innovation is cumulative, narrow patents are better). See also Mark F. Grady and Jay I. Alexander, "Patent Law and Rent Dissipation," *Virginia Law Review* 78 (1992): 305 (arguing that patents reduce rent dissipation from races to initial invention, races to improvements, and wasteful efforts to keep secrets). For a critique of Grady and Alexander, see Robert P. Merges, "Rent Control in the Patent District: Observations on the Grady-Alexander Thesis," *Virginia Law Review* 78 (1992): 359.

[92] As Professor Julie Cohen describes it:

> Kitch based his "prospect" theory on an analogy to nineteenth-century mining claims, which reserved for first-comers all rights to explore the described terrain. Under the prospect theory of patent scope, issued patents would operate as broad reservations of rights in the technical landscape. As a result, patentees could credibly seek to exact royalties for nearly all improvements, whether literally infringing or not. Improvers, meanwhile, would need to think twice before refusing such demands. To a greater degree than ever before, second-comers would need permission to develop and market their innovations.

Julie E. Cohen and Mark A. Lemley, "Patent Scope and Innovation in the Software Industry," *California Law Review* 89 (2001): 1, 14–15.

[93] Ibid., 15. ("It assumes that owners can readily identify, and would readily license, successful improvers; that the gains from coordination would outweigh the costs of any strategic behavior by owners and improvers; and that the initial allocation of stronger property rights to the prospect owner would not adversely affect improvers' incentives [or that an overall increase in productivity would outweigh any such adverse effect].")

[94] Cf. Rai, 121 (criticizing patents because of the "losses in creativity and high transaction costs that such grants generate").

[95] This point is not specific to the Internet or to software technologies. Professor Arti Rai has made a similar point in the context of basic scientific research:

Bargaining between the patent holder and improver would face a variety of obstacles. First, there would be very substantial difficulties in valuation. It is by no means clear how one goes about valuing an EST of unknown function, let alone uncertain but potentially highly lucrative research using that EST. Disagreement about the value of the patented invention relative to the value of the research project might make it very difficult for the parties to agree on the terms for a license. This disagreement might well be exacerbated by cognitive biases that could lead the EST patent owner to overvalue its asset. In particular, the owner might overestimate the possibility that the EST would lead to the finding of a valuable drug therapy and then negotiate based on this irrational estimation. Negotiation would also be hampered by Arrow's information paradox: it might be impossible for the subsequent researcher to get a license *ex ante* without disclosing to the patent holder valuable information about its own research plans. But because this research plan would not be protectable as intellectual property, the competitor might fear that the patent holder would appropriate the information for its own use, with no compensating benefit to the competitor. Even if these difficulties did not lead to bargaining breakdown, they would create transaction costs that reduced the cooperative surplus to be gained from a license and would thus deter at least some inventors and improvers from negotiating in the first instance. Transaction costs would be compounded by the likelihood that the would-be follow-on improver would likely have to negotiate licenses not simply with one owner of basic research but with many such owners. For example, in order to develop a commercial treatment for a genetic disease (particularly a polygenic disease), it may be necessary to have access to a large number of ESTs and SNPs, each conceivably patented by a different entity. Similarly, in order to screen potential pharmaceutical products for therapeutic effects and side-effects at the pre-clinical testing stage, it may be very useful to have access to a large number of different receptors, each potentially controlled by a different owner. Some of these difficulties might be addressed if the bargaining occurred *ex post*, after the follow-on improver had already developed the improvement. In that case, both the initial inventor and the follow-on improver would have greater knowledge of the value of the improvement relative to that of the original invention. Moreover, in the *ex post* situation, the possibility of "blocking patents" might provide a way around Arrow's information paradox. Blocking patents arise when a follow-on improver takes a patented product and improves it in a nonobvious way. Although the follow-on improver can then secure a patent on that improvement, the improvement may nonetheless infringe the original patent. In the blocking patent situation, neither the initial patent holder nor the follow-on improver can sell the improvement without cross-licensing. But, if the improvement is truly significant, such that the initial inventor would want to sell the improvement itself, it would presumably have a financial incentive to cross-license the improver.

Ibid., 125–26. Rebecca Eisenberg makes a similar point: "Michael Heller and I argue that too many patent rights on 'upstream' discoveries can stifle 'downstream' research and product development by increasing transaction costs and magnifying the risk of bargaining failures." Rebecca S. Eisenberg, "Bargaining over the Transfer of Proprietary Research Tools," 224. See also Robert P. Merges, "Institutions for Intellectual Property Transactions: The Case of Patent Pools," in *Expanding the Boundaries of Intellectual Property*, Rochelle Cooper Dreyfuss and Diane Leenheer Zimmerman, eds. (Oxford: Oxford University Press, 2001), 127–28.

96 Bessen and Maskin, "Sequential Innovation, Patents, and Imitation."
97 Steven Levy, "The Great Amazon Patent Debate," *Newsweek* (March 13, 2000): 74

("I asked Bezos if Amazon would have developed 1-Click even if there were no patent system to protect it and anyone could legally rip it off. 'Yes,' he responded without hesitation. 'Very definitely.' "). This point suggests a related reason to be skeptical about these patents. Patents can induce overinvestment in patent protection; the low additional cost to get the protection may induce too much patent duplication. See Posner, *Economic Analysis of Law*, 39.

[98] For skepticism about software patents, see, e.g., Pamela Samuelson, "Benson Revisited: The Case Against Patent Protection for Algorithms and Other Computer Program–Related Inventions," *Emory Law Journal* 39 (1990): 1025; A. Samuel Oddi, "Beyond Obviousness: Invention Protection in the Twenty-first Century," *American University Law Review* 38 (1989): 1097 (arguing that patents should be issued only for major innovations); Pamela Samuelson et al., 2308. See also Cohen and Lemley (arguing for narrowing to permit reverse engineering). On business method patents, see, e.g., "One-click Monster," *American Lawyer* (May 2000): 51; Rochelle Cooper Dreyfuss, "Are Business Method Patents Bad for Business?," *Computer & High Technology Law Journal* 16 (2000): 263 ; William Krause, "Sweeping the E-Commerce Patent Minefield: The Need for a Workable Business Method Exception," *Seattle University Law Review* 24 (2000): 79; Jared Earl Grusd, "Internet Business Methods: What Role Does and Should the Law Play?," *Virginia Journal of Law & Technology* 4 (1999): 9.

[99] "In the United States, despite the long-standing controversy around software patents, there has been virtually no government effort to study the economic effects of expanded patent protection. The one government-commissioned study of which I am personally aware was suspended at the request of a multinational company with a unique position in software patents." Brian Kahin, comments in response to "The Patentability of Computer-Implemented Inventions," available at http://europa.eu.int/comm/internal_market/en/intprop/indprop/maryland.pdf. The National Academies has launched a study, "Intellectual Property Rights in the Knowledge-Based Economy," http://www.nationalacademies.org/ipr.

[100] See "Internet Society Panel on Business Method Patents," http://www/oreillynet.com/lpt/a/434 ("Property, the first of the three debates I argued, I would argue is beyond reproach and the burden of proof is not on those who would need to say property should be but on those who say property should not be because historically societies that did not respect property rights, all rights, ended up in the dust bin of history." [Jay Walker]).

[101] Friedrich A. von Hayek, "Free Enterprise and Competitive Order," in *Individualism and Economic Order* (Chicago: University of Chicago Press), 107, 114. Nobel Prize–winning economist Milton Friedman expressed similar skepticism. "[T]rivial patents . . . are often used as a device for maintaining private collusive arrangements that would otherwise be more difficult or impossible to maintain." Milton Friedman, *Capitalism and Freedom* (Chicago: University of Chicago Press, 1962), 127.

[102] Lest too much of my own bias become apparent, I should note that there are some who argue strongly (and in some ways convincingly) that between a well-functioning copyright and well-functioning patent system, a patent system for software may well be better. As Mark Haynes argues, "[U]nlike copyright, the patent system encourages improvement patents, through which competitors are able to neutralize the patent portfolios of others." Mark A. Haynes, commentary, "Black Holes of Innovation in the Software Arts," *Berkeley Technology Law Journal* 14 (1999): 567, 574. Likewise, as Mark Lemley and David O'Brien have argued, patents would encourage the deployment of reusable software "components." Mark A. Lemley and David W. O'Brien, "Encouraging Software Reuse," *Stanford Law Review* 49 (1997): 255. Thus, conceivably, a patent sys-

tem would encourage innovation. And Professor Scott Kieff has argued quite convincingly that patents spur not just innovation, but also commercialization. See F. Scott Kieff, "Property Rights and Property Rules for Commercializing Inventions," *Minnesota Law Review* 85 (2001): 697. Commercialization, Kieff argues, depends upon property rules protecting invention, not liability rules. Compare Ian Ayres and Paul Klemperer, "Limiting Patentees' Market Power Without Reducing Innovation Incentives: The Perverse Benefits of Uncertainty and Non-Injunctive Remedies," *Michigan Law Review* 97 (1999): 985 (arguing for liability, rather than property protection, for patent rights).

I'm skeptical, but not a committed skeptic. These accounts don't (and don't purport to) account for the full costs of a patent system, or the particular costs that would affect software developers. Nor do they deny the burdens imposed by the current patent system. Thus, while such a benefit is possible, that it is possible in the current regime has not, in my view, been shown.

[103] Telephone interview with Bob Young, November 14, 2000. See also Kahin, 3–4 ("At the level of individual patents, patents may benefit small firms more than large firms because small-firm options for appropriating returns from innovation are fewer. For example, small firms may be less able to exploit first-mover advantages. At the portfolio level, large firms with large portfolios benefit disproportionately from network effects and economies of scale and scope. This includes their ability to manage transaction costs, which is the subject of the third perspective that I will explore at greater length."); Kahin, 4 ("Small firms [with some exceptions] are generally disadvantaged because they lack in-house patent counsel and their business focus can be easily distracted by litigation or even claims of infringement.").

[104] "In the short run, individual patents work to [the benefit of small firms], while in the long run and in the aggregate, patents favor large firms. The more pervasive patenting becomes, the more the long-term, portfolio-level effects dominate." Kahin, 4.

Patents have also been said to be a useful tool for old companies to protect themselves against the new. As Gary Reback, Silicon Valley entrepreneur and attorney, describes the history in the Valley, "[W]e went through a long period like that where I saw companies like IBM going around Silicon Valley . . . leaning on the new generation of companies like Sun . . . to develop a revenue stream out of their patent portfolio." Telephone interview with Gary Reback, November 21, 2000.

[105] Tim Berners-Lee, *Weaving the Web: The Original Design and Ultimate Destiny of the World Wide Web by Its Inventor* (San Francisco: HarperSanFrancisco, 1999), 196.

[106] Richard Stallman, "The GNU Operating System and the Free Software Movement," in *Open Sources: Voices from the Open Source Revolution*, Chris DiBona, Sam Ockman, and Mark Stone, eds. (Beijing and Sebastopol: O'Reilly, 1999), 53, 67.

[107] Robert Young and Wendy Goldman Rohm, *Under the Radar: How Red Hat Changed the Software Business—and Took Microsoft by Surprise* (Scottsdale, Ariz.: Coriolis Group Books, 1999), 135–36.

[108] Peter Wayner, *Free for All: How Linux and the Free Software Movement Undercut the High-Tech Titans* (New York: HarperBusiness, 2000), 223–24.

[109] Kahin, 5.

[110] Telephone interview with Bob Young.

[111] Ian Mount, "Would You Buy a Patent License from This Man?," *eCompany*, April 2001, available at http://www.ecompany.com/articles/mag/0,1640,9575,00.html.

[112] Carl Shapiro, "Navigating the Patent Thicket: Cross Licenses, Patent Pools, and Standard-Setting," in *Innovation Policy and the Economy*, vol. 1, Adam Jaffe, Joshua Lerner, and Scott Stern, eds. (Cambridge, Mass.: MIT Press, 2001), 8. Shapiro recom-

mends that antitrust authorities permit packaging licensing for complementary, but not substitute, patents, as a way to reduce the transaction costs associated with the hold-up problem created by patents.

113 C. Shapiro, 7. A related argument is summarized by Denise Caruso. As she argues in "Patent Absurdity," New York Times, February 1, 1999, available at http://www.nytimes.com/library/tech/99/02/biztech/articles/01digi.html, "Ideas are given their literal currency through patent and copyright laws, originally intended to stimulate innovation by protecting inventors from idea snatchers and allowing them to profit more easily from their talents. But some experts worry that an increasing number of individuals and companies are perverting that original purpose with increasingly specious claims to ownership, as well as by stockpiling patents into competitive arsenals." Ibid. Caruso identifies such things as "[a] patent for using a book as a teaching tool" and "a patent for downloading files over the Internet for a fee" as some of the more ridiculous recent developments in intellectual property law and adds that "various technology companies, including IBM, Intel and Hewlett-Packard, use their vast holdings of patents as competitive weaponry in seeking to disable each other with infringement charges. . . . Today's relaxed rules for granting patents, and the greater ease with which arsenals can thus be amassed, gives a decided battle advantage to industry heavyweights. . . . In today's business environment, in which a company's market value is measured with increasing frequency by the intellectual property it owns, arsenals of patents—specious or not—make an unfortunate kind of sense." Ibid.

114 Warshofsky, The Patent Wars, 170–71 (emphasis added).

115 Michael A. Heller, "The Tragedy of the Anticommons: Property in the Transition from Marx to Markets," Harvard Law Review 111 (1998): 621. The general issue of patents in sequential, or cumulative, innovation is addressed by Suzanne Scotchmer, "Standing on the Shoulders of Giants: Cumulative Research and the Patent Law," Journal of Economic Perspectives 5 (Winter 1991). James Bessen and Eric Maskin argue that this is precisely the kind of innovation that is harmed the most by strong patent protection. See Bessen and Maskin. See also Merges, Institutions for Intellectual Property Transactions, 125.

116 James M. Buchanan and Yong J. Yoon, "Symmetric Tragedies: Commons and Anticommons," Journal of Law & Economics 43 (2000): 1.

117 I've not discussed two other critical aspects of intellectual property law—either trade secret law or trademark law. Both are relevant to the issues of control that I have described, and trademark law in particular has expanded significantly. See, e.g., Alanna C. Rutherford, "Sporty's Farm v. Sportsman's Market: A Case Study In Internet Regulation Gone Awry," Brooklyn Law Review 66 (2000): 421, 437 (describing the proliferation of trademarks on the Net and its undermining of the original justification for trademark law); Matthew A. Kaminer, "The Limitations of Trademark Law in Addressing Trademark Keyword Banners," Santa Clara Computer & High Technology Law Journal 16 (1999): 35, 61–62 ("We should not contain the growth of the Internet, but instead support it") (quote on 62); Glenn A. Gunderson, "Expansion of Trademark Law Yields Trickier Search: Development of Unusual Marks, Dilution Law and the Internet Complicate Clearance Process," National Law Journal, May 31, 1999, C9 (describing the near doubling of trademark applications from 1990 to 1998), cited in Kathleen Donohue, "Trademark Vigilance in the Twenty-first Century: A Pragmatic Approach," Fordham Intellectual Property Media & Entertainment Law Journal 9 (1999): 823, 828, n.18; Claire Ann Koegler, "Here Come the Cybercops 2: Who Should Police Cybermarks?," Nova Law Review 22 (1998): 531, 532–33 (explaining how trademark law has greatly expanded in the context of the Internet).

CHAPTER 12

[1] Thomas W. Hazlett, "Spectrum Flash Dance: Eli Noam's Proposal for 'Open Access' to Radio Waves," *Journal of Law & Economics* 41 (1998): 805.

[2] See Hazlett, "The Wireless Craze," 17 ("Allocation and 'technical' rules protected broadcasters from competition as well as from fees or competitive bidding"). The examples include AM radio's protection from FM, ibid., 50–53; the artificial scarcity in VHF-TV licenses, which produced just three national networks, ibid., 53–55; VHF-TV blocking CATV, ibid., 55–62; AM and FM radio's blocking of digital radio, ibid., 62–65; NAB and NPR's blocking of low-power FM radio, ibid., 68–82.

[3] Eli Noam, "Beyond Spectrum Auctions: Taking the Next Step to Open Spectrum Access," *Telecommunications Policy* 21 (1997): 461, 462, n. 5.

[4] Ibid. How this market system might work is not yet clear. Presumably, users would bid in real time to get access to available spectrum. Bidding in turn would require that users have some form of identification. The ID need not be a real identity. But every transaction has a name. You generate less overhead validating every request if laying unknown bids elsewhere is allowed. How those requests are handled would determine how efficiently the system could work.

[5] See, e.g., Yochai Benkler, "From Consumers to Users: Shifting the Deeper Structures of Regulation Toward Sustainable Commons and User Access," *Federal Communications Law Journal* 52 (2000): 561; Eli Noam, "Spectrum Auctions: Yesterday's Heresy, Today's Orthodoxy, Tomorrow's Anachronism," *Journal of Law & Economics* 41 (1998): 765; Yochai Benkler, "Overcoming Agoraphobia: Building the Commons of the Digitally Networked Environment," *Harvard Journal of Law & Technology* 11 (1997): 287.

[6] See Hazlett, "Spectrum Flash Dance"; Gregory L. Rosston and Jeffrey S. Steinberg, "Using Market-Based Spectrum Policy to Promote the Public Interest," *Federal Communications Law Journal* 50 (1996): 87.

[7] *Turner Broadcasting System, Inc.* v. *F.C.C.*, 520 U.S. 180, 189 (1997). I am assuming (and I would argue) that ordinary First Amendment analysis should apply to the rules allocating spectrum. That assumption, however, is not obvious. You might take the view that spectrum is just like paper (both are used to communicate), and there's not a First Amendment problem with the government's nationalizing paper production. Cf. *Arsberry* v. *Illinois*, 244 F. 3d 558 (7th Cir., 2001) (examining tax as applied to the telephone company).

But in my view, the appropriate analysis begins with the speaker, who would speak using spectrum but for regulations by Congress of that spectrum. That is the same posture the Court has adopted when explaining why regulation of cable television is subject to First Amendment analysis. In both cases, the issue is properly framed: What justifies the state-imposed interference with the speaker's ability to communicate? That question, I expect, will be resolved through the same level of analysis as applied to cable. This is because, as Benkler writes, "enclosure of information . . . affects different organizations engaged in information production differently. This is so because information is not only an output of information production, but also one of its most important inputs." Yochai Benkler, "The Commons as a Neglected Factor of Information Policy," (paper presented at the Telecommunications Policy Research Conference (October 5, 1998): 70. Thus, "the availability of a commons creates incentives that make possible decentralization of content-production." Benkler, "The Commons," 68.

[8] "These units are so small as to make the transaction costs involved in negotiating allocation of exclusive property rights to them prohibitive." Benkler, "Overcoming Agoraphobia," 174.

[9] See, e.g., Andy Kessler, velcap.com, "Steal This Bandwidth!," e-mail on file with author, June 19, 2001 ("The FCC should set aside some not-for-profit spectrum specifically for wireless access, probably at the same time they auction 3G licenses, and keep encouraging the grassroots to run with new technology.").

[10] Telephone interview with Alex Lightman, January 31, 2001.

[11] Ibid.

[12] Telephone interview with Dave Hughes, November 13, 2000.

[13] Federal Communications Commission, "Creation of Low Power Radio Service," January 27, 2000, at http://www.fcc.gov/Bureaus/Mass_Media/Orders/2000/fcc00019.doc.

[14] Harry First, "Property, Commons, and the First Amendment: Towards a Core Common Infrastructure" (White Paper of the First Amendment Program at the Brennan Center for Justice at New York University School of Law, 2001), 42–44.

[15] Departments of Commerce, Justice, and State, the Judiciary and Related Agencies Appropriations Act, 2001, H.R. 4942, enacting into law H.R. 5548, 106th Congress, Title VI §632 (2000) (enacted).

[16] See Bob Brewin, "Airports Ground Use of Wireless: Safety, Loss of Income from Pay Phones Cited," Computerworld (February 19, 2001): 1, http://computerworld.com/cwi/story/0,1199,NAV47_STO57817_NLTpm,00.html.

[17] The real aim of the airports, organized under "wirelessairport.org," appears to be to develop a proprietary, exclusive architecture for wireless technologies within airports, to permit them to extract rents from the technology's use.

[18] See, e.g., Hazlett, "The Wireless Craze," 42 ("The burden of proof is on the potential entrant. No incumbent must show that less competition serves the public in order to preserve the status quo, it must only rebut proponents of competition. The default position is that entry does not occur."); Net@EDU, Position Paper on WLAN Radio Frequency Interference Issues ("FCC Part 15 devices like wireless access points must accept all interference that may be caused by the operation of an authorized radio station, by another intentional or unintentional sources [sic]."), 1, available at http://www.educause.edu/asp/doclib/abstract.asp?ID=NE+T0014 (visited June 11, 2001); ibid. (discussing ham radio). For a site collecting the FCC's Technical Advisory Committee's work on spectrum, see http://www.jacksons.net/tac/.

[19] Hazlett, "The Wireless Craze," 45.

[20] Thus, in setting aside 300 MHz within the U-NII band, the FCC stated:

> We note that it may also be appropriate to reassess the technical parameters governing U-NII devices in light of second generation MSS systems. For example, second generation MSS systems may be more sensitive and therefore more susceptible to interference from U-NII devices.

Amendment of the Commission's Rules to Provide for Operation of Unlicensed NII Devices in the 5 GHz Frequency Range, 12 F.C.C.R. 1576, ¶96 (1997). But why should U-NII devices respond to second-generation MSS devices, rather than the other way around? See Yochai Benkler, "Overcoming Agoraphobia," 338, n. 225.

[21] FCC Regulations, part 97, subpart A, section 97.1, available at http://www.arrl.org/FandES/field/regulations/news/part97/.

[22] As Hazlett argues, the current regime does not actually sell the right to spectrum. Instead, it sells the right to a certain kind of business, since the license received is a license to use certain equipment at a certain time for certain business purposes. Hazlett, "The Wireless Craze," 102. Thus the criticism of spectrum auctions that I offer here is

not a general criticism of auctions; it instead is critical, as Hazlett is, of the particular mode of auctions currently pursued.

[23] Ibid., 105.

[24] S.J. Res. 125, 69th Cong., 1st Sess. (1926) (Clarence C. Dill).

[25] Telephone interview with Dave Hughes.

[26] A distinct but related concern is that the relative demand for different uses of spectrum can't be known in advance. As Reed puts it, "[W]hether HDTV or more cellular telephone service would be more useful to society" is not something we can know in advance. Telephone interview with David Reed, February 7, 2001. Yet the existing system of allocation presumes as much.

[27] Noam, "Beyond Liberalization II," 473.

[28] Telephone interview with Alex Lightman.

[29] John Naughton, A Brief History of the Future: The Origins of the Internet (London: Weidenfeld & Nicolson, 1999), 107.

[30] Telephone interview with David Reed.

[31] As well as other great books. See, for example, Orwell's Revenge: The 1984 Palimpsest (New York: Free Press, 1994).

[32] Huber, Law and Disorder in Cyberspace, 75.

[33] As Carol Rose argues, however, commons traditionally are not regulated by the state or through law. They instead are regulated through norms. Indeed, their nonstate character is an important element of their status a commons. Rose, "The Comedy of the Commons," 720–21. But today, the most important commons are built by the state and regulated under general law. The highways and parks, for example, are not found by the state anymore. For more on the role of highways in engendering growth because of their commonslike character, see "Toll Roads and Free Roads," 76th Congress, 1st Sess., House Document No. 272, 98 (1939) (Serial Set at 10339) ("The business-generating potentiality of a heavy traffic stream is so great that there is an immediate development of a great variety of roadside establishments all along every new heavily traveled route that is created. Every new highway also, especially in the vicinity of cities, immediately encourages residential development and attracts commercial establishments more interested in the new facility provided by it than in catering to its traffic."); Clay Committee Report, "A 10-Year National Highway Program," 84th Cong., 1st Sess., House Document No. 93, 7 (1955) (Serial Set at 11840) ("An adequate highway system is vital to the continued expansion of the economy. The projected figures for gross national product will not be realized if our highway plant continues to deteriorate. The relationship is, of course, reciprocal; an adequate highway network will facilitate the expansion of the economy which, in turn, will facilitate the raising of revenues to finance the construction of highways.").

[34] The origin of this idea is a 1959 paper by J. P. Costas, "Poisson, Shannon, and the Radio Amateur," 47 Proc. IRE 2058 (December 1959). See also Shepard, "A Channel Access Scheme for Large Dense Packet Radio Networks."

[35] Hazlett, "The Wireless Craze," 136–37. Thomas W. Hazlett, "An Essay on Airwave Allocation Policy," AEI-Brookings Joint Center for Regulatory Studies (2001).

[36] See, e.g., International Bandwidth 2001 (Washington, D.C.: TeleGeography, 2001).

[37] As David Reed describes it:

We don't understand how the capacity of communications relates to the number of users. [The historical model assumes] capacity is constant. So if you have ten users, you'll be able to divide it up ten ways and each user will get one-tenth at most. . . . [But] there are two . . . plausible arguments from physics that describe constructible systems where, as the number of users of that same spectrum in the same volume of space increases, the amount of available spectrum [increases as well] . . . which means that if you have one hundred times as many stations in that same volume, you can get ten times (or maybe even a hundred times) as much communication capacity.

Telephone interview with David Reed.
[38] Noam, "Beyond Spectrum Auctions."
[39] Ibid., 465.
[40] Ibid., 466.
[41] George Gilder, *Telecosm: How Infinite Bandwidth Will Revolutionize Our World* (New York: Free Press, 2000), 159.
[42] Ibid., 159–60. Gilder's point is correct whether or not there is a true "winner's curse." A "winner's curse" exists only when the bid was irrationally high. Richard H. Thaler, "Anomalies: The Winner's Curse," *Journal of Economic Perspectives* 2 (1988): 191, 192. Whether or not the bid was irrational, it can still create this pressure on the system.
[43] The story is told in Lawrence Lessing, *Man of High Fidelity: Edwin Howard Armstrong* (New York: J. B. Lippincott, 1956).
[44] The best example is the slow deployment of ultrawideband (UWB) technologies. A kind of spread spectrum technology, UWB uses extremely low power transmissions that do not rise above the noise floor. The application process at the commission has slowed the approval process of UWB, as incumbents who would be affected by this new competition can slow the process merely by raising questions about the potential interference from this new technology. This shifts the cost of demonstrating the value of UWB to the entrant, which significantly slows (and can kill) the entry process. Thus, "despite the enormous spectrum efficiencies of UWB . . . UWB is going nowhere fast." Hazlett, "The Wireless Craze," 87–88.

CHAPTER 13

[1] Telephone interview with Pat Feely (July 18, 2001).
[2] Interview with John Seely Brown in Stanford, Calif. (May 2, 2001).

CHAPTER 14

[1] George Gilder, *Telecosm: How Infinite Bandwidth Will Revolutionize Our World* (New York: Free Press, 2000), 163 ("[T]he FCC should not be in the business of licensing spectrum. It should instead issue driver's licenses for radios"); telephone interview with Bill Lane, November 15, 2000 (describing regulatory role); telephone interview with Dave Hughes, November 13, 2000 (describing regulatory role).
[2] Software-defined radios were first demonstrated in 1995. Federal Communications Commission, "In the Matter of Inquiry Regarding Software Defined Radios," ET Docket No. 00-47, FCC 00-103 (March 21, 2000), par. 4.
[3] See, e.g., 42 U.S.C. 7601 (2001), Title III, Sect. 5(A) (granting a six-year compliance extension only to air polluters who appreciably reduced their emissions before the EPA deadline); Title IV, Sect. 3(b) (allowing factory owners' only "substitution" of SO_2 facility reduction requirements to a separate facility under the same ownership).
[4] 47 U.S.C. §301 (2001).

[5] FCC Regulations, part 97, available at http://www.arrl.org/FandES/field/regulations/news/part97/. Yochai Benkler proposes that the FCC reopen U-NII proceedings to further free spectrum about the 6 GHz layer. Benkler, "Overcoming Agoraphobia," 297. Similarly, the FCC could allow part 15 unlicensed operations in the other ISM bands—such as that allocated under part 18 to 24.05–24.25 GHz. FCC Regulations, part 18, available at http://www.access.gpo.gov/nara/cfr/waisidx_98/47cfr18+_98.html.

[6] See, e.g., First, "Property, Commons and the First Amendment," 9 ("Just as municipalities provide sidewalks, roads, and sewers, so too it is important to revive an interest in designing the best possible approach towards public investment in the core infrastructure. This would require careful selection of the right level of public investment. At present, some municipalities are acting in ways that suggests that such public investment could entail deploying conduits and dark fiber [fiber without the electronics attached] cables in municipal streets or sewage systems.").

[7] See ibid., at 54–55.

[8] Canada has been experimenting extensively with this mode of providing connectivity. Through the development of "customer-owned IP networks," the government is supporting low-cost provision of IP services. For a description, see Timothy Denton, "Customer-Owned IP Networks," March 2001, available at http://www.tmdenton.com.

[9] In the first half of 2001, Microsoft launched a campaign against government support for what it called "open source" projects. These projects were "intellectual property-destroyers," since the license under which the code is distributed requires that derivative work also be distributed subject to the same license. This destroys intellectual property, Microsoft argued, because it means that no company can use "open source" products without losing control over its own code. See, e.g., Ben Charny, "Microsoft Raps Open-Source Approach," CNET News, May 3, 2001, available at http://news.cnet.com/news/0-1003-200-5813446.html (Mundie); interview with Bill Gates, Comdex, Fall 2000, available at http://www.key3media.com/comdex/fall2000/daily/keynotes/gates_interview.html (Gates); Paula Rooney, Balmer: "Linux Is Top Threat to Windows," TechWeb, January 10, 2001, available at http://content.techweb.com/wire/story/TWB20010110S0006 (Balmer).

If you're this far into this book, then the mistakes in this argument should be patent. The only open source or free software license that has a "viral" component is the GNU GPL. "Open source" software is not software governed by the GPL. Thus Microsoft's argument has nothing to do with "open source" software such as the Apache server or BSD Unix. The only possible target of Microsoft's attack is software licensed under the GPL—namely, GNU/Linux.

But even here, Microsoft's claims are just false. It is not the case that any software that runs with Linux thereby becomes subject to the GPL, any more than any software that runs on the Windows platform becomes subject to the license of Microsoft. The GPL requires that only derivative work be licensed under the GPL—if you take the Linux operating system and modify it in a particular way and then publish it to others, then the product you publish must be under the GPL. That is, no doubt, a restriction on the freedom of developers. They can't simply "take" Linux and do with it as they wish. But neither can anyone simply "take" the Windows operating system and do with it as they wish.

The essence of Microsoft's arguments is simply that the government should not support GPL research. Government funds should not promote a coding project that is not wholly free for anyone to take and do with as they wish. Thus, Microsoft should have no complaint if the government supports coding projects that are dedicated to the public domain (like TCP/IP or the protocols of the Web). Its only complaint should be when the government supports projects that are restrictive of citizens' freedom—in any way.

This is not an argument against open source, it is an argument against GPL. And if it is a strong argument against GPL, then it is also an argument against the government supporting proprietary projects as well. If it is wrong for the government to support Linux because I am not free to do with Linux as I wish, then it is wrong for the government to support Windows because here too I am not free to do with Windows as I wish.

If that is the principle Microsoft is advancing, it is an interesting and valuable point to consider. But only if it is a principle, as opposed to FUD designed to scare the market from a competitor's products. We'll have to see more before we can tell whether this is principle or something less.

[10] There may be a constitutional limitation on this form of regulation. At least one court has concluded that requiring open access on cable lines violates the First Amendment. See *Comcast Cablevision of Broward County, Inc.* v. *Broward County, Fla.*, 124 F. Supp. 2d 685 (S.D. Fla., 2000). For a powerful, if depressing, analysis, see Brandan I. Koerner, "AT&T's First Amendment Problem, and Ours," *The New Republic* (May 14, 2001): 18.

[11] This is related to the National Research Council's suggestion that the government push "open IP services"—meaning a policy to preserve the essential features of end-to-end IP. See National Research Council, 138–39.

[12] Report of the National Broadband Task Force, *The New National Dream: Networking the Nation for Broadband Access* (2001), 96. The OECD report is described in "Broadband Blues," *The Economist* (June 21, 2001).

[13] Jessica Litman, *Digital Copyright* (Amherst, N.Y.: Prometheus Books, 2000), 78.

[14] Some of the changes I propose here would require changes to or the abrogation of some treaties. Four treaties are especially relevant. The first is the Berne Convention for the Protection of Literary and Artistic Works, 828 U.N.T.S. 221, S. Treaty Doc. No. 99-27, which the United States joined in 1989. The Berne Convention provides for national treatment of foreign authors, meaning that each signatory nation is required to protect foreign authors to the same degree that it protects domestic authors. Additionally, the Berne Convention sets a limit on the minimum level of protection that a signatory nation can offer and requires that materials be automatically protected from the moment of creation, rather than being protected only once they are registered.

The second treaty is the Agreement on Trade Related Aspects of Intellectual Property Rights, Including Trade in Counterfeit Goods, of the General Agreement on Tariffs and Trade, 33 I.L.M. 83 (1994), better known as the TRIPs agreement. The TRIPs agreement was adopted as part of the Uruguay Round of GATT. It sets out minimum standards of protection for intellectual property and is unusual in providing sanctions for copyright violations. Member nations must enact laws giving foreign authors legal remedies for copyright infringement. The agreement not only sets standards for those remedies, but also subjects member nations to trade sanctions if they do not meet the standards. TRIPs also narrows the scope of fair use by requiring that exceptions to copyright protection must occur only in special cases, must not conflict with the normal exploitation of the work, and must not unreasonably prejudice the interests of the holder of the copyright.

The third and fourth treaties were adopted at the UN's World Intellectual Property Organizations (WIPO) Diplomatic Conference in 1996. They are, respectively, the

WIPO Copyright Treaty, December 20, 1996, WIPO Doc. CRNR/DC/94 (December 23, 1996), and the WIPO Performances and Phonograms Treaty, December 20, 1996, WIPO Doc. CRNR/DC/95 (December 23, 1996). The WIPO treaties expand the protection afforded to on-line works by requiring countries to extend copyright laws to the Internet. In the United States, this extension took the form of the Digital Millenium Copyright Act of 1998 (DMCA), which prohibits both acts circumventing copy protection and the importation, manufacture, or sale of technologies developed primarily for such circumvention. Willful violation of these provisions is subject to criminal penalties, and both criminal and civil sanctions may be applied to violators even if the underlying use is privileged (even if, for example, the use were to fall within traditional fair use).

[15] There is an obvious, and important, problem of security raised by such a system, though there are also obvious and feasible ways to minimize any security risk. For an example of a secure system that was used to effect a settlement between IBM and Fujitsu, see Robert H. Mnookin and Jonathan D. Greenberg, "Lessons of the IBM-Fujitsu Arbitration: How Disputants Can Work Together to Solve Deeper Conflicts," *Dispute Resolution Magazine* (Spring 1998): 16.

[16] Under existing law, "if the intended use is for commercial gain," the likelihood of market harm can be presumed. See *Sony Corp. of America v. Universal City Studios, Inc.*, 464 U.S. 417, 451 (1984). This presumption could be modified in the context of the Internet so that innovators could defend a new use by demonstrating that no substantial likelihood of harm to existing markets exists.

[17] Of course, it is not as if artists are really being paid under the existing system—or at least, not most of them. In 1999, eighty-eight recordings accounted for 25 percent of all record sales. Charles C. Mann, "The Heavenly Jukebox," *Atlantic Monthly* (September 2000).

[18] The proposals for this are many. As Jon Potter describes it:

> Once the art is disseminated to a single reseller, then other resellers can also have that art for resale for the same terms and conditions, so maybe you can have a standardized nondiscriminatory license provision rather than a compulsory statutory scheme of royalties. So, if Sony needs to sell something through a Sony store, and tries to really control all distribution, then Barnes & Noble gets to do the same deal—whatever the Sony store does with Sony music, or whatever Barnes & Noble gets, Tower gets, but something so that compensation is ensured. And competition is ensured.

Telephone interview with Jon Potter, December 7, 2000.

[19] See, for example, "Artists' Contribution to American Heritage Act of 2001," 107th Cong., 1st sess., H.R.1598; Artist-Museum Partnership Act, 107th Cong., 1st sess., S.694; Arts and Collectibles Capital Gains Tax Treatment Parity Act, 107th Cong., 1st sess., S.638; Artists' Contribution to American Heritage Act of 1999, 106th Cong., 1st sess., H.R.3249; 106th Cong., 1st sess., S.217.

[20] Stephen Fishman, *The Public Domain* (Berkeley, Calif.: Nolo, 2000), 2/9 ("Claiming copyright in public domain works is a federal crime, but the maximum penalty for engaging in this sort of criminal conduct is a fine of $2,500 [17 U.S.C. § 506(c)]. Moreover, no one has ever been prosecuted for violations [of this provision]").

[21] David Lange, "Recognizing the Public Domain," *Law & Contemporary Problems* 44 (1981): 147, 166.

[22] See Gail E. Evans, "Opportunity Costs of Globalizing Information Licenses: Embedding Consumer Rights Within the Legislative Framework for Information Contracts," *Fordham Intellectual Property, Media & Entertainment Law Journal* 10 (1999):

267. For competing views on UCITA (most of them negative), see "Symposium: Intellectual Property and Contract Law in the Information Age: The Impact of Article 2B of the Uniform Commercial Code on the Future of Transactions in Information and Electronic Commerce," *Berkeley Technology Law Review* 13 (1998): 809.

[23] L. Ray Patterson, "Understanding the Copyright Clause," *Journal of the Copyright Society U.S.A.* 47 (2000): 365; L. Ray Patterson and Stanley W. Lindberg, *The Nature of Copyright: A Law of Users' Rights* (Athens, Ga.: University of Georgia Press, 1991); L. Ray Patterson and Judge Stanley F. Birch, Jr., "Copyright and Free Speech Rights," *Journal of Intellectual Property Law* 4 (1996): 1; L. Ray Patterson, "Copyright and 'The Exclusive Right' of Authors," *Journal of Intellectual Property Law* 1 (1993): 1, 137; L. Ray Patterson, "Free Speech, Copyright, and Fair Use," *Vanderbilt Law Review* 40 (1987): 1.

[24] Litman, 12–14.

[25] The law does not ordinarily have an interest in forcing an owner of a property right to "use it or lose it." For example, I should not have to drive my car all the time to ensure no one else gets to take it. But where property is not exhaustible, and is nonrivalrous, then the balance in favor of the "use it or lose it" rule can shift. Litman's rule is related to a French requirement that if a publisher fails to exploit an assigned right, then, under certain circumstances, the original author can reclaim the right. See Neil Netanel, "Copyright Alienability Restrictions and the Enhancement of Author Autonomy: A Normative Evaluation," *Rutgers Law Journal* 24 (1993): 347, 390–91.

[26] On the role of damage remedies in patent infringement cases, see Mark Schankerman and Suzanne Scotchmer, "Damages and Injunctions in Protecting Intellectual Property," *Rand Journal of Economics* 32 (2001): 199 (in the context of research tools, damages underdeter infringement, but that nondeterrence may be a good thing for the patent holder, since it prevents a hold-up problem). Carl Shapiro, "Navigating the Patent Thicket: Cross Licenses, Patent Pools, and Standard-Setting," in *Innovation Policy and the Economy*, vol. 1, Adam Jaffe, Joshua Lerner, and Scott Stern, eds. (Cambridge, Mass.: MIT Press, 2001), 8.

[27] Professor John Barton, for example, has proposed that Congress (1) raise the standards for patentability (such that an invention is nonobvious only "when the approach seemed quite unlikely to work and still proved successful"); (2) decrease the use of patents to bar research; and (3) improve the U.S. Patent Office to reduce invalid patents. John H. Barton, "Reforming the Patent System," *Science* 287 (2001): 1933.

[28] See Brian Kahin, comments in response to "The Patentability of Computer-Implemented Inventions," 2000, 5 (noting that patent attorneys discourage software professionals from reading patents to avoid "willful infringement"), available at http://europa.eu.int/comm/internal_market/en/intprop/indprop/maryland.pdf.

[29] See, e.g., Daniel R. Harris and Janice N. Chan, "Case Note: *Wang Laboratories, Inc.* v. *America Online, Inc. and Netscape Communications Corp.*," *Computer & High Technology Law Journal* 16 (2000): 449, 457.

[30] See, for example, Robert P. Merges, "As Many as Six Impossible Patents Before Breakfast: Property Rights for Business Concepts and Patent System Reform," *Berkeley Technology Law Journal* 14 (1999): 577 (poor-quality patents, especially business patents, reveal need for PTO reform; PTO jobs and incentives should be restructured; third parties, especially the applicant's competitors, should be consulted early and thoroughly through a European-style opposition system).

[31] See A Bill to Amend Title 35, U.S. Code, to Provide for Improvements in the Quality of Patents on Certain Inventions, H.R. 107th Cong., 1st Sess., 1932, §4 (nonob-

viousness). Congressman Berman's bill also proposes useful changes to facilitate early challenge of business method patents before a patent on these methods is granted. See A Bill to Amend Title 35, U.S. Code, to Provide for Improvements in the Quality of Patents on Certain Inventions, H.R. 107th Cong., 1st Sess., 1332, §3.

[32] Pamela Samuelson et al., "Manifesto Concerning the Legal Protection of Computer Programs," *Columbia Law Review* 94 (1994): 2308, 2331.

[33] In March 2000, the U.S. Patent Office launched a Business Method Patent Initiative designed "to ensure high quality patents in this fast-emerging technology." Available at http://www.uspto.gov/web/offices/com/sol/actionplan.html. Fifteen months later, the U.S. Patent Office asked for comment on Prior Art Sources for Business Method Patents. See http://www.uspto.gov/web/offices/com/sol/notices/ab26.html.

CHAPTER 15

[1] Orrin G. Hatch, Address of Senator Orrin G. Hatch Before the Future of Music Coalition, Future of Music Coalition, January 10, 2001, available at http://www.senate.gov/~hatch/speech020.htm.

[2] *Eldred* v. *Reno*, 239 F. 3d 372, 375 (D.C. Cir., 2001).

[3] Testimony of Professor Peter Jaszi, The Copyright Term Extension Act of 1995: Hearings on S.483 Before the Senate Judiciary Committee, 104th Cong. (1995), available at 1995 WL 10524355, *6.

[4] Oral arguments, *United States* v. *Microsoft*, February 26, 2001, available at http://www.microsoft.com/presspass/trial/transcripts/feb01/02–26.asp.

[5] E-mail from John Gilmore, January 19, 2001, to EFF list, on file with author, 6.

[6] Telephone interview with Marc Andreessen, December 15, 2000.

[7] As Timothy Wu commented to me, "[T]he real successes on the Internet have not been killer *apps*, but killer *platforms*." E-mail from Tim Wu, June 28, 2001. Not, in other words, amazing but proprietary applications that do extraordinary things, but amazing and open platforms upon which others have been free to build. E-mail and the Web are examples, Wu suggests, of killer platforms. Napster and Instant Messaging, while popular, have none of the equivalent open platform characteristics.

[8] David Bank's recent book, *Breaking Windows*, argues that there is more reason to be hopeful about Microsoft. According to Bank, "[I]nteroperability, not lock-in, has become the winning strategy" for Microsoft. David Bank, *Breaking Windows: How Bill Gates Fumbled the Future of Microsoft* (New York: Free Press, 2001), 237. In June 2000, Microsoft "embraced XML and made it the centerpiece of its new Internet platform." The platform was designed, at least initially, to be a "complot for interoperability." Ibid., 198. Following Christensen's recommendations in *Innovator's Dilemma*, the strategy was born from a spin-off that Microsoft created with executive Adam Bosworth. Ibid., 196. To "his credit," as Bank writes, "Gates never shut the XML effort down." Ibid., 198.

[9] Gordon Cook, "The Meaning of Current Events," *The COOK Report*, June 20, 2001, available at http://cookreport.com

Index

THE NEXT FIFTY YEARS
Science in the First Half of the Twenty-First Century
edited by John Brockman

A brilliant ensemble of the world's most visionary scientists provides twenty-five never-before-published essays about advances that could happen within our lifetimes. *The Next Fifty Years* includes essays that examine the likelihood of establishing a continuing human presence on Mars, the ramifications of engineering high-IQ, genetically happy babies, the probability of obtaining a genome printout that predicts our natural end (Will we want to read it? And will insurance companies have access to it?), and much more.

Science/0-375-71342-5

FASTER
The Acceleration of Just About Everything
by James Gleick

Most of us suffer some degree of "hurry sickness," a malady that has launched us into a need-everything-yesterday sphere dominated by cell phones, computers, faxes, and remote controls. Yet for all the hours, minutes, and even seconds being saved, we still lack time for such basic human activities as eating, sex, and relating to our families. Written with fresh insight and thorough research, *Faster* is a wise and witty look at a harried world not likely to slow down anytime soon.

Current Affairs/Technology/0-679-77548-X

THE INGENUITY GAP
Facing the Economic, Environmental, and Other Challenges of an Increasingly Complex and Unpredictable World
by Thomas Homer-Dixon

Despite society's advances, global problems proliferate. The Internet and other media help to disseminate knowledge, but they've also created an "info-glut." What's more, advances in technology have made the world so fast-paced and complex that fewer people are able even to grasp the problems, let alone generate solutions. As he explores the possible consequences of the gap between the problems that arise and our ability to solve them, Thomas Homer-Dixon offers an absorbing assessment of the state of the world.

Current Affairs/Technology/0-375-71328-X

THE SUPREME COURT
Revised and Updated
by William H. Rehnquist

This new edition of Chief Justice William H. Rehnquist's classic book offers a lively and accessible history of the Supreme Court. His engaging writing illuminates both the high and low points in the Court's history, from Chief Justice Marshall's dominance of the Court during the early nineteenth century through the landmark decisions of the Warren Court. Citing cases such as the *Dred Scott* decision and Roosevelt's Court-packing plan, Rehnquist makes clear that the Supreme Court does not operate in a vacuum, that the justices are unavoidably influenced by their surroundings, and that their decisions have real and lasting impact on our society.

History/Law/0-375-70861-8

THE UNWANTED GAZE
The Destruction of Privacy in America
by Jeffrey Rosen

The Unwanted Gaze is an important book about one of the most pressing issues of our day: how changes in technology and the law have combined to demolish our rights of privacy, and what we can and must do to re-secure them. In a world in which Ken Starr can subpoena Monica Lewinsky's bookstore receipts, and deleted e-mail messages can be used as justification for firing employees, it's clear that private information of all kinds can be taken out of context and wielded against us. In superbly lucid prose, Jeffrey Rosen explains not only where our privacy rights went, but also how we can get them back.

Current Affairs/Law/0-679-76520-4